M000286914

Free Speech and Unfree News

FREE SPEECH AND UNFREE NEWS

The Paradox of Press Freedom in America

SAM LEBOVIC

Harvard University Press
Cambridge, Massachusetts
London, England
2016

Copyright © 2016 by the President and Fellows of Harvard College
All rights reserved
Printed in the United States of America

First printing

Library of Congress Cataloging-in-Publication Data

Lebovic, Sam, 1981–
Free speech and unfree news : the paradox of press freedom in America / Sam Lebovic.
pages cm
Includes bibliographical references and index.
ISBN 978-0-674-65977-3 (alk. paper)
1. Freedom of the press—United States—History—20th century.
2. Journalism—Political aspects—United States—History—20th century.
3. Press and politics—United States—History—20th century. I. Title.
Z658.U5L43 2016
323.44'509730904—dc23
2015026926

For my parents

CONTENTS

Free Speech and Unfree News

Prologue

The Problem of Press Freedom

In 1938, to celebrate the sixtieth anniversary of the *St. Louis Post-Dispatch,* Franklin Delano Roosevelt sent a public letter to the newspaper. He used the opportunity to reflect on the state of American press freedom. "In these past few years," the president declared, "there has been so much resounding thunder about freedom of the press that one sometimes wonders what it is all about." Roosevelt was adamant that there was no threat to the press from government censorship—the importance of a free press was "an axiom from which no thoughtful person will dissent." But he also suggested that an absence of state censorship did not guarantee that the press was fulfilling its role in democratic life. In fact, he continued, the government "has rightfully and necessarily an interest in freedom of the news as well as in the preservation of a free press."[1]

Roosevelt was distinguishing "freedom of the news" from "freedom of the press" for quite particular political reasons. His New Deal was under assault from many conservative newspaper publishers, who had accused FDR of regulating the press in an effort to undermine American democracy. In his 1938 letter, Roosevelt was returning fire, accusing the newspaper industry of editing the news in the interest of the "counting room" rather than the general public. But in distinguishing freedom of the news from traditional press freedom, FDR was also participating in a much larger and much longer debate about the meaning of press freedom in the twentieth century. In speaking of "freedom of the news," Roosevelt was attempting to expand the meaning of press freedom beyond a First

Amendment right to speak without government interference. If press freedom meant simply the absence of state censorship, Roosevelt implied that a truly democratic press had to mean something more. To meet its obligations to inform the public, the press also had to have "freedom of the news."

FDR never developed the idea of "freedom of the news," but he was neither the first nor the last American to try to articulate a concept of press freedom that went beyond a First Amendment right to free speech. Over the course of the twentieth century, a wide variety of lawyers, journalists, philosophers, and politicians grappled with the same problem: How could one guarantee that informative and accurate news would flow to the public through the press? The notion that First Amendment rights did not produce a truly free press may seem jarring to us, but in the quite recent past, Americans of diverse political inclinations were concerned that press freedom had to mean something more than freedom of expression.

This book is the history of surprisingly wide-ranging attempts to clarify and expand the meaning of press freedom in the twentieth century. These efforts are largely forgotten today, because they were almost entirely unsuccessful. The idea of a positive right to the news never found firm footing in American law, politics, or culture. Press freedom still means only the right to speak without government interference. But understanding why that notion of press freedom seemed inadequate in the past offers new insight into the tangled relationships between the press, the First Amendment, and liberal democracy in America's twentieth century.

The distinction between press freedom and freedom of the news also helps us to better understand the crises that besiege the press today, when the First Amendment is used to protect corporate speech, the newspapers are dying, and the government is waging a "war on whistleblowers." All three of these trends had their origins in the middle decades of the twentieth century. Until the interwar years, the First Amendment languished as a legal protection for free speech. The Supreme Court only rediscovered it in 1919, and only began using it to meaningfully protect press freedom in the 1930s. By that time, the newspaper industry had begun a century-long process of consolidation and decline—the nation had its highest number of newspapers in 1909, and the falling numbers of papers has been the subject of debate and anxiety ever since. And it was only in the 1940s that the United States began to build the laws and practices of classification that are now used to keep so much information secret.

To understand the ambiguities of modern American press freedom, we need to understand its ambiguous past.

* * *

In the middle decades of the twentieth century, the problem of press freedom was a central concern in American political life. Journalists, editors, and publishers reflected publicly on the state of their craft. Lawyers wrote treatises and briefs, and took landmark First Amendment cases to the Supreme Court. Politicians and intellectuals argued about the abstract meaning and current state of American press freedom. "In the last six months of 1933," observed University of Wisconsin journalism professor Willard G. Bleyer, "there was more discussion of the freedom of the press in this country than in the 135 years since the violent debate about the Sedition Act of 1798." In his 1938 letter to the *Post-Dispatch,* FDR was already calling freedom of the press a "greatly overworked phrase," but he nevertheless called for a "national symposium" on the subject. One hundred twenty intellectuals, politicians, and journalists responded to this call with their own letters to the paper, and the *Post-Dispatch* issued the exchanges as a symposium on press freedom. Five years later, a multiyear investigation into press freedom was launched at the University of Chicago. One of its participants thought the timing of the inquiry "almost miraculous": "There is a tremendous interest in the problem of the freedom of the press. You hear people talking about it almost anywhere."[2]

Debate about the meaning of American press freedom took place in a variety of arenas and focused on a range of issues. In the agencies of the New Deal, government reformers tried to use the state to regulate the newspaper industry and ensure that a vibrant newspaper market would provide a diverse range of news to the public. Publicity agents in the New Deal bureaucracy argued that government had an obligation to issue press statements about its activities—they soon found themselves accused of issuing propaganda that undermined press freedom. In the newsrooms of the nation's press, journalists asserted that only unionization would provide them with the economic security necessary to fearlessly report the news to the public. In the national security branches of the state, administrators sought to simultaneously preserve free speech and military secrets, even as they were criticized by lawyers and journalists committed to abolishing state secrecy. In the halls of the young United Nations, American diplomats argued that press freedom required global flows of free information, and tried to write international laws that would abolish propaganda and censorship.

This was not a unified movement, and proponents of these measures rarely agreed with one another. But they were all trying, in different ways, to expand the meaning of press freedom to guarantee the circulation of information to the public. And they all agreed that traditional understandings of press freedom were inadequate to modern conditions. The notion that press freedom meant simply the absence of government censorship had been inherited from the classical liberal philosophy of the eighteenth century. By the 1930s and 1940s, a number of Americans worried that it was out of date, incapable of preserving a free flow of information to the public amid the challenges of the twentieth century: the industrialization and corporate consolidation of the newspaper industry, the rise of a centralized state, and the waging of total war. In seeking to guarantee that the public would be provided with accurate and varied news, midcentury press reformers were thus seeking to modernize the concept of press freedom.

As they tried to reform the flow of information in their polity, Americans were led to compare their press freedoms with the new regimes of totalitarian censorship and propaganda they saw emerging in Nazi Germany, Fascist Italy, and the Soviet Union. At first, the emergence of totalitarianism heightened American concerns about the state of domestic press freedom and encouraged Americans to reform their press to ensure the ongoing vitality of American democracy. But over time, the fear of totalitarianism came to blunt domestic press reform. Centralized efforts to regulate the flow of information in the polity seemed to open the door to dictatorship at home. And new practices of state secrecy and propaganda seemed necessary to protect American liberty from international threats.[3]

Antitotalitarianism ultimately led Americans to elevate the importance of individual free speech to American democracy and to shy away from reforming the flow of information in the press. Rather than modernizing the concept of press freedom, Americans retreated to a bedrock commitment to classical First Amendment speech rights. Journalist Raymond Clapper captured this sentiment in 1941. "It is difficult for me to be dogmatic about this problem of the press," he admitted, "but I am dogmatic on one point. There must be no government tampering with the news."[4] By 1970, Thomas Emerson, the nation's leading First Amendment theorist, encapsulated the failed effort to rethink the meaning of press freedom when he observed that "the basic theory underlying the legal framework [of the First Amendment] has remained substantially unchanged since its development in the seventeenth and eighteenth centuries."[5] This classical theory was based, at least, on a clear principle—it was uncompromising, straightforward, and comprehensible. The opposition to government censorship not only provided a lodestar through troubled political times; above all, it helped to produce an unprecedented level of respect for free expression.

But in Cold War America, such noble sentiments also had unintended consequences: there would be no formal government censorship of the news, it was true, but there were no guarantees that newspapers would have access to information held by the state, or that the public would have access to a diverse range of newspapers.[6] The quality, diversity, and accuracy of the information in the nation's press were not protected by law. They were left unregulated and unprotected, subject to the outcome of competition between state officials and newspaper publishers, all of whom acted according to their own political and economic interests. The flow of information in the American polity came to be controlled by an ever-growing national security state and ever-larger, more consolidated media corporations. By the end of the twentieth century, Americans' ability to access diverse and accurate information through the press faced unprecedented challenges—even though First Amendment rights had been greatly expanded.

* * *

Paying attention to the failed effort to guarantee freedom of the news recasts the history of the First Amendment. The modern history of the First Amendment is normally told as a tale of rising liberalism, with more and more speech becoming constitutionally protected over time.[7] Problems of access to information rarely impinge on this story. From the perspective of classical liberal philosophy and First Amendment jurisprudence, the problem of news freedom is barely perceptible: there is no right to the news that is distinct from the right to speech; the right to a free press is synonymous with the individual right to free expression. John Stuart Mill, for instance, thought it "impossible to separate the cognate liberty of speaking and writing," and early American state constitutions referred to a singular "right to speak, to write, or to publish."[8] Following this tradition, the U.S. Supreme Court has refused to distinguish the press clause of the First Amendment from the jurisprudence of speech rights—it too has used

"Freedom of Speech" and "Freedom of Press" interchangeably.[9] But if we descend from the heights of First Amendment jurisprudence and abstract theorizing to the everyday politics of information, new questions about press freedom come to light. So do the considerable contingency and uncertainty that attended the rise of the modern First Amendment. Byron Price, a leading press executive and World War II censor, had experience with these problems. Celebrating the installation of the Bill of Rights at the Library of Congress in 1945, he reflected that "it is only when we depart from the abstract and begin to speak about details that Americans differ about freedom of the press."[10]

Exploring anxieties about the meaning and practice of press freedom provides a unique window into the political and intellectual history of liberal democracy in the modern United States.[11] The press is the only private enterprise specifically mentioned in the Bill of Rights. As both a formal political institution and an economic enterprise, it uniquely straddles the sphere of the state and the sphere of the market. As Americans argued about freedom of the press, they were therefore forced to come to terms with the major economic and political transformations of their day: the corporate consolidation of the economy, the rise of the New Deal, the growth of the executive branch, and the emergence of the national security state. As a result, debates about the press were at the center of political life from the New Deal through the Cold War and onto the crises that brought down the Nixon administration. Tracking debates about press freedom across this tumultuous half-century allows us to witness the remaking of liberal democracy.[12] Founding a multiyear philosophical inquiry into the meaning of press freedom in 1944, publishing magnate Henry Luce understood this point perfectly. "An inquiry into the freedom of the press," he declared, "is an inquiry into the whole problem of freedom."[13]

And understanding the increasing gulf separating the well-respected freedom of speech and the neglected freedom of the news provides us with a better understanding of the current crises of the American press. From the death of the daily in the age of the Internet, to the role of the press in the War on Terror, to the controversies over WikiLeaks and Edward Snowden, the problem of press freedom is still at the heart of American political life. First Amendment rights to speech have never been more highly protected, but the free flow of news to the public is far more tenuous, and rests on more fragile foundations. Americans have a well-entrenched right to free expression, but no right to the news. This book explains how this paradoxical situation developed.

1

The Inadequacy of Speech Rights

Reflecting on the relationship between free speech and democracy in the fall of 1919, Walter Lippmann came to a troubling conclusion. Less than a month had passed since Oliver Wendell Holmes's evocative dissent in the *Abrams* case had articulated a new understanding of the importance of the First Amendment. Liberals around the country had welcomed the dissent as a charter for modern speech rights, and saw in it the promise of a more vibrant and robust democracy. But the precocious Lippmann—Holmes had declared the young journalist and intellectual a "monstrous clever lad"—was not so sure. Contrasting John Milton and John Stuart Mill's classic arguments for free speech with the realities of modern American life, Lippmann realized that "traditional liberties of speech and opinion rest on no solid foundation." Liberty of opinion, Lippmann observed, was in fact "a subsidiary phase" in the production of democratic politics because opinions were "derived . . . from the stream of news that reaches the public." Opinions, in other words, were based on the information that people received from the news. To try to resolve the "privileges and immunities of opinion" without "going behind opinion to the information which it exploits" was, according to Lippmann, "missing the point and trying to make bricks without straw."[1]

At a time when most free speech theorists were still articulating the need for a right to free expression, and free speech advocates were just beginning to win recognition in the courts, Lippmann had already decided that speech rights were no democratic panacea. Protecting only the right to free expression, Lippmann realized, provided no guarantees that the public would be provided with the information necessary for self-government. The reasons were simple, if unsettling. By 1919, the free flow of information to the public was threatened by new forms of power—by an increasingly consolidated newspaper industry, intertwined with the business elite, and by a modern state that had discovered new capacities for censorship and propaganda in the recent Great War. The classical free speech philosophies of Mill and Milton provided little guidance in dealing with the corruption of the flow of news to the public. Therefore, Lippmann concluded, it might be impossible to meaningfully protect democratic public opinion "simply by imitating the earlier champions of liberty."[2] Even as Holmes was setting the agenda for the modern jurisprudence of speech rights, Lippmann argued convincingly that speech rights were inadequate to modern conditions. At the moment of its birth, the modern First Amendment already seemed insufficient.

In trying to articulate what was missing from the modern vision of free speech, Lippmann was inaugurating a debate that would continue throughout the century. The vision of First Amendment speech rights articulated by Oliver Wendell Holmes had a long genealogy—the idea that democracy rested on a free marketplace of ideas could be traced back to canonical liberal theorists of the seventeenth and eighteenth centuries. But it had never before been actively implemented in the law, and by the time the Supreme Court finally embraced this notion of free speech in the twentieth century, it seemed curiously abstract, out of touch with contemporary problems. In the first place, the newspaper market—the literal marketplace in which ideas circulated—had undergone profound transformations in the late nineteenth century. The newly industrialized press, argued a generation of muckrakers and media critics, bore little relation to the liberal cacophony of voices presumed by traditional democratic theory. Moreover, by the time the Supreme Court began to recognize the individual right to free speech, progressive critics were generally doubtful that protecting individual rights was an adequate way to preserve democracy in an industrial age. In the 1920s, in response to these problems, democratic theorists such as Lippmann and John Dewey began to grope toward a new conceptualization of press freedom. They struggled to articulate a modern vision of press freedom that respected the individual right to free speech while also guaranteeing the quality of information circulating in the polity. Their efforts revealed the need to modernize the antiquated conception of press freedom at the heart of the First Amendment. And their difficulties in accomplishing that task foreshadowed the difficulty of reimagining freedom of the press for the twentieth century.

* * *

Freedom of the press had, of course, been a foundational guarantee of political liberty for centuries. The presses in the early American colonies were subject, as were the presses in England, to censorship by the representatives of the Crown. But over the eighteenth century, inspired by radical English theorists, the American press increasingly advocated for a right to publish without government interference. In 1722, a young Benjamin Franklin reproduced an essay on free speech by two English theorists writing under the pseudonym of Cato. That essay, in which Cato declared that free speech was essential to political liberty and threatened by tyrannies, was widely republished in the middle decades of the eighteenth century—the *Boston Gazette* alone published it seven times between 1755 and 1780. And such sentiments were more than theoretical. In the important 1735 trial of John Peter Zenger for the seditious libel of New York governor William Cosby, one of Zenger's lawyers argued, in language akin to Cato, that "freedom of speech is a principal pillar in a free government." Zenger's eventual acquittal, on the novel grounds that one could not be found guilty of libel if one's criticisms of the government were true, suggested that American respect for press freedom was developing more rapidly than liberties in England.[3]

In the revolutionary crises of the 1760s and the 1770s, press freedom became strongly associated with the cause of patriotic liberty. The odious Stamp Tax fell heavily on printers, creating an economic motive to overthrow the repressive hand of the Crown that dovetailed with political concerns. Patriots relied heavily on the press to mobilize and unite anti-British sentiment and to bind the colonists together as a nation.[4] And with the coming of independence, the right to press freedom was enshrined in American law. Of the twelve new state constitutions written during the Revolutionary War, ten guaranteed a right to press freedom.[5] The first, drafted by George Mason in Virginia, declared in terms borrowed directly from Cato that "the freedom of the press is one of the greatest bulwarks of liberty, and can never be restrained but by despotick Governments." And once a decision was made to include a Bill of Rights in the new federal constitution, the First Amendment declared that "Congress shall make no law . . . abridging the freedom of speech, or of the press."[6]

It remains unclear precisely what the drafters of the First Amendment meant by "freedom of the press." We know very little about the drafting of the language, but it appears that early Americans were divided on such fundamental questions as whether press freedom was simply the absence of censorship before publication or whether press freedom also required protection from postpublication retribution. Determining the substance of the guarantee of press freedom, in fact, would be the political and legal work of more than a century.[7] But whatever the specific legal contours of press freedom were, its central place as a bedrock principle of American democracy was unquestioned. As James Madison put it, the "right of freely examining public characters and measures, and of free communication thereon, is the only effectual guardian of every other right." Or as Thomas Jefferson explained when fears of mobocracy were raised in the 1790s, "the way to prevent these irregular interpositions of the people is to give them full information of their affairs through the channel of the public papers, and to contrive that those papers should penetrate the whole mass of the people. The basis of our government being the opinion of the people, the first object should be to keep that right."[8]

It was significant that Jefferson saw "public papers" as the medium through which information was to circulate to the public—he went on to observe that he would have preferred to have newspapers without government rather than to have had government without newspapers.[9] Jefferson was not alone in seeking to ground press freedom in an arena of free exchange unregulated by the state. Classical theories of press freedom were predicated on an assumed homology between liberal economics and liberal politics. In a political analog to the "invisible hand" regulating liberal economics, it was presumed that removing the hand of the state would allow truth to emerge from the harmonious and equal exchanges of individuals who were presumed to possess a natural rationalism.

Even in John Milton's *Areopagitica* of 1644, the language of the market was beginning to undergird the conceptualization of the right to a free press. "Truth and understanding are not such wares as to be monopolized and traded in by tickets and statutes and standards," Milton argued; "we must not think to make a staple commodity of all the knowledge in the land, to mark and license it like our broadcloth and our woolpacks." To modern ears, that sounds like an effort to distinguish the press from commodity exchange, but Milton was trying to elevate information from the seventeenth-century market, which was a place of bounded, organized, and regulated exchange. He complained, for instance, that censorship was like the blocking of "havens and ports and creeks, it hinders and retards the importation of our richest merchandise, truth." And the rise of the liberal market was entirely compatible with Milton's famous conceptualization of the unfettered exchange of ideas: "And though all the winds of doctrine were let loose to play upon the earth, so Truth be in the field, we do injuriously, by licensing and prohibiting, to misdoubt her strength. Let her and Falsehood grapple; who ever knew Truth put to the worse, in a free and open encounter?"[10]

The presumption that the free exchange between truth and falsehood would naturally result in the favor of truth became the linchpin of the classically liberal theory of free speech. By the nineteenth century, John Stuart Mill was openly comparing the case for liberty of speech with the case for free trade.[11] But a relationship between capitalist exchange and the idea of democratic liberty was there from the beginning. Cato, for instance, declared that "trade and naval power [are] the offspring of civil liberty," thought that "the security of property and freedom of speech always go together," and reasserted the necessary relationship between unregulated exchange and enlightenment: "whilst all opinions are equally indulged and all parties equally allowed to speak their minds the truth will come out."[12]

In America, too, capitalist exchange suggested the conceptual tools for the most liberal defenses of the right to free speech. A prominent antifederalist pamphlet argued that the First Amendment was necessary because "a free press is the channel of communication as to mercantile and public affairs."[13] In a 1791 essay on democratic public opinion, James Madison similarly declared that liberty was improved by "whatever facilitates a general intercourse of sentiments, as good roads, domestic commerce, a free press, and particularly a circulation of newspapers."[14] And it was a lesser known American theorist who made most explicit the subtle analogies between the market and politics that underpinned the democratic theory of free speech. In 1800, New York lawyer and political activist Tunis Wortman wrote the most extensive early account of the right to speech. Wortman's book was promoted by Albert Gallatin, Republican secretary of the treasury, and Wortman's theory of free speech bore a close resemblance to Adam Smith's theory of free trade. In both Smith's and Wortman's theorizing, the unfettered pursuit of natural inclinations would produce natural harmony and progress:

> Neither prejudice, authority or terror should be suffered to impede the liberty of discussion; no undue influence should tyrannize over mind; every man should be left to the independent exercise of his reflection; all should be permitted to communicate their ideas with the energy and ingenuousness of truth. In such a state of intellectual freedom and activity, the progress of mind would infallibly become accelerated; we would all derive improvement from the knowledge and experience of our neighbor; and the wisdom of society would be rendered a general capital, in which all must participate.[15]

That reference to capital was no slip, and as Wortman expounded his defense of freedom of expression, he returned to economic metaphors: "Improvement is the constant law of our intellectual nature. Knowledge is a general fund, of which all have a right to participate: it is a capital which has the peculiar property of increasing its stores in proportion as they are used." The exchange of ideas "united the powers of individual intellect into a common bank."[16]

The loose equation between free speech and free markets was plausible in the eighteenth century, because, as Jefferson had put it, opinion and information circulated through the press, and the early press was a creature of the market. Beginning as internal reports of the merchant and banking houses of southern Germany and Venice in the sixteenth century, time-sensitive and increasingly regular news-sheets were produced by printers seeking profit through the sale of political and commercial information.[17] In the American colonies, too, the newspapers flourished in the market economy. America's first paper had been published in Boston in 1690, and ran for precisely one issue. But in the early eighteenth century, newspapers sprouted up throughout the colonies, clustering particularly in the northern commercial hubs. From the first, newspapers were run for profit, and heavily dependent on advertising. Up to 50 percent of column space in the early newspapers seems to have been devoted to ads, and by 1800 the word "advertiser" was featured in the title of twenty out of the twenty-four daily newspapers in the nation.[18] The first page of the eighteenth-century *Connecticut Gazette* called for articles that would advance virtue, liberty, and commerce.[19] By the early years of the republic, the newspaper market was growing rapidly, propelled by the expanding economy and by favorable governmental postage rates that ensured the easy circulation of newspapers throughout the young nation. In 1790, there had been 106 newspapers in the United States, but by 1835 there were 1,258—an elevenfold increase that radically outstripped the growth of the population.[20] In the 1820s, an impressed Alexis de Tocqueville observed that there "were more newspapers [in America] than [in] any other country in the world."[21]

In two senses, then, early American free press advocates rested their theory of democratic public opinion on capitalism: the concept of a "free exchange" of ideas rested on a sequence of analogies to capitalist exchange; and the literal exchange of ideas was to take place in a capitalist newspaper market. Out of the free exchange of ideas and information, out of the rough-and-tumble of rational debate between formally equal individuals, the alchemy of the market would produce democratic public opinion. Eventually, this theory of free speech would be embraced by Oliver Wendell Holmes, and become foundational to liberal politics in the twentieth century.

* * *

But throughout the eighteenth and nineteenth centuries, Americans would understand and implement press freedom in ways that departed sharply from this liberal theory. To begin with, the early newspaper economy was not a pure experiment in laissez-faire, hermetically sealed from the state. Rather, postal subsidies from the state underwrote the profits of the press, and many newspaper publishers in the early years of the republic earned their bread from government or party patronage—functioning as government printers, or party propagandists.[22]

And for all the talk of a free exchange of ideas, no one believed in complete freedom of expression. The right to a free press and the right to free speech were understood to have limits. Because the purpose of the right was to advance the common good, one had no individual right to harm the common good. In 1753, lawyer and publisher William Livingston explained his understanding of Cato's vision of press freedom in an essay titled "Of the Use, Abuse, and Liberty of the Press." Livingston, who went on to serve as governor of New Jersey and sign the U.S. Constitution, argued that liberty of the press did not mean an "equal unrestraint in writing," but "a liberty of promoting the common good of society and of publishing any thing else not repugnant thereto"—"the Liberty of the Press is always to be restricted from becoming a prejudice to the common weal." Thomas Jefferson had a similar understanding, and wrote to Madison to suggest that the First Amendment should be redrafted to exclude any right to publish "false facts affecting injuriously the life, liberty, property, or reputation of others or affecting the peace of the confederacy with foreign nations." Jefferson was in good company with other advocates of classical press liberty—Milton did not extend the right of free speech to Catholics, and served as a state censor in 1651; John Locke would not tolerate the right to express opinions "contrary . . . to those moral rules which are necessary to the preservation of civil society." The liberal belief in the unregulated exchange of ideas, in other words, was enveloped in a cocoon of republican values—only certain types of ideas, uttered by men of a certain class, were virtuous enough to be allowed to circulate freely. During the U.S. War of Independence, patriots tarred, feathered, and repressed the loyalist presses, because illiberally Tory sentiments were not worthy of the right to free expression.[23]

After independence, all Americans agreed that there were limits to speech—the divisive issue was how a republic could police those limits. In 1798, the Federalist administration of John Adams passed the Alien and Sedition Acts in an effort to limit criticism of the government during the Quasi-War with France. Prosecuting journalists for defaming the government was unpopular, and the backlash they provoked helped sweep Jefferson into power in the revolution of 1800. But opposition to the Sedition Act was not motivated by a heightened respect for speech rights in the abstract. Rather, Republican opposition emphasized that the act was odious because it imposed federal jurisdiction over an issue that should have been left to the states. Edward Livingston, Republican representative for New York, for instance, opposed the Sedition Act on the ground that "there is a remedy for offences of this kind in the laws of every state in the Union." Thomas Jefferson agreed, writing to Abigail Adams in 1804 that "while we deny that Congress have a right to control the freedom of the press, we have ever asserted the right of the states, and their exclusive right to do so."[24]

The First Amendment, in other words, protected the right to free speech only from congressional interference. James Madison's original draft of the Bill of Rights had included an additional amendment preventing states from violating the freedom of the press. But although Madison declared this "the most valuable amendment in the whole list," it was killed in the Senate.[25] Regulation of speech was left to the states, and states were quite happy to limit speech. The free speech guarantees in state constitutions often made the limits to free speech explicit. New York's Constitution of 1821, which was representative, declared that although "every citizens may freely speak, write and publish his sentiments on all subjects," citizens would be "responsible for the abuse of that right." As late as 1900, the Connecticut Court stated plainly that "the liberty protected is not the right to perpetuate acts of licentiousness, or any act inconsistent with the peace or safety of the state." In practice, therefore, the nineteenth-century right to free expression was hedged in by a thicket of state laws. Libel of public officials was met with strict punishment; blasphemy and obscenity were banned. And such regulations of speech fell heavily on minorities espousing opinions that challenged the political and social order. In the antebellum South, abolitionist material was outlawed in the 1830s. In the late nineteenth century, a host of states passed antianarchy laws making it illegal to advocate the forceful overthrow of the government. Beneath all of these laws was a deep assumption that states had sweeping police powers that allowed the regulation of individual rights in the interests of protecting the common good. For individuals seeking to express ideas unpopular with the elite, that meant censorship.[26]

Increasingly, even the First Amendment's protection of speech from federal regulation was understood to have limits. The U.S. Constitution included no language about the "abuse of liberty," but Joseph Story was dismissive of claims of unlimited liberty in his influential 1833 *Commentaries on the Constitution of the United States:* "that this amendment was intended to secure to every citizen an absolute right to speak, or write, or print, whatever he might please, without any responsibility, public or private therefor, is a supposition too wild to be indulged by any rational man." In 1877, the Supreme Court held that the federal government had the right to prohibit a host of "immoral" material from the mail, such as "lewd" books and information about contraceptives. And during World War I, amid the heated debates of patriots and pacifists, this repressive impulse reached a crescendo with the passage of the Espionage Act of 1917 and the Sedition Act of 1918. Combined, the two acts made it illegal to interfere with the war effort or the draft or criticize the government, the army, the Constitution, or the war. There were approximately 2,000 prosecutions for speech crimes during the war, which yielded roughly 1,000 convictions. Individuals went to jail for expressing even mild opposition to the war—their convictions capped the nineteenth century's long neglect of meaningful protections for individual rights of expression.[27]

After the war, the Supreme Court heard appeals on some of these convictions, and began to seriously ponder the meaning of the First Amendment for the first time. At first, the court was dismissive of claims to free speech. In the three First Amendment cases decided in the spring of 1919, the court unanimously upheld the convictions of all three speakers. Charles Schenck went to jail for distributing leaflets that encouraged drafted men to protest or register as conscientious objectors. The court found that such speech created a "clear and present" danger of disrupting the draft and that regulating such speech was not a violation of the First Amendment but appropriate state action (the speech was deemed the moral equivalent of falsely shouting fire in a theater). Socialist Party leader and perennial presidential candidate Eugene Debs went to jail for a speech that promoted socialism and criticized the war. And Jacob Frohwerk, editor of a small German-language newspaper in Kansas City, went to jail for publishing a sequence of critical articles about Britain and the war effort. The last decision suggested how much censorship the clear and present danger test allowed. The court conceded that Frohwerk had not made "any special effort to reach men who were subject to the draft," but argued that it was "impossible to say that it might not have been found that the circulation of the papers was in quarters where a little breath would be enough to kindle a flame." Such logic threatened to turn the Espionage Act into a general censorship bill—"clear and present danger" to the war effort could be discerned in any generally circulating publication, for who could say that it would not end up reaching a training camp?[28]

All three decisions were penned by Oliver Wendell Holmes, and all three reflected accurately Holmes's attitudes to free speech. To the extent that the aging justice was considered a liberal, it was because of his belief that judges should defer to legislatures rather than strike down democratically made law. In economic cases, that meant that Holmes favored state economic regulation rather than individual rights to freedom of contract, and on these grounds his opinions were welcomed by progressive commentators who were looking to use the state to mitigate the inequalities of Gilded Age capitalism. But in civil liberties cases, judicial deference meant supporting the state's right to regulate speech. In 1907, Holmes had upheld the conviction of a Denver newspaper for criticizing the Colorado Supreme Court; in 1915 he had upheld the conviction of an advocate of nudism for encouraging violations of laws against indecent exposure. And privately, Holmes confessed that "free speech stands no differently than freedom from vaccination."[29]

In the wake of World War I, however, progressives had come to a new appreciation of the threat that state regulation posed to civil liberties. Holmes's 1919 decisions were met with criticism, and in the summer of 1919, progressives mounted a campaign to change his mind about free speech. Lower court judge Learned Hand sent letters to Holmes about the need for civil liberties—the two had run into each other on a train in 1918, and had been arguing about free speech ever since. The progressive *New Republic,* ordinarily a great champion of Holmes, published articles critical of his free speech decisions, including one written by Zechariah Chafee Jr., a young law professor at Harvard, who began to outline a new defense of free speech in a series of influential publications. Harold Laski, who had a close relationship with Holmes, provided the judge with a steady summer reading list of material arguing for free speech, including Chafee's articles. In July, Laski arranged for Chafee and Holmes to meet over tea.[30]

By the time Holmes returned to the court in the fall of 1919, he had changed his mind about the meaning of the First Amendment. In his famous dissenting opinion in the 1919 *Abrams* trial, Holmes decisively broke from his earlier decisions. He argued that even radical pamphleteers trying to obstruct war production should be afforded First Amendment protections in order to promote public, democratic debate. His new vision of the role of free speech in the polity harkened back to the classical theories of Milton, Mill, and Wortman. Since his student days at Harvard, Holmes had been a careful student of John Stuart Mill's philosophy, and he had met the English philosopher on a trip to London in 1866. As he was deciding the post–World War I speech cases, Holmes reread *On Liberty* and came to a defense of speech rights that echoed Mill's classical liberalism: "The ultimate good desired is better reached by *free trade in ideas*—that the best test of truth is the power of the thought to get itself accepted in the competition of the market."[31]

The opinion was hailed immediately as a landmark in the emerging struggle for civil liberties. Roscoe Pound, dean of Harvard Law School, declared it a "document of human liberty" that was worthy of comparison with the work of Mill and Milton; Felix Frankfurter thought the dissent would "live as long as the *Areopagitica.*"[32] Over the course of the twentieth century, Holmes's rhetorical and conceptual coupling of free speech and free trade would, in fact, provide the animating principle behind the liberal development of the First Amendment—it was soon encapsulated by the powerful metaphor of a "marketplace of ideas."

Although that metaphor was an invention of the twentieth century—it seems to have been coined in the interwar period, and became ubiquitous after World War II—it crystallized the loose connection between speech and trade from earlier centuries, and created the impression of a consistent and long-lived liberal tradition.[33] By 1945, one philosopher of press freedom could refer straightforwardly to the "Milton-Mill-Holmes First Amendment formula"; in 1956, another declared that "from Milton to Holmes" the "libertarian theory" of press freedom had taken the "free market place of ideas" as its "slogan."[34] The democratization of American political discourse in the twentieth century, as well as the extension of free speech rights to a wide variety of minority groups, was attributable in no small part to this post–World War I rearticulation of a "classical" theory of free speech.

* * *

But there were deep ironies here. The "marketplace of ideas" had never been just a metaphor. The early American vision of press freedom had rested on two analogies to liberal economics. The theories of men such as Jefferson and Wortman had assumed that free public opinion required the absence of state censorship—that a free market of information would provide the basis for democratic politics. But their understanding of a free market of information in turn presumed the existence of a liberal newspaper market—as Jefferson had put it, "public papers" would be the mechanism to provide the citizenry with "full information." Holmes shared with earlier theorists of public opinion an assumption that democracy required a free flow of information untrammeled by state interference. But Holmes paid less attention to the *quality* of the literal marketplace of ideas. In fact, Holmes quite self-consciously didn't even read newspapers—as a jurist and a reader he preferred the abstraction of philosophy to the gritty particularity of facts.[35] Holmes paid little attention to the fact that the newspaper market, like other markets, had industrialized over the course of the nineteenth century.[36] By the time of Holmes's 1919 embrace of the "marketplace of ideas," the newspaper market bore little resemblance to the "public papers" that were so central to Jefferson's defense of freedom of the press.

From Gutenberg to Jefferson, the technical capacities of the printing press had remained largely unchanged. But in the nineteenth century, the nature of printing was revolutionized. Hoping to sell larger numbers of papers to the new mass markets of an increasingly urban and increasingly literate America, newspaper owners embraced a host of technological developments: the invention of newsprint, the development of linotyping and stereotyping, and the application of steam power to the printing press. By the late nineteenth century, publishers had both the desire and capacity to massively expand the circulation of their papers. For a time, the newspaper industry flourished. In the last decades of the nineteenth century, the number of daily newspapers in the country quadrupled. And circulation boomed. In 1870, there were 34 daily papers circulating for every hundred households; by 1910, it was up to 121 papers.[37]

The new mass press operated according to a new economic logic. With the rise of modern consumer culture, the advertising industry was expanding, and it turned to the newspapers to hawk a new range of products and brands. In 1890, T. H. Cahill boasted in the advertising trade journal *Printer's Ink* that newspapers had evolved beyond their traditional mission of "collecting and disseminating current intelligence" and that they now served as "agent and servant of the advertising spirit." The revenues from modern advertising dwarfed revenues from subscriptions, sales, and commercial printing contracts—and the more readers a paper had, the higher the fees it could charge the advertisers. Newspapers seeking a larger market and a competitive edge sunk more and more money into increasingly expensive printing technologies. In 1835, James Gordon Bennett had established his trailblazing mass-circulation *New York Herald* in a basement with a $500 investment. By 1890, when the *Chicago Tribune* established a new office, it cost the newspaper $750,000—$250,000 of which was spent on the machinery alone. As the press reached ever-greater numbers of readers, more and more capital was required to start a competitive and financially viable newspaper.[38]

In the newspaper industry, as in so many other late nineteenth-century industries, the increase in productivity thus became joined to a decline in competition. The lion's share of advertising revenue in any city flowed to the paper with the largest circulation, and with more revenue it could afford to grow its circulation even further. Smaller newspapers began to close. The largest number of daily newspapers in the nation's history was reached in 1909—it has been falling, more quickly in some periods than others, ever since.[39] And where newspapers remained, they were increasingly local monopolies. In 1910, 689 cities had competing daily newspapers—New York alone had boasted fifty-five newspapers in 1889. By 1930, only 288 cities had competing dailies. At the same time, newspaper chains began to emerge as wealthy publishers expanded to new cities to increase their market share. In 1909, press critic James Edward Rogers observed that "with the need of large capital, newspapers ceased to be owned and edited by one man. . . . Newspaper syndicates with trust methods have sprung into existence everywhere in our midst." In 1923, the Scripps-Howard chain paid $6 million for a paper that had been bought for $51,000 in 1892.[40]

Just as the industrialization of the press led to a decline in the diversity of the newspaper market, it also transformed the diversity of political information in the newspapers. The quest for mass markets was the deathknell for the old era of the partisan press—it no longer made sense to risk alienating half of the newspaper-buying public. As the *Cincinnati Tribune* made clear in 1895, political independence made a great deal of economic sense—the "old time servile party organs are neither profitable nor influential. The newspaper which is independent, and which is not merely partisan in its utterances, is sure to be the most profitable, for the reason that it enjoys the largest degree of popular approval." Such self-interest dovetailed with Progressive Era concerns about partisan political corruption, and newspapers began to declare their objectivity and independence. Although the new commercial papers expanded the range of their coverage—crime, sports, gossip, and comics all rose in importance—the political news began to become standardized. In the middle of the nineteenth century, the Associated Press (AP) formed, so that newspapers could share their stories and bring down the costs of reporting. An objective, authoritative, impersonal tone emerged in the news columns, so as to appeal to the widest audience. And the politicized commentary of the editor was quarantined in the new opinion columns, which were themselves syndicated across many newspapers. The newspaper industry was thriving, but it was also becoming clearer that the press was developing into a new and distinctive kind of political institution—authoritative, rationalized, standardized.[41]

Eighteenth-century theorists of press freedom had seen little need to distinguish between the rights of the press and the rights of the public—the right to speak, write, and print were presumed to be interchangeable, and freely available to all. (Given the gender, class, and racial limits to political participation, and the relatively low costs of printing, this was not an unwarranted assumption: the set of those who could participate in political life was not radically different than the set of those who had access to the press.)[42] But the industrialization of the press and the democratization of the country had introduced a new distinction between the printers and the public. As the polity had grown in scale, control of the press had consolidated in the hands of a small class of publishers; the formal equality of the "marketplace of ideas" was belied by the unequal power of the publishing class. Most Americans would participate in the free exchange of ideas in the newspaper market not as writers, but as readers. And they would depend for news on papers that were being produced as standardized, industrial commodities. Witnessing a display of American newspaper printing at the Paris Universal Exposition in 1900, one foreign commentator could not help but compare the making of a newspaper to the mass production of another infamous product of the industrial age—"it is as rapid and complete as the transformation of a pig into pork in the great factories of Chicago."[43]

American commentators, too, began to dwell on the unsettling comparison between the newspaper industry and the industrial corporations of the Gilded Age. Indeed, the new trends in publishing suggested the emergence of a new class division between the publishers, bound closely to the world of business, and the reading public who consumed mass news products. In the wake of his 1896 presidential defeat, William Jennings Bryan complained that "all the newspapers of the country [were] against us" and declared that there was "no greater menace than the predatory interests which own newspapers and employ brilliant editors to chloroform their readers while the owners pick their pockets." In 1911, he summed up a nascent critique of the newspaper industry's dereliction of democratic duty: "So many newspapers are owned by, or mortgaged to, speculators, capitalists and monopolists, and are used for advocating or excusing legislation, having for its object the conferring of special privileges upon a few of the people at the expense of the rest of the people, that the press has been robbed of much of its legitimate influence."[44] Henry George agreed, arguing in 1906 that "the large majority of the dailies, weeklies and monthlies turn pleader and champion for Privilege in this, that or the other respect"—a "bondage of the press" he attributed to the high costs of running a modern newspaper and the concomitant reliance on advertising support.[45]

Given such sentiments, it was only a matter of time until the muckrakers turned their attention to their own industry—they, too, thought the press was monopolizing the flow of information in the polity to the benefit of a self-interested class elite. Will Irwin, a famed muckraker who more or less invented modern press criticism in a series of 1911 articles in *Collier's,* expressed the point in representative language:

> The "system" in the American newspaper proceeds from the fact that the subscriber who buys the newspaper that it may teach him about his times and fight his battles against privilege, is not paying for that newspaper. *The advertisers are paying*—about one per cent of the population, and often the very one percent united, in the present condition of American society, with the powers most dangerous to the common weal. That, however, is not quite the taproot of the trouble. The American newspaper has become a great commercial enterprise. . . . Men and companies controlling such funds look at business in the business way. It has followed inevitably that the controlling head of most newspapers, the so-called publisher, is not an editor with the professional point of view, but a business man.[46]

Like so many Progressive Era reformers, Irwin was concerned that a class system of interlocking business interests had come to dominate American political life. "Big business," he observed, "is a complex web, binding this near department store to that remote trust company, this near insurance company to that far bank. Since the metropolitan newspaper also is a large commercial venture, involving millions in capital, hundreds of thousands in annual profit or loss, it follows the rule. Its capital is a thread in the same fabric."[47] The newspaper's incorporation into this capitalist fabric posed fundamental challenges to the possibilities for democratic politics. Elsewhere in the muckraking corps, journalist Charles Edward Russell argued that newspapers were "gagged through the irresistible medium of the advertising business," which created a "kind of concealed autocracy" at the heart of the American public sphere.[48] Upton Sinclair agreed. In 1919, the author of *The Jungle* set out to do for the newspaper industry what he had earlier done for meatpacking. "Journalism," Sinclair concluded, "is one of the devices whereby industrial autocracy keeps its control over political democracy."[49]

By the time the Supreme Court rediscovered the "marketplace of ideas," then, the actual marketplace that most mattered to the First Amendment had been transformed. It bore little apparent relation to the marketplace of ideas that lay at the heart of the democratic theory of public opinion. A capitalist media market, it now seemed, did not straightforwardly produce democratic public opinion—if anything, it seemed to Progressive Era commentators, the capitalist development of the newspaper industry might undermine democracy. Insofar as Holmes's embrace of the "free trade in ideas" reproduced the classical faith in a free newspaper market, it seemed out of touch with the transformations taking place in the actually existing newspaper industry.

* * *

Holmes's articulation of the modern faith in free speech was anachronistic in a more abstract, philosophical sense as well. The belief in natural individual rights that simply needed to be protected from state interference had been widely discredited by the politicized jurisprudence of the Gilded Age. As judges struck down collective bargaining and social welfare legislation as interferences with individual rights of contract, and as the corporate form was declared a legal person and issued a host of individual rights, progressives launched a full-throated critique of laissez-faire theories based on natural rights. The philosophy of liberalism was undergoing its own revolution. Whereas the "classical liberalism" of the eighteenth and nineteenth centuries emphasized the importance of individual autonomy from state intervention, the "new" or "social" liberalism that emerged in the early twentieth century sought to use the state to create the possibility of autonomous individuality.[50] At the level of political philosophy, the distinction between the two was captured in the opposition between classical liberalism's negative freedoms ("freedoms from") and social liberalism's emphasis on positive freedoms ("freedoms to").[51]

Paradoxically, calls to protect an individual right to speech came from precisely the same actors who otherwise wanted to transcend a politics centered on laissez-faire and individual rights. Holmes, for instance, had famously critiqued laissez-faire jurisprudence in his dissent in the *Lochner* case. Roscoe Pound, who welcomed Holmes's *Abrams* dissent as a continuation of a classically liberal tradition, elsewhere argued for an updated jurisprudence attuned to modern social interests rather than formal individual rights. This paradox was not lost on early free speech advocates. As legal historian Laura Weinrib has shown, the early American Civil Liberties Union was deeply ambivalent about relying on the courts to enforce an individual right to speech because its members were so committed to overcoming the jurisprudence of individual rights in the labor struggles that centrally concerned them. Zechariah Chafee, heavily influenced by Pound, even felt the need to declare that "it is useless to define free speech by talking about rights" as he was arguing for a more robust First Amendment right to speech.[52]

To square the paradox, Chafee attempted to identify a "social interest" in speech rather than simply an individual interest—speech should be free, he suggested, because it allowed societies to better determine political truths. But this effort to avoid the logic of individual rights failed to modernize First Amendment jurisprudence. Rather, in suggesting that a free exchange of ideas would produce truth, it reproduced the classical arguments for speech entirely. Mill, Cato, Wortman, and Jefferson had also assumed that protecting individual rights would produce public goods. For all of his rhetorical commitment to modernizing the jurisprudence of rights, it was telling that Chafee presented the case for free speech as an effort to preserve the vision of the founders.[53] Despite their hesitation, other advocates for free speech also ended up transferring classically liberal ideas about negative freedom and individual rights into the heart of the modern First Amendment. Holmes, for instance, was no free-market apologist. He argued for a marketplace of ideas less out of a naïve faith that truth would naturally emerge than from a world-weary fatalism and a Darwinian resignation to letting the chips fall where they may. For all that, the metaphor he chose to express the exchange of ideas harkened back to classical liberalism and laissez-faire—it was appropriate that he had been reading a biography of Adam Smith as he rethought the meaning of free speech in the summer of 1919.[54]

Justice Louis Brandeis, Holmes's civil libertarian ally on the Supreme Court, was more optimistic than Holmes, and argued that the free exchange of ideas would produce truth, democracy, and civic virtue. He valorized free speech as a positive contribution to democratic governance, arguing that "public discussion is a political duty. . . . This should be a fundamental principle of the American government. . . . It is the function of speech to free men from the bondage of irrational fears." That encapsulated a new idealization of the role of the individual in creating public opinion; as an affirmative, civic-minded gloss on free speech theory, it helped drive the modern embrace of individual speech rights. Still, even this most modern of legal thinkers was curiously traditional when it came to the First Amendment. In his famous opinion in the *Whitney* case, Brandeis sought to defend free speech with reference to the founders' republican faith in democratic dialogue. And, in the back of his mind,

Brandeis was thinking of politics in even older terms—classical Greek civilization provided his model of the good political life.[55]

In all, the modern jurisprudence of speech rights was framed in remarkably traditional terms. Modern civil libertarians had drawn on an eighteenth-century metaphor to justify their novel arguments for an unlimited right to speech, and they regularly made their case for civil liberties by presenting it as the heir to a long and consistent liberal tradition—even if that tradition was actually stitched together from often idiosyncratic philosophers who had little else in common. (In 1938, for instance, a district court judge would refer to Spinoza, Locke, Aristotle, Mill, Jefferson, and Holmes in deciding a case about the right to picket in New Jersey.)[56] Coming in the second decade of the twentieth century, this turn to a classically liberal philosophy of speech rights was doubly surprising. It seemed out of step with the interests of modern liberals in moving beyond the world of laissez-faire, rights-based jurisprudence. And it seemed strangely disinterested in the actual operations of a newspaper industry that had become stratified by new hierarchies of wealth and power.

* * *

The leading interwar theorists of democratic public opinion took on precisely these issues. Walter Lippmann and John Dewey's writings on public opinion in the 1920s have been elevated into something of a set piece in modern intellectual history—Lippmann questioning the traditional theory of democratic public opinion, Dewey quarreling with Lippmann's pessimistic conclusions.[57] What has been ignored, though, is the extent to which their work emerged from a particular and focused discussion of the inadequacy of First Amendment rights in the context of an industrializing newspaper market. Both scholars were attempting, in their own ways, to articulate a vision of press freedom that would transcend the traditional focus on speech rights. Both were concerned with guaranteeing the quality of information in the polity, rather than simply guaranteeing the individual right to express an opinion. Both sought to update democratic theory to account for the operation of the marketplace of ideas in fact, as well as in theory. And both were attempting to create a theory of press freedom that was appropriate to the twentieth century. Their efforts simultaneously articulated the problem of modern press freedom and foreshadowed the intellectual and political difficulties that their descendants would face when trying to reform the press.

Although *Public Opinion* and the *Phantom Public,* published in 1922 and 1925, respectively, are Lippmann's famous books, they were really the final two installments in a trilogy of works on the problem of public opinion. The first volume, *Liberty and the News,* was issued in 1920. Until very recently, it has been slighted—presumably on the grounds that as a collection of three essays, two of which had been previously published in *The Atlantic,* it was itself a rather slight volume.[58]

But *Liberty and the News* reveals Lippmann's central preoccupation with the challenges that the modern newspaper industry posed to the theory of free speech, and thus to the theory and practice of modern democracy. "In an exact sense," Lippmann declared in the book's opening pages, "the present crisis of western democracy is a crisis in journalism." In part, Lippmann argued, this was a function of the new modes of state propaganda that had first piqued his interest in the subject. But it was also, he realized upon closer reflection, a product of the economic basis of the newspaper industry. "Everywhere today," Lippmann observed, people "are wondering whether government by consent can survive in a time when the manufacture of consent is an unregulated private enterprise." Scanning newspaper coverage of the Great War and modern politics, and clearly influenced by muckraking critics of the press as well as his own studies of the *New York Times'* inaccurate coverage of the Bolshevik revolution, Lippmann worried that the public was not being provided with sufficiently accurate information. The public, Lippmann suggested, was "baffled because the facts are not available." Because "all news comes at second hand," he concluded, the public was responding not to objective political realities, but to "a pseudo-environment of reports, rumors and guesses. . . . Under the influence of headlines and panicky print, the contagion of unreason can easily spread through a settled community."[59]

The inadequacies of information in the news led Lippmann to rethink the relationship between free speech and modern democracy. He argued that the modern focus on protecting freedom of opinion was of less importance than protecting the flow of information upon which opinions were based. Opinions were derived from the "stream of news that reaches the public," so "the protection of that stream is the critical interest in a modern state. In going behind opinion to the information which it exploits, and in making the validity of the news our ideal, we shall be fighting the battle where it is really being fought." In short, Lippmann suggested that "the axis of the controversy needs to be shifted": "it may be bad to suppress an opinion but the really deadly thing is to suppress the news."[60]

At base, Lippmann was attempting to transcend the assumptions of the classical theory of democratic public opinion that was in the process of being enshrined in First Amendment jurisprudence. Given the actual operations of the press, Lippmann argued, it was possible to protect individual speech without ever touching the central issue for democratic government. "Protection of the sources of its opinion," Lippmann insisted, "is the basic problem of democracy. Everything else depends on it." By 1922, Lippmann was openly critical of the "classic doctrine of liberty" as embodied in the Bill of Rights and as articulated by Chafee, Mill, and Milton. "Democrats have treated the problem of making public opinions as a problem in civil liberties," Lippmann complained. While civil liberties were important, they did not "guarantee public opinion in the modern world," for they made a false assumption that true public opinion emerged spontaneously and naturally.[61]

Lippmann's intellectual moves bore all the hallmarks of the social liberals' efforts to move from a world of individual rights preserved by a faith in laissez-faire to a world of politically regulated social rights. The problems in the stream of news were, Lippmann suggested, the result of the laissez-faire nature of the newspaper market: "the mechanism of the news supply has developed without a plan." Modern democracies relied on individual self-interest to produce public opinion, but when those who owned the "common carriers" of information "arrogate to themselves the right to determine by their own consciences what shall be reported and for what purpose, democracy is unworkable." These problems could not be resolved through protecting a formal right to speech, free from government interference. "We cannot successfully define liberty, or accomplish it, by a series of permissions and prohibitions," Lippmann reiterated, "for that is to ignore the content of opinion in favor of its form."[62]

True liberty required a rejection of the abstract concern with form and a newly concrete effort to positively guarantee the sources of news upon which opinions were based. Or, as Lippmann put it, "liberty is the name we give to measures by which we protect and increase the veracity of the information upon which we act." *Liberty and the News* thus concluded by sketching a range of press reforms that Lippmann hoped would positively improve the content of democratic public opinion: improved professional standards and training for journalists; increased social responsibility among newspaper publishers; newspaper transparency about their sources of information; the replacement of libel laws with courts of honor; and the creation of government bureaus to provide information to the press. Each of these areas of practical reform would become widely debated over the course of the twentieth century.[63]

But even as he was calling for press reform, Lippmann was beginning to nurse deeper doubts about the problems of democratic public opinion. The ideas were only partly worked through in *Liberty and the News,* and they were largely submerged in his analysis of the press. But the seeds for Lippmann's later critique of mass democracy could be seen sprouting in his questioning of the possibilities of democratic governance. Unlike the muckrakers, Lippmann was not willing to lay the blame entirely on the corruption of the press by capitalism: "I do not agree with those who think the sole cause is corruption. There is plenty of corruption to be sure, moneyed control, caste pressure . . . and yet corruption does not explain the condition of modern journalism." Lippmann struck out for more fundamental problems, for more troubling criticisms: "The modern news problem is not solely a question of the newspaperman's morals. It is, as I have tried to show in what follows, the intricate result of a civilization too extensive for any man's personal observation."[64]

Over the coming years, Lippmann would come to treat the problems of the press as epiphenomenal to what he increasingly saw as the real problem of modern democracy—the fact that it had grown too vast and intricate for the capacities of the "omnicompetent" citizen of traditional democratic theory. In *Liberty and the News,* for instance, Lippmann argued that the economic structure and professional practices of the press created a distorting "pseudo-environment" that prevented citizens from "responding to reality as it is." But by 1922's *Public Opinion,* Lippmann had elevated the notion of a "pseudo-environment" from a particular problem of a disorganized newspaper industry to an ontological and epistemological dilemma—an inherent problem of psychology, or modern life, or language. Seeing the problem of the press in this way led Lippmann to dismiss his earlier hopes for press reform. "The problem of the press is confused," Lippmann now declared, because people hoped that the press would "make up for all that was not foreseen in the theory of democracy" and because "democrats [regarded it] as a panacea for their own defects." Such sentiments were naïve, Lippmann asserted, because "newspapers necessarily and inevitably reflect . . . the defective organization of public opinion." The crisis of western democracy was no longer a crisis of journalism caused by the economics of the newspaper industry. Instead, the crisis of journalism reflected a deeper problem for democracy—the impossibility of organizing mass democratic public opinion rationally. As Lippmann now saw it, the problem of the press was epiphenomenal: "the quality of the news about modern society is an index of its social organization."[65]

Looking back on his earlier thinking, Lippmann now argued that he had mistakenly conflated "news" and "truth." In reality, he had always made that distinction—the basis for his critique of the news (as it was) was its divergence from truth (or news as it *should* be). But what he now did was call into question the possibility that the news could *ever* represent the truth, and in the process he discarded his earlier hopes for a rational, truthful press. By opening up an unbridgeable conceptual distance between news and truth, he saw that the problem of the news was but a stand-in for the broader problem of democracy—"the troubles of the press, like the troubles of representative government . . . go back to a common source: to the failure of self-governing people to transcend their casual experience and their prejudice, by inventing, creating and organizing a machinery of knowledge. . . . This is the primary defect of popular government, a defect inherent in its traditions, and all its other defects can, I believe, be traced to this one."[66]

It was therefore necessary to turn away from hopes that the press could provide a panacea to the problems of democracy. It was necessary to explore the primary defect of what Lippmann was coming to call the "original dogma of democracy"—the idea that the public was supposed to be self-governing. In reframing the problem in such deep and intractable terms, Lippmann was drawn to pessimistic conclusions. "How," Lippmann asked, "is any practical relationship established between what is in people's heads and what is out there beyond their ken in the environment? How, in the language of democratic theory, do great numbers of people feeling each so privately about so abstract a picture, develop any common will? How does a simple and constant idea emerge from this complex of variables?" His answer, put simply, was that it couldn't. Not, at least, so long as democrats clung "to the intolerable and unworkable fiction that each of us must acquire a competent opinion about all public affairs." This was a repudiation of *Liberty and the News*'s hope for a revitalized press. The restructuring of the institutions of the public sphere now required not the reform and rebirth of journalism, not a more involved public, but the development of new expert organizations: "representative government . . .

cannot be worked successfully . . . unless there is an independent expert organization for making the unseen facts intelligible to those who have to make decisions." The beginnings of Lippmann's plans for a bureaucracy of experts had been present in *Liberty and the News,* but their purpose had been to increase the flow of news to the public. Now they began to seem a way to displace the public from direct democratic governance—they were to advise only those "making the decisions."[67]

By 1925, when he published the "sequel to *Public Opinion,*" Lippmann had followed this position to its logical, gloomy conclusion. In the new work, entitled *The Phantom Public,* Lippmann was in full retreat from the theory of democratic public opinion being articulated by civil libertarian advocates of the right to free speech. Building on his work in *Public Opinion,* Lippmann argued that "the ideal of the sovereign and omnicompetent citizen" at the heart of their theory of democratic public opinion was "unattainable," a "false ideal" that was "misleading" when pursued. The arguments remained the same, but the language had become stronger, the metaphors more contemptuous. Given the complexity of society, Lippmann pointed out that no citizen could know enough to make informed decisions and "given his inherently amateurish equipment, he will be as bewildered as a puppy trying to lick three bones at once." The only solution to these facts was to "abandon the notion that democratic government can be the direct expression of the will of the people. We must abandon the notion that the people govern." Instead, Lippmann argued, we should concede that on every issue there were "insiders" and "outsiders," and that only the former had the knowledge and competence to govern or make substantive decisions. If outsiders tried to govern directly it would be a disaster, and so it was necessary that "the public must be put in its place . . . so that each of us may live free of the trampling and roar of the bewildered herd." And the place of the public, Lippmann argued, was to intervene to adjudicate on the practice of "insiders" on an occasional, sporadic, and delimited basis—in short, to occasionally vote in broad terms on the actors who were to make all the important technical and substantive decisions.[68]

That was a fairly accurate, if deeply cynical, account of the trajectory of electoral politics and administrative governance in the modern United States. But it was significant that in the mid-1920s, Lippmann understood it to be a retreat from his earlier hopes for a more free and democratic press, as well as a critique of the valorization of public opinion that defined the new civil liberties discourse. In a few short years, Lippmann had so radically diminished his assumptions about the capacity for public opinion, so radically scaled back his democratic optimism, that *The Phantom Public* could appear almost undemocratic. "While one might cite passages which, if divorced from their context, would give the impression that Mr. Lippmann was permanently 'off' democracy," liberal philosopher John Dewey noted in a review of the book, "Mr. Lippmann's essay is in reality a statement of faith in a pruned and temperate democratic theory." But in the mid-1920s, it seemed that Lippmann was not so sure about even his "pruned and temperate" democracy. Writing to Judge Learned Hand shortly after the Scopes Trial, Lippmann confessed "My own mind has been getting steadily anti-democratic." Shortly thereafter, he told the readers of his daily newspaper column that "the plain fact is that democracy has had more failures than successes."[69]

* * *

However Lippmann had thought it through, it was not necessary to move directly from critiquing the role of the press in American politics to revising one's theories about the role of public opinion in democratic governance. In 1926, John Dewey turned his attention to the problems of democratic public opinion in a series of lectures at Kenyon College that were subsequently published as *The Public and Its Problems*. The lectures were, in part, a direct response to Lippmann. Dewey acknowledged his "indebtedness" to Lippmann's *Public Opinion* and *Phantom Public* "for ideas involved in my entire discussion even when it reaches conclusions diverging from his."[70]

Dewey, as always, worked at a degree of abstraction—Justice Holmes notoriously observed that Dewey wrote as "God would have spoken had He been inarticulate but keenly desirous to tell you how it was."[71] So there was much in *The Public and Its Problems* that seemed distant, colorless, and vague compared with the crisp, cynical realism of Lippmann. Dewey reflected at great length, for instance, on the importance of human associationalism, on the need for experimental reasoning, and on the problems of defining a "state." But at its heart, the work echoed Lippmann's analysis in *Liberty and the News*. Like Lippmann, Dewey was worried that modern conditions had created vast, distended, and complicated chains of interconnection that outstripped political ideas and practices that were anachronistic holdovers from an earlier era of small-town democracy. The "prime difficulty" for democratic life, Dewey suggested, "is that of discovering the means by which a scattered, mobile and manifold public may so recognize itself as to define and express its interests." Like Lippmann, Dewey thought that the increasing judicial protection of classical speech rights failed to guarantee a free and democratic public opinion: "the belief that thought and its communication are now free simply because legal restrictions which once obtained have been done away with is absurd. Its currency perpetuates the infantile state of social knowledge. . . . No man and no mind was ever emancipated merely by being left alone. Removal of formal limitations is but a negative condition; positive freedom is not a state but an act which involves methods and instrumentalities for control of conditions."[72]

Like Lippmann, Dewey was highly critical of the role of private economic interests in corrupting the flow of information in the news: "As long as interests of pecuniary profit are powerful and a public has not located and identified itself, those who have this interest will have an unresisted motive for tampering with the springs of political action. . . . The gathering and sale of subject matter having a public import is part of the existing pecuniary system." Like Lippmann, Dewey was concerned with the distorting influence of publicity agents, "advertising, propaganda, invasion of private life, the 'featuring' of passing incidents in a way which violates all the moving logic of continuity." And like Lippmann, Dewey wanted to dig beneath such obvious forms of corruption to articulate the deeper problems of modern democracy.[73]

But here, the two parted ways. Whereas Lippmann worried that members of the public could never be the omnicompetent citizens that democratic theory presumed them to be, Dewey argued that such concerns were mistaken. Of course individual citizens could not be omnicompetent, Dewey suggested, but to expect omnicompetence from every individual citizen was a holdover of a misguided belief in individual autonomy. Public knowledge could never be held individually; knowledge was social, a product of associations and communication. For Dewey, the root problem of modern democracy was the failure to acknowledge these truths, and the persistence of the false belief in individual autonomy. Because knowledge was associational and communicative, Dewey therefore argued that what was required was not less communication, as Lippmann had held in *The Phantom Public,* but more and better communication, as Lippmann had held in *Liberty and the News.*

So Dewey maintained that one could reform the press to create a closer relationship between news and truth. He thought that "Lippmann seems to surrender the case for the press too readily—to assume too easily that what the press is it must continue to be."[74] And by maintaining a distinction between the news media as they were and the news media as they ought to be, Dewey suggested that there were real possibilities for improvement—"the assembling and reporting of news would be a very different thing if the genuine interests of reporters were permitted to work freely." Unlike the later Lippmann, Dewey maintained that reforming the press was not a misguided and naïve panacea that would only exacerbate the inadequacies of democratic governance. It was a necessary step in a broader process of democratic revitalization. There was no need, therefore, to dismiss the democratic theory of public opinion. In fact, a "democratically organized public is a kind of knowledge and insight which does not yet exist"; it remained a project to be realized, not a reality to be transcended. And for a democratically organized public to emerge, "an obvious requirement is freedom of social inquiry and of distribution of its conclusions." Then, and only then, Dewey prophesied, "democracy will come into its own, for democracy is a name for a life of free and enriching communion. . . . It will have its consummation when free social inquiry is indissolubly wedded to the art of full and moving communication." This was what Dewey meant when he declared that "the cure for the ailments of democracy is more democracy."[75]

But Dewey was exceedingly vague about the practical measures that needed to be taken to create "full and moving communication." What, precisely, did he mean when he argued that "the highest and most difficult kind of inquiry and a subtle, delicate, vivid and responsive art of communication must take possession of the physical machinery of transmission and circulation and breathe life into it?"[76] The lack of prescription was tied to the nature of his project and to his experimentalist, pragmatic philosophy. It was far easier for Lippmann to critique or rationalize what existed than it was for Dewey to outline mechanisms that had to emerge from the trial and error of political life.

The fuzziness, however, was also a product of a deep tension in Dewey's thinking about the problem of the press, a tension that would haunt the politics of press freedom throughout the twentieth century. As a leading advocate of social liberalism, Dewey was committed to transcending classical liberalism's emphasis on individual rights. He wanted to move beyond the nineteenth century's focus on negative liberties by using the state to cultivate a social environment conducive to individual liberty. But when it came to the issue of press reform, Dewey's social liberalism faced quite a conundrum. Negative protections against censorship of opinion, both he and Lippmann had held, were insufficient to produce a genuinely liberal and democratic polity. They were inadequate guarantees of the quality of information in the press, and they could not reform the inequalities and inefficiencies that corporate power had introduced to the "marketplace of ideas." In this, the argument followed the standard line of the new liberalism. The normal course of action would be to use the state to break the corporate stranglehold and regulate the content of the market and thus create the possibilities for genuine liberalism through positive social action.

But in the case of press reform, such a move seemed unthinkable. What separated social liberals like Dewey from their progressive forebears was a reticence about the general applicability of centralized state action to resolve social problems.[77] The excesses of World War I had revealed that the prewar belief in collective action could go too far, that it could end up undermining rather than protecting liberty. And a key check on statist overreach was freedom of speech, expression, and opinion as outlined in Holmes's line of dissents in the Supreme Court. In *Liberty and the News,* Lippmann acknowledged that the "whole subject" of press reform was a "subtle and elusive matter," "immensely difficult and full of traps."[78] Lippmann had sidestepped the problem by retreating from press reform. Instead, he had reformed his theory of democracy—and he was never, in any case, a First Amendment absolutist.[79]

For those who maintained a belief in the traditional theory of democratic public opinion and an absolutist commitment to civil liberties, however, the problem of press reform was rather more intractable. Dewey, for instance, believed that the Supreme Court's defense of free speech was the "creed of a fighting liberalism," and he valorized Holmes as the embodiment of the "liberal mind."[80] In 1932's *Ethics,* Dewey argued that "ultimate authority [in a democracy] is to reside in the needs and aims of individuals as these are enlightened by a circulation of knowledge, which in turn is to be achieved by free communication, conference, discussion."[81] But how was such free communication to be created? By the mid-1930s, Dewey was insistent that democracy was a radical cause, that it "requires great change in existing social institutions, economic, legal and cultural"—that "the ends to which liberalism has always professed can be attained only as control of the means of production and distribution is taken out of the hands of individuals who exercise powers created socially for narrow individual interests."[82] At the same time, Dewey continued to insist on the need for "eternal vigilance" to protect the Bill of Rights—"he who would put the freedom of others in bond, especially freedom of inquiry and communication, creates conditions which finally imperil his own freedom."[83] Dewey never made it clear how he would reconcile those two commitments. How was one to decide whether the press was exercising its rights for "narrow individual interests" or to further the social interest in free inquiry and communication? And what political action could be taken to prevent the former while promoting the latter? Dewey never said.[84] But even Upton Sinclair, a less subtle thinker than Dewey, balked at the prospect of using the state to reform the press. "As a socialist," Sinclair had declared in 1920, "I advocate public ownership of the instruments and means of production, but I do not entirely rely upon that method where intellectual methods are concerned." "Have the state make all the steel and coal and oil, the shoes and matches and sugar," even have them distribute and print the press, Sinclair argued. "But for the editing of the newspapers I cast about for a method of control that allows free play to the development of initiative and the expression of personality."[85]

It thus seemed almost impossible to resolve the deeper problem of press freedom without trampling on the right to a free press—state intervention with the press was both the most obvious cure for the inefficiencies of the marketplace of ideas, and the one measure that was widely regarded as a death sentence for a free marketplace of ideas. A theory and program for press reform remained elusive. How, practically, could one create a free marketplace of ideas when the actually existing marketplace of ideas fell short of the ideal? The closest Dewey ever came to proffering an answer was a vague hope that the problem of press freedom would simply dissolve under a new economic order. "Does anyone," he asked in 1935, "imagine that under a cooperative economic system, controlled in the interest of all, it would be necessary to have official censorship of, say, the Hearst press? Would not such a press under such a social system be inherently impossible?"[86] It was appropriate that such sentiments were framed hypothetically and rhetorically—for all of his careful analysis, Dewey's effort to reformulate press freedom produced more questions than answers.

* * *

On the cusp of the Depression, then, basic tensions in the meaning and practice of modern press freedom had opened up. Despite the nascent development of First Amendment protections at the Supreme Court, the industrialization of the press meant that individual speech rights did not seem to ensure a free and democratic flow of information to the public. No longer, it seemed to critics like Dewey and Lippmann, could democratic public opinion be straightforwardly assured by restricting the intervention of the state in the marketplace of ideas. Such a classical understanding of press freedom seemed inadequate to modern conditions—it seemed a holdover of the eighteenth century, not a solution to the problems of the twentieth. It was thus necessary to rethink the meaning of press freedom, to find a way to guarantee the quality of the information that the public received. In the 1920s, this was a problem that was grasped primarily by the most perceptive theorists of democracy and a clutch of media critics. Even in purely intellectual terms, the need to outline a modern, positive theory of press freedom posed a difficult challenge. Neither Lippmann nor Dewey, after all, succeeded in outlining a new understanding of press freedom: Lippmann's efforts on this front led him to delimit the role of public opinion in democracy; Dewey's resulted in increasingly vague abstraction. And the problem of press freedom was also practical. In 1920, Lippmann had predicted "that in some form or other the next generation will attempt to bring the publishing business under greater social control [because] there is everywhere an increasingly angry disillusionment about the press, a growing sense of being baffled and misled."[87] Lippmann was prescient. Following the crash of the stock market, anger, disillusionment, and bafflement would explode.

2

Interwar Threats to Press Freedom

On January 12, 1939, New Deal secretary of the interior Harold Ickes and Frank Gannett, president of the Gannett newspaper company, engaged in a heated debate on the subject "Do We Have a Free Press?" Conducted before a sold-out New York Town Hall and broadcast nationally on NBC, the exchange revealed how divisive American press freedom had become in the 1930s. Ickes argued that "the lack of a free press is the most serious threat confronting our democratic government and our social order." Although the press was free from government regulation, Ickes asserted, the "financial and economic tie-ups" of the press meant it was not a "free servant of democracy." Gannett suggested that the threat to press freedom came not from the counting office—"financial strength" had led to "greater independence"—but from a New Deal plot to regulate and censor hostile newspapers. "This will bring about a situation," Gannett warned ominously, "where the one great essential of democracy, a free press, will no longer fearlessly inform the public about the public's business. Government propaganda, unrestrained and unchecked by the vigilance of the newspapers, will become the people's main source of information." The debate captured the deep uncertainty that many Americans felt about the state of their press. Indeed, if the applause and boos of the 2,000-strong audience were anything to go by, it seemed to one observer that the crowd was "about evenly divided in its sympathies."[1]

In the context of the global crisis of democratic governance in the 1930s, as well as the challenges and conflicts that roiled the New Deal polity, the state of American press freedom became a central and heated political issue. Troubled times gave old sentiments about the importance of press freedom both a new urgency and a new uncertainty. Frank Knox, publisher of the *Chicago Daily News,* felt that "as in many other fields, in the newspaper field the times demand a careful revaluation of concepts we once thought fundamental." Marlen Pew, a leading spokesperson for the newspaper industry, agreed: "We speak of 'free press' as one of the established facts of modern life in America, copper-riveted in the federal constitution and the constitution of the states. But nothing in the age-long battle for human rights is as simple as that." Thomas Mann, in exile at Princeton in 1938, expressed the problem of the press in appropriately epic terms: "The flag still stands, but the meaning has totally changed. A century ago freedom of the press was a demand; today it is an endangered right. A century ago the press had to break chains; today it has to defend itself against being enchained. . . . The shrinking power of democracy in Europe portrays itself in the decay of its press which is neither able nor willing to keep the public informed."[2]

As Americans concerned about the future of democracy turned their attention to the problems of the press, many became aware of the tensions between the theory and practice of American press freedom that had first been spied by such theorists as Walter Lippmann and John Dewey. In the context of the rise of fascism, the Great Depression, and the emergence of the New Deal state, uncertainties about the role of the press in the production of democratic public opinion became charged sites of political anxiety. Although the Supreme Court would begin to extend meaningful First Amendment protections to the press during the decade, leaving the press free from formal political censorship, this did not resolve the problematic relationships among the press, a newly activist state, and a corporate economy in crisis. Instead, the state of press freedom was interpreted by Americans in light of their diverse political commitments, and according to splintering understandings of the threats to the free press. In particular, two distinct developments threatened to monopolize the flow of political information in the Depression-era polity. Economic collapse and the growing consciousness of the American class divide heightened the sense of a distance between the publishers and the public, suggesting to New Dealers and those in the Popular Front that the flow of information had become monopolized by rich and venal publishers acting in their own self-interest. Alternatively, for conservative critics of the New Deal, the rise of the activist, regulatory state suggested the ways that a state could sculpt the flow of information in the polity without censorship—

through measures such as public relations bureaus, press handouts, and expanding economic regulation. Dictatorship, it seemed, would not come to America via formal censorship of the press. But it might come via either of these other channels. In the shadow of totalitarianism, the meaning of American press freedom became fraught.

* * *

The manifold crises of the interwar years produced deep doubts about the future of American democracy. In 1932, *Commonweal* observed that "the times are rich in talk of the passing of democracy." The next year, historian and diplomat Lewis Einstein agreed: "Mentally the world crisis has everywhere undermined faith in democratic institutions." Even before the Crash, leading intellectuals and commentators had wondered whether democracy could handle the challenges of modern politics: the apparent irrationality of the mass, the terrors of total war, and the turbulence of the international economy. On the global stage, liberal democracy had begun to retreat in the 1920s. In the United States, pragmatic liberals, radical communists, and corporate leaders alike flirted with the promises of governmental and economic efficiency they saw shimmering in Mussolini's Italy and Soviet Russia.[3]

Following the shock of the Depression, and the apparent inability of American politics to steer a stable course toward recovery, these democratic doubts deepened. Some called for a revision of traditional democratic commitments. In September 1932, the editor of the *American Political Science Review* wrote an article answering a startling question: "Does America need a dictator?" He decided in the negative, but both the question and the article revealed that others were not so sure. In June 1932, as mainstream a magazine as *Vanity Fair* ran an article entitled "Wanted: A Dictator! A Solution to the National Difficulty." In that article, which was nestled between glossy ads extolling the benefits of Gantner "knit to fit" swimsuits and Cliquout Club's "delicately dry ginger ale with piquant personality," the editors argued that Congress had proven utterly ineffective in the face of crisis, and that the "salvation" of European nations had come only with the rise of dictatorship. "We must," they concluded, make the "perfectly feasible . . . grant of dictatorial powers to the next President." *Barron's Business Weekly* agreed, arguing blandly that "a mild species of dictatorship will help us over the roughest spots in the road ahead." Walter Lippmann counseled a recently elected Franklin

Delano Roosevelt that "you may have no alternative but to assume dictatorial power." In late 1932, William Randolph Hearst's movie company adapted a British novel, *Gabriel over the White House,* in which an ineffective president became a divinely inspired dictator after suffering a car accident, and rapidly solved America's economic and social problems.[4]

Ultimately, the American people would rally behind a rebirth of democratic values, fashioning themselves as champions of democracy in an illiberal world. Hitler's rise to power in the heart of European civilization, and his dismantling of the liberties of the Weimar Republic, particularly encouraged Americans to renew their opposition to dictatorship. And the rise of the Nazis powerfully dramatized to Americans how quickly democratic institutions could be subverted, and how precarious their civil liberties were. Early interpretations of Nazi rule came primarily from foreign correspondents, who keenly felt the emergence of speech and press restrictions and amplified this image of oppression to their stateside readers.[5] In March and April 1933, the Nazi regime suppressed oppositional papers, threatened foreign correspondents, and promised punishment to nonconformist writers. On April 1, American reporter Robert Desmond observed that "freedom of the press in Germany . . . is at an end," while *Editor and Publisher* charged that Hitler had "decreed one of the most sinister censorships on record." Three weeks later, observing the effects of censorship combined with the rise of the Ministry of Public Enlightenment and Propaganda under Joseph Goebbels, American editor Mark Ethridge mourned that "until a few months ago, no press in the world was freer in the right to criticize than the German press" and that "never in history has a once proud press taken so humiliating and degrading a part in organized brutality." By the beginning of 1934, *Editor and Publisher* could sum up the state of German journalism as a "grotesque picture to American eyes. . . . What is left of the German press [has been flattened] into a mere servile, flattering, fawning and viciously deceptive organ of the dictatorship."[6]

From that moment forward, Americans began to call the new dictatorships "totalitarian," adopting a term that originated in Italian fascist circles. The totalitarian concept became the interpretive tool by which Americans determined the state of liberty in the world as well as the moral contours of geopolitics. And it heightened American concern with the problems of public opinion—the essence of totalitarianism was the erasure of individual rights to thought, speech, and publication. In 1939, philosopher Sidney Hook—a student of John Dewey—established the

Committee for Cultural Freedom (CCF) to marshal intellectual support against the "tide of totalitarianism" that was "washing away cultural and creative freedom along with all other expressions of independent human reason." The CCF's declaration of principles, written by Hook and signed by ninety-six prominent figures, placed liberty of thought and discussion at the center of their opposition to totalitarianism. Totalitarian systems, they argued, shared an "unvarying hatred for the free mind." Columbia historian Carlton J. H. Hayes agreed with these sentiments, noting that totalitarianism "is the antithesis of ideals of spiritual and mental freedom."[7]

The structure of public opinion therefore became the quality through which Americans could distinguish dictatorships from democracy. Modern dictatorships ran sham elections, which meant, according to University of Chicago professor of international law Quincy Wright, that elections "do not disclose a democracy because the opinion which is reflected in the election is one which is determined by the dictator." Instead, "in a democracy, opinion is determined by the people as individuals." In 1939, Julius Yourman of New York University summed up the prevailing logic neatly: "The extent to which the propaganda machinery of a country has been brought under the control of one organization or of a group of related organizations is a useful measure of the degree to which absolutism dominates it, and of the extent to which democracy has been eliminated."[8]

The sharp comparison between totalitarian and democratic regimes of public opinion heightened the importance of the conjoined liberties of press, speech, and thought within America. As FDR put it in 1937, "the whole structure of democracy rests upon public opinion. . . . Only through the full and free expression of public opinion can the springs of democracy be renewed." In a 1938 University of Chicago Roundtable on the future of democracy, a Swiss professor of law expressed the modern political binary crisply: "When you have an effective opposition, based on freedom of speech and thought and on information, you have a democratic government. Where you have no authorized public opposition, you have dictatorship." His American interlocutor, a University of Chicago economics professor, understood the lesson perfectly. "In other words," Professor Harry Gideonse replied, "we have a free democracy in proportion to the extent to which we protect minorities in expressing their views of what the dominant group is doing."[9]

Because the experience of Germany had revealed how a once liberal public sphere could become its monstrous opposite, understanding

America's press system became all the more crucial. Observing that "a 'free press' is in greater danger today all around the world than ever before in one hundred years," Republican senator Arthur Vandenberg, himself an editor and publisher before his turn to politics, argued that "we have no automatic immunity against this hazard." On the other side of the political spectrum, New Dealer Rexford Tugwell warned a meeting of editors that they should be primarily concerned with the "nationalist movements which have extinguished democracy and written warped definitions of freedom," because "three hundred and fifty million people who thought that they were free fifteen years ago are now living under dictatorships of one kind or another." Managing editor of the *Christian Century* Paul Hutchinson summed up the connection between dictatorship and the heightened importance of American press freedom. "There will probably be little debate among Americans these days as to the importance of a free press," Hutchinson argued. "If any among us have had doubts on the subject, recent events in Europe should have settled them. More and more we see that the fate of American democracy is tied up with the fate of the First Amendment."[10]

* * *

In the 1930s, the First Amendment was about to enter a new era. First Amendment rights had languished in the nineteenth century. Out of deference to federalism, individual states had been free to censor newspapers without raising constitutional questions. At the federal level, the Supreme Court had only begun to consider constitutional rights to speech in 1919, and only the dissenting opinions of Holmes and Brandeis had adopted a civil libertarian perspective. But in 1931, the Supreme Court found that state laws censoring the press violated the First Amendment. Its decision in *Near v. Minnesota,* although a close-run affair, was a victory for classical speech rights. It breathed new life into the First Amendment's protection of press freedom.

The origins of the case could be traced to 1925, when Minnesota had quietly approved a Public Nuisance Law that allowed a judge to perpetually enjoin a newspaper or magazine from publication if it was "obscene, lewd, and lascivious . . . or malicious, scandalous and defamatory." In 1927, the *Saturday Press,* run by Jay Near and Howard Guilford, became the first newspaper to be enjoined under the law, which had become known as the "gag law." Near and Guilford's stock-in-trade were scandalous attacks on the city's Prohibition-era government and its links with organized crime. They repeatedly attacked the sexual impropriety of the city's ruling elite, were not above using their paper for blackmail, and had a penchant for using anti-Semitic, anti-Catholic, and racist rhetoric. In the summer and fall of 1927, the *Saturday Press* began running a series of stories on the shakedown of a dry cleaner by a local gang. The stories fixated particularly on the inadequate policing of the matter, which the *Saturday Press* attributed to the corruption of law enforcement by Jewish gangsters. "We have Jew Gangsters," the *Press* howled, "practically ruling Minneapolis. . . . I simply state a fact when I say that ninety per cent of the crimes committed against this society are committed by Jew gangsters. . . . It is Jew, Jew, Jew, as long as one cares to comb over the records." (The *Saturday Press* was quieter on the fact that the aggrieved dry cleaner was also Jewish.) In November, the paper was charged under the gag rule.[11]

Liberal defense attorney Thomas Latimer picked up the case for Near and Guilford. Challenging the law's constitutionality, he connected the matter to the general crisis of democracy. "There are only two countries in the world today with a statute similar to the one at issue," Latimer asserted—Russia and Italy. The immediate constitutional question was whether the law was compatible with the Minnesota Constitution, which held that "the liberty of the press shall forever remain inviolate, and all persons may freely speak, write and publish their sentiments on all subjects." The matter was referred to the Minnesota Supreme Court, which held unanimously that the gag law was constitutional. The decision reflected the lingering hold of a delimited, republican vision of press freedom from the nineteenth century. In the first instance, the Minnesota court held that "our constitution was never intended to protect malice, scandal and defamation when untrue or published with bad motives or without justifiable ends." Rather, it was "liberty of the press that is guaranteed—not the licentiousness." Given that the disreputable, licentious *Saturday Press* fell outside the limits of protected speech, the court concluded that the regulation of such a nuisance fell within the state's police powers, and could be straightforwardly compared with the regulation of other public nuisances—houses of prostitution, noxious weeds, dogs, and carnivals.[12]

Such a decision not only reflected nineteenth-century attitudes about the limits of press freedom; it also reflected nineteenth-century attitudes about the right of states to regulate behavior within their borders in the interests of preserving what they held to be the public good. With one important exception, the Supreme Court had been highly deferential to such state regulation in the late nineteenth and early twentieth centuries. That exception was the regulation of economic activity, where the *Lochner*-era court repeatedly struck down efforts to regulate commerce on the grounds that such regulations violated Fourteenth Amendment rights to property and freedom of contract. But First Amendment rights had not yet been incorporated into the Fourteenth Amendment, so even as it protected individual property rights, the Supreme Court deferred to state regulation targeting speech. Only eight years earlier, in 1920, the Supreme Court had upheld the conviction of Joseph Gilbert under a Minnesota statute barring speech that interfered with military recruitment. Gilbert had suggested that Americans had been "stampeded into this war [World War I] by newspaper rot to pull England's chestnuts out of the fire for her"—for that, he had been fined $500 and imprisoned for a year. Refuting Gilbert's claim that his First Amendment rights had been violated, the majority of the court found that such a statute was "a simple exertion of the police power." In dissent, Louis Brandeis articulated liberal disgust with both the court's use of the Fourteenth Amendment to shore up property rights and its neglect of free speech claims against censorious states: "I cannot believe that the liberty guaranteed by the Fourteenth Amendment includes only liberty to acquire and enjoy property."[13]

Near's lack of success at the Minnesota state court was thus unsurprising; it reflected the jurisprudential status quo. But as Brandeis's 1920 dissent suggested, momentum was building for a more robust understanding of the First Amendment, and a variety of political actors were mobilizing to defend and extend the right to free speech. Looking for champions for his cause, and increasingly desperate, Near reached out to these new free speech advocates. (Guilford, recovering from gunshot wounds from a run-in with Minneapolis gangsters, had lost interest in the case.) First to respond to Near's entreaties was the most unlikely of allies for the anti-Semitic, antiradical publisher. In July, the American Civil Liberties Union (ACLU) announced that it would appeal to the Supreme Court to overturn the Minnesota gag law, because the endorsement of the "prior restraint" of the press was "a menace to the whole principle of the freedom of the press." Until now, as the ACLU pointed out, even the most limited readings of the First Amendment had held that at least prior restraints on publication were unconstitutional (punishment after publication, of course, was completely legitimate). The ACLU thus understood that "if the Minnesota Law is constitutional, then the Fourteenth Amendment and inferentially, the First Amendment, no longer protects the press against previous restraints."[14]

The young organization, however, was cash strapped, and it found itself squeezed out of Near's case by a much wealthier benefactor: Robert McCormick, archconservative publisher of the *Chicago Tribune*. McCormick's support for Near's case was no doubt eased by the fact that Near's anti-Semitism and conservatism were rather less distasteful to him. (McCormick, apparently, felt that the *Saturday Press*'s articles were "fairly temperate and possessed of some literary merit.") But McCormick was also emerging as a leading advocate for a robust First Amendment. Forced to defend his paper from libel charges brought by Henry Ford and Chicago mayor William Hale Thompson in the early 1920s, McCormick had begun to articulate a classically liberal understanding of the need for a press free from government restraint. With his lawyers, McCormick began to think about the right to press freedom in sweeping historical terms; in preparing Near's defense, he consulted with University of Illinois journalism professor Frederick Siebert, and encouraged Siebert to work on a history of press freedom from British common law to the present. Both McCormick's public statements about the gag law and his lawyers' briefs on behalf of Near abounded with references to Milton, the Tudors, the Renaissance, and the death of Socrates (one *Tribune* headline boasted, "History of 2,300 Years Cited in 'Gag' Law Brief"). Given these interests, in 1928 McCormick had been named chairman of the American Newspaper Publishers Association's (ANPA) newly created Committee on Freedom of the Press (the new committee reflected the increased interest in the First Amendment, and was also, at least in part, a direct response to the Minnesota gag law). In his 1929 report to ANPA, McCormick declared the gag law "tyrannical, despotic, un-American and oppressive." The *New York Times* similarly opined that the "vicious law" was the envy of "Soviet Commissars" and "Oriental despots" and threatened "the end of a free and honest press." By April 1930, McCormick had convinced ANPA to back an appeal of the case to the Supreme Court, on the understanding that the *Chicago Tribune* would foot much of the bill.[15]

Argued in late January 1931, a Supreme Court decision in favor of Near was handed down five months later. By striking down a state law for violating an individual's right to speech, it was a breakthrough decision that extended First Amendment protections against the states, and ushered in a new era in which press freedom was fully incorporated through the Fourteenth Amendment.[16] The court had been flirting with such a finding for the past five years, but there was no good reason to expect that it would protect Near's right to free speech. In 1925, en route to upholding Benjamin Gitlow's conviction for publishing a radical pamphlet in violation of a New York statute, Justice Sanford had declared that First Amendment rights were among those rights protected by the due process clause of the Fourteenth Amendment, at least in the abstract. And in 1927, a conviction under a Kansas criminal syndicalism law had been set aside because the application of the act had violated the Fourteenth Amendment rights of an IWW organizer—but in this case the court had carefully stopped short of ruling the law itself unconstitutional.[17] The extent to which First Amendment rights could be practically defended from state regulation was thus unclear, as was the likely success of a legal strategy focused on speech rights. It was significant that Near's lawyers and some of his public advocates simultaneously made the argument that by depriving him of his livelihood, the gag law had violated Near of his right to property under the Fourteenth Amendment.[18]

Writing for the majority of the court, however, Chief Justice Charles Evans Hughes made it abundantly clear that the gag law violated press freedom. Hughes declared straightforwardly that there was no doubt that the First Amendment applied to the states through the due process clause of the Fourteenth Amendment. The question thus turned on whether the gag law interfered with "the essential attributes" of press freedom—whether the law was "consistent with the conception of the liberty of the press as historically conceived and guaranteed." Casting his mind back to classical defenses of press freedom, and citing a long line of commentary from Blackstone through Madison and onto Chafee, Hughes argued that the gag law's use of prior restraint was the "essence of censorship." It was settled law, Hughes argued, that the First Amendment was designed to protect against such previous restraints. However odious a particular publication might be, Hughes continued, prior restraint was not a constitutionally valid remedy; "the fact that the liberty of the press may be abused by miscreant purveyors of scandal does not make any the less necessary the immunity of the press from previous restraint."[19] Nor did it matter whether or not the publication would cause public outrage or whether it was based on truth—for allowing prior restraint for reasons of falsehood or public reaction would open the door to widespread censorship. The ruling of the Minnesota Supreme Court was reversed and the Gag Rule was struck down.

But it was a closer affair than the cogent and apparently commonsensical decision suggests. The case was decided by the slimmest of margins—five votes to four. The dissenting opinion was written by Justice Pierce Butler, who observed correctly that despite Hughes's historical mode of argumentation, the decision was novel: "it gives to freedom of the press a meaning and a scope not heretofore recognized and construes 'liberty' in the due process clause of the Fourteenth Amendment to put upon the States a federal restriction that is without precedent." If Hughes had embraced a new way of thinking about the abstract right to free speech, Butler, who hailed from Minnesota, continued to focus on the offensive content of the particular speech at issue. Unlike Hughes, Butler quoted extensively from the *Saturday Press,* and observed that "slanderous and defamatory matter predominates [in its pages] to the practical exclusion of everything else." And if Hughes sought to protect an abstract right to speech from abuse by the states, Butler continued to argue that the regulation of such slanderous speech fell within the police powers of the states. "It is of the greatest importance," Butler asserted, "that the States shall be untrammeled and free to employ all just and appropriate measures to prevent abuses of the liberty of the press."[20] Such a vision came incredibly close to carrying the day in 1931. In fact, had it not been for the retirement of Chief Justice William Howard Taft because of ill health in 1930, and his replacement by Hughes, the Butler position would likely have been the majority holding. As McCormick wrote to a fellow publisher in the aftermath of the decision, "If Taft were still occupying Hughes' place, we would have been beaten."[21]

Even the majority position contained significant loopholes in its protection of press liberty. The decision turned on the unconstitutionality of prior restraints, and Hughes explicitly noted that it remained perfectly acceptable to punish a newspaper after publication via libel laws. More importantly, the decision also asserted that "protection even as to previous restraint is not absolutely unlimited." The court opined that prior restraint might be constitutional if it was necessary to protect national security during war, public decency in the face of obscenity, or orderly government from violent revolution. Even as it struck an unprecedented blow for the right to free speech, then, the court was legitimizing prior restraints for the first time in the nation's history. And the logic of the first of these exceptions—the wartime requirements of national security—would come to play a significant role in delimiting modern American press liberty.[22]

But in the short term, neither the contingency of the outcome nor the lacunae within the decision could tarnish what was undeniably a reestablishment of the First Amendment's protection of press freedom from prior restraint as well as an unprecedented application of the First Amendment to protect press liberty from encroachments by the states. The decision was widely interpreted as a "great charter of freedom" for the American press and as a sign that the Supreme Court had embraced a newly liberal conception of free speech. Throughout the remainder of the decade, the court *would* increasingly protect First Amendment rights from state censorship. And forty years later, the promise of the *Near* decision was fulfilled when it played a central role in the Supreme Court's decision to overturn restraints on the publication of the *Pentagon Papers*.[23]

But although the *Near* decision represented a breakthrough in modern First Amendment jurisprudence, commentators at the time correctly understood that the case instantiated a classical vision of press freedom, that it indicated "a resurgence of the eighteenth century doctrine of the privilege of free speech." Judge Leon Yankwich, quoting from the increasingly obligatory John Milton, explained that *Near* was a great victory for free speech, the "traditional concept of the English-speaking world."[24] The decision, then, was simultaneously a leap forward and a throwback. In practical terms, it created federally enforceable speech rights against state governments for the first time. But symbolically, it represented, 150 years later, the final ratification of Madison's failed effort to include a prohibition on state censorship in the Bill of Rights. Colonel McCormick, fairly giddy with success, certainly understood the decision as part of a classically liberal tradition. To celebrate his victory—which he thought would "go down in history as one of the greatest triumphs for free thought"—he organized a party at Monticello at which 200 editors and journalists gathered to dedicate Jefferson's study as a "perpetual shrine to freedom of the press." (McCormick seemed oblivious to the irony that Jefferson had championed state regulations of speech.) McCormick subsequently had a section of Hughes's decision chiseled into the marble of the *Chicago Tribune*'s lobby, where Hughes's sentiments took their place among the pantheon of free press advocates—John Milton, Benjamin Franklin, and Thomas Jefferson.[25]

The press freedom protected by the *Near* decision, then, was viewed in traditional terms—as merely the absence of state control. In the classical theory of press freedom that was being elaborated in the 1930s, a free newspaper market would provide the basis for democratic public opinion so long as it was shielded from state oppression. "A hundred years ago," Baltimore journalist Gerald W. Johnson declared in 1938, "this might have been accepted as the conclusion of the whole matter." But now, the professor and practitioner of journalism pointed out, even though freedom of the press "had been established as far as the law and the courts can establish it . . . he who would call the press of the United States absolutely free is either reckless or not well informed." Indeed, in the age of the Depression and the New Deal, transformations in both the market and the state ushered in new threats to press freedom. Developments in First Amendment jurisprudence did little to convince Americans that their press was free, and debate about the actual operation of the press mushroomed. As the *New Republic* put it in 1937, Americans wanted their press to "be free in fact as well as in theory."[26]

* * *

The crisis of the American economy provided many reasons to think that the press was not, in fact, free. The mere fact of the financial crash suggested that something was amiss in the press. Journalism had been unable to provide the information necessary to ward off the speculative bubble and the panicky crash that had decimated the nation's economy, and there was evidence to suggest that this was more than simple incompetence. In April 1932, New York congressman Fiorello La Guardia had offered testimony to the Senate Banking and Currency Committee that suggested widespread "ballyhooing of stocks" by financial journalists. Assisted by two other men, La Guardia "carried into the committee room a large trunk containing scrapbooks of newspaper articles, cancelled checks and other data"—proof that financial writers from such papers as the *Wall Street Journal* and the *New York Times* had been paid to promote the public sale of stocks by companies such as Savage Arms, Indian Motocycle, and Pure Oil. One press agent, Newton Plummer, was alleged to have spent $268,000 to have his promotional pieces rewritten for newspapers. "This only goes to show," La Guardia concluded, "what lengths such forces will go to humbug the public mind."[27]

At the same time, federal forays into the world of the power industry revealed a vast propaganda apparatus that the power trusts were using to manipulate press coverage and further "humbug the public mind." Press critic George Seldes, for instance, claimed that the Federal Trade Commission (FTC) investigation had "disclosed one of the biggest scandals in the history of the United States and certainly the greatest scandal in the history of the American press." Between 1928 and 1932, the FTC investigations produced forty-four volumes of reports, which contained some 25,000 pages of testimony and analysis and exhibits documenting the shady economic practices of the modern power companies. According to one commentator, the FTC had "hewn its way . . . to the very heart of our modern monopoly system and laid it bare."[28]

Among the revelations in the FTC reports was evidence that the public utility industry was deploying "one of the greatest propaganda machines in the history of the country," designed to ensure that the industry received favorable publicity and to ward off the threat of public regulation. Centrally coordinated information bureaus issued press releases and ghost-written editorial copy to newspapers across the country, which quickly found their way into print. The Illinois Public Utility Information Committee, for instance, sent out a regular news bulletin to 900 newspapers in the state, which produced about 5,000 column inches per month. Similar material found its way onto the wire services. ("The AP sends out practically everything we give them," boasted one Missouri publicist.) At the same time, power companies sought to purchase newspapers, while power company PR agents wined and dined editors, trying to curry favorable editorial coverage with the promise of exorbitant advertising contracts. It all added up to a sustained and apparently successful effort to manipulate press coverage of an important industry. "Only one of the 600 newspapers in Missouri," declared publicist J. B. Sheridan, "is opposed to the electric industry." What was more, he continued, power industry publicity had "done much to change and direct the economic thought and economic practice of the American people."[29]

For the heirs to the muckraking critique of corporate newspaper corruption—men such as Harold Ickes and radical journalist George Seldes—such revelations confirmed earlier fears that monopolistic money interests were controlling the press and distorting the formation of public opinion. As Seldes put it in 1937, the power industry propaganda campaign was waged by "the powers known as the capitalist system or Wall Street, or the Money Trust, or Plutocracy, or Special Privilege, the System, the Beast or what you will by any other name." Ickes referred simply to a "Utilities Octopus." Even conservative congressman John Rankin, hardly a radical critic of capitalism, thought the FTC hearings raised questions about the autonomy of the press: "We ask for and demand a free press in this country, and yet the power trust owns or controls some newspapers in every state in the Union, some of which deliberately distort the news, deceiv[ing] the public with misleading headlines or with editorials written by or at the request of these utilities."[30]

The FTC investigation certainly confirmed that the corporate, profit-seeking press was suffering from the same problems that afflicted the broader economy. As one close observer of the FTC hearings put it, the public utilities industry had worked its influence on the press because "the concentration of ownership and control in the newspaper field [was] similar to what is going on elsewhere."[31] In the first place, newspaper diversity was declining. Between 1930 and 1940, the number of cities with competing dailies fell from 288 to 181—in 1936, over 1,200 cities had only monopoly newspapers.[32] Even in more diverse media markets, the change was clear. In 1890, there had been eleven newspapers in Chicago. Since then, the population had doubled, but the number of newspapers had more than halved, dropping to five.[33] The background trend was the ongoing decline in the absolute number of newspapers in the nation. There had been 2,078 newspapers in 1919. By 1942 there were only 1,787—a 14 percent decline despite a 29 percent increase in population.[34] Over the same period, newspaper circulation was growing—between 1904 and 1947, it increased some 56 percent.[35] And the decline in papers was not caused exclusively, or even primarily, by Depression-induced problems in the industry. In fact, a 1933 government report on the newspaper industry concluded that "the last two decades have seen a rapid and even accelerating increase in the circulation of individual publications. The financial position of the newspaper industry appears to be excellent. It is indeed an unusual industry in which a random selection of 14 concerns reveals not one that sustained a loss during 1932."[36] While advertising and circulation were down from pre-Crash heights, the newspaper industry was weathering the storm fairly well, and there were more newspaper closures in the booming 1920s than there were in the 1930s. The press was declining because it was simply more profitable to own a monopoly newspaper.[37]

Counting up individual newspapers, moreover, overstated the diversity of the American newspaper market. In 1933, industry watcher Marlen Pew conducted a survey of "hundreds of newspapers . . . published in cities scattered from coast to coast" and found them "as alike as so many peas in a pod." In part, this was a function of reliance on syndicated material and standardized wire services—essential if smaller papers were to fill their news holes economically. But diversity was also undermined by the continuing growth of newspaper chains. The first national study of newspaper chains had been conducted in 1924, and discovered thirty-one chains controlling 153 newspapers and 30 percent of the daily circulation. By 1933, there were sixty-three newspaper chains in the country, which controlled 361 newspapers and over 37 percent of the daily circulation. On Sundays, the chains controlled 46 percent of circulation. This decline in diversity posed a threat to the vibrancy of American press freedom.[38]

At the same time, the growth of chains and newspaper monopolies had turned journalism into a big business. Journalist and New Deal staffer Irving Brant observed that "the press, though it never admits, and the public at large does not realize it, is a part of American big business." John E. Stempel, head of the Department of Journalism at Indiana University, stated that "no one denies that economic growth has resulted in shifting the direction of the policy of an increasing number of newspapers from publishers who were editors to publishers who are primarily business men."[39]

The facts did seem undeniable—publishers were now men of big business. When *Time* magazine profiled *Los Angeles Times* publisher Harry Chandler in 1935, it revealed that he was an officer or director of thirty-five corporations in California, including oil, shipping, and banking interests. In 1934, the owner of the *New York Tribune* passed away, leaving a will that revealed an estate holding securities in excess of $16,000,000 in such industries as electricity, oil, gas, and steel. In 1941, Vernon McKenzie, director of the University of Washington School of Journalism, observed calmly that "many owners are not really newspapermen . . . [but] they are not influenced by the pressures of a big bad wolf called Big Business. They are *a part of* big business. So they tend, quite naturally, to dress like, act like, and think like big bankers and big corporation lawyers and big private utilities men." McKenzie was untroubled by this development. "In stiffly competitive days," he thought, it was lucky that newspapermen were now economically savvy businessmen.[40]

But in the context of economic catastrophe, as well as the growing awareness of the American class divide between the haves and the have-nots, many were concerned that the wealth and power of a small class of newspaper publishers posed a threat to press freedom. Bruce Bliven of *The Nation,* for instance, believed that chain owners such as Gannett, Hearst, and Roy Howard "wield more power than is safe in a democracy." Many others grappled with the economic transformations of the press by fixating on the threat that the figure of the publishing baron posed to

American democracy. In Sinclair Lewis's dystopian 1935 novel about the rise of American fascism, *It Can't Happen Here,* the power behind the dictator's throne was a successful and mysterious newspaper editor. Lewis's outmatched protagonist was the editor-publisher of a small Vermont paper, who struggled to resist the dictatorship—but his "smearily printed newspaper, seemed futile against the enormous blare of . . . propaganda."[41]

In his Depression-era films about American democracy, Frank Capra was similarly preoccupied with the power of newspaper barons. In 1939's *Mr. Smith Goes to Washington,* the villain is a corrupt senator in the pocket of Jim Taylor, a newspaper publisher who runs the state political machine. In the film's climactic sequence, as Capra's everyman hero, Jefferson Smith, tries to take on the Taylor Machine with an epic filibuster to stop the passage of a corrupt bill, the action turns on Smith's ability to explain his actions to the public. But Smith's efforts are defeated by Taylor's newspaper machine, which misrepresents Smith and violently suppresses Smith's efforts to circulate accurate information through an old-fashioned associational newsletter. In 1941's *Meet John Doe,* another newspaper baron tries to build a third-party movement to replace democracy with dictatorship, and once again uses his newspaper holdings to misrepresent and marginalize the hero. In both films, Capra relied on characters having improbable changes of heart to preserve democracy, but the real message was bleak: the corporate newspaper barons seemed to hold all the trump cards. In the opening sequence of *Meet John Doe,* Capra showed an old newspaper motto ("A Free Press means a Free People") being jack-hammered from the façade of a newspaper building and being replaced by a new phrase: "A Streamlined Press for a Streamlined Age."[42]

One real-life publisher, William Randolph Hearst, became a lightning rod for such fears about the undemocratic power of newspaper barons. The wealthy publisher—*Fortune* reckoned him to be worth $140 million in the middle of the Depression—was both a larger-than-life character and an increasingly reactionary political player. Hearst's media holdings were vast: twenty-six daily newspapers and more than 20 percent of Sunday circulation, a news syndicate, a wire service, thirteen magazines, eight radio stations, and two motion picture companies. Amid the squalor of the Depression, his lifestyle was flamboyant: Hearst's California estate was an ostentatiously eclectic homage to European aristocracy, replete with fifty-six bedrooms, multiple swimming pools, and a vast private menagerie. After briefly supporting FDR's 1932 election, Hearst attacked the

New Deal with vigor, calling it a communist threat to traditional American liberty. From the floor of the Congress, loyal Democratic senator Sherman Minton returned the insult, declaring that "the dictatorship we have to fear in this country is that of a purse-proud, insolent, arrogant, bull-dozing newspaper publisher like William Randolph Hearst." In all, Minton charged, Hearst was "the greatest menace to freedom of the press in this country."[43]

In the era of the Popular Front, Hearst hardly helped his cause by vigorously opposing labor, hounding radical academics, and publishing articles sympathetic to Hitler and Mussolini. In early 1935, a series of mass protests indicted the publisher. Fifteen thousand gathered in a Madison Square Garden "hung with red streamers proclaiming the Soviet cause and condemning Hearst" for editorializing against the USSR. The same week, an unofficial caucus before the National Education Association meeting gave historian Charles Beard a standing ovation for a vitriolic attack on Hearst, passed a resolution in favor of freedom of the press, and called for congressional inquiry into the connection between Hearst's anti-Red campaign and his industrial interests. The Communist Party organized People's Committees against Hearst that were so successful in their boycotts that they caused Hearst to change the name of his newsreels from *Hearst Metronome News* to *News of the Day.* Norman Thomas declared Hearst "Public Enemy no. 1," the League Against War and Fascism called him "Hitler's man in America," and Raymond Gram Swing thought Hearst one of the "forerunners of American fascism." Activism against Hearst revealed that the broader political networks of the Popular Front were deeply concerned about the corrosive effects of a capitalist-dominated press on the future of American political liberty. It was no accident that the masterpiece of Popular Front cultural politics was a thinly veiled attack on the publisher—Orson Welles's *Citizen Kane.*[44]

Even beyond Hearst's ill-fated orchestration of the 1936 Alf Landon campaign for the presidency, the press's role in presidential elections suggested that newspaper publishers were following their own economic interests and drifting away from the people. In 1932, FDR had been elected with 57 percent of the popular vote but had received editorial endorsement from only 41 percent of daily newspapers. In 1936, FDR captured 60 percent of the popular vote but had received editorial support from only 37 percent of the dailies—a number that slumped to one in four daily newspapers by 1940, when he received 55 percent of the vote.[45] Such evidence suggested that newspaper editorials did not shape public political consciousness anywhere near as directly as most media pundits presumed. But most commentators instead read these figures as proof of the increasing chasm separating the elitist press from the people's interest.[46] Journalist Irving Brant, for instance, argued that the sheer magnitude of capital invested into a newspaper had "given the newspaper publisher all the fears and prejudices which make the business world reactionary in politics." Looking over newspaper behavior in the 1940 political campaign, Brant charged that the "alliance between the press and Big Business throws into the political scales, all on one side, a crushing weight of propaganda and money."[47]

In short, in a decade wracked by class conflict, the growing wealth and apparent conservatism of newspaper publishers seemed to place them in opposition to the people. Both liberal and radical critics began to wonder whether press freedom could survive. Publisher William Allen White, a widely respected sage of small-town political values, worried that the press was becoming controlled by the "innate conservatism of property interests"—a fact that "may constitute a new threat to freedom of the press." Radical press critic George Seldes was rather more direct: "The press needs free men with free minds intellectually open; but its leadership consists of moral slaves whose minds are paralyzed by the specter of profits." In his 1939 debate with Frank Gannett, Ickes drew on the FTC investigations to charge that Gannett's papers had been temporarily owned by the International Power and Paper Company. "During the time that this company had a very large interest in the Gannett newspapers," asked Ickes, "was Mr. Gannett free?" Warming to his theme, Ickes argued that newspapers' "vast financial investment, running high into the millions, binds them closely to the business world from which they draw their sustenance. Freedom is impossible . . . when the counting office holds the whip hand."[48]

In the polarizing economic conflicts of the 1930s, the traditional connection between the economic and political functions of the press had become a contentious site. Whereas the capitalist basis of the press had once been the foundation for its independence and liberalism, the industrialization of the press now seemed to suggest that press economics had made it subservient to undemocratic forces. It all raised new questions about the meaning of the First Amendment. "What benefit of a free press," asked liberal publisher J. David Stern, "if that free press gangs up on one side?" Observing that the press was acting much like any other business in "treating information as a commodity like shoes and butter," Pulitzer

Prize–winning historian Herbert Agar posed a more troubling problem. "If the press operates like other forms of private business," Agar asked, "why should the press have special protection under the Constitution?"[49]

* * *

While liberal critics worried that the market undermined press freedom, conservative critics of the New Deal began to worry that the press faced renewed subservience to the state. The Supreme Court decisions of the 1930s made clear that the First Amendment protected newspapers from explicit censorship. But the modern state no longer sought to shape opinion only through prohibition; a firewall against censorship was no protection against an increasingly active state shaping the circulation of information to the public. As journalist Bryant Putney observed, "under the New Deal, administrative agencies have made greater efforts than under any previous administration to create public support for their acts and policies through the use of such instruments of explanation and persuasion as are available to them."[50] The rise of administrative publicity raised new questions about the relationship between the modern state and press freedom, and became enmeshed in partisan clashes over the expansion of the New Deal state.

The New Deal public relations apparatus was certainly vast. It is tempting to focus on the most visible developments—but as important and richly symbolic as the fireside chats may have been, it should be remembered that there were only thirty-one of them in twelve years.[51] The real activity took place elsewhere in the bureaucracy, where each of the new executive agencies established publicity departments and held regular press conferences. These publicity departments churned out a huge amount of verbiage—a 1936 report revealed that in three months alone, federal agencies had prepared 4,794 news releases, which were issued in a total of 7,139,457 copies to 2,280,963 persons.[52] In less than a year, the National Recovery Administration (NRA) alone issued 5,200 handouts, and the Agricultural Adjustment Administration almost 5,000. At the receiving end, the system produced the regular "swish of an envelope being dropped through the slot in the door" of the Washington correspondent.[53] By March 1940, it was estimated that the Washington bureau of the *St. Louis Post-Dispatch* was receiving seventy-three pieces of federal publicity a day. Such a flood of information found its way quickly into print. A 1937 study of the *New York Times* found 1,281 items that appeared to have been "released or influenced by federal administrative publicity offices"—a number that amounted to 15 percent of all wire items.[54]

An ever-expanding staff of publicity workers was responsible for producing this stream of handouts—some 146 full-time staffers in 1936, assisted by 124 part-timers. The staff for these positions came overwhelmingly from the ranks of working journalists and editors. Press relations for Harold Ickes's Department of the Interior were handled by the "red-faced burly philosopher" Michael Strauss, a former Hearst employee whose "ménage for a number of years was a haven of refuge for competent journalists who found themselves out of a job." "Seasoned newspaper man" William Lawson headed up the press service of the NRA, where he "organized a full staff on the pattern of a newspaper room with himself as a managing editor." The new government positions offered higher salaries and greater job security than Depression-era newsrooms, and the new jobs promised liberal journalists, particularly those working for a conservative publisher, a chance to participate in the New Deal rather than swipe at it. Senator Glass of Virginia, himself a newspaper publisher, quipped that there were "more newspapermen in the departments and bureaus than there are newspapermen outside." Indeed, for all of the talk of the brains trust, one observer felt that the newspapermen outnumbered the professors in the New Deal by nearly two to one. As Harvard political scientist E. Pendleton Herring observed in 1935, "the public relations of the federal administrative agencies is predominantly the relationship between newspaper men speaking for the Government to their erstwhile fellow journalists"—"to an extraordinary degree the bureaucracy has taken the newspapermen into its own camp."[55]

The rash of New Deal activity, filtered through this new information apparatus, transformed Washington, DC, into the news capital of America. A DC press corps had been growing throughout the second half of the nineteenth century—in 1840, press galleries had been organized in Congress for the first time; in the 1860s, a stretch of 14th Street became known as Newspaper Row because of the growth of bureaus that had sprung up in proximity to both government buildings and a telegraph service; by the 1870s and 1880s, the press correspondents were organizing social and professional societies. Still, reporters in DC covered the Senate, not the White House. And until 1932, New York had generally been considered the plum domestic job for journalists—Washington at best a detour, at worst a hardship post. In the first decade of the twentieth century, a *Chicago Tribune* reporter assigned to DC had hesitated because Washington's news "did not bulk large compared with the news of Chicago." In the 1930s, though, Washington became the reporters' town it is today. By 1934, the United Press (UP) wire service carried three times more news from DC than it had in 1930; 25 percent of all AP wire stories were coming from DC. As the New Deal began to dominate the nation's political agenda, so too did it begin to dominate the news agenda.[56]

Ever since, there has been an understandable tendency to interpret the development of the New Deal publicity system in personal and partisan terms. The presidential press conference was the undisputed symbolic center of DC's press relations—seen as a uniquely American equivalent for parliamentary question time and, with varying degrees of irony, a "showpiece for democracy." In a theatrical arena where presidential personalities ruled, none reigned more supreme than FDR. By abandoning Hoover's requirement that questions be submitted in writing in advance of the conference, FDR signaled a new openness to the press, a trusting candor that seemed confirmed by his habit of talking "off the record" or providing "background information" that could be used without attribution. Of course, FDR would prove a master at using his press relations not only to inform but also to manipulate, cajole, and seduce the press. Whether one thought of FDR as a saint or a Svengali of the press, however, the modern press conference had actually begun decades earlier, when the first Roosevelt was in the White House. It had been evolving, in fits and starts, ever since.[57]

New Deal press relations, too, were a broader development of what came before. The first publicity agent to work for an administrative agency was Joseph Bishop, who had worked for the Panama Canal Commission in 1905. In 1908, Gifford Pinchot of the Forest Service pioneered the use of press handouts. By 1913, when almost every cabinet department had at least one press relations specialist, Congress was sufficiently concerned about executive publicity branches that it passed a law prohibiting the use of federal funds for "publicity experts." (The ban was wholly ineffective, because it applied only to the specific job title of "publicity expert," hence the use of euphemisms like "director of information," "director of publications," or "chief educational officer" for the publicity agents of the New Deal.) With the coming of World War I, the Creel Committee became a major producer of government propaganda and news releases, and the employment of press agents hardly waned in the 1920s. Secretary Hoover's Department of Commerce, for instance, continued to expand and modernize its press relations. The number of press releases it issued had increased tenfold under his watch, to 3,658,000 in 1928. The Department of Agriculture, too, was a pioneer in providing information to the public. By 1930, it issued 25 million publications alongside 3,000 news and interpretive articles. Given such output, it was little wonder that a journalist facing a ten-pound pile of ninety-six papers on his desk—the "twenty four hour output of the great battery of government press agents"—should conclude in 1931 that the federal government was "the greatest propaganda establishment in the world."[58]

All of this took place before the New Deal, which meant, as Leo Rosten observed in his landmark 1937 study, *The Washington Correspondents,* that DC's emergence as the "matrix of political news . . . was no sudden phenomenon." Rather, it was a function of the "movement of political power to a central point, the most striking characteristic of contemporary political life [and] a manifestation of an historical trend which began on the plane of the economic and invaded the sphere of politics." The rise of federal publicity was a necessary part of the rise of the modern administrative state. As political scientist Harold W. Stoke explained in 1941, the executive had displaced the legislature as the center of policy making, and it needed a mechanism to build public support for its activities. Journalists, too, were coming to rely on executive publicity to make sense of the dizzying array of federal activity. "Such a thing as really 'covering' Washington in the old newspaper sense is now out of the question," confessed the political editor of the *Baltimore Sun;* "the press agents alone make it even relatively possible."[59] The shift in the mode of governance disrupted the traditional channels through which political information circulated to the public, and raised new questions about the relationship between the press and the state.

Historically, the main mechanism for informing the public had been the partisan press. The emergence of the party system in the early decades of the nineteenth century had been bound up with the proliferation of newspapers in the early republic. Editors helped to organize political parties, and partisan papers provided the ideological and organizational ties needed to bind nascent parties together. The relationship between parties and press was mutually beneficial. For the politician, a friendly press was a necessity—feeding information to a loyal newspaper guaranteed good coverage come election time, and the press provided unrivaled insight into the mood in the electorate. For the editor, a friendly politician provided an easy source of news, and a channel to the economic lifeblood of the early American press—government printing contracts.

This system began to disintegrate in the middle decades of the nineteenth century. The newly commercial press began to rely on mass circulation rather than printing contracts for revenue, and it became more profitable to present a paper as objective in order to appeal to the greatest number of readers. As a result of a series of corruption scandals and the expanding scale of state printing needs in the middle of the nineteenth century, the state stopped awarding printing contracts to newspapers. Instead, from 1861 on, a new Government Printing Office handled the printing of government documents, laws, and releases. Still, the older partisan system continued in sections of the country, particularly the solid Democratic South.[60]

By the time of the New Deal, then, political information circulated to the public via a number of channels—from congressional members with ties to local newspapers, from commercial presses keen to display their independence, and from nascent administrative agencies publishing releases printed by the government. During the New Deal, the administrative agencies continued to grow in importance, and administrative publicity was a necessary part of the broader state-building activity of the FDR administration, which sought to displace the party and Congress in favor of executive governance.[61]

As a result, opposition to federal publicity became intertwined with partisan opposition to both executive reorganization and the substantive goals of New Deal reform. The charge against executive reorganization was led by representatives of two older systems for circulating political information to the public. Representing the partisan network was Virginia senator Harry F. Byrd, head of the Byrd political machine and publisher of a number of partisan papers. Byrd was the key figure in congressional opposition to both executive reorganization and federal publicity: his investigating committee in the mid-1930s, intended to roll back the proliferation of executive agencies, was the first to publicize the scale of New Deal publicity, and he continued to champion laws banning federal publicity well into the 1950s. Representing the commercial press was Frank Gannett, who used his chain of newspaper holdings to fund a Committee to Uphold Constitutional Government and launch a vast publicity campaign against executive reorganization. Gannett, who had hopes for the presidency, was not alone among newspaper publishers in attacking executive reorganization and publicity, or in arguing that the New Deal was ushering in a dictatorship. In 1938, one businessman wrote to FDR to complain that the newspapers had taught his employees to "unconsciously group four names, Hitler, Stalin, Mussolini, and Roosevelt."[62]

More broadly, attacks on federal publicity became a central front of anti–New Deal politics, as conservative politicians charged FDR with orchestrating a national propaganda system that would lead America down the path to dictatorship. As early as January 1935, Red-baiting congressman Martin Dies, soon to be chair of the infamous Dies Committee, introduced a resolution to the House calling for a seven-man commission to investigate charges "that the present administration is seeking to control the press through a well-organized and highly developed plan of employing hundreds of newspapermen as press agents for various federal activities; and that the administration requires such press agents to exercise favoritism and partiality in giving news releases to such newspapers that favor the administration." Inspired by Dies's resolution, two conservative writers soon published a sensationalist exposé attacking New Deal handouts. In 1937, the chairman of the Republican National Committee blamed his party's 1936 electoral defeat on federal publicity; in 1938, J. Parnell Thomas began a one-man investigation into the "hornet's nest" of New Deal publicity agents. By 1940, Thomas Dewey was charging that the expansion of the New Deal "propaganda machine" represented "the most staggering bid for power in our history" and "the trend toward centralization of power in the national government." In all, Dewey argued that the "propaganda mills" of the New Deal "constitute[d] a dangerous trend toward totalitarianism."[63]

New Dealers responded to such accusations by doubling down on claims that there was nothing insidious about New Deal publicity. Liberal journalist Elmer Davis conceded that the current administration had "enormously expanded the practice" of government publicity, but asserted that that was natural for a government that was "trying to do more things than any administration had tried before." In the first academic study of administrative publicity, political scientist James McCamy argued that despite the hostile rhetoric of government critics, there was no terrifying centralized propaganda apparatus—in fact he was dejected to find little coordination among the various branches of the government, and a high degree of overlap, inefficiency, and improvisation in New Deal publicity bureaus. McCamy, who had studied under proponents of administrative centralization at the University of Chicago and would soon move into the administration himself, hoped that a greater coordination of publicity would enhance the efficiency of federal governance, which was the "chief hope of making the necessary social adjustment to urban-industrial conditions."[64]

On another level, the New Deal response was more partisan. Against the neutral, technical and democratic work of the state publicist, McCamy juxtaposed the self-interested propaganda of the corporate newspaper press. He argued that newspapers reflected the view of business, and were opposed to the New Deal because it challenged their private monopolies. Democratic public opinion, McCamy asserted, was "more likely to be drowned in the flood of publicity issued not by bureaucrats but by demagogues who speak the people's language and serve other gods than freedom." State publicity was simply providing a democratic counterbalance to the undemocratic propaganda of the corporate press; the state was merely "competing with private propaganda" to provide true information to the public. Leading New Deal politicians made the same case. When a Republican senator called for an investigation of government publicity in 1935, Hugo Black countered that the investigation should be extended to "include propaganda issued by any agency of any kind in the US, including the Chamber of Commerce and the power companies." Harry Hopkins justified Works Progress Administration (WPA) publicity spending as a necessary mechanism to spread truth about the program to a public that was being misled by false stories in the press. In 1939, when justifying the establishment of a New Deal publicity program on the radio, FDR asserted that it was only possible to transmit the truth through the radio and implied that the capitalist press had fallen short of its democratic duty—"the press is as free as it cares to be or as its economic condition permits it to be."[65]

In the hyperbolic partisan crossfire, an opportunity to conduct a serious debate about the relationship between administrative publicity and press freedom was missed. Depression-era journalists often lacked the specialized training to interpret the policy decisions of the New Deal state. In the mid-1930s, 86.6 percent of DC correspondents felt that doing their job properly required more knowledge about economics than they had. But when journalists became dependent on official handouts to cover the activities of the government, it raised important questions about the possibilities for independent, critical journalism. And for all the concern about propaganda, in the longer term, the rise of the administrative state would not threaten press freedom by propagandizing the public directly. Rather, the administrative state would increasingly conduct its affairs in secret, a fact that McCamy noted in passing in 1939: "The need for secrecy in some activities where advance publicity might spoil valuable preparation occurs in practically all fields of federal administration."[66] But the 1930s saw almost no discussion of the problems of secrecy and transparency. Instead, there was a heated debate about whether or not it was appropriate for the state to provide information to the people. Both sides conceptualized a public besieged by biased propaganda, differing only on whether that propaganda was being produced by the state or by the corporate press. The debate continued, unresolved, into World War II.

* * *

In all, the global crisis of liberal democracy had led Americans to worry about the state of their domestic liberties. But what *was* the state of press freedom in the 1930s? Americans did not agree about the answer, or even about the terms in which the question should be posed. From the perspective of First Amendment jurisprudence, the Supreme Court had extended press freedom in the 1930s, and the press increasingly had the legal right to publish without state censorship. But the decade witnessed new challenges to the practical ability of the press to circulate information to the public. Liberal and progressive press critics argued that press freedom was threatened by corporate consolidation. They thought that the press was biased toward business, tending toward monopoly, and dominated by antidemocratic newspaper barons. For conservative critics of the New Deal, the independence of the press was challenged by the flood of government propaganda swamping the nation, a sign of the looming growth of the state. The inadequate flow of information to the public was a problem that had first been raised by John Dewey and Walter Lippmann in the apparently placid 1920s. In the turbulent thirties, the problem had been given new urgency. And as reformers within the New Deal state sought to regulate the crisis-ridden newspaper industry, the problem of modern press freedom became sharply political.

3

A New Deal for the Corporate Press?

In the fall of 1933, a number of newspaper publishers gathered at St. Paul's Church in Mount Vernon, New York, to celebrate the 200th anniversary of the Zenger trial. Their paeans to the glories of that eighteenth-century struggle for press freedom had a distinctly modern edge. Indeed, reported *Editor and Publisher,* "seldom, if ever, since the early days of the Republic has there been such a unified and insistent demand from newspapers that their constitutional rights be reaffirmed officially."[1] The publishers gathered at St. Paul's insisted that the First Amendment protected the press from any state regulation. Thinking of themselves as heirs to Zenger's classically liberal fight against state censorship, they sought to block New Deal efforts to regulate the economics of the modern newspaper industry. But men such as Robert McCormick and William Hearst were not simple craftsmen like Zenger. And the state they opposed was not an absolutist monarchy.

Could the state regulate the modern newspaper industry without violating the First Amendment? The question was new, a product of the simultaneous industrialization of the press and rise of the modern First Amendment. In the classical theory of press freedom, state regulation of the press automatically violated civil liberties. The theory had emerged in the eighteenth century, when the public and printers had struggled together against the absolutist state. But by the 1930s, the interests of the public and the printers had diverged. The publishers at the Zenger ceremony continued to presume that the public interest in a free flow of information was best served by protecting their own rights to economic and political autonomy. Others, convinced that the corporate press was undermining democratic dialogue, began to wonder whether public rights to information should trump the economic rights of the publisher. As Frank Knox, editor of the *Chicago Daily News,* put it, "Pre-eminently and most emphatically the news columns of a modern newspaper do not belong to the owners of the publication. They belong to the readers of the newspaper just exactly as the streets of a city through which a streetcar system operates belong, not to the streetcar company, but to the citizens who are its customers."[2]

But what could be done if the publishers abused their responsibilities to the public? In the case of the streetcars, as in any other modern industry, the public could turn to the state or municipality to regulate or take ownership of the cars. But in the case of the press, such state intervention was a fraught business, because it seemed to risk squashing press freedom in order to save it. It was an "illogical situation," according to labor journalist J. B. S. Hardman: "The Bill of Rights is our sacred inheritance. The freedom of the press is a basic right. But the newspapers are an industry. And while we don't want any meddling with our civil rights, our industrial enterprises can and more often need to be regulated for the safety of our social traffic."[3] The state could not avoid regulating a major industry, yet it could not interfere with freedom of the press.

These complex relationships between the modern state, the newspaper industry, and the First Amendment were resolved during the New Deal. In an effort to democratize the press industry, reformers tried to apply to the press a variety of policies they used in other industries: corporatist regulation, consumer protection, and trust-busting litigation. The NRA tried to regulate the newspaper industry like all other industries—according to federal codes on pricing and production practices. The Food and Drug Administration (FDA) attempted to regulate deceptive advertising, both to protect consumers from dangerous products and to loosen the hold of the advertising industry on the nation's press. And the Justice Department brought an antitrust suit against the AP in an effort to restore competition to an increasingly monopolistic newspaper market. None of these proposals were particularly radical. New Deal reformers were sensitive to concerns about state censorship, and proposed narrowly drawn regulations that were intended to reform newspaper economics without interfering with civil liberties. Nevertheless, they argued that such technocratic regulations were appropriate for what was, after all, a major industry. And they suggested that state action might be essential to the preservation of a diverse and vibrant press.

Even so, their arguments were almost entirely unsuccessful. New Deal efforts to reform the press were defeated by a newspaper industry that argued that any government regulation of the press would lead to totalitarian censorship. This was a novel use of the First Amendment, pioneered by the conservative, pro-business lawyers of the newspaper industry. In particular, these arguments were developed by the general counsel for the American Newspaper Publishers Association (ANPA)—the "chubby, suave [and] immensely clever" Elisha Hanson. Hanson criticized New Deal publicity handouts, and argued that government regulation of business was "an octopus that is constantly stretching out its tentacles in an effort to completely enmesh us." He prepared legal briefs and offered congressional testimony to protect the newspaper industry from economic regulation. And he successfully fused his antiregulatory politics to antitotalitarian commitments. If the New Dealers regulated the press, he argued in 1943, the "people of the US will be confronted just as the people of Germany today are confronted, with a government-controlled press."[4]

By using the First Amendment to ward off New Deal press reform, Hanson and his allies played a central role in bringing classically liberal speech rights into the twentieth century. They pioneered the use of civil liberties as a tool for free-market politics. In the end, although there was little reform of the press, the New Deal did transform the meaning of press freedom. It produced a heightened respect for laissez-faire press freedom, and a new resignation to the corporate consolidation of the press.

* * *

The problematic relationship between the First Amendment and the New Deal first crystallized around the attempt to regulate the newspaper industry under the NRA. On June 16, 1933, Franklin Delano Roosevelt signed into law the National Industrial Recovery Act. A signature program of the early New Deal, the new law sought to bring all industries—including, presumably, the press—under the aegis of a national regulatory apparatus. In an effort to stabilize the economy, it allowed the president to approve industrial codes that had been drawn up by trade groups. The details of these codes—price and trade regulations, labor conditions, production policies—were to be developed in consultation with a newly created government apparatus: the NRA. The law led to an explosion of bureaucratic activity. In two years, the NRA issued 13,000 pages of codes and issued 11,000 interpretive rulings. And it produced contradictory outcomes. It sought simultaneously to transcend industrial competition—FDR privately admitted that it was an "enormous step away from the philosophy of equalitarianism and laissez-faire"—and to hold the line against monopoly. It made promises to protect the interests of labor, business, and the nascent consumer movement, even though those interests were often mutually exclusive. Its boards were soon dominated by business.[5]

In the case of the newspaper industry, the uncertainties and contradictions of the process may have reached their greatest heights. The day after the National Industrial Recovery Act was signed into law, newspaper trade journal *Editor and Publisher* observed that "there is considerable question as to whether newspapers come under the provisions of the act." There was debate about whether the newspaper industry should write a code, what such a code should cover, and whether a newspaper code was even compatible with the First Amendment. The ANPA, for instance, initially advised papers to neither prepare nor subscribe to an NRA code "because the publishing of newspapers is not an industry but an enterprise of such peculiar importance as to be especially provided for in the constitution of the U.S. and of the several states whose independence must be jealously guarded from any interference which can lead to or approximate censorship." The NRA, declared *Editor and Publisher* in July, had handed the newspaper industry "a jigsaw puzzle of a thousand pieces with about half of them missing. The result is confusion thicker than we have ever witnessed."[6]

Proponents of a newspaper code, both within the newspaper industry and within the NRA, thought it was actually a rather simple matter. The modern mass press, they argued, was an industry like any other. It was therefore appropriate and necessary to subject it to industrial regulations. The liberal *Milwaukee Journal* dismissed ANPA's advice as simply a "plea for special privilege" and argued that, as industrial enterprises, newspapers needed economic regulation to prevent the rise of press monopolies. Lindsay Rogers, charged with administering the newspaper code for the NRA, thought a code was completely compatible with press freedom, for it would deal exclusively with economic issues and would have no impact on editorial affairs. After all, Rogers pointed out, no newspaper had ever relied on a constitutional guarantee of press freedom to ignore workers' compensation or maximum hour laws.[7]

NRA chief Hugh Johnson knew that publishers were particularly worried about section 4(b), which gave the president power to license industries that engaged in "destructive wage or price cutting" and other practices contrary to the spirit of the act. A licensed press, argued *Editor and Publisher,* would violate press freedom: "The press cannot be free unless it is economically free. The President or Congress that puts it under license will control it and will have declared a dictatorship." Shortly after the launch of the NRA, in an effort to appease the publishers, Johnson announced in a press conference that the licensing provisions would be clearly unconstitutional if applied to the press. (In fact, he had been given advice that this power was broadly unconstitutional and it would never be used in any industry.) Then he took the offensive. The free press issue was a "synthetic dead cat," he asserted. It was raised only to mask the economic self-interest of the publishers—"even my gentlest and most loyal terrier will growl at me if I try to take his bone away, and these few gentlemen fear the loss of the biggest bone of all—the preferred place at the table—the right to practice their own form of racketeering and chiseling."[8]

But publishers continued to insist that NRA regulation of the newspaper industry threatened press freedom and American democracy. The publisher of the *St. Louis Star and Times* worried that if the NRA was "literally applied, the US would have no more free press than Italy." The national newspaper fraternity saw in the NRA a "similar betrayal of democracy" to the violations of press freedom in totalitarian nations. Referencing Milton, Voltaire, and Jefferson, as well as the rise of dictatorships in Russia, Italy, and Germany, trade journal *Editor and Publisher* argued that publishers opposed to the code were "not such grotesque fools in attempting to throw a few anchor ropes around the civil liberty." In an age of democratic crisis, publishers insisted, economic regulation would lead automatically to censorship. "The strength of a newspaper as a public service institution," asserted *Editor and Publisher,* "is in large part due to its fierce individualism and resistance to central control."[9] It was becoming difficult to distinguish the economic self-interest of the publishers from antistatist liberalism.

Although ANPA originally opposed the drafting of any NRA code, it soon shifted strategy, and sought to neutralize the issue of industrial reform by drafting a code that was sufficiently weak to win the approval of its members. When ANPA drafted a provisional Newspaper Code in August 1933, it inserted a unique clause specifying that newspapers signing the code did not agree to "waive any constitutional rights or consent to the imposition of any requirements that might restrict or interfere with the constitutional guaranty of the freedom of the press." It also exempted the newspaper industry from the ban on child labor, to protect the hiring of delivery boys, and committed the newspaper industry to the open shop. Johnson, disgusted, declared that "this thing is nothing but an exception." The *Milwaukee Journal* excoriated it as "a disgrace . . . shot through with loopholes for publishers who may want to dodge the spirit and the purpose of the NRA; and it is covered over with weasel words about the 'freedom of the press.'" Once newspapers began to publicly announce their support, however, the code was temporarily adopted on August 14, 1933, pending further hearings later in the year.[10]

During those hearings, publishers continued to argue for a uniquely limited code. Elisha Hanson, general counsel for ANPA, testified that "many of the provisions of the NIRA [National Industrial Recovery Act] could not be applied to newspapers" because of the "limitations of the First Amendment." Dismissing charges of self-interest, Hanson argued that publishers had drafted the code "not as a matter of privilege to themselves, but as a sacred duty to the public whom they serve." To protect the public interest in a free press, the publishers had proposed a voluntary code "to which the publishers may or may not subscribe, as their judgment dictates," had exempted professional journalists from the code's labor provisions, and had avoided instituting any provisions regulating fair trade practices.[11]

The lack of fair trade regulations was particularly striking. In the words of one internal NRA memo, it meant that the newspaper industry was "the only industry of any importance in the entire country which has refused to recognize this plain purpose of the law." During the September hearings, NRA consumer advisor Dexter Keezer pushed Hanson to consider whether the newspaper industry's concern for freedom might not lead it to "use this freedom in such a way through this code as to help you in dealing with the unfair practices in your industry." Hanson was nonplussed, reiterating that federal regulation violated the First Amendment. Offering testimony later that day, the president of the National Association of Better Business Bureaus noted archly that it was a "rare treat . . . to find an industry such as the American newspaper publishers wherein there are no unfair trade practices which apparently need to be mentioned in a code recommended by the industry."[12]

Of course, there were widespread rumblings about unfair practices in the newspaper business. An internal NRA memo made clear that "the newspaper publishing business for many years, and particularly since the war, has been the victim of as many unfair competitive methods as any industry in the country"—such as "the development of a large number of newspaper monopolies, discrimination between advertisers, secret rebates of various kinds to advertisers and news dealers." In particular, a number of smaller publishers complained that larger papers were able to take advantage of their market share to manipulate advertising rates and squeeze their smaller rivals out of business. In August, for instance, the small Suffolk News Company had written to the NRA to call attention to the fact that "the small daily newspapers in metropolitan areas such as the *News Herald* are constantly menaced by the large corporations which invade their fields by reducing their advertising rates." Rather than allow big corporations to use their size in the market and their diversified holdings to undercut the sale of advertising space, the Suffolk News Company asked that the code regulate advertising sales rates, and prevent publishers from combining rates across multiple newspapers. In the same month, two Pennsylvania publishers drafted an alternative NRA code that included articles promoting competition by protecting smaller papers and banning special deals with advertisers. In Omaha, the vice president of the *World-Herald* made a similar cry for help. The rival Hearst paper in Omaha was losing money, and had been since Hearst had bought it. But normal competitive economics was not working in Omaha. Hearst could take advantage of his other newspapers to maintain a volume of advertising in the paper by setting special rates, by giving rebates, and by carrying a loss. The only way to rectify the situation, the beleaguered *World-Herald* executive felt, was to ban such unfair trade practices in the code. "Possibly," he noted glumly, "this is the reason some newspapers are so vehement in their desire not to have any fair practice code."[13]

The vehemence of the publishers was successful in neutralizing the newspaper code. After the September hearings, the development of the code proceeded behind closed doors. As the official NRA historian observed, "the daily newspaper publishing business code was not handled through the normal channels of NRA after it had been submitted. Practically all of the negotiations leading up to approval were carried on directly with General Johnson by the publishers." No records of these informal conferences were kept, but when a final version of the code was approved during the holiday season of 1933–1934, the publishers had won all the concessions they desired. The final code was voluntary, the only voluntary code in the country and therefore, according to an NRA memo, "unsatisfactory . . . [and] completely out of harmony with the intent of the entire NRA system." The code barely touched newspaper economics. The one area of business operations that was covered by the code was labor relations—and substantive regulations for wages and hours were deferred to yet another industry board. It contained no fair trade practice regulations. It even had large exemptions from the NRA's usual ban on child labor.[14]

Expressing the general disgust of reformers, the *New York Evening Post* dismissed the code as "a chiseling performance. . . . Big business, through its organs which object to the regulation of business practices and labor conditions through NRA codes has merely raised the freedom of the press issue as a smokescreen." When FDR issued the newspaper code on February 17, his rhetoric suggested that he agreed with these reformers. The freedom of the press clause in the code, he asserted, was "pure surplusage" that had "no more place here than would the recitation of the whole Constitution or of the Ten Commandments." The First Amendment should not exempt publishers from general regulations—it was not "freedom to work children, or do business in a fire trap, or violate the laws against obscenity, libel and lewdness."[15]

But Hanson and the newspaper industry had argued successfully that press freedom did require exemption from general economic regulations. For all of FDR's rhetoric, even NRA reformers had been convinced by these arguments. In June 1934, Attorney General Homer Cummings explained to the White House that "the regulatory provisions of the newspaper code are confined to wages, hours and conditions of employment. . . . It contains no unfair practice provisions and nothing whatsoever which might be construed as abridging freedom of the press." Hugh Johnson later recalled that he had asked for a newspaper code that would "leave the elimination of unfair practices to the [industry's] own self-governing bodies" because such government intervention was not appropriate for the press. When an Alabama newspaper publisher complained to the NRA about unfair advertising practices in 1934, the NRA rejected his complaint because the code did not cover trade practices. "This omission in the formulation of the code," the NRA explained, "was to protect the independence and freedom of the press from restrictions and regimentation that would be more harmful than any benefits possibly derived from commercial trade practices."[16] Elisha Hanson couldn't have put it better himself.

It is important not to overstate the impact of the code's shortcomings. This was not a missed opportunity to remedy once and for all the inadequacies of the modern press. In other industries, too, the NRA ended up serving business interests much more than reformist hopes. And the entire NRA apparatus soon fell into disrepair; in 1935, it was declared unconstitutional. But the idiosyncrasies of the newspaper code—its voluntary nature and its complete eschewal of fair trade practices—suggested that the regulation of the newspaper industry was becoming almost unthinkable. Although the newspaper was a modern business, publishers had successfully mobilized classically liberal arguments for press freedom to ward off government economic regulation. This was the ultimate significance of the NRA controversy. Economic concentration and inequality, however unpleasant, were coming to be seen as a necessary cost of a press free from state intervention.

* * *

Alongside their effort to oppose the NRA, newspaper publishers were also using First Amendment arguments to defeat an FDA attempt to pass truth-in-advertising regulation. The FDA had been disappointed by the absence of advertising regulations in the NRA code, but in June 1933, Secretary of Agriculture Henry Wallace had introduced a bill intended to ban false advertising. The bill had been prepared by Assistant Secretary of Agriculture Rexford Tugwell, who had entered the New Deal from academia. Tugwell, an economist, had links to the nascent consumer rights movement, an interlinked group of journalists and intellectuals that had been writing exposés of the advertising industry since the 1920s. Advertising, they argued, irrationally distorted the market, sapped consumer power, and misled the public. It had even taken control of the means of mass communication. "Advertising," declared James Rorty, "perverts the integrity of the editor-reader relationship essential to the concept of a democracy." The consumer rights movement hoped both to protect the consumer from false advertising and to begin to dislodge advertising from its central place in modern America.[17]

For all of the ambition of the antiadvertising movement, the bill that Tugwell prepared in 1933 was narrowly drawn. It responded to pressing needs to expand the 1906 Pure Food and Drug Act, which regulated package labeling, but left advertising unregulated. The FDA, therefore, had no jurisdiction over ads, and while the Federal Trade Commission (FTC) had some regulatory powers over advertising, it could act only to prevent unfair business practices, not to protect consumers. The limitations of this approach became clear in 1930, when the Supreme Court overturned an

FTC ban of advertising for a fraudulent diet product that killed a number of its consumers—killing one's customers, after all, could not be considered an unfair trade advantage.[18]

The Tugwell bill, as it quickly became known, sought to remedy these problems. It allowed the FDA to ban anything that "by ambiguity or inference creates a false or misleading impression" and threatened fines and jail time for breaches. Anticipating resistance from the advertising industry, Tugwell spent extra time ensuring that the bill was "carefully drawn" and "airtight" so that it could "placate as much opposition as possible." But he needn't have bothered taking the time, for the advertising industry quickly mobilized against the bill. Even if predictable, their arguments against a ban on false advertising had a certain irony. As Henry Wallace wryly observed, the whole attack on the bill by Madison Avenue "logically proceeded from the amazing assumption that honest advertising does not pay."[19]

More surprising were suggestions that the bill was a dictatorial assault on press freedom. The *St. Joseph News-Press* thought that the Tugwell bill promised the "imposition of so complicated and unpredictable a system of censorship" that America's "free press was threatened." Opponents to the bill turned Tugwell himself into a symbol of power-mad, dictatorial, academic elitism—the poster boy for the un-American, East Coast radical of the anti–New Deal imaginary. According to Sumner Welles, no member of the early New Deal "was more bitterly derided and more unjustly pilloried as a strange amalgam of a Fascist, a Communist and a menace to the liberties of the American people." The *Wall Street Journal* suggested that the bill would make Tugwell the "dictator of cosmetics, food and drug standards"; the New York Board of Trade argued that the bill promised to "set up in the country an absolute dictator over private business . . . [and] create an absolute czar." In Congress, an opponent of the bill asked his colleagues whether they wanted to place advertising regulation under "Dr. Tugwell and give him a whip lash not only over business, but over the press of this country?"[20]

Alongside such antitotalitarian hyperbole, Elisha Hanson continued to develop legal arguments that turned the First Amendment into a general shield against state regulation. Offering congressional testimony against the Tugwell bill, Hanson asserted the interests of the press in the regulation of advertising: newspapers were the "most extensively used advertising medium in the U.S. So, naturally, any measure which affects advertising is of vital interest to publishers." Moreover, Hanson suggested that

Section 17 of the bill threatened to hold publishers liable for false ads that ran in their papers. Hanson thought this a clear threat of state intervention in the press, but he was jumping at shadows. Section 17(d) explicitly exempted publishers from prosecution—it had been written out of concern that the bill not interfere with civil liberties, and the FDA testified that it was happy to continue rewriting it to guarantee that there was no ambiguity on this front.[21]

Hanson, however, was relying on ambiguity to cast any assault on advertising as an assault on the press, for that would allow him to stretch the First Amendment's protection of press freedom to cover the advertising industry. Section 19 of the bill, he pointed out, allowed the FDA to suppress the further circulation of false advertisements. Hanson moved quickly to play out the implications of the provision: "The advertisement being an integral part of the newspaper printing it, this power of injunction, as this sentence is written, gives an unlimited power of suppression. Of course, insofar as newspapers are concerned, the section is in direct conflict with the First Amendment of the Constitution." Forty years before the Supreme Court would recognize advertising as protected speech under the First Amendment, Hanson argued that state regulation of advertising was de facto regulation of the press.[22] Such government powers, Hanson concluded, were "not only unwarranted and unjustified but un-American."[23]

Hanson never had an opportunity to test these legal arguments in court, however, because the Tugwell bill was defeated by lobbying pressure. Amon Carter, president of the *Fort-Worth Star-Telegram,* wrote to FDR's presidential secretary to convey ANPA's unanimous opposition to the bill. (Carter adopted the increasingly fashionable pose of free press martyr: "Our taxes have been increased, hours shortened, wages increased, ink, metal, paper, twine and everything which goes into the making of the newspaper has gone up and we cannot increase our advertising rates at this time and now they are trying to pass a measure to make it almost impossible for the publisher to survive. In the name of the good lord when are we going to stop. We are almost like the country dog in town.") In 1933, *Business Week* observed that country editors with "immense political weight" were opposed to the bill, posing the "biggest hump" to its passage. The Democratic representative from Oklahoma, for instance, had become worried about reelection and pleaded with FDR to go slow on the bill because "the newspapers, advertising agencies and druggists are up in arms against this legislation."[24]

News columns, meanwhile, reflected newspaper opposition to the bill—it was generally ignored, misrepresented, or criticized. One New Dealer wrote to FDR to complain that it was "impossible for me to find out through our 'free press' " which measures were included in a later version of the bill. A survey of Washington correspondents in 1935 and 1936 found that 42.6 percent thought that "most papers printed unfair or distorted stories" about the Tugwell bill, with only 21.6 percent disagreeing with the statement (a very high number were not sure, which reflected the vagaries of the question, according to the analyst). And eight of the reporters told the writer of the survey that they "wrote around the story" or avoided it because they knew of their publisher's opposition to the bill.[25]

In early 1934, in an effort to end the controversy, FDR met with Tugwell and Senator Royal S. Copeland, who was steering the bill through Congress. Siding with the publishers over the objections of Tugwell, FDR instructed Copeland to redraft the bill to water down the false advertising regulations and more explicitly exempt newspaper publishers from its provisions. The change gutted the bill. In an angry memo to FDR, Tugwell fumed that Copeland had "handed the measure over to our opponents who would have been regulated under it." This was a pointed barb at Copeland, who was moonlighting as a paid radio spokesperson for Fleischmann's Yeast—advertising exactly the sort of product his bill was supposed to regulate.[26]

But the matter was out of Tugwell's hands. The FDA was cut out of further amendments to the bill from 1934 on, as the FTC sought to wrest control of advertising regulation back into its jurisdiction. In the end, in 1938, a decision was made to separate advertising regulation from the Food and Drug amendments. The FTC was provided new powers to regulate advertising by the Wheeler-Lea Amendment; the Food, Drug and Cosmetics Act updated the 1906 Food and Drugs Act. The new FTC powers were lackluster: the new law defined false advertising in terms even narrower than the already watered-down Copeland bill, and the FTC relied on slow and ineffective cease and desist orders to enforce them. Remarkably, Elisha Hanson remained outraged at even these FTC powers. In 1940, he suggested that the FTC was acting like a "Bureau of Censorship of Knowledge" more appropriate for Nazi Germany or eighteenth-century England. But that was in keeping with the heightened sensitivity of the newspaper publishers, and their defense of advertising as essential to a free press. "If advertising is destroyed, a free press will be destroyed," the president of ANPA had warned in 1934; "a tax on advertising was one of the favorite old world methods of destroying a free press."[27]

Afterward, Tugwell was incredulous at the outcome of the failed quest for advertising regulation. "What was proposed," he suggested, "could not have seemed very drastic to the detached observer. But the patent medicine and cosmetic manufacturers were shocked beyond sanity by the threatened changes. The shock very quickly communicated itself to the newspapers and the magazines. . . . It was a very short jump, indeed, from a threat to publisher's profits from advertising, to un-Americanism. And the publishers were not long in making it." The affair suggested just how difficult economic regulation of the press had become. The newspaper industry had successfully mobilized against a fairly innocuous piece of reform legislation. It had found a way to deploy First Amendment arguments to protect its economic interests from a general piece of regulation that would have done nothing to interfere with its editorial affairs. In all, the newspaper industry had successfully argued that even marginal and limited economic regulation of the press could be defeated as a threat to press freedom. A free press, the clash over the Tugwell bill revealed, meant a press with complete economic autonomy.[28]

* * *

In both the NRA and Tugwell debates, political arguments about the sanctity of First Amendment rights had been so successful in defeating state regulation that there had been no need to test them in court. Serious jurisprudential consideration of the relationship between the regulatory state and the modern news industry came only during World War II when, in a late spasm of the reform impulse, the Justice Department brought an antitrust suit against the AP wire service. The case was appealed to the Supreme Court, and although the Justice Department ultimately prevailed, both the logic of the decision and the context of the case actually undermined the efficacy of state-based press reform. The lone success of New Deal press reform highlighted how difficult it was to regulate the newspaper industry while preserving a commitment to classical First Amendment speech rights.

By the time of the New Deal, there was a widespread belief that the power of the AP posed a threat to press freedom. The AP had been founded in the 1840s as a cooperative news-gathering organization—member newspapers agreed to share their news stories exclusively with other members. Joining the AP allowed newspapers to receive a diverse array of news from across the world without having to bear the cost of gathering news in all those locations, which was a considerable competitive advantage. By 1942, the AP had over 1,200 members, and AP subscribers dominated the nation's newspaper industry. Almost all of the large newspapers had an AP subscription; of the 373 morning papers, only sixty-two relied exclusively on one of the two rival wire services, the UP or the International News Service (INS). AP members commanded 96 percent of circulation among morning dailies, and 77 percent of evening circulation. And AP members jealously guarded access to the service; the service had been accused of antitrust violations more than once in its life. By the 1940s, it was still difficult to join the AP. If a current member protested a new paper's membership, the new member needed the support of 80 percent of existing members to join. That proved a prohibitive barrier for papers seeking to challenge the market share of an existing AP member. Between 1900 and 1942, over one hundred papers had tried. Only six were approved to join the AP.[29]

Muckrakers and radical press commentators, moreover, had long argued that the AP service reflected the pro-business bias of its large and profitable members. George Seldes, Oswald Garrison Villard, Walter Lippmann, and Upton Sinclair had all excoriated the AP for passing off biased stories on race relations, labor disputes, and foreign affairs as objective wire reports. Seldes, for instance, argued that the AP had run stories on the Bolshevik influence in Mexico that had been planted by the State Department, an abuse, he suggested, akin to what the "Wolff bureau did in Nazi Germany or the Stefani does in Fascist Italy." In 1913, *The Masses* accused the AP of taking the substance of current history and holding it "in cold storage, adulterated, colored with poisonous intentions, and sold to the highest bidder to suit his private purposes." Will Irwin called the AP "a force of reaction," and Eugene Debs declared that "if there is in this country a strictly capitalist class institution it is the Associated Press."[30]

But the Justice Department's 1942 antitrust suit was not intended to deal with the quality of the service. Rather, it emerged from economic rivalries within the Chicago newspaper market, and focused on problems of membership and access. In 1941, department store heir Marshall Field III challenged Robert McCormick's hegemony in the Chicago morning newspaper market. He founded the *Chicago Sun,* intending to offset the

Tribune's anti-FDR isolationism with a paper supporting both the president and an interventionist foreign policy. When Field applied for an AP membership, McCormick unsurprisingly used his influence to block the application of his new rival. So, in early 1942, Field took his case to the government. Seeking to head off litigation, the AP adjusted its bylaws, but Field was again denied membership in April. On August 28, the AP was charged with violations of the Sherman and Clayton Acts. Because the First Amendment stakes of the matter were clear, the case was heard before a special three-judge expediting court in the summer of 1943 in anticipation of an expected appeal to the Supreme Court.[31]

Both Field and the Justice Department argued that the AP rules were a threat to press freedom. Field began by noting the challenge that a lack of access to the AP service posed to his fledgling newspaper. "Much of the energies and imagination of the staff," he complained, "have had to be consumed in equalizing deficiencies due to our not having the coverage furnished as a matter of routine by AP to its members." Just to match the AP's coverage, he had to employ ten correspondents in DC; it was almost impossible to match the AP's coverage of specialized subjects that required expert journalists, let alone its sports coverage. Such practical difficulties, Field suggested, made the lack of an AP subscription an "almost insuperable obstacle" to starting a newspaper. That meant that the AP membership rules allowed a "few men" to "dictate" which organizations could supply the news to Americans by restraining the emergence of new newspapers in the market. Field concluded that the restraints on new papers posed by the AP "strikes peculiarly at fundamental American conceptions": "freedom of the press can have its full fruition only if new persons, with fresh points of view, can become the publishers of newspapers and compete effectively with existing newspapers." In an affidavit supporting Field's case, journalism scholar Alfred McClung Lee made much the same point—freedom of the press required a diverse newspaper market, which required that newspapers' access to news sources should be "unhampered by any artificial or unnecessary restraints, public or private." The Justice Department, too, thought that the "broad objective" of its suit was to "promote freedom of the press" by promoting free access to news sources and thus greater diversity in the newspaper market. But it also insisted that this was "an ordinary garden variety of anti-trust case," intended "only to purify the AP's operations," and not a sweeping effort to regulate the newspaper industry.[32]

Unsurprisingly, AP members responded that any state intervention in the newspaper market threatened the freedom of the press. The AP also thought that press freedom required economic competition, but it argued that if the antitrust suit prevailed, then the government would be forcing AP members to sell their stories to all comers, which would replace competitive news gathering with government-enforced standardization. And if the government became the "economic arbiter of the newspaper field," the AP warned darkly, then "it would regulate that field no less effectively than did the English kings through their systems of licensing and taxation." "Freedom of the press has been extinguished in practically all other countries," the AP cautioned. The court should learn the lessons from what had happened "universally throughout the world" and hew closely to a First Amendment that was "designed to avoid these ends by avoiding these beginnings." Regulate us, was the takeaway argument, and you begin a process that ends with Hitler.[33]

Other publishers joined in defending the AP, deploying the classically liberal arguments they had developed in the press struggles of the 1930s. Robert McCormick declared that "the First Amendment was intended solely as a protection of the press against government encroachments." Taking particular umbrage with the arguments of Professor Lee, McCormick suggested that the antitrust case threatened American democracy: "Under such specious arguments have dictatorial governments everywhere subjected the press to their control. Under guise of freeing the press they have dominated the press. In my opinion the most dangerous modern threat to free speech and press are those academic thinkers who desire the government to control, regulate, and regiment the press in order to obviate some imagined or comparatively insignificant evil of the press." Amicus briefs prepared by the *Chicago Times* and by Elisha Hanson on behalf of ANPA reiterated classically liberal arguments for free speech and explicitly cautioned against updating the classical conception of press freedom in the First Amendment. "The public interest" in a diverse newspaper market, declared the *Chicago Times,* "was the same at the time the First Amendment was adopted as it is today."[34]

The issues were clear, if knotty. Was it possible to use antitrust action to promote a more competitive press? Or did such prosecution destroy classical liberal competition by opening the door to government control? In October, the judges split in answering these questions, ruling two to one in favor of the Justice Department. Composing the majority, Learned

Hand and Augustus Hand declared that the current bylaws rendered the AP an unlawful combination, and the AP was enjoined from enforcing them. The majority decision adopted the expansive vision of press freedom articulated by Field and the Justice Department. It was not enough, Learned Hand wrote, to consider simply economic questions when thinking about monopolies in the newspaper industry, because "neither exclusively, nor even primarily, are the interests of the newspaper industry conclusive; for that industry serves one of the most vital of all general interests: the dissemination of news from as many different sources, and with as many different facets or colors as is possible. That interest is closely akin to, if indeed not the same as, the interest protected by the First Amendment; it presupposes that right conclusions are more likely to be gathered out of a multitude of tongues."[35]

The opinion reveals two eminent judges, both influential in developing the modern jurisprudence of speech rights, trying to express the widely felt sense that the First Amendment had to guarantee not just classical speech rights, but some kind of positive flow of information to the public ("an interest closely akin to, if indeed not the same as, the interest protected by the First Amendment"). To deprive a paper of a wire service, Hand wrote, "is to deprive the reading public of means of information which it should have." Thus Hand found for the Justice Department not on the grounds of restraint of trade and harm to rival publishers, but on the grounds of public interest. This was a noble sentiment, one that called out for a liberal and diverse press leading to an enlightened public: "It is only by cross-lights from varying directions that full illumination can be secured." In the context of a newspaper market trending toward monopoly, First Amendment interests could be protected only if the state interfered with the economic rights of individual publishers. The Justice Department had won the first round.[36]

On April 29, 1944, members of the AP voted unanimously to "continue the fight for the preservation of First Amendment ideals" by appealing to the Supreme Court. There, the justices decided, five to three, to uphold the lower court's ruling. But it was a messy decision that produced five separate opinions, a welter of disagreement, and a fracturing of the usual jurisprudential alliances of the court. The *Chicago Daily News* suggested that "if eight newspaper reporters on an assignment turned in as confusing and contradictory a report as that made by the Supreme Court on the AP case, any editor would be justified in firing most of them."[37] But the confusion was understandable. Following the "Constitutional Revolution of 1937," the Supreme Court had upheld sweeping new federal powers to intervene in the economic sphere via the Commerce Clause. And it had simultaneously sought to counterbalance these new centralizing powers with an enhanced protection of the political liberties enshrined in the Bill of Rights. The AP case forced the court to trade off between its newfound commitments to both First Amendment rights and federal economic regulation.[38]

Hugo Black's majority opinion combined these commitments in a surprising manner; its odd nature is revealed by contrasting it with the more straightforward opinions of two of his colleagues. In dissent, Justice Roberts defended the antistatist, classically liberal understanding of press freedom. He decided for the AP: "The decree here approved may well be, and I think threatens to be but a first step in the shackling of the press, which will subvert the constitutional freedom to print or to withhold, to print as and how one's reason or one's interest dictates. When that time comes, the state will be supreme and freedom of the state will have superseded freedom of the individual to print." In a concurring opinion, by contrast, Felix Frankfurter adopted the antimonopoly vision of press freedom articulated by the Justice Department and Learned Hand. Because a "free press is indispensable to the workings of our democratic society," Frankfurter argued, the press was a unique industry—it had a "relation to the public interest unlike that of any other enterprise pursued for profit." It was necessary "to have the flow of news not trammeled by the combined self-interest of those who enjoy a unique constitutional protection precisely because of the public dependence on a free press." Viewed from that perspective, it made sense to Frankfurter that one should use the state to strike down "private restraints" that offended "the basic functions which a constitutionally guaranteed free press serves in our nation."[39] Frankfurter's position flowed directly from his broader jurisprudential and political inclinations: no great stickler for First Amendment rights, Frankfurter firmly believed in judicial deference as well as antitrust state action. But by reasoning from the point of view of the public interest in free information, Frankfurter had articulated a press corollary to the new social liberalism—one in which the state had an obligation to produce a free flow of information for the public.[40]

Hugo Black, writing for the majority, produced a more complex decision than either Robert's classically liberal dissent or Frankfurter's socially liberal concurrence. He was committed to both individual rights and state regulation of the market, and he was a firm advocate of antitrust action.[41]

Now he sought to combine these commitments. His first and most significant step was rethinking the economic implications of the AP bylaws. Hand had argued that public interest rendered the press a unique industry because he felt that the AP's actions did not have sufficient impact on other publishers to constitute an illegal monopoly in simple economic terms. Judges on both sides of the issue had agreed that the AP bylaws fell short of violating the antitrust laws unless one was willing to consider an expansive public interest in a diverse press.

Black broke with this consensus. He held that "the restraints on trade in news here were no less than those held to fall within the ban of the Sherman Act with reference to combinations to restrain trade outlets in the sale of tiles, or enameled ironware, or lumber, or women's clothes, or motion pictures."[42] Black upheld the ruling against the AP, but not on the grounds of protecting a public interest in the free flow of information. Rather, he upheld the ruling to protect the rights of publishers to free and equal competition. "The net effect" of the AP bylaws, according to Black, "is seriously to limit the opportunity of any new paper to enter those cities. Trade restraints of this character aimed at the destruction of competition, tend to block the initiative which brings newcomers into a field of business and to frustrate the free enterprise system which it was the purpose of the Sherman Act to protect."[43]

The First Amendment was not entirely irrelevant to this reasoning, but it was a subsidiary matter. Black argued that "it would be strange indeed . . . if the grave concern for freedom of the press which prompted adoption of the First Amendment should be read as a command that the government was without power to protect that freedom." Black flirted here with the logic of Frankfurter, suggesting that the language of the First Amendment might actually provide a positive argument to apply the Sherman Act to the case. But the First Amendment was not central to his decision. He raised it only to dismiss classically liberal objections as insincere efforts to defend anticompetitive business practices: "Surely a command that the government itself shall not impede the free flow of ideas does not afford non-governmental combinations a refuge if they impose restraints upon that constitutionally guaranteed freedom."[44]

At its core, therefore, Black's decision protected the rights of the publishers to compete freely, and assumed that such competition would contribute to democratic life. It neither opened the door to state regulation of newspaper economics nor retained faith in the existing economics of the newspaper industry. Instead, Black sought to use state action narrowly, to return the newspaper market to the competitive conditions presumed by democratic theory. In some ways, the decision might have seemed the best of both worlds. But in assuming that competition between publishers was the key to a vibrant democracy, Black actually sacrificed the interests of the reading public and, ironically, encouraged the AP's monopolization of the newspaper field.

In his thoughtful lower-court opinion, Hand had foreseen the possibility that "if all be allowed to join AP, it may become the only news service, and get a monopoly by driving others out." But he considered this an "exceedingly remote possibility" and, even if it came to pass, nothing to fear. "The essence of monopoly is exclusion," he asserted, and if all newspapers could subscribe to the AP, there was no exclusion and no monopoly.[45] But Hand's reasoning was faulty. No newspaper publishers would suffer from such a monopoly, but Hand had justified the opening of AP membership for the good it would do for the public. By allowing more newspapers to compete in the market, open access to the AP would theoretically enhance the diversity of information provided to the public. The irony, of course, was that if all papers relied on the AP service, the information that reached the public would become less diverse, not more diverse. Indeed, the entire logic of Hand and Black's decision ignored the widespread accusations that the problem with the AP was not its restrictive membership laws, but the extensive spread of the service's biased news. Many critics were worried that there was entirely too much AP information circulating, not that there was too little. But neither Hand nor Black took into account the quality of information in the press, or the interests of the reader-consumer.

The paradoxical nature of the decision had two important consequences for the history of the press. In the first case, forcing open AP membership did, in practice, lead to an ever-greater market-share held by the AP. AP membership jumped from 1,274 in 1943 to 1,708 in 1949. In 1934, 54 percent of newspapers received the AP wire service. By 1948, 68 percent did so, and this number remained remarkably constant through the 1960s. And between the 1940s and 1960s, the newspapers that received the AP news service became more dependent upon it for content. In 1948, there were three wire services—the AP, the UP, and INS—and papers could subscribe to multiple services (10 percent subscribed to all three). But in 1958, the UP and INS merged. By 1966, 84 percent of dailies received their out-of-town news entirely from one of the two remaining services.[46]

And secondly, although the Justice Department won the case, the limited nature of the decision made it a poor platform upon which to construct a robust jurisprudence of trust-busting, populist press freedom. It did little, in practice, to arrest the decline of newspaper diversity in the postwar period. And for all the soaring rhetoric suggesting that the First Amendment protected a broad public right to receive diverse information, and for all the intimations that the First Amendment could sanction economic regulation of the press, the actual decision was incredibly narrow. As Zechariah Chafee observed, the AP case, like antitrust actions in the radio industry and the motion picture industry, had worked to "protect the retailer against the power of the manufacturing wholesaler." It said little if anything about the rights of the public vis-à-vis the retailer. (Just "because the Associated Press has to behave like a railroad," Chafee pointed out, "this does not mean that the *Chicago Tribune* must behave like a railroad.")[47] And even that narrow field of state action was too broad for some of the justices. In a concurring opinion William Douglas emphasized what he called the "narrow compass of the decision": it applied strictly to the particular AP bylaws in question. In dissent, Frank Murphy was sufficiently worried about opening the door to "despotic governments" that he recommended returning the matter to a full trial so the facts could be more fully established.[48] The First Amendment, it was clear, did not automatically render antitrust actions in the newspaper industry unconstitutional. But where and when antitrust action was appropriate state action remained entirely uncertain, an ambiguity to be resolved in the postwar years.

* * *

Even though the Justice Department had technically won the case against the AP, the decision stopped well short of reorienting the First Amendment away from the economic privileges of the publisher and toward the interests of the public. In justifying antitrust action to protect the interests of the publisher, in fact, the resolution of the AP case contributed to the most significant trend to emerge from New Deal efforts at press reform: the language of press freedom was monopolized by publishers who used it to protect their own autonomy. "Who has this freedom of the press?" asked journalist turned New Deal administrator Lowell Mellett in 1938. "The answer is: those persons who own the press. Nobody else. Freedom of the press is a property." Tom Wallace, editor of the *Louisville Times*, agreed: "Freedom of the press is the owner's freedom to publish news and express opinion unimpeded by the central government or any unit of subordinate government."[49]

The legal implications of that attitude had been developed by Elisha Hanson. By 1943, he had established that press freedom rendered the newspaper industry uniquely exempt from all state regulation: "The press is not like a stock exchange, a commodity exchange, a stockyard, a railroad, an electric utility that can be required to take out a license, obtain a certificate of convenience, or procure a charter with special limitations before it can operate. . . . The public good requires that the press shall not be subject to such a control. And our forefathers determined that question when they ratified the First Amendment." Hanson's transformation of the First Amendment into an antistatist tool was soon influential through a broader network of conservative lawyers. In 1938, when lawyer Grenville Clark began to argue that conservatives needed to support civil liberties, he quickly met with ANPA. Clark soon founded a new organization, the American Bar Association's Committee on the Bill of Rights. It continued and broadened ANPA's use of the First Amendment as a shield against a variety of government regulations. Chafee, an early committee member, joked in one letter to Clark that "some newspapers evidently expect us to oppose all the policies of the New Deal on the ground that they deprive American citizens of all their rights, the most important of which appears to be the right to be taxed low."[50]

Publishers had successfully fused their interest in protecting their individual economic rights with classically liberal arguments against state regulation. "Freedom of the press," Hanson proclaimed to the New York Advertising Club in 1940, "is just as essential to the preservation of our economic liberty as it is to the safeguarding of our political freedom, for the two go hand in hand." Many thought this was simply cynical. Two-thirds of reporters in a mid-1930s survey thought that the "publisher's cry of 'freedom of the press' in fighting an NRA code was a ruse." By 1937, the *New Republic* thought that the publishers had made their argument about press freedom "so often it has practically lost all meaning in their mouths."[51]

Still, the publishers' defense of press freedom was not an entirely unsalutary development. Anti–New Deal publishers did produce some of the signal First Amendment victories of the 1930s. McCormick, for instance, had helped win the *Near* case. And, in 1936, newspaper lawyers convinced the Supreme Court that Huey Long's newspaper tax was an unconstitutional interference with the freedom of the press. Long's tax, which had been targeted at newspapers critical of his increasingly demagogic rule, was a prime example of the way that state regulation of economics could provide a mechanism for unsavory interferences with democratic debate. The nature of that victory, though, was telling. At first, most of the lawyers for the Louisiana papers had wanted to argue that the tax was unconstitutional because it discriminated against larger papers; it was on these grounds that a three-judge lower court enjoined the tax. But one of the Louisiana lawyers was more ambitious, and he called in legal advice from Elisha Hanson and the lawyers for the *Chicago Tribune.* Drawing analogies between Long's tax and the taxes imposed on the eighteenth-century press by the English Crown, they prepared a sweeping defense of the need to protect the press from all state regulation. When the State of Louisiana appealed the matter, Elisha Hanson represented the newspapers in front of the Supreme Court, arguing in familiar terms that the First Amendment protected the press from all methods of restraint—"censorship, licensing, taxation, seditious libel, injunction, writ of attachment or anything else." A unanimous Supreme Court agreed, as liberals and conservatives on the fractious 1936 bench briefly united to extend First Amendment protections against government harassment. It was significant that the decision was written by the conservative Justice Sutherland, who had first drafted an opinion focusing on statist interferences with economic liberty; he reframed the decision around the First Amendment to bring liberal justices on board. Still, liberal commentators welcomed the decision—*The Nation,* for instance, thought it "excellent" and good "to have on the record for future use in a fascist emergency." But the fact that the case had been won by Elisha Hanson gave *The Nation* pause. Hanson's "presence" in the Grosjean victory, *The Nation* worried, "also foreshadows the uses to which the decision may be put." The First Amendment, the magazine suggested, might soon be used to block state regulation of the economy, for Hanson was simultaneously opposing the Social Security Act. It was becoming almost impossible to distinguish victories for classical press freedom from antiregulatory victories for the newspaper industry.[52]

And more broadly, the power of the publishers' antitotalitarian arguments led Americans to abandon the prospect of state-based press reform. "So long as the only working models of alternatives to the American press are found in the Axis countries," declared Richard L. Wilson, president of the National Press Club, "it is difficult for those who say the press is corrupt to demonstrate how they would improve the situation." By 1941, even Freda Kirchwey, liberal editor of *The Nation,* found it difficult to articulate a program of press reform. Kirchwey understood the classical arguments of the anti–New Deal press. And, "in simple, eighteenth century terms," she conceded, "the newspapers [making this argument] are right: they are free as long as they can go on saying what they please without interference from the authorities." Kirchwey pointed out that 1941 was not the eighteenth century, but she conceded that the press could not be improved by government regulation, because this would itself be an "intolerable interference with freedom." Kirchwey summed up a general feeling of inadequacy to face the problem. Radical redistribution of wealth seemed one, albeit unlikely, solution. Apart from that, she confessed, "I don't know how we are to create the sort of free press America needs."[53]

New Deal efforts to regulate newspaper economics had hardly threatened government control of the newsrooms. There had been no general effort to establish trade regulations for the newspaper industry, no effort to regulate the quality of the news, no effort to abolish newspaper chains, and no effort to encourage the founding of new newspapers. Instead, there had been an attempt to regulate costs and prices through a corporatist industry agreement, a move to ban fraudulent advertising, and a successful endeavor to promote free competition among newspaper publishers by abolishing a restraint on the purchasing of a wire subscription. But the firestorm of controversy meeting even such limited proposals suggested the impossibility of articulating a positive conception of press freedom or of achieving any program of state-backed press reform. When a socially liberal vision of press freedom clashed with a classical vision of laissez-faire press liberty, the classical vision won out. The negative liberties of the First Amendment were sacrosanct, and Americans resigned themselves to the corporate consolidation of the newspaper market as the necessary cost of a press free from state intervention. "Freedom of the press today has one practical meaning," declared Richard Wilson. "Whatever else the press may be subservient to, it is not subservient to the government."[54] Any reform of the press, then, was not going to come from the state—it would have to come from within the industry itself.

4

Dependent Journalists, Independent Journalism?

In late 1930s Chicago, journalists employed by two Hearst newspapers waged a seventeen-month strike to forestall firings and pay cuts as their papers were merged. The intensity of the strike dramatized the deep conflict between publishers and journalists over the labor relations that determined the production of the nation's news. "Blood was spilled in the shadow of Chicago's civic opera theater," as strikers were shot at and beaten. Publishers backed delivery trucks up to the picket lines and left the engines running, forcing strikers to wear gas masks. On the night of February 12, 1939, Hearst-hired thugs stole the strikers' sound truck, and tossed it into the icy Chicago River.[1]

The striking journalists were members of the Newspaper Guild, a newly formed union of journalists. The guild had been founded in 1933, and had grown rapidly; by 1940, it had more than 16,000 members and had signed 122 contracts, covering almost 150 papers. It had also raised controversial and difficult questions about the labor of journalism, and about the political and professional obligations of journalists. In 1941, Louis Stark, the founding father of the modern labor beat, reported that the "city rooms of newspapers in many cases divided sharply on the merits of the Guild." His own *New York Times,* for instance, "exhibited some of the aspects of a seething volcano about to erupt." In a 1937 forum on press freedom, the dean of Columbia's School of Journalism, Carl Ackerman, focused his remarks exclusively on the problem of the guild. The guild, Dean Ackerman declared, had "precipitated the greatest crisis in the history of modern journalism."[2]

The profession of journalism had a short and unsettled history. The growth of the commercial press in the late nineteenth century had produced a new class of waged journalists, a vast labor pool necessary to cover the news of the nation. This raised new questions about the relationship between the work of journalism and freedom of the press: Could the public trust the information that journalists were placing before them? How could the public be sure that journalists were reporting accurately, honestly, and skillfully? Efforts to professionalize journalism in the first decades of the twentieth century were an attempt to address these concerns. Through journalism education and new codes of ethics, the professionalization movement hoped to guarantee that the press was circulating high-quality information, produced by a high caliber of skilled individuals, reporting objectively and without bias. By the 1930s, however, the professionalization movement had had limited success, and it had not settled broader anxieties about the labor of journalism.

The Newspaper Guild proposed a different method to improve the quality of information in the nation's press. Journalists should not professionalize, the guild argued, but unionize. Unionization would provide journalists with the political and economic independence required for independent and truly objective reporting. The guild suggested that unionization would make two changes to the labor of journalism. First, they argued that working journalists needed to wrest control of hiring and firing away from editors and publishers, so that journalists had the economic security to report without fear of losing their jobs. Second, they argued that working journalists had an obligation to build democracy not only within their newsrooms but also in society as a whole. Responding to the pressures of the Depression, and inspired by the leftist politics of the Popular Front, the guild argued that journalists should become politically engaged citizens, not merely passive stenographers. Making those changes, the guild argued, would ensure that journalists had greater freedom to report, and that the public would receive more accurate information from their papers.

This was a radical and controversial effort to reform the labor relations of journalism; as Ackerman put it, the clashes over the guild constituted "a turning point in the evolution of the profession of journalism."[3] In the end, although the guild won higher wages for journalists, its attempt to reimagine journalism failed. By the 1940s, the guild had abandoned both of its reform policies. In the face of publisher resistance in the mid-1930s, it traded control over employment for wage gains. And in the late 1930s, an anticommunist movement within the guild successfully argued that political engagement by journalists did not produce truly independent journalism; rather, they argued, the radical politics of the guild had produced a doctrinaire press that undermined American press freedom.

The guild failed to promote a positive theory of press freedom based on the labor of the journalist, but its failure clarified the professional norms of objective journalism in the liberal theory of press freedom. After World War II, the flow of information to the public, the positive content of America's free press, would continue to depend on the labor of a curiously unregulated class of workers: neither formally disciplined as a profession nor ensured independence by a militant union.

* * *

How did the work of a journalist contribute to press freedom? The answer was uncertain throughout the first half of the twentieth century. The new figure of the waged reporter entered the world of journalism with the mass commercial press of the late nineteenth century. Before this, newspapers had small staffs, often no more than an editor and possibly an assistant or two. The editor gathered news, wrote reports and editorials, handled the business side of the papers, and, at least at first, was an essential cog in the machinery of his political party. The paper's content was thus the product of the editor's individual labor, and it bore the stamp of his judgment. But as the commercial press of the late nineteenth century aimed to provide news to a mass market, news gathering became a collective enterprise, conducted by a growing staff of waged reporters. A new set of labor practices emerged—the beat system, the interview, an increasingly strict division of labor between reporters and editors. No one could agree what kind of work the journalist did. Some thought it a form of art, some a profession, others a craft, yet others a deskilled trade (one commentator argued that the journalist was "not a thinker, but a worker; a human machine like a steam potato-digger" who was paid to mindlessly dig for information). Even the name of the job was unclear—some preferred to be called newspapermen, and dismissed the title of journalist as a pretension. "A journalist," ran one joke, "is a newspaperman out of work." Whatever one called the job, there was clearly a new social role. The reporter, declared Will Irwin, was "wholly an outgrowth of modern life . . . the newest arm of this newest power in civilization."[4]

And it soon became clear that a new occupational norm defined the work of the reporter. Reporters prepared news stories that were "objective"—they took the mess of reality and through a set of labor practices and ethical judgments they produced an accurate summation and representation of reality for the reader. The precise origins of the norm of journalistic objectivity remain unclear, but many factors contributed to its rise to prominence: the standardization produced by the growth of the wire services; the desire of the commercial papers to transcend partisan lines and reach ever-larger audiences; the new responsibilities placed on monopoly papers; the Progressive Era's broader rejection of "corrupt" partisanship in favor of rationality, scientism, and expertise.[5] Whatever the origins of this broad and ill-defined norm, by the early twentieth century, reporters had begun to carve out a distinct role with a distinct set of responsibilities to the public. Unlike the partisan commentators of an earlier era, and unlike the publicity agents rising to prominence in both the administrative state and the corporate economy, the reporters would be disinterested in their provision of information to the public.[6] The reporter had to be autonomous, free from outside pressure to fulfill this task—as one commentator put it in 1893, "the special mark of the journalistic temperament is a horror of dependence."[7] As readers came to rely on increasingly monopolistic newspapers for their news, they came to increasingly rely on the independent labor of journalists.

That independent journalism, however, was to be produced by a class of dependent workers. In the early twentieth century, most journalists were poorly paid, often at space rates or by the word (as late as the 1930s, that meant that an eleven-hour day of interviewing, research, and writing might produce $4 for 400 words—if the editor saw fit to publish the story at all). And they lacked job security—they could be dismissed or reassigned at the whim of the publisher. Press critics were concerned that such economic dependence undermined the quality of American journalism, making the job less appealing to high-caliber workers and undermining the reporter's independence. With their wages, hours, and livelihood at stake, journalists quickly learned what stories and angles their bosses preferred, and which they did not. In 1909, a New York newspaperman made explicit the threat that waged dependency posed to press freedom: "The business of a New York journalist is to distort the truth, to lie outright, to pervert, to vilify, to fawn at the foot of mammon, and to sell his country and his race for his daily bread. We are the vassals of the rich men behind the scenes. Our time, our talents, our lives, our possibilities are all the property of other men. We are intellectual prostitutes."[8]

The important question, then, was how to ensure that dependent journalists would be guaranteed the independence required for objective reporting. In the first decades of the twentieth century, there were efforts to professionalize journalism to ensure that America's free press was produced by a skilled and regulated labor force that could resist outside pressure. Professional journalism associations argued that reporters had professional obligations to the public just as a lawyer or doctor did. Drawing inspiration from the professionalization of law and medicine, they sought to raise the standards and pay of journalism by regulating the newspaper's labor pool. Their main hope was the promotion of journalism education. Universities and colleges had been experimenting with journalism courses since the 1870s, but the first school of journalism was only created in 1908, at the University of Missouri. Journalism education subsequently flourished. In 1910, only twenty-two universities were teaching journalism in any capacity; by 1940, 60 percent of the nation's four-year universities were offering journalism courses, and a number of specialized journalism schools existed. Alongside educational programs, journalism associations across the country also began issuing codes of ethics. In 1923, the American Society of Newspaper Editors (ASNE) issued a national "Canons of Journalism." And in the early twentieth century, a number of state governments proposed the establishment of licensing systems, in which a state board would issue licenses to journalists who had passed an exam and certain levels of training, and which could revoke licenses to punish unethical behavior. Trained journalists, reporting according to standardized and enforced ethics of objectivity, seemed to guarantee that the labor of journalism would place accurate information before the reading public.[9]

But the hopes of the professionalization movement were never realized. State licensing plans were soon abandoned. The professional codes of ethics were simply statements of ideals—the professional societies did not license journalists, and could not disbar journalists for violating professional ethics. Hiring and firing therefore remained the prerogative of the publisher. And journalism schools, unlike schools of law and medicine, never monopolized access to the labor market. In fact, editors remained ambivalent about hiring journalism school graduates. Many preferred to hire graduates with general college degrees or to recruit workers who had not gone to college at all, and could receive all their training on the job. Only 51 percent of DC correspondents had college degrees in the mid-1930s. In 1934, only five of the fifty-three reporters on the city staff of the *New York Herald Tribune* had gone to journalism school. (And with one exception, their editor reported, they were "not by any means among the best men on the paper.")[10]

Journalism could not be fully professionalized because that would have interfered with press freedom. There could be no consensus about professional ethics—even the effort to decide on the curriculum within journalism schools reopened debates about the best training for reporting. Any centralized regulation of the work would, of necessity, constitute an interference with individual freedoms. As a leading journalism educator put it in 1930, "any law or state board for the regulation of journalists, of course, suggests a jeopardy to the freedom of the press."[11]

So the uncertain status of the waged journalist continued. As late as 1934, the former head of the leading publishers' association could only define the job in the negative: "it is neither an art, a craft or a profession." And that uncertainty continued to raise questions about the quality of information in the nation's press. The journalist, Will Irwin observed in 1911, "furnishes the raw material for public opinion. . . . If the strand be shoddy, how can the finished fabric be sound?" Walter Lippmann agreed, arguing in 1920 that "no amount of money or effort spent in fitting the right men for this work could possibly be wasted, for the health of society depends upon the quality of the information it receives." Press critics had unloaded much of their anxiety and hope about the problem of press freedom onto the figure of the journalist; if the journalist was sufficiently skilled, the press could be sure to contain high-quality information. Expectations for journalists grew ever higher, as Carl Ackerman noticed in 1933: "What our critics desire is a superhuman institute. . . . They would employ reporters possessing the skill and precision of a surgeon, the patience and resourcefulness of chemists, the spiritual idealism of the church, the unhurried study and power of reflection of an educator . . . a thorough knowledge of history and an understanding of public affairs possessed at present only by members of the 'brains trust.' Our critics would engage as editorial writers only men capable of being president of the United States in the millennium."[12] Ackerman's bitter caricature was accurate. Many of his colleagues in the press no doubt looked on with a mixture of envy and desire when Clark Kent turned up at the Daily Planet each morning.

* * *

Instead of Superman came the crises of the Depression and the New Deal. These gave material and political teeth to the problematic status of the waged journalist. New Deal investigations into labor conditions confirmed that journalists were poorly paid; a 1935 Bureau of Labor Statistics survey found that the average weekly income of a reporter was $41.81—roughly equivalent to that of a bricklayer in Alabama. But it conceded that the figures were skewed high by the salaries of a small group of star reporters, columnists, and editorial figures. Rival studies produced by newspaper industry groups suggested that average wages were between $34 and $36.[13]

More importantly, income and work conditions deteriorated in the Depression. Wages fell an average of 12 to 16 percent. Some newspapers paid reporters advertising scrip or hotel vouchers; others granted reporters the right to use by-lines in lieu of raises. But hours stayed long—a six-day, fifty-hour week was common. And many journalists lost their jobs. Hundreds did so when the venerable *New York World* went out of business in 1931. The arbitrary and absolute firing power of publishers became legendary: one allegedly drew a line down the center of the editorial room and fired all those to the left. Like all apocryphal stories, its potential plausibility to contemporaries makes it revealing. As one news worker complained in 1933, "Newspaper reporters are fired from their jobs more quickly and more arbitrarily than any other class of men in America. . . . They suffer more from the autocracy of capitalism than any other class I know."[14]

Reporters responded angrily, contrasting the social and political importance of their labor with their precarious economic conditions. They bore, one complained, "tremendous responsibility without the comforting walking aid of a stout financial staff." A journalist earning $9.80 a week, down from his pre-Crash salary of $100, was one of many who wrote to FDR for relief: "Our work on which so much admittedly depends is valuable in a nearly direct proportion to our personal welfare. Our self-respect is being torn to pieces as we find ourselves, month after month, going deeper and deeper into debt, wearing clothes . . . which are now becoming shabby, worn and torn."[15] Another, assuming a mixture of professional and masculine privilege that might be more repugnant if it didn't speak to shattered hopes, informed the president that he had a college education and was "a competent member of a highly trained profession," but was forced by "economic stress" to wander the country looking for work and suffering the "ignominy of allowing my wife to support me."[16]

When this last letter arrived in Washington, a bureaucrat attached a brief, dismissive cover letter: "Shall I tell him he's lucky to have a wife to support him and to stay put instead of traveling all over the country?"[17]

Despite its reputation as a champion of the worker, the FDR administration was distinctly cold to the plight of the journalist. Because of publisher pressure, the NRA newspaper code contained no regulations to improve economic conditions for journalists. It did not prescribe minimum wages or maximum hours, or even assert that all reporters were subject to code rules (publishers, taking advantage of ongoing uncertainty about the status of the journalist, had argued that reporters should be exempted from code provisions as "professionals"). Instead, FDR simply asked that wages and hours provisions be determined within sixty days, and "requested" that large papers within urban areas implement a forty-hour, five-day week. The task of actually reforming the labor conditions of journalism was deferred to a Newspaper Industry Board, and the board—dominated by representatives of the publishers and the mechanical unions—largely ignored the question of reportorial labor. In any case, deadlocked between publisher and union factions, it was mostly ineffective.[18]

* * *

The New Deal state could not provide relief to journalists. So Heywood Broun proposed a different solution: unionization. Broun was a major national figure in the 1930s. His fiercely opinionated and liberal column, *It Seems to Me,* was circulated nationally. A socialist socialite and a perpetual guzzler of gin, the spectacularly ill-groomed Broun was in many ways a quintessential figure of the Popular Front. He had supported Sacco and Vanzetti and run as a Socialist candidate for Congress. A former drama critic, he was a member of the Algonquin table. Hemingway, Dos Passos, Sherwood Anderson, and Archibald MacLeish all paid tribute to him on his death in 1939.[19]

Broun's column of August 7, 1933, was entitled "A Union of Reporters." Given that publishers were "planning to cheat NRA re-employment aims," he declared, there had to be "a newspaper writer's union." "Beginning at nine o'clock on the morning of October 1," he continued, "I am going to do the best I can to help in getting one up." Poking gentle fun at his own pampered condition (no matter how short the working day, he noted, it would be much longer than the time it took to write the column for which he got paid $40,000 p.a.), Broun challenged the self-image of his fellow editorial workers who "never look upon themselves as they really are—hacks and white collar slaves." The column ended on a note of playful militancy: "I think I could die happy on the opening day of the general strike if I had the privilege of watching Walter Lippmann heave half a brick through the *Tribune* window at a non-union operative."[20]

Broun's personality and national celebrity helped spread the idea of a reporter's union. But, as guildsmen later recalled, the idea's time had come. There had been some short-lived efforts at unionization decades earlier, and Depression-era journalists had already begun to meet and organize in Cleveland even before Broun's call went out. Newspapermen across the country soon began meeting in speakeasies, hotels, press clubs, and apartments. They organized local guilds, issued draft NRA codes, and offered testimony in NRA code hearings. The New York guild began issuing a national newsletter, the *Guild Reporter,* in November. And on December 15, thirty-six delegates representing twenty cities met in Broun's room at the Willard Hotel in DC and formed the American Newspaper Guild. Broun was named president.[21]

At first, publishers were almost entirely hostile to guild demands, and refused to recognize the unions forming in their newsrooms. And the machinery of what one guildsman called the "NRA quagmire" was largely useless to the young organization. So the guild became more organized and more militant. At its first convention in June 1934, it drew up a national contract program, calling for recognition of the guild; forty-hour, five-day weeks with overtime and no split shifts; limitations on space work; minimum wages; dismissal notices; and sick pay.[22] It waged strikes against the *Long Island Daily Press,* the *Newark Ledger,* and the *Wisconsin News* to win recognition and protest the firing of guild organizers. In 1936, the guild voted to affiliate with the American Federation of Labor. The next year, it committed itself to industrial unionism and moved to the more radical Committee for Industrial Organization.[23] In only four years, previously unorganized editorial workers had moved into open affiliation with the progressive wing of the labor movement.

Publishers and professional boosters responded to the radicalization of the guild with horror, arguing that unionization was inappropriate for creative workers and a threat to press freedom. Regulation of hours and work conditions was fine for mechanical crafts, they argued, but it was not viable for the skilled and individualistic work of reporting. "Editorial workers are essentially artists," opined *Editor and Publisher,* and "artists enjoy freedom." If reporters unionize, another news industry spokesperson warned, we "will have sacrificed individuality. We will have become button makers and toothpick whittlers." And the unionization of journalists threatened not only individual liberties but also freedom of the press. Such a union, declared *Editor and Publisher,* would "mark the end of independent journalism in this country." Hearst argued that as soon as a newspaperman "joins a radical guild [he] becomes a radical propagandist," undermining the objectivity of the press. Or, as another editor put it, a union in control of the newsroom "becomes an absolute political boss the equal of which can be found only in a totalitarian state."[24]

The guild's opponents saw their worst fears realized when the Seattle guild united with the Teamsters to wage a successful three-month strike against the Hearst-owned *Post-Intelligencer* in the summer of 1936. "There is the same kind of dynamite in the Seattle situation that flamed into the revolution in Spain," one editor declared. Another argued that "it becomes increasingly evident that democracy is dying in America. . . . The great city of Seattle is virtually under a dictatorship today—a dictatorship of thugs and other base fellows." The California Newspaper Publishers Association, representing 300 papers, condemned the strike as "contrary to the American principle of majority control, and as a violation of the right of the freedom of the press."[25]

The guild, on the other hand, argued that it was working to create a truly free press. One 1937 guild manifesto declared that "the maintenance of a free press and its extension beyond present conditions to a *genuine* free press is of vital importance to the trade union movement. The Guild . . . should take the leadership in the fight to ensure a *real* free press." The guild dismissed claims that America already had a free press, arguing that "avaricious" publishers were pretending to care about press freedom "as a cloak for the preservation of their own profits and dividends."[26] One satirical guild song, "The March of the Publishers," ran as follows:

On to Chicago to fight for our freedom—
Freedom to hire men, work 'em and bleed 'em—
Freedom to chisel to heart's content—
Freedom to make thirty-seven per cent.
On to Chicago—but don't fail to stress—
That our battle, of course, is for freedom of press.[27]

The guild was thus participating in the broader Popular Front assault on the figure of the dictatorial publisher. The guild, too, argued that capitalist self-interest had undermined press freedom. Guild members particularly focused on the biased and incomplete coverage of labor and progressive political movements, arguing that the publishers represented an organized class faction threatening to create newspaper dictatorship.

The unionization of journalists did not threaten to end the impartiality of the press, the guild believed, because the press had never been impartial. Rather, control of the press currently "lies in the hands of men whose economic and political ties must continually tempt them to present an incomplete and distorted picture of what is going on in the world."[28] In song, guild members dressed as Hearst, McCormick, and Patterson linked arms and ridiculed the publishers' claims to represent a diversity of opinion and a free press:

> We are the publishers three, are we,
> United we represent li-ber-ty
> . . .
> (McCormick): it's very objective when *we* combine
> I'll let you two in on my free press line
> But men writing news aren't entitled to views
> Unless they happen to be mine.[29]

In place of this, the guild argued that a truly free press would provide an accurate flow of news to the public. It was thus attempting, like so many other press critics in the 1930s, to guarantee that the press was free to spread accurate information to the public. But whereas others had rested their reform program on state regulation, or on an enlarged sense of publisher responsibility, the guild argued that a truly free press depended on reforming the labor relations of the newsroom. This claim brought together older concerns about the dependence of the hireling reporter and new concerns about the crises of American press freedom.

The guild was proposing, in short, a labor theory of press freedom. In a crucial formulation, Broun argued that "a free press can be maintained only through the support of free men" and that it "is not possible to have a free press in any circumstance where the men and women who get the news feel insecure or terrorized." A New York guildsman suggested that a lack of security made journalists "subservient to outside influence" and "impairs the strength of the press."[30] At the first national convention one month later, the guild passed a resolution tying an expansive vision of a free press to the employment conditions of reporters:

> Whereas reporting is a high calling which has fallen into disrepute because news writers have been so often degraded as hirelings, compelled by their employers to serve the purposes of politicians, monopolists, speculators in the necessaries of life, exploiters of labor

> and fomenters of war; therefore be it resolved that the ANG strive tirelessly for the integrity of news and opportunity for its members to discharge their social responsibility: not stopping until the men and women who write, graphically portray or edit news have achieved freedom of conscience to report faithfully.[31]

The guild also hoped that unionization would transform the journalist into a crusader for a more vibrant press and a more vibrant democracy. One guild manifesto argued that "a genuinely free press" could emerge only when reporters abandoned "the old tradition of bored, weary and usually alcoholic indifference and cynicism" and embraced "an aroused social conscience, a clear realization of the duty which [they] owe to the democracy in which they live." An early issue of the *Guild Reporter* denounced the reporter of yesteryear for his naïveté: "He was an individualist, and if things got too intolerable he could always remind himself of the romance of his work, or get drunk, or both. He was an individualist and he was also something of an ass." Welcoming the signing of a contract as "a step towards the economic liberation of the newspaper editorial worker," the president of the New York guild hoped that "very soon it will be possible to bid a final farewell to the slapstick or Hollywood reporter whose sustenance was reputed to be equal parts of glamour, gin and graft." Broun thought a new attitude might lead to the "perfect newspaper." This was heady stuff, and moved one journalism student to conclude a 1941 term paper: "The day will come when Guildsmen will be worshipped as martyrs. . . . They are on the 'side of angels' and they promise to come through with a better deal for men whose profession should rank with the foremost workers for the betterment of the public weal."[32]

* * *

The first challenge for the guild was gaining economic security for its members. To do so meant challenging the publisher's otherwise unlimited authority to hire and fire journalists. Following standard union practice, the guild tried to sign contracts that would ensure that all employees of the newsroom were members; this would provide its members with economic leverage as well as job security. There were also some efforts to require that publishers first come to the guild when trying to fill vacancies. Publishers, unsurprisingly, resisted any effort to interfere with their hiring prerogatives. They argued that the only way to preserve independent journalism was to hire "on merit and without regard to external affiliations and influences." "Effective and responsible newspaper publication," argued Wilbur Forrest, an executive at the *New York Herald Tribune,* "requires complete freedom in the selection by the editor of a diversified staff." Any form of a closed shop would undermine press freedom. By 1937, *Editor and Publisher* was describing the closed shop as the "essential difference" between publishers and the guild. The disputed relationship between hiring rights and press freedom even found its way into a Roper public affairs survey in 1938: 35 percent of the public believed membership in a union impaired a journalist's impartiality; 56 percent believed a journalist's impartiality was impaired by "fear of displeasing his boss."[33]

In 1937, this dispute about the relationship between press freedom and newspaper employment rights went to the Supreme Court. The AP had fired Morris Watson in 1935 when he tried to organize a guild unit within the New York AP offices. The AP argued that Watson's guild activities undermined the integrity of his reporting. The guild protested, charging that such punitive dismissal of a union organizer violated labor's right to organize under the newly passed Wagner Act. By the time the case reached the Supreme Court, it had partially evolved into a general decision about the constitutionality of the Wagner Act. The Supreme Court ruled against the AP, and ordered Watson's reinstatement. It was one of five rulings, handed down simultaneously, that upheld the constitutionality of the Wagner Act.[34]

But the Supreme Court also considered the more specific issue of the relationship between reporters' unionization and the First Amendment. The AP and ANPA's Elisha Hanson argued that any state interference with the publisher's right to determine who was fit to work on a paper violated the First Amendment; if a news organization believed union membership undermined journalist objectivity, no law could interfere with the publisher's right to fire the individual. A minority of four justices agreed with this argument, holding that under the First Amendment, publishers could not be restrained "in respect of employment in the editorial force." If the state could force the reinstatement of a journalist, it would "abridge the freedom of the press." The majority of the justices did not go so far. They argued that union activity did not necessarily undermine a reporter's ability to do their work, so there could be no automatic First Amendment exemption from the Wagner Act's general protections for union organizations. The reasoning upheld the right of journalists to unionize, but it also made it clear that Watson could be fired if membership in the guild did *in fact* cause him to fall short of the publisher's understanding of good journalistic practice. As Justice Roberts put it, "The restoration of Watson to his former position in no sense guarantees his continuance in petitioner's employ. The petitioner [AP] is at liberty, whenever occasion may arise, to exercise its undoubted right to sever his relationship for any cause that seems to it proper save only as a punishment for, or discouragement of, such activities as the [Wagner] Act declares permissible."[35]

The Supreme Court had both recognized the publisher's authority to fire journalists and declared the First Amendment neutral on the question of newspaper unions. The future of the guild would be determined in clashes between the guild and the publishers. A few months after the Watson decision was handed down, "one of the largest gatherings of newspaper editors and publishers ever held" declared a closed guild shop "the most dangerous threat to press freedom that has arisen." Eleven different associations of publishers and editors formally declared their "unalterable opposition" to any such agreement with the guild. At the same time, some publishers started to offer journalists more favorable economic terms. And the guild, flush from success in the Seattle strike, was keen to sign many more contracts. In the end, they reached a compromise. In a "concession to the freedom of the press," the guild clarified that it would claim no control over hiring; publishers could hire whomever they liked. The guild still tried to insist that all new employees would subsequently become guild members (it called this a guild shop). But by 1940, only one in three guild contracts provided such guarantees. And many guild contracts conceded that the publisher had unilateral rights to fire journalists for a wide variety of reasons, provided only that the journalist was issued severance pay.[36] In exchange for recognition and much-needed wage gains, the guild had conceded that publishers retained the right to hire and fire journalists.

* * *

If the guild had failed to take control of the hiring process, it nevertheless continued to argue that unionization would improve the quality of the nation's press by transforming the ethics of journalism. Superficially, the argument was akin to those of professional boosters and journalism educators—the conditions of the waged journalist needed improvement to produce a truly free press (or, as Broun put it, "better working conditions do not impair a free press but promote it.") But there was a crucial difference. The guild explicitly rejected the notion that journalism was a profession. Instead, guild members were part of the working class. "Newspaper editorial knowledge is not professional knowledge," declared one early member, "but the same type of knowledge as that possessed by the bricklayer who has learned by practice to build a wall to plumb. Editorial workers are not professional men but skilled artisans and hired hands." "We are not professionals but craftsmen," announced another; "we are laboring persons." In part, the rejection of professionalism was a product of the minimum wage provisions of the early NRA code, which exempted professional workers. (As the guild put it, "We would much prefer to be classed as simply craftsmen and taken up to the heights of the Blue Eagle rather than be abandoned in the valley of rugged individualism.")[37]

But in rejecting professionalism in favor of class consciousness, the guild was also attempting to redefine the ethics of journalism. Publishers argued that press freedom was best preserved when the journalist had no outside affiliations, and was loyal only to his newspaper. ("A born newspaperman," declared one editor, "is as loyal to his paper as a good Mohammedan is to Allah.") But the guild argued that the journalist had ethical obligations to the broader working-class mobilization of the Popular Front. "Guild members SHOULD be loyal to their paper," declared one circular, "but Guild members MUST be loyal to their fellow members in matters within the clear scope of union activity as well as loyal to organized labor as a whole." Collective political activity would produce both a more objective journalism and a more vibrant democracy. No longer would the journalist be "compelled to be a bystander, assuming an air of lofty detachment" or forced to "make close daily scrutiny of the seamiest side of modern society without doing one solitary thing to remedy the abuses which he observes." Far "from being strait-jacketed by the Guild," the journalist was "in fact set free." He was free to report without the straitjacket of what had passed for objectivity in the business-dominated press. "If you do color your news reports in favor of organized labor," one guild meeting was informed, "it would be colored in the interest of a larger number of Americans than it has been colored for in the past."[38] The guild was, in short, attempting to advocate a populist theory of journalistic ethics.

Interestingly, the guild's populist labor politics led it to underemphasize gender and racial inequalities in the newsroom. The guild made overtures to women and racial minorities in the press, but claims for workplace equality did not make their way into the mainstream of the guild's vision of revitalized press freedom. An early *Guild Reporter* article pointed out women's unequal work conditions and limited opportunities for advancement, and the first guild convention passed a resolution calling for equal pay for equal work, but journalism remained "predominantly a man's job" for decades. Not until feminist reporters filed a class-action lawsuit in the early 1970s, for instance, was the *New York Times* forced to remedy its unequal pay, promotion, and hiring practices.[39] And while the guild's own constitution barred racial discrimination, and while it helped organize units in some African American papers, the guild made no real effort to end discrimination in newsrooms until the mid-1950s. At that point, a guild survey could find only thirty-eight African Americans among the 75,000 newsroom employees of the nation's general circulation papers. By 1960, only 30 percent of guild contracts contained fair employment or antidiscrimination provisions.[40]

Nevertheless, in the mid-1930s the guild did become active in a gamut of Popular Front causes: court reform and a third term for FDR; an independent farmer–labor party; support for the Wagner Act, the WPA, and the antilynching bill; opposition to the Dies committee, antialien legislation, and the attacks on Harry Bridges. And the guild repeatedly supported organized labor.[41] It understood all of these activities not as a violation of press freedom, or of objectivity, but as a populist recapturing of the press from corporate interests. It expressed these sentiments in the populist nationalism so prevalent in the 1930s.[42] One guild organizer argued that the guild was "making [changes] within the framework of traditional American ideals about freedom, democracy and the right of each man to follow the dictates of his own mind." The guild saw itself as reclaiming press freedom from the publishers, whose vision of the free press was "not the sort of thing that Tom Jefferson or Tom Paine conceived for America." Guild members, declared one flyer, "determine to fight, as their American forefathers fought, for the elementary rights of free speech, assemblage and free press."[43]

* * *

Such a broad vision of political engagement did not last long. In 1937, the guild convention passed a number of resolutions committing the guild to a more activist agenda, and then put all of them to a referendum among the national membership. Guild members affirmed all of the resolutions bar one: a resolution supporting the Republican cause in the Spanish Civil War. Guild leadership had assumed that its members would support what was, in many ways, *the* cause of the Popular Front. The first American to die volunteering in Spain was a member of the Newspaper Guild—Ben Leider, an airman who was quickly claimed as a leftist martyr after he was "shot down by fascist gun fire as he fought for the freedom and rights of workers in the cause of democracy." Leider's body was returned to America in 1938; 3,000 people attended his funeral at Carnegie Hall. In Spain, a children's home was named after him.[44] But when Heywood Broun sent out a circular calling for guild contributions to a Leider Fund, he received some unexpectedly vitriolic responses. Forty-three out of forty-four members of the *Boston Daily Record* guild unit signed a letter from Harry Benwell arguing that instead of contributing,

> I'm going to continue minding my own damn business. . . . The late Mr. Leider may have been a hero as you say, but the fact he gave his life fighting for Spanish communists is nothing for American newspapermen to get excited about. . . . What does arouse my ire is this nauseating comparison with Abraham Lincoln, and the drivel about "liberty, justice and democracy." Newspaper people of this country have enough to do in fighting their own battles right here in this country.[45]

The membership's refusal to support Republican Spain was the first indication of a growing antiradical backlash among the guild rank and file. The guild had been accused of un-American internationalism since its founding. And the guild's political progress had alienated some journalists for just as long. As it moved leftward, it had lost reporters to more conservative organizations: when the guild affiliated with the American Federation of Labor (AFL), a professional society sprung up; following the guild's move to the Congress of Industrial Organizations (CIO), a number of AFL craft unions emerged. Others simply quit the guild to protest its radicalization. When the guild joined the CIO, Walter Lippmann publicly turned in his guild card: "As long as the Guild stands committed to the political opinions adopted at the St. Louis convention, or any other political opinions, I shall not pay any membership dues."[46]

But in the late 1930s, members organized an antiradical faction within the guild itself. Local elections in 1939 and 1940 saw the victory of anti-Red tickets in such cities as Philadelphia, Seattle, DC, and the Twin

Cities. Anti-Red delegates at the 1940 convention tried to expand an older resolution condemning fascism and Nazism to include an explicit denunciation of communism. Although their efforts were defeated on the convention floor, the Youngstown Newspaper Guild successfully lobbied for a national referendum on the issue, and in early 1941 the guild membership voted three to one to denounce communism. It was a symbolic defeat for the radical leadership.[47]

In 1941, the guild's politics were remade by members who believed that its radicalism posed a totalitarian threat to American press freedom. Ever since, the question of communist domination of the early guild has been controversial. At least some of the guild's early leaders were Communist Party members. Nat Einhorn, executive secretary of the New York guild and chairman of the heavily communist *Brooklyn Eagle* unit, was widely known to be a member, for instance.[48] And key guild leaders were certainly involved with "communist front" organizations. But it is hard to say anything more definitive about who was and was not a member, let alone about more elusive questions of intent: Who knew "the truth" about the party? Who was a naïve fellow traveler, and who an unwitting dupe? It is impossible to see through all the accusations, counteraccusations, hazy memories, and highly politicized assertions.

The key historical question, however, is not whether the leaders of the guild were dupes of the Communist Party, but why that charge became so persuasive to unionized journalists in the late 1930s. The accusation had been made before, entirely unsuccessfully. But in the late 1930s, the rapid deterioration of the geopolitical climate allowed the antiradical faction to take control of the language of populist Americanism, and to present guild radicals as part of an un-American conspiracy. *Editor and Publisher* observed, with some glee, the emergence of a "rank and file rebellion against anything that smacks of un-Americanism." Anti-Red activists self-consciously tied guild radicals to an un-American internationalism. As one anti-Red player strategized, "I got over very thoroughly the idea that I was against all internationalism in the Guild." To break apart a local meeting, he continued, an effective tactic was the introduction of resolutions attacking communism and condemning the Soviet invasion of Finland. In the wake of the Hitler-Stalin pact, guild tie-ups with Popular Front pacifist organizations such as the American Peace Mobilization (APM) were used to discredit guild leaders as thoroughly un-American: "In the APM matter the guild leadership is putting the guild on the big-league battlefield, against the American people. For the American people are girding themselves to halt the inroads of totalitarianism. The APM wants to cripple the right arm of the American people." Apparently worried that the key point could be missed, one anti-Red ticket passed a resolution instructing "those who like the American way [to] offer a unanimous vote of confidence and support for the election of . . . [the] Americanized slate to take over the guiding of our guild for Americans."[49]

Crucially, the anti-Red faction also argued that the radical internationalism of the guild was nothing more than biased propaganda, and thus a violation of the journalist's professional obligations to the public. The guild had been founded to improve working conditions for journalists in order to free journalism from undemocratic control by the publisher, and to thus improve the flow of objective information to the public. But now, it seemed, political engagement by a union of journalists led not to individual autonomy, but to an even more insidious form of domination—one orchestrated by an un-American conspiracy. Anti-Red activists accused the guild leadership of mindless devotion to Moscow, of reporting with "closed minds," and of falling short of professional standards. The *Guild Reporter* was repeatedly held up as outrageously biased, sectarian, and dogmatic, and it was asserted that the best newspapermen had left the guild, to be replaced by party functionaries, hacks, and careerist graspers. Leadership policy maneuverings were dismissed as "unworthy of newspaper people" and as "primarily concerned with a narrow circle of outside interests . . . [that] are also the special concerns of the Communist Party." One report on communist influence made clear that the guild "is obligated to resist this delegation with more spirit than the layman for as newspapermen we know how vital is a free press to the service of majority and minority rights."[50]

The balance of power tipped to the anti-Red faction in June 1941. On June 22, as the guild was gathered for its annual convention, Nazi Germany invaded the Soviet Union, scuttling the Hitler-Stalin pact and scrambling the antiwar stance of the Communist Party. Anti-Red activists in the guild made great hay of the fact that they had watched the guild leadership run to grab copies of the *Daily Worker* to determine "what the new communist party line would be." In the lead up to the October 1941 election for the national board of the guild, anti-Red activists fixated on the communist orthodoxy of the current leadership. The guild had been eaten away by "red termites," they charged. It had become a Communist Party "transmission belt" and had a "rosy pink hue." They called on members to elect "guild officers and not Moscow errand boys." One pamphlet—entitled *Are Their Faces Red!*—asserted that the "hairpin turn" of the leadership into support for the war confirmed "what we have said time and time again"—"the present guild leadership slavishly followed the Communist Party line."[51]

On October 15, by a vote of roughly 5,500 to 3,500, the entire pro-guild slate would be elected to national office. Two weeks later, on the first afternoon of its first meeting, the new board fired the three paid officers of the guild.[52] Before Pearl Harbor, the guild had purged its radicals from leadership. There would be no rapprochement with the communists during the Good War. The guild, devoted to anticommunism, was already prepared for the Cold War.

* * *

The interwar clashes over the guild defined the relationship between waged journalists and American press freedom for the postwar period. In 1959, reporter and critic Judith Crist observed that the guild had been responsible for professionalizing journalism, and for elevating the journalist into the bourgeoisie. It "took a union," Crist declared, "to make a profession out of newspaper reporting simply because the union achieved the economic security that frees a man to work in a truly professional manner in any field."[53] That was an ironic statement, for the guild had been founded to challenge the professionalization of the journalist. But Crist was only partly correct. The guild had helped to professionalize journalism insofar as it raised wages and embraced an ethics of apolitical neutrality. But it had not transformed the dependent status of the journalist, or found a way to collectively enforce professional ethics. The labor that produced the flow of information in the postwar press remained curiously unregulated, subject to the whims of the publisher.

After 1941, the new guild leadership was certainly successful in winning unprecedented wage gains for reporters, elevating them into the middle class. Anti-Red activists had presented themselves as more militant on wage issues than the communist leadership, arguing that a focus on unpatriotic politics had distracted from union organizing. In 1946, they proposed an ambitious wage program calling for $100-a-week minimums across the nation. Within two years, the guild had increased national salaries by a combined $22 million. The guild's first contract had guaranteed a starting journalist $20 per week; in 1940, starting New York journalists were guaranteed $25 per week. By 1958, a starting journalist in New York was guaranteed $90 per week; by 1964, that had risen to $160. Those raises radically outstripped inflation—in constant 1940 dollars, the difference from 1940 to 1964 was a raise from $25 a week to $72 a week.[54]

But for all that those wages did for the living conditions of journalists, they did not transform the economic relations at the heart of the modern press. The guild eschewed any effort to involve journalists in questions of newspaper management—it asked for higher pay as straightforward recompense for journalists' "contribution to the immense wealth and prestige of the press in the U.S." At the 1946 annual convention, guild members were told to expect boom-times ahead, and instructed to insist on their fair share: "The newspaper industry is in an era of unparalleled prosperity. Its current and future volume of business and profits greatly exceed even the immensely profitable war years. There can be no question of ability to pay." But one year later the *Philadelphia Record* went out of business, throwing 500 guild members out of work.[55] It had been the first newspaper to sign a contract with the guild.

As early as 1950, some members of the guild came to the "sudden realization that the American press is actually in danger of becoming extinct." Arguing that the guild was the only organization that could "reverse the trend toward fewer papers and fewer jobs," they proposed that the guild levy funds to endow a nonprofit newspaper. But the proposal was defeated by a greater than two-to-one margin in a membership referendum. The guild's task was to win wage gains, not to launch new papers. Management, and management alone, was responsible for economic policy. By 1960, 90 percent of all guild contracts granted the publisher rights to fire journalists if the publisher considered it necessary for the financial health of the newspaper.[56] The economic status of the waged journalist remained precarious.

Just as the postwar guild retreated from any effort to establish journalist control over newspaper management, it also retreated from any effort to expand the meaning of objectivity. Whereas the early guild had argued that political engagement would produce a truly objective press for the first time, the postwar guild argued that apolitical neutrality was essential to ensuring the flow of objective and accurate information to the public. Journalists, they argued, should adopt "middle of the road" and "unbiased" coverage of controversial issues. The guild should stick to straightforward union issues, and avoid politics. As an anticommunist candidate in New York put it, "We've got to make the Guild an out and out trade union and concentrate on wages, hours and working conditions. It is my own personal business what I think on China or Russia or Spain, but now it has nothing whatever to do with the Guild." "Sam Gompers had it right," agreed Republican-voting guild member Chester Norris; "a labor union had no business playing politics." The guild retreated to an affirmation of the objectivity of the American press: "Even the entrenched tory press in America is evolving towards freedom. . . . The doctrinaire press is not."[57] Press freedom, in other words, depended on objective journalism.

But the ethics of objectivity would remain unregulated in the postwar period. The guild did not police the professional behavior of its journalists, and professional associations still lacked enforcement mechanisms. Journalism education continued to expand in the booming postwar universities, but the standards of instruction remained uneven, and paths into journalism remained diverse: as late as 1958, fewer than 60 percent of American journalists were college graduates. The responsibility for enforcing professional ethics remained the sole prerogative of the publisher. As a leading postwar exploration of press freedom put it, "The writer works for an employer, and the employer not the writer takes the responsibility. . . . The effective organization of writers on professional lines is almost impossible." Although the journalist was "the first link in the chain of responsibility" of providing information to the public, "his employer has the duty of training him to do his work as it ought to be done."[58]

In practice, therefore, neither the guild nor the professionalization movement had succeeded in reforming the labor of journalism to ensure that the waged journalist was guaranteed the freedom to report independently. A sociological study of newsrooms in the mid-1950s observed that publishers still set editorial policy, and that the guild "has not interfered with such matters." Journalists still learned to internalize the political tastes of their bosses in order to maintain their jobs, advance their careers, and see their names in print. In 1960, press critic A. J. Liebling returned to the old critique of the hireling reporter. "Freedom of the individual journalist," he declared, "corresponds exactly with what the publisher will allow him."[59] The effort to improve American press freedom by reforming the labor of journalism had failed. The flow of information in the nation's press still relied on a dependent class of workers.

The success of the anti-Red faction in the guild in the fall of 1941 was thus a turning point in the history of journalism and the politics of press freedom. The new guild leaders had argued, successfully, that the early guild's labor theory of press freedom was a violation of the journalist's obligations to objectively report the news to the public. But an important question remained. If radicalism and internationalism were violations of objectivity in an era of geopolitical turmoil, what were the journalist's obligations to the nation? When America entered World War II only weeks after the ascension of the new guild leadership, this became a crucial problem. Reiterating its antitotalitarian beliefs, the guild committed itself to the war effort. Members flowed into armed service, and threw their support behind the bond drive, the no-strike pledge, and the emerging propaganda and censorship agencies of the wartime state.[60] As it became involved in the war effort, new questions about the political and professional obligations of the journalist arose. Almost ten years to the day since Broun's 1933 call for a newspaper union, the *SS Heywood Broun* set out to aid the American war against fascism.[61] The United States had gone to war to protect American liberties in an illiberal world. And so had the press.

5

The Weapon of Information in the Good War

One year after the attack on Pearl Harbor, *Chicago Times* editor Richard J. Finnegan addressed his local City Club on the "dual obligations" of the press during wartime. On the one hand, Finnegan observed, newspapers "owe it to their readers to print the truth." On the other, newspapers owed it "to the leaders of the armed services not to divulge, prematurely, military information." But this produced a paradox. When a liberal democracy goes to war, Finnegan continued, "the people expect—yes, demand—that their government construct an economic and military totalitarianism equal to that of their enemy to guarantee victory. As to political and civil liberties, however, they insist on preservation of democracy with all its freedoms." As a common World War II formulation put it, news was a "weapon" that had to be strategically managed to build morale and deceive the enemy. But Americans were also waging the war to defend their vision of freedom—and "freedom of speech and expression" was the first of the Four Freedoms that FDR had pledged to defend early in 1941.[1]

As Americans sought to resolve this paradox during World War II, they were guided by a desire to distinguish their war effort from those of their totalitarian foes. And they hoped to avoid repeating what were widely viewed as the excessive censorship and propaganda programs of World War I's Creel Committee. The World War II state would not create a centralized information agency, and Americans on the domestic front were subject to remarkably little direct state propaganda. And in stark contrast to the earlier war, the "Good War" featured very little censorship or prosecution of speech. There were some minor violations of the right to free speech: domestic Fascist William Pelley served jail time for his offensive opinions about Jews, FDR, and the war effort; approximately twenty black activists were convicted for seditious statements in support of the Japanese; eighteen Trotskyists in Minneapolis went to jail for subversive advocacy. But the general pattern was one of prosecutorial restraint and increasing judicial respect for First Amendment rights. In 1944, the Supreme Court even overturned a rare Espionage Act conviction of a man who had written an anti-Semitic pamphlet that called for a Nazi victory. The decision was made on narrow grounds, and by a close five-to-four vote, but it nevertheless symbolized the distance the court had traveled since the *Debs, Frohwerk,* and *Schenck* decisions twenty-five years earlier.[2]

Throughout the war, the American public sphere was subject to surprisingly little direct interference by the state. Americans retained their rights to express their opinions, the press retained its right to publish what it pleased, and the state did little to propagandize the public. But although the press retained its essential autonomy, the pressures of total war led the state to institute a host of new practices centered on the regulation of information. The state did not issue propaganda directly to the public, but it became increasingly strategic about what information it disclosed to the press. While journalists were free from formal censorship, they were encouraged to practice voluntary self-censorship to prevent vital information from circulating in the press. And although the state did not censor public discourse, wartime agencies began to develop a new regime of secrecy and classification that kept information from ever reaching the public. As the state retreated from overt regulation of the press, in other words, it began to exercise new powers over the flow of information in the polity. While Americans largely retained their right to express their opinions during the Good War, their ability to access information held by the state began to decline.[3]

* * *

In the early years of the war, in an effort to avoid creating a centralized propaganda agency akin to the Creel Committee of World War I, the FDR administration created a host of specialized agencies devoted specifically to morale work, or issuing handouts, or measuring public opinion. But it soon became clear that the system was chaotic and dysfunctional. In June 1942, FDR created a new Office of War Information (OWI). Under the leadership of liberal journalist Elmer Davis, the new organization united all the preexisting propaganda agencies under one roof. It took responsibility for clearing speeches and press releases from the agencies to assure an "accurate and consistent flow of war information to the public," it produced content to "facilitate the informed and intelligent understanding" of the war effort, and it coordinated informational policy throughout the administration. The OWI still had far less power than the Creel Committee had wielded. The OWI, importantly, never had censorship powers, which fell to a different agency. And in the long run the OWI would be most significant for its role in developing international propaganda. But at first, the OWI promised to remake the domestic relations between state and press as well. By February 1943, the domestic branch of the OWI had a budget of $8 million, and a staff of 1,500.[4]

The OWI was the culmination of New Deal efforts to bypass the press and speak directly from the administrative agencies to the people. Earlier wartime informational agencies had avoided direct propaganda. The Office of Facts and Figures (OFF), the direct precursor to the OWI, was intended, in the words of Director Archibald MacLeish, "to act as a sort of attorney for the public in bringing out the official facts concerning the progress of the war." It limited its activities to coordinating background press releases from the bureaucracy—what MacLeish called "pre-news."[5] But by early 1942, only months after the OFF had been created, MacLeish realized that such limited activities would not adequately inform the public about the war effort. In the first place, the OFF lacked the authority to coordinate releases from agencies committed to maintaining their own agendas. After Pearl Harbor, MacLeish could not force the Army or Navy to release information—he was so deprived of access that he was dependent on radio reports to learn about the events in Hawaii. And more importantly, releasing only "pre-news" meant that the OFF relied on the commercial press to interpret the war effort. That meant relying on archisolationists like Robert McCormick to present the administration's war programs to the public.[6]

Dependency on what he called "reactionary newspapers" was anathema to MacLeish's militant liberalism, as it was to the generation of patriotic antifascists for whom he was spokesperson. MacLeish was a man of many talents, and his career exemplified the trajectory of an important strain of midcentury American liberalism. At seventeen, MacLeish wrote an essay on John Milton, ruminating on the tension between his desire to write poetry and his calling to political engagement. The tension defined

MacLeish's life, as—he argued—it had defined the life of his seventeenth-century muse. In the 1920s, MacLeish decamped to Paris to write poetry in the company of Hemingway and Dos Passos; in the 1930s, he returned to the United States to work as an economic journalist alongside Dwight Macdonald and James Agee at *Fortune* magazine. By the second half of the 1930s, MacLeish was preoccupied with international politics and the threat that fascism posed to liberalism. In a series of intellectual salvos he called for a renewed commitment to a fighting liberal idealism, which brought him to the attention of FDR, then gearing up for World War II. In 1939, MacLeish was appointed Librarian of Congress, where he became colloquially known as FDR's "minister for culture."[7]

So MacLeish brought to his duties as head of the OFF a particular understanding of the importance of antifascism to liberal politics. He had constructed his political philosophy around the concept of "responsibility." In an illiberal world, MacLeish argued, a responsible liberal had to make a full-throated defense of democracy. Those who doubted such sentiments were dismissed as "irresponsibles." Calling for American intervention in the Spanish Civil War in 1937, MacLeish attacked the "hypocrites and the cynical and the frivolous who do not wish to understand what is happening in Spain—who do not wish to accept the *responsibility* of understanding."[8] Confronted by newspaper criticism of the war effort and conservative slanting of his "pre-news" releases, MacLeish interpreted them as signs of irresponsibility.

On April 17, 1942, MacLeish outlined his understanding of the wartime "responsibility of the press" to the ASNE. As MacLeish saw it, the press was responsible for the formation of public opinion in a democratic society. And a liberal democratic state could not police irresponsible press behavior, even if it threatened national security, for that would violate press freedom. Therefore, MacLeish instructed his audience, the press was confronted with a new problem—would newspaper editors "accept, as a consequence of its traditional right to influence American opinion, a responsibility for the opinion which results?" "There was a time," MacLeish conceded, "when the chief and almost only concern of a free press in a free country was to protect its freedom against the encroachments of its own government." MacLeish believed that time had passed, but "a part of the press acts today as though we still lived in that time." A new understanding of press freedom was needed, one appropriate to the existential struggle with fascism. "It is not enough for any man, journalist or other, to fight for the freedom of ideas," MacLeish suggested; "it is necessary now to fight for the idea of freedom. It is not enough to claim the right to influence opinion. It is necessary to accept responsibility for the opinions which result." Such responsibility required self-discipline and self-policing among the press to weed out irresponsibility. And it also meant, as MacLeish elaborated three days later in a speech to the AP, press participation in an active campaign to spread positive information about the war. MacLeish called it the "strategy of truth."[9]

MacLeish's understanding of press responsibility resonated among liberals committed to the war effort. In 1940, Attorney General Francis Biddle had argued that liberals needed to "brush away a good deal of the eighteenth century negative attitude which has been part of the decadence of the liberal tradition"; rather, they should "have faith" in the ability of the government to issue antifascist propaganda to help defeat the Axis. Max Lerner called for a "bold and affirmative attempt to use democratic persuasion . . . as a form of political warfare." Stephen Vincent Benet said, "I am neither afraid nor ashamed of the word propaganda. I am neither afraid nor ashamed of the fact that American writers are speaking out today for a cause in which they believe."[10]

And MacLeish's ideas became central to the early operations of the OWI, for the OWI had been intentionally created, with input from MacLeish, to overcome the shortcomings of the OFF. In September 1942, Elmer Davis articulated the philosophy of the OWI in terms that echoed MacLeish. Propaganda, Davis insisted, was a neutral instrument that "may employ truth instead of falsehood." To "condemn the instrument because the wrong people use it for the wrong purposes is like condemning the automobile because criminals use it for a getaway." The OWI would provide the propaganda of truth, outlining both the successes and failures of the war effort. But it had to do more than simply issuing information, because that could produce confusion and a lack of understanding. So the OWI would also "from time to time issue a general survey of our own to try to tell the people how the total picture looks." Continuing the argument of New Deal publicists, Davis asserted that there was no risk to democratic debate in such interpretive releases, for if the OWI's spin looked one-sided "there is no law against standing up and saying so—in Congress, or on the radio, or in the newspapers, or on a soapbox." OWI propaganda would be but one more voice in America's free market of ideas. On a personnel level, too, the OWI expressed MacLeish's liberal vision of propaganda. A gaggle of liberals had come to work for the OFF and the OWI. Such men as Arthur Schlesinger Jr., Henry Pringle, and Ben

Shahn took part in some seventy campaigns to inform the public about the war program, producing pamphlets and press releases that outlined war aims and policies as part of a New Deal crusade.[11]

Such liberal propaganda quickly came under attack from conservatives. The *Chicago Tribune* had called MacLeish's views on press responsibility a totalitarian effort to "destroy the independence of the press by terrorizing it." And the OWI was criticized by the same conservatives who had called New Deal publicity a form of propaganda. In 1943, Harry Byrd, among others, once again promised to investigate the "entire propaganda field," while Alabama's Joe Starnes complained that "America needs no Goebbels sitting in Washington to tell the press what to publish." Congressional conservatives took particular offense at a series of OWI pamphlets: a magazine for foreign distribution that was attacked as pro-Roosevelt, fourth-term propaganda; a pamphlet on tax policy that caught the OWI "red-handed dealing in political propaganda"; and a pamphlet titled *Negroes and the War* that southern Democrats accused of attempting to "glorify one race in the war." As appropriations for the OWI were debated in the summer of 1943, there were increasing calls to defund the organization. There was a certain irony in the congressional fixation on these pamphlets; they had largely been the work of a group of OWI staffers who had very publicly quit the organization to protest what they felt was the OWI's retreat from New Deal commitments and its infiltration by corporate executives and shills for capitalism. The OWI was retreating from full-throated liberalism even before the conservative assault in Congress.[12]

But the damage had been done, and in June 1943, the House of Representatives voted to abolish the appropriation for the Domestic Branch of the OWI. That proved too drastic for the Senate, and the Domestic Branch was funded for the remainder of the war, albeit at a low level. More important than the gutting of the budget, however, was an earmark that banned the use of the funds to create any material that would be issued directly to the public. In practice, that meant that the OWI Domestic Branch would live on as an organization that cleared releases from government agencies and issued government handouts to newspapers. The News Bureau became the heart of the Domestic Branch: it was organized to mirror a "metropolitan newspaper editorial staff," and its forty-seven employees were responsible for issuing some 35,000 news releases from government agencies as well as preparing a smaller number of factual reports about the war effort. The rump of the OWI, as Elmer Davis testified to Congress in 1944, was much like "it had been in some degree heretofore"—that is to say, it looked like the OFF, a coordinating agency issuing handouts.[13]

So when the dust had settled after the OWI dispute, a large publicity apparatus remained in place, pumping vast amounts of verbiage to the nation's press. As Davis astutely observed, the congressional assault on the OWI had not abolished government information altogether. Rather, the "action was chiefly of partisan motivation; by providing that all information issued to the American people by OWI had to be filtered through newspapers (most of which were politically opposed to the administration) or other media, the Congress guaranteed that the people would be trusted with no more information than newspaper editors chose to give to them." After all the fireworks about handouts and propaganda, congressional conservatives were happy to settle for the New Deal handout system so long as private interests could frame and interpret government information. Provided that the state could not speak directly to the public, they seemed to believe, America's press would remain free. And since handouts remained only partially centralized, and individual agencies issued their own information, the system favored larger news organizations that could afford to send large staffs to cover all the agencies in DC. The formal independence of the commercial press was thus assured.[14]

The gutting of the OWI had two further consequences for press-state relations during the war. First, because it did not end the need to explain the meaning of the war to the public, private agencies rushed to fill the void. Most notable of these was the advertising industry, which organized a War Ad Council to coordinate publicity drives with the OWI. Donating advertising time and talent, the Ad Council kept the advertising industry in business amid the consumer shortages of the war economy and rehabilitated advertising's status as a democratic form of communication after the challenges of the Tugwell bill. Depicting America's war aims had been outsourced.[15]

Second, as the administration lost control of the ability to determine the way its releases were interpreted, it exercised the only power it still exclusively held—it became increasingly stingy and increasingly strategic about what information it released to the press. The president's press conferences, for instance, were no longer the garrulous affairs of the early New Deal. Instead, as one observer put it, they were "pretty newsless." Journalist and government press agent Eben Ayers kept a daily diary of the wartime conferences, in which he complained regularly about their lack of information and their dull, tedious formalism. He was not alone. Instructed by Press Secretary Stephen Early to "join the marines and see the world," one frustrated correspondent snapped back, "Cover the White House and don't see anything."[16]

The release of information was increasingly regulated throughout the administration. Decisions about what to release and what to suppress were inherently political, and as the war continued this became clearer and clearer. Images of casualties were banned from the press until late 1943, but as the administration became worried about public complacency, it cleared those images for release in order to maintain militaristic patriotism. In 1943, too, a decision was made to release previously restricted information about war production—with the war economy humming, such information was now seen as a way to intimidate the Axis. In January 1944, Elmer Davis justified the release of information about Japanese atrocities on the grounds that such releases "would nullify any voices which might be raised here if we should undertake bombing of Japanese cities." Suppression could also serve more partisan ends. In 1942, FDR sent a directive to the heads of all agencies and departments instructing them not to air out policy debates in public. The next year, a follow-up directive cautioned that anyone expressing a policy disagreement to the press would be expected to resign from the administration.[17]

* * *

Strategically managing news releases was a useful tool for promoting morale, but it provided no guarantees that sensitive military information would be kept from public circulation. That problem fell to another organization—the Office of Censorship (OC), which had been created on December 12, 1941. The OC represented an ingenious solution to the paradox of defending liberalism with wartime censorship: it made censorship a form of voluntaristic self-policing. As FDR put it shortly after establishing the new office, "Americans abhor censorship . . . [but] some degree of censorship is necessary in war time, and we are at war." The challenge now, FDR held, was to ensure "that such forms of censorship as are necessary shall be administered effectively and in harmony with the best interests of our free institutions." In an executive order issued on December 19, FDR granted the OC broad powers to censor the mail and international cables. But he did not grant the OC legal authority to censor the press. Rather, the president "called upon a patriotic press and radio to abstain voluntarily from the dissemination of detailed information of certain kinds, such as reports of the movement of vessels and troops." The newly appointed director of censorship, AP managing editor Byron Price, was verbally instructed to administer this voluntary self-censorship. "No law," Price proudly declared, "forms the basis of the voluntary censorship of the domestic press and radio. It is entirely cooperative, a patriotic contribution by editors and broadcasters to the national security."[18]

Cooperative press censorship had begun almost a full year earlier, when Secretary of the Navy Frank Knox had sent a sequence of letters to the press asking them to "impose a voluntary censorship" on news relating to maritime vessels, navy construction projects, navy contracts, and the repair of British ships under Lend-Lease. The letters had been met with some reportorial grumbling, particularly when papers were asked to suppress stories about the arrival of the British vessel *Malaya* in New York (some of the discontent was motivated by isolationist resentment, but much reflected incredulity at the attempt to suppress news of a highly visible boat). But overall, the requests had been met with incredible compliance. The navy reported a response "within one quarter of one percent unanimous." And the program provided a way to secure information without recourse of formal censorship. As the navy put it, a true definition of the practice would be "voluntary cooperation," not "voluntary censorship." FDR's press secretary, Stephen Early, concurred: "This is not censorship but an effort to avoid censorship."[19]

The new OC expanded this program of voluntary self-censorship. It began by developing a Code of Wartime Practices for the American Press. After two weeks of consultation with the army, navy, State Department, Maritime Commission, Weather Bureau, War Production Board, and FBI, the OC issued its first code on January 15, 1942. It was a five-page pamphlet that listed the "specific information which newspapers and magazines are asked not to publish" for the effective prosecution of the war: the character and movements of troops, ships, planes, and fortifications; information about war contracts, the location of production sites, estimated supplies of strategic or critical materials and national round-ups of procurement data; weather forecasts other than those officially issued; casualty lists; information about damage to military and naval objectives from enemy action; transportation of materials; the movement of the president or of official military and diplomatic missions of the allied nations. Categorical exceptions were made for information that had already been published, or information that had been released by an appropriate government source. Crucially, the code was not intended as a blanket prohibition on the publication of such information, or as a blank check to publish any information not listed in the pamphlet. And "nowhere was there a mandatory paragraph" within the code—it had no force of law. Instead, "a maximum of accomplishment will be attained if editors will ask themselves with respect to any given detail, 'is this information I would like to have if I were the enemy?' and then act accordingly."[20]

In short, when 50,000 copies flooded out through the press via wire services and professional organizations, the OC effectively outsourced the practice of censorship. As Price put it, "Every editor, every copy-reader, every reporter and writer becomes his own censor." The OC's main job was to inculcate the habits of self-censorship. In a 1942 censorship school the OC ran for forty editors, one Mr. Smith proved a model student when he noted that no matter who released information, "there has to be some judgment, some authority, whether or not specific information . . . should or should not be used." The OC instructor was ecstatic: "Good for you Mr. Smith, that is the attitude we would like to get out of every editor. Don't look on this office as something giving you a permit to print. Look on yourself as allies or associate members of the OC and make up your own mind what you think should be properly published in wartime in this country." It was, as Price astutely noted, "a system of self-discipline under the leadership of government."[21]

Given the emphasis on voluntarism, the OC did not formally censor or edit news stories, and it did not prosecute or punish the infrequent violations of the code. It acted as a "policy making body and not a direct censor of news." Much of the OC's time was spent handling queries from concerned publishers as to whether they should run certain items. In an effort to avoid becoming an official clearing house, the OC did not formally "approve" or "disapprove" stories sent to it (it fielded some 7,814 inquiries in 1942 alone). Instead, it marked the copy "No objection to publication or broadcast" or suggested deletions or other changes. Although there were no penalties for noncompliance with these suggestions, one OC employee reported that "in the end [the papers] always acquiesced."[22]

The OC relied on a rhetoric of patriotic sacrifice to produce such a culture of self-censorship. Editors and journalists were asked to consider the battlefield consequences of their publications. A favored expression of the OC came from the *New York Times* London Bureau chief, who had declared, "There isn't any story in the world that is good enough to justify risking the life of a single American soldier." The head of army PR had forwarded the quote to the OC, observing that it was a "sentence which might well be trumpeted to the American press as a keynote of patriotic reportorial thought. . . . Personally, I think it might well be emblazoned in every city room in the US." The OC plastered it on posters and used it in memoranda and requests to the press. A typical memorandum from the OC explained that the press was "cooperating with the government to deprive the enemy of certain information which would help him to kill Americans." The success of that effort, and the safety of the soldiers and the nation, depended on the individual decisions of journalists and editors. As one OC note to editors put it, "Ask yourself, 'is this information I would like to have if I were the enemy?' then let your conscience and your patriotism guide your decision."[23]

The OC's message was spread particularly effectively because it flowed out through the professional and social networks of the press. It was OC policy to employ only journalists of "unquestionable professional standing" to run the voluntary censorship program. Byron Price, heading the organization, was a longtime DC correspondent and AP executive; he was well known throughout the press. To staff the rest of the Press Bureau, Price employed men of similar pedigree, such as John Sorrells, president-publisher of the *Memphis Commercial Appeal* and executive news editor of the large Scripps-Howard chain; Nat Howard, editor of the *Cleveland News;* and William H. Mylander, DC correspondent of the *Toledo Blade* and *Pittsburgh Gazette.* Taking leaves of absence from their private-sector jobs, and working on reduced salaries, the OC staff were well positioned to speak to the press as colleagues. Indeed, personal and professional remembrances often slipped into official OC correspondence with the press. The close relationship between the press and the state was further consolidated as journalists poured into the expanding informational agencies of the wartime state. By 1944, it was reported that some 15,000 individuals had worked in the information agencies—many of them serving only briefly before returning to work in the private sector. The line between the press and the state was becoming blurry.[24]

In keeping with its voluntarist philosophy, the press division of the OC had a light institutional footprint—it sought to marshal the press of the nation with a tiny annual budget, a fifteen-person staff, and an aversion to branch offices. Instead, it relied on networks of volunteers in the press to spread the practice of self-censorship. In January 1942, the OC created an Editorial Advisory Board composed of representatives from the prominent professional organizations, which successfully spread OC messages to the major newspapers. By November 1942, Nat Howard could describe the daily newspapers as "pretty well indoctrinated with the rules of the game." That allowed the OC to turn to its attention to the thousands of smaller country weeklies that existed throughout the nation—papers that did not subscribe to a wire service or belong to an association, and that might dismiss or ignore OC requests as one more piece of mail from DC, or assume that they could not know any military secrets.[25]

The OC was adept at converting private networks into conduits through which OC instructions could reach even the smallest papers in the nation. Journalism schools helped spread the OC message: one OC staffer convinced his alma mater to send out the code in a statewide style book; in Nevada, OC instructions were included in a university journalism bulletin that got "into nooks and crannies" that the OC could not reach; at Oklahoma State University, the code was distributed to seniors and made part of the graduating exam. OC instructions even found their way into the "house magazine for house magazine editors," *Stet.* The centerpiece of the OC's mobilization of the press, however, was its creation of what it called a group of "OC Missionaries." To spread the OC message more widely, the OC asked for a volunteer from each state "who has a wide newspaper acquaintance and a fairly eminent standing to introduce our purpose and ideas as personally as possible." In April 1942, forty editors from forty states came to DC at their own expense to study censorship problems with the OC. They were instructed to use their "initiative and judgment" to spread the practice of self-censorship, and they proved enthusiastic. They made appearances at district meetings, and sent out OC material with personal entreaties to their colleagues and through state editorial associations. In the Upper Peninsula in Michigan, the publisher of a small paper in Escanaba drove "with his own gas and his own rubber" to all sixty-seven weekly newspapers to talk to editors about the code.[26]

The work of the OC's missionary in Indiana captured the essence of the OC's operations. Tom Keene, editor of the small *Elkhart Truth,* wrote to each of the 309 weeklies in the state multiple times, stressing the OC's patriotism and voluntarism: "The OC, after all, is in a sense our own organization, for it is directed and manned by practical newspaper men, and the censorship is voluntary. And certainly there is no newspaper in this state which for one moment wishes to be helpful to the Hitlers or the Hirohitos. The press is patriotic." In a 1943 New Year's Day memo, Keene reiterated the stakes of patriotic self-discipline: "Surely you aren't one of those newspaper editors who is unwittingly endangering the lives of his neighbor's sons?" But even such pleading was not enough for Keene. Five months later, he wrote to the OC to complain that they were "not close enough to the weeklies" and lacked a "more thorough grass-roots organization." He suggested the creation of a network of regional missionaries below him, who would spread OC practices "personally" through each of their territories. The OC considered Keene to be a "solid gold friend" and through his zeal for proselytizing one can clearly see the OC's success in ideologically mobilizing the press of the nation. It was all too appropriate that the OC referred to men such as Keene as "missionaries," to the wartime code as a "bible," and to Price as the "Bishop." As Howard put it, the OC was "spreading the gospel of voluntary censorship."[27]

Voluntary censorship won many converts. By May 1942, after newspapers had successfully kept the lid on diplomatic visits by Churchill and Molotov, press commentators and OC workers were noting that "the acceptance of the operations of the Press Division by newspaper publishers everywhere was of a surprisingly high degree." The press complied with requests to suppress even the most banal of military information: weather reports, which censors feared could provide information of aid to hypothetical enemy air raids. Papers were limited to reporting only on local weather, ostensibly to prevent spies triangulating from multiple reports. The *Kansas City Star* published Missouri weather reports on Monday, Wednesday, and Friday, and the Kansas weather on Tuesday, Thursday, and Saturday. Not even the First Lady was exempt—when she mentioned "rain and showers" in one of her nationally syndicated columns in 1942, she received "a very stern letter about my remarks on the weather and from now on I shall not tell you whether it rains or whether the sun shines where I happen to be." And so successful was voluntary censorship that the OC could turn its attention to the smallest of infractions. Major newspapers kept information about the Doolittle Tokyo raid carefully under wraps, but the OC discovered that details had appeared in "a small church paper, having been forwarded circuitously from a missionary." In May 1942, observing that "things pop up where one least expects to find them," Nat Howard of the OC asked the publisher of a stamp column to refrain from listing the cancellations from army and navy bases because this might give information regarding the location of forces abroad. "This entrance into the stamp column," Howard believed, "has seen censorship in the society column, the want ads, in fact about every place but the comic strips. Let's hope Homer Hoopee doesn't get drafted and sent to Australia, or we're liable to find ourselves in a new field." By 1944, Price could boast to a House Appropriations Committee that "magnificent cooperation" by the press meant that he had "been able to find no case in which any newspaper, or any publisher of a newspaper, magazine, books, house organ, church organ or any other class of publication has deliberately violated the code." "Literally thousands of items," Price boasted, "are eliminated every hour on a voluntary basis."[28]

If anything, voluntary censorship was too successful. Letters flowed into the OC complaining that there was too much information being published in the papers, and asking for more censorship. One irate citizen complained about an AP article on Czech saboteurs that could easily be forwarded to the Nazis from their stateside spies. The letter encapsulated the widespread desire to curtail press freedom in order to defeat the Axis—"We had all rather have the Associated Press with a muzzle on once in a while than the nazisatied [*sic*] press unmuzzled all the time." In late 1943, Price had to write to the press to cool the flames of patriotism he had earlier fanned. "In addition to your loyal and generally excellent cooperation under the voluntary code," Price lectured, "many of you have been led by overzealousness to withhold information having no security value, on the advice of persons having no authority." So effective was patriotic self-discipline as a regulatory device that Price now asked for continued cooperation to see, "in this instance, that a dangerous psychology of over-censorship is not created throughout the land by the activities of a miscellany of volunteer firemen."[29]

The success of voluntary censorship came as a particular surprise to one of the system's few early critics—George Creel, head of World War I's Committee for Public Information. In the middle of 1941, Creel had argued that the size and diversity of the U.S. press meant that voluntary censorship was doomed to failure. Creel spoke with considerable authority on the issue, for his committee had attempted, and failed, to institute just such a system during the last war. The failure of voluntary censorship had led quickly, and regrettably, to more severe interferences with free speech as fears about spilled secrets added fuel to the "hysterical 'shush-shushing' that warned against unguarded speech."[30]

Although historians normally juxtapose the World War I state's violation of press freedom with the preservation of press freedom during World War II, the actual story is more complicated. Creel thought that the scale and diversity of the U.S. press had defeated his effort at voluntary self-censorship. Twenty-five years later, the press that confronted Price was less sprawling, and far more easily managed. The growing power of the wire services, the emergence of chain publications, and the rise to prominence of industry groups like the ASNE, established in 1922, provided channels through which instructions could easily be sent from the OC to an increasingly concentrated and integrated media. That made it easier to regulate the flow of information in the polity while preserving freedom of expression. The booming African American press remained free to criticize domestic racism in its "Double-V" campaign, for instance, and the Negro Newspapers Publishers Association cooperated with the OC. And with the radical reduction of immigration after 1924, the foreign language press that had posed particular problems during World War I was in steep decline by the outbreak of World War II. While the rump of that press was carefully monitored by new national security agencies within the Department of Justice, they were generally left free to express their opinions about the war.[31]

Combined with greater public enthusiasm for the war in the wake of Pearl Harbor, this increasingly integrated national flow of information guaranteed that voluntary censorship was more effective in World War II than in World War I. What Creel had attempted, Price now accomplished. (Significantly, Price thought that the OC "demonstrates the continuing strength of the ideals of freedom represented" by the Creel Committee.) But the nature of the endeavor, the inculcation of a practice of self-censorship, served to mask the accomplishment. Legally prosecuting speech, as Creel had discovered, was a visible, controversial state action. But self-censorship was not. The state became an organic part of the press's war effort, not an imposition upon it. Reflecting on the success of the OC shortly after the war, University of Chicago president Robert Hutchins wondered whether the new system was more insidious than the last. Creel's system, Hutchins suggested, was highly visible—"the interference with publication was itself public and could be criticized and attacked." "In this war," Hutchins concluded, "you never could find out why certain information could not be published."[32]

* * *

Hutchins was right: during World War II, censorship began to retreat from public view. In making decisions about what information to suppress, editors were guided by their internalization of the OC's patriotic guidance. That provided one filter that prevented the circulation of information to the public. But as the war continued, editors and journalists were increasingly thought of as a safety net for the protection of state secrets. The primary mechanism became censorship at the government source. In fact, the entire logic of voluntary self-censorship was built on press deference to state decisions about what information could be disclosed; the OC Code explicitly assured the press that any information that had been released by an "appropriate authority" in the government was fine for republication. OC censorship thus rested on and reinforced a prior moment of censorship—the state's decision to release or suppress information.[33]

During World War II, an increasing amount of information was declared classified and unfit for disclosure. The army and navy had well-established cultures of secrecy—the first military classification orders had been issued in 1869, and as warfare had become increasingly technological, and as communications technology had become increasingly rapid, those rules had expanded. FDR conferred presidential recognition on this classification system for the first time with a 1940 executive order. During World War II, the army and navy tightly controlled the release of information from a vast domain: from war fronts and domestic training camps, from ports and industrial sites, from Japanese internment camps, and from Hawaii, where the press operated under martial law. But in a total war, information pertinent to the war effort was also issued from nonmilitary agencies—information on production, nutrition, and agriculture, among other things. Declaring the "necessity for a uniform practice" of classification to "be a matter of some urgency," Elmer Davis issued an OWI regulation on September 28, 1942, that for the first time established one set of information-handling practices for the federal government.[34]

Establishing codes for classification was one thing, but unless those codes could be implemented they would provide little practical security. Earlier efforts to maintain state secrecy had been poorly enforced. Although the Senate debated nominations and treaties in secret until 1929, leaks were habitual, and congressional investigations were lackluster. Executive efforts to conduct secret negotiations were similarly unsuccessful—James Polk's "secret" diplomatic missions during the Mexican-American war were closely reported in the nation's newspapers. And as late as World War II, most importantly, there was little culture of secrecy within the federal administration. In May 1943, the OWI established a Security Advisory Board (SAB) to coordinate security throughout the government. Composed of representatives from the OWI, the navy, the army and the OC, the SAB was the first centralized office to handle security matters in the federal government. The SAB ran training sessions through the government, audited government security practices, and developed the practices and policies of state secrecy. (In a training program within one war agency, a military officer lectured new employees on the Axis propensity for espionage: "My mental picture of a Jap is a little fellow with buck teeth and thick glasses taking a picture of something.") In the first two months of 1945 alone, over 11,000 government employees in some eighteen agencies were shown a film on proper security practices.[35]

But as security officers fanned out across the government, they discovered a lack of security consciousness among federal employees. Classified information was being left unattended on desks, safes were not being locked at night, access to secret information was provided to unscreened personnel, and secret documents were being sent to unapproved commercial printing firms. Employees were reading classified documents on trams and streetcars, and taking copies of information home for personal use. Reviewers of security practices at the Government Printing Office worried that proofreaders of unclassified documents might hear proofreaders of classified documents reading their work aloud; that shredding secret documents was not as secure as pulping them; and that the faces of electroplates were not being destroyed before their transmittal to the refinery for reprocessing. The quotidian nature of these security violations suggests the novelty of the classification regime—employees were unaware of basic security practices, and the SAB was fixated on achieving unprecedented levels of secrecy. They also reveal the difficulty of inculcating a new culture of secrecy throughout the state. As late as December 1944, an internal OWI document complained that it was "obvious" that "complete security-consciousness in every federal department and agency" had not been achieved: "the physical security and the care given to classified documents in some areas still leaves much to be desired."[36]

A large part of the problem was that the classification regime was, remarkably, unsupported by any law—there were no clear legal penalties for disclosing information that was marked secret. This was largely attributable to the rising respect for First Amendment speech rights in the twentieth century. Until the rediscovery of the First Amendment during World War I, government officials had sought to secure secrets by regulating the press. When Benjamin Franklin Bache published secret diplomatic correspondence in the 1790s, he found himself prosecuted by a Federalist government that saw no distinction between his crime of leaking and his crime of seditious editorializing—both fell beyond the pale of protected speech. And during the Civil War, the Union Army had no general system to ensure the secrecy of military information. Rather, after a brief and halfhearted attempt to institute voluntary censorship, the Lincoln administration tried to enforce secrecy by barring newspapers from circulating in military zones, banning certain periodicals from the mail, censoring the telegraph cable, jailing hostile editors, and using military force to close a number of Democratic newspapers.[37]

In the twentieth century, such interferences with the press became politically anathema, and laws that sought to regulate the press to secure state secrets were dead on arrival. The first draft of the 1917 Espionage Act, for instance, had included a sweeping authorization allowing the president to ban the circulation of "any information relating to the public defense, or calculated to be, or which might be useful to the enemy"—but it was met with vehement criticism both in Congress and in the press, where it was identified as "Prussian," an effort to "muzzle the press," and "an absolute overthrow of a free press." The offending section of the Espionage Act was struck out of the final bill. In the short term, of course, wartime censorship flourished under other sections of the act.[38]

In the longer term, the amendment of the Espionage Act introduced a foundational uncertainty into the jurisprudence of state secrecy. The 1917 act included a number of measures aimed at regulating the disclosure of government information. Some of these covered classic espionage scenarios, such as the smuggling of secret information to a foreign government. But the law also prohibited a wide range of other acts—collecting information about national defense by entering military installations, failing to surrender government documents under orders, and, most importantly, communicating or possessing information about national defense without authorization. These sections have stayed on the books until the present day, where they can be found as Sections 793–798 of the U.S. Criminal Code. Their meaning is still not clear. During World War II, they were almost entirely incoherent, and largely untested in court.[39]

The basic confusion was an unintended consequence of congressional revisions to the Espionage Act in 1917. Although the 1917 act had made it illegal to disclose information related to the national defense without authorization, it neither defined the phrase "related to national defense" nor established the procedure for authorizing access to that information. Both definitional issues had originally been vested in the president, but Congress had struck out these clauses in order to protect the freedom of the press, and no new clauses had replaced them. The Espionage Act created sanctions for the criminal disclosure of national security information. But it said nothing about what national security information actually was, or about how access to such information should be regulated.[40]

Congressional efforts to grapple with this uncertainty in the interwar period failed to clarify the law. But they began to develop a distinction between the acceptable regulation of information and the unacceptable regulation of speech. In April 1933, for instance, a bill was introduced to the House to criminalize the leaking of information gleaned from foreign code. The bill was so loosely drawn that it risked rendering criminal the publication of almost any government document, and it was heavily criticized. (Newspaper trade journal *Editor and Publisher* protested that the passage of the bill "serves notice upon journalism, and readers who feel like freemen, that their constitutional liberties hang by slim threads" because the bill "dragged the free press by the heels deliberately, mercilessly, in the very spirit of a Hitler, Mussolini or a Stalin.") The bill was redrawn to more narrowly cover the specific problem at hand, and the final bill regulated only government employees who had access to code (the initial impetus for the bill, it had become clear during the furor, was the impending publication of a book by a former code-breaker). *Editor and Publisher* breathed a sigh of relief. Narrow regulation of the government employee, the trade journal concluded, meant that there was no chance that the "measure can now be construed as an attempt to muzzle the press in any way."[41]

In 1942, the uncertain legal status of government information was raised again, when the Justice Department attempted to prosecute three individuals who had stolen information from Civil Service Records in order to sell it to a marketing firm. The prosecution had collapsed when it became clear that although there were general prohibitions on concealing, mutilating, or destroying government documents, there were no general prohibitions on stealing or disclosing the information within them. Attorney General Francis Biddle thus wrote to congressional leaders to ask for a new bill to punish the disclosure of government information and "plug the loophole." Introduced in February 1942, the bill was heavily criticized for threatening the ability of journalists to publish state information (it threatened fines or jail time for revealing or communicating secret information). The White House Correspondents Association and a number of journalists protested—*Editor and Publisher* thought the bill was "one of the most iniquitous stabs at freedom of press and speech that had ever come before an American legislature." It died in committee.[42]

The jurisprudence of the Espionage Act was equally unsettled. In 1941, two men convicted of spying for the Soviets had challenged the constitutionality of the Espionage Act, arguing that the naval intelligence reports they had sent to the USSR contained innocuous and publicly available information about Japanese-American citizens and fishing vessels. If such publicly available information fell within the meaning of "national defense" information in the Espionage Act, the lawyers for the pair argued, then the Espionage Act was unconstitutionally broad and threatened to spill over to regulate all sorts of discussion and exchanges of information. The courts were having none of this argument, and a unanimous Supreme Court upheld the convictions of the pair in the *Gorin* decision. Writing for the court, Justice Stanley Reed argued that the relevant sections of the Espionage Act did not interfere with freedom of discussion because one could be found guilty only if one had reason to believe that sharing the information would "be used to the injury of the U.S. or the advantage of any foreign nation." The court was satisfied that relying on this test of mental intent would limit the sweep of the Espionage Act and protect "freedom of discussion of matters connected with national defense."[43]

Despite this decision, the line between protecting secrets and violating press freedom was far from clear, and wartime efforts to apply the *Gorin* framework were far from straightforward. In June 1942, in the most famous leak of military information during the war, the *Chicago Tribune* published a story about Japanese naval forces in the Battle of the Midway. Based on a classified naval memo that journalist Stanley Johnston had read without authorization, the story revealed that the United States had broken Japanese naval code. The administration charged Johnston with violating the Espionage Act, but because the jurisprudence of the act was so unclear Attorney General Biddle sought guidance from the Office of Legal Counsel. Based on his reading of the *Gorin* decision, Assistant Solicitor General Oscar S. Cox concluded that Johnston had violated the Espionage Act on two counts: he had taken information relating to the national defense and, by publishing it, he had provided information to people who were not entitled to receive it. Johnston's behavior, Cox believed, had the necessary intent to meet the *Gorin* requirements, for Johnston's actions were "characterized by real turpitude and disregard of his obligations as a citizen" and "thoroughly deserve punishment." Such a reading threatened to turn the Espionage Act into a broad authority for prosecuting the press—Cox entertained the possibility that Johnston's editor, as well as publisher Robert McCormick, might also be guilty of Espionage Act violations. In the end, nothing would come of the opinion, which remained classified until 2013. Although Johnston was charged with Espionage Act violations before a grand jury, the charges were dropped when it became clear that the Japanese, amazingly, had not realized their code had been broken; pursuing the case further risked alerting the Japanese to the secret the prosecutions were intended to protect. But the case demonstrated both the danger that the *Gorin* construction of the Espionage Act could pose to press freedom and the practical difficulties of protecting secrets by punishing their publication after disclosure.[44]

A second Espionage Act decision also suggested that *Gorin* underprotected freedom of speech. It emphasized the importance of regulating secrets at the source rather than prosecuting publication after disclosure. The case concerned a naturalized German automotive industry executive, Edmund Carl Heine, who had compiled information about the American aviation industry on behalf of Volkswagen, then associated with the Third Reich. Heine admitted preparing the reports, but appealed his conviction under the Espionage Act on the grounds that he had not intended to harm the United States. He argued that he could not have harmed the United States because the reports had been prepared from publicly available information. (Heine had pored over magazines, technical catalogues, and handbooks; corresponded with employees at airplane factories and world's fair exhibits; and paid a member of the armed services $5 for photos of planes.) In December 1941, this carried little weight; he was sentenced to eighteen years for violating the Espionage Act. But when Learned Hand heard an appeal of the case in late 1945, he overturned Heine's conviction on the grounds that information had to be kept secret to fall within the provisions of the Espionage Act. Contrary to the *Gorin* decision, Hand argued that the phrase "national defense" was too broad to be limited simply by intent—in a total war it could refer to almost anything, and even sending harmless information to an ally could be seen to be an "advantage" to them. On such a reading, Hand worried that the Espionage Act would make it "criminal to send to a subject of Britain or to a citizen of France a railway map, a list of merchant ships, a description of automobile assembly technique, an account of the latest discoveries in antisepsis." In short, the *Gorin* test risked "a drastic repression of the free exchange of information." Hand subtly adjusted the test in *Gorin;*

the necessary mental intent could be found only if the information involved was secret.[45]

Hand was trying, admirably, to curtail the sprawl of the Espionage Act and to preserve freedom of discussion. And in the case at hand, the test did that. Ironically, however, the logic of the decision opened the door to an increasing deference to governmental secrecy. Although he was aware that "'secret' is an equivocal word whose definition might prove treacherous," Hand concluded that "the services must be trusted to determine what information may be broadcast without prejudice to the 'national defense.'" His limiting test, in short, would remain a limiting test only if the practices of state secrecy remained limited. The decision put the onus on the state to both formally declare and practically enforce state secrecy if it wanted to prevent the spread of defense information. In a 1946 appeal of the case that the Supreme Court declined to hear, the Justice Department argued that if Hand's decision was allowed to stand then security officials would need to impose stricter regulations on the publication of military information.[46]

Indeed, as the war entered its final stages, security-minded officials were becoming increasingly dissatisfied with their limited ability to enforce state secrecy. The system was a patchwork: the OWI and the agencies tried to keep information secure at the source; the OC acted as a safety net, catching material before it went into print. With the multiplication of authority came opportunities for abuse and error. In July 1944, for instance, the *Wall Street Journal* published a story that featured classified details about government stockpiles of strategic metals and materials. The SAB contacted the OC to find out why the story had been cleared for publication. The OC responded that the journalist had received the information from Bruce Catton, information officer for the War Production Board. That meant that the information had been released with "appropriate authority" and there was nothing the OC could do. The SAB asked the WPB to strengthen security in-house, but there was little formal sanction for Catton. And there the matter ended, despite the fact, as one irate military officer pointed out, that "the *figures were published.*" Members of the SAB were frustrated. Catton, despite being flip and casual in his treatment of information, had suffered little sanction. And the voluntary nature of censorship gave "the OC a big out every time." So in the waning stages of the war, moves were afoot to simplify the secrecy regime by changing the legislative basis of classification. The SAB, after consulting with the Department of Justice, began to draft a general classification order. When the OWI was abolished in the immediate aftermath of the war, the SAB was a rare institutional survivor, and it continued to develop secrecy laws in the early Cold War as part of a new State-War-Navy Coordinating Committee.[47]

* * *

Nevertheless, during the war the patchwork system of censorship proved effective in keeping the lid on important military and diplomatic secrets. Journalists knew, for instance, about the North African, Sicilian, and D-Day invasion plans in advance, but stayed mute to aid the element of military surprise.[48] A combination of classification at the source and self-censorship in the press even kept the most important secret of the war—the development of the atomic bomb. General Leslie R. Groves, director of the Manhattan Project, carefully compartmentalized knowledge among his employees in order to keep the secret from leaking out. But he also relied on the OC. On June 28, 1943, following consultation with the OWI and military intelligence, the OC issued a confidential message to editors warning against the publication of information about "the production or utilization of atom smashing, atomic energy, atomic fission, atomic splitting." The science of atom splitting and the potential of uranium had been the subject of wide speculation in the interwar period, but now the OC sought to erase all mention of them from the press. After the *Schenectady Gazette* ran a letter that mentioned the power of U-235, the paper received a stern explanation of the OC's ambitions. Not content merely to regulate technical details of the bomb, or the location of bomb development, or the status of American progress, the OC was "trying to lead the enemy to believe we never think about such a thing" as atomic energy. So while the OC conceded that its censorship efforts were not entirely successful—it counted 104 references to atomic bombs in the wartime press—it was concerned primarily about vague references to atomic power, such as a briefly run Superman comic that featured a cyclotron and a reference to atom smashing.[49]

Technical and strategic details were kept secure throughout the war. Even the occasional slip by a government official could be covered by calling on the press to patriotically restrain itself. On December 11, 1943, Tennessee's Selective Service director publicly commented that a weapon was being made in Oak Ridge that would end the war. The AP sent the story out over the wire at 12:24 P.M., and at 1:23 P.M., the *Knoxville*

News-Sentinel checked with the OC if it could publish the item. The OC rushed to intervene, and by 2 P.M., the AP had sent out a bulletin asking its subscribers not to publish the story. Presses had already begun printing the afternoon edition, but at substantial cost, the item was removed, and secrecy was preserved. After 1946, atomic secrecy would be preserved by the unprecedented classification provisions of the Atomic Energy Act. But during World War II, atomic secrecy was preserved by a patchwork of censorship both at the source and in the voluntary compliance of the press. And as a result of such efforts, one OC worker later crowed, "the Japanese literally did not know what hit them at Hiroshima." The American public had been kept equally uninformed.[50]

Repression of information about the bomb was only half the story. The other half was the military's role in pumping propaganda about the bomb to the American public in the wake of Hiroshima. Grove's preferred channel for that propaganda was at first OC Press Division chief John Lockhart, but in the process of turning down the gig, Lockhart put forward the name of the *New York Times* science writer, William Laurence. From his position within the military, Laurence helped to cover up the development of the bomb with press releases passing off tests as ammunition dump explosions. And he played a unique role in explaining the atomic bombings to Americans. In a sequence of ten articles, Laurence helped to justify the bombings by casting Hiroshima and Nagasaki as military targets, dismissed reports of radiation poisoning as Japanese propaganda, and reveled in the scientific accomplishments of the military. Indeed, Laurence was bewitched by the "millions of man hours" and "most concentrated intellectual effort in history" that had produced the bomb. "It is," he wrote, "a thing of beauty to behold, this 'gadget.'"[51]

In fact, there could be no more evocative image of the press's wartime accommodation to military prerogatives than that of Laurence, riding with the B-29 bomber to Nagasaki on August 9, 1945. As the only journalistic witness to the earlier Trinity test explosion, Laurence was under no illusions about the havoc that the beautiful "gadget" was about to unleash. "In about four hours from now," he wrote, "one of its cities, making weapons of war for use against us, will be wiped off the map by the greatest weapon ever made by man. In one-tenth of a millionth of a second . . . a whirlwind from the skies will pulverize thousands of its buildings and tens of thousands of its inhabitants." But Laurence was unabashed in viewing the war through the lens of patriotic militarism, and according to the moral economy of battlefield sacrifice, "does one feel any pity or compassion for the poor devils about to die? Not when one thinks of Pearl Harbor and of the death march on Bataan." For such reporting, produced on the military payroll and subject to military censorship, Laurence won the 1946 Pulitzer Prize.[52]

In general, too, wartime press practices won plaudits for exemplifying press freedom. Byron Price declared the OC a "heartening example of democracy at work" and received a Medal of Merit from President Truman and a special Pulitzer citation. Even the American Civil Liberties Union, the national organization most likely to critique any interference with freedom of the press, noted that "censorship arising out of the war has raised almost no issues in the US." In 1945, *Editor and Publisher* was not alone in opining that "our press and radio operating under democratic principles and voluntary censorship have established further proof of why our free press system is the best in the world."[53]

* * *

It was certainly true that there had been remarkably little formal censorship of speech rights during the war. But in other ways, the meaning of press freedom had subtly evolved during the war. In the interwar period there had been widespread fears that the press was too irresponsible to serve the public good—the Right had feared the press too liberal, too crusading, and too enchanted with the New Deal and internationalism; the Left had thought the press reactionary, venal, and corrupted by capitalist self-interest. During the war, the press was repeatedly reminded of its responsibilities to the nation: two days after Pearl Harbor, FDR had instructed the press of its "grave responsibility" in the war; Byron Price repeatedly called for the press to exercise responsible self-censorship. And the press had proved remarkably willing to comply with such requests. "Tell us what should not be printed," said the managing editor of the *LA Times* early in 1941; "we will play ball." In 1942, Archibald MacLeish had called for a press both free and responsible, and though he had lost his particular battle to establish a liberal propaganda organ, MacLeish's ideas had won the war: self-censorship had come to seem proof of the vitality of American press freedom. As Byron Price put it in a speech marking the installation of the Bill of Rights at the Library of Congress in 1945, "a free press cannot endure unless it is a responsible press."[54]

Relying on the patriotic responsibility of the press, moreover, was only one element of the wartime state's effort to regulate the flow of information in the polity. Increasingly important was the new emphasis on securing secrets at the source, of carefully policing the release of information, and regulating access to classified information. The distinction between the censorship of speech and the classification of information had been building through the interwar period, but it found new expression during the war, particularly in the institutional division of labor between the OWI and the OC—the former developing the legal and institutional capacity to regulate information at the source, the latter relying on voluntary self-censorship to regulate the sphere of publication. Such a patchwork regime of censorship revealed modern American press freedom at a moment of evolution: the growing respect for speech rights precluded any legal censorship of the press, but the legal and institutional capacity to secure information was not yet so effective that the state could afford to free the press entirely. After World War II, as a more robust secrecy regime was established, the protective cocoon of patriotic self-censorship would fall away, leaving the press free to publish what it wanted, but increasingly cut off from access to information. Even during the war, Byron Price was promoting this delimited vision of press freedom. Free speech, Price opined in 1942, "does not mean and never has meant the right to play fast and loose with information, as distinguished from opinion." Or, as he put it in 1944, "freedom of the press was freedom to express your opinion, criticize, advocate and complain, but not freedom to disclose information."[55]

In the short term, however, these subtle transformations went unremarked. Instead, the absence of formal censorship and propaganda, combined with the heady euphoria of victory and peace, seemed to affirm the freedom of America's press. The press's patriotic contributions to the war effort, and its responsible self-censorship, seemed to calm interwar fears that the capitalist press was an unmanageable, undemocratic institution. And compared with the odious censorship regime of World War I, and the extreme censorship and propaganda regimes of the Axis nations, the American reliance on handouts, self-censorship, and classification seemed remarkably democratic and remarkably liberal.

Just weeks after the cessation of conflict, during 1945's Newspaper Week, Harry Truman expressed the triumphalist attitude to American press freedom that had emerged during the war. "In this hour of exultation," he declared, "we should dedicate ourselves anew to the perpetuation of one of our cherished heritages—freedom of the press." He called American attention to a "singular triumph of our war experience": "The

American free press through the stress of the most horrible of all wars withstood subversive and open attack and operated under a voluntary code of censorship." Such liberal exceptionalism led directly to a new global mission. "Ours then," Truman concluded, "is the plain duty . . . to work without ceasing to make a free press the true torch of world peace." Appropriately, the leading architects of the press's war effort would soon be helping to construct a liberal international order—Archibald MacLeish would draft the Preamble to the United Nations charter; Byron Price would become assistant secretary general at the United Nations. As America rose to world power in the wake of World War II, it was fashioning itself as the exemplar and champion of universal liberal values.[56] Such global ambitions would produce new, and newly geopolitical, reflections on the meaning of American press freedom.

6

The Cold War Dilemma of a Free Press

For Zechariah Chafee Jr., the years after World War II were busy. Three decades earlier, in the wake of the previous World War, Chafee had played an influential role in developing the modern jurisprudence of speech rights—his articles had helped shape Oliver Wendell Holmes's embrace of the free market of ideas. In the 1940s, Chafee was once again involved in debates about postwar press freedom. He was a central member of the illustrious Hutchins Commission on Freedom of the Press, which met for several years to resolve the press debates of the 1930s and propose new understandings of press freedom. He also served as an official U.S. delegate to UN conferences that attempted to construct a global right to press freedom. Earlier in his career, Chafee had been part of a small network of lawyers and intellectuals arguing about the importance of the right to free speech. Now, in his sixties, he put forward the same vision of free speech as a representative of a global superpower. And he did so with gusto. On his first day at a 1946 UN conference, Chafee enthusiastically seconded every motion.[1]

The United States sought to globalize its vision of liberty as it rose to power after World War II.[2] Individual freedom of speech was, of course, a crucial component of the American view of freedom; the right to free expression distinguished free states from totalitarian ones. But the problem of press freedom remained: could the simple guarantee of free speech ensure that the press was meaningfully free in an age of corporate media consolidation and an existential clash between liberal and totalitarian political systems? In the 1940s, both the Hutchins Commission and the

United Nations took up this question, and debates in both places centered on the relationship between classical press freedom and the press's responsibilities to the public. Classical liberals like Chafee emphasized negative rights to free speech. Their interlocutors, both domestic and foreign, argued that only a well-regulated press could improve the flow of information to the public.

In the end, the Hutchins Commission recommended against state regulation of the press, and the UN Declaration of Human Rights protected only an individual right to free speech; the antitotalitarian commitments of American liberals carried the day. But in the late 1940s, protecting only a right to free speech had ironic outcomes. Absent regulation, the corporate consolidation of the press continued. And the desire to combat totalitarianism led the American press both to participate in state propaganda campaigns in the early Cold War and to collaborate in the McCarthy-era policing of radicals. The antitotalitarian vision of press freedom preserved a formal right to free expression. But it also, paradoxically, helped new forms of corporate and state power take control of the flow of information within the American polity.

* * *

If the global rise of totalitarianism had raised new questions about the freedom of America's press in the 1930s, the defeat of the Axis during World War II seemed to answer them. Heady from military victory, newly assured of the liberal might of the United States, Americans increasingly contrasted the apparently exceptional freedom of their press with the unfree polities they observed elsewhere in the world. In 1946, Earl Warren contrasted American press freedom with "the many other countries in the world [where] this condition does not exist." *Editor and Publisher* agreed, asserting that "people in other lands do not have the century and a half of experience with a free press that we enjoy." The American press, journalist Wilbur Forrest stated bluntly in 1947, was simply the "fairest and the most honest and accurate in the world. . . . The press of no other country, and no other age in history, can compare with the newspapers now published daily in the United States."[3]

A widely believed platitude attributed the rise of militarist dictatorships to propaganda and the absence of press freedom; on a 1946 radio program, one thirteen-year-old New Yorker distilled this political fable to its essence by declaring that "Hitler would have been stopped in his tracks with one free paper." Spreading press freedom throughout the world thus seemed to be the obvious antidote to dictatorship and war, so Americans sought to export their vision of a free press. As early as 1943, newspaper publisher and OWI administrator Palmer Hoyt argued that the U.S. press "represents the one great oasis of objectivity in an international desert of propaganda and government influence." "There is only one thing that can save civilization," Hoyt concluded, "and that is the unhampered release of objective news—American style—between the nations."[4]

Such triumphalism was accompanied by a retreat from any criticism of the actual state of midcentury American press freedom. In part this was a consequence of domestic developments—the failures of interwar press reform, the patriotic accomplishments of the press during World War II, and the political marginalization of left-wing and progressive voices. But the retreat was also a result of the new sense of liberal exceptionalism and the new sense of global mission. In 1944, the ASNE sent a Committee on Freedom of Information on a four-month, forty-thousand-mile tour to "spread the gospel of the First Amendment among the people of foreign lands." The group came "face to face with the effects of some American muckraking of a dozen or more years ago" when Indian editors, quoting from Upton Sinclair and George Seldes, argued that the American press was dominated by business interests. But those arguments could be dismissed as irrelevant relics that were "hoary with age."[5] After World War II, press freedom was no longer an ideal to be attained, as it had been in the tumultuous 1930s. It was an actually existing set of practices, ready to be exported wholesale.

Coming so soon after the heated press debates of the past decade, such liberal triumphalism struck some as jarring, if not hollow. Liberal lawyer Morris Ernst argued that if America was to take its "rightful place" as global leader of press freedom it had to "clean [its] own house" and confront the threats posed by corporate monopoly. Even Henry Luce, who had recently proclaimed an "American Century" and boasted that "the American people are by far the best informed people in the history of the world," nursed doubts about press freedom. So he donated $200,000 to the University of Chicago to establish the Hutchins Commission, a multiyear inquiry into the "present state and future prospects of freedom of the press." This was necessary, Luce believed, because the widely observed "troubles of my occupation were related to philosophy and morals" that were in a "somewhat acute state of confusion." Under the leadership of University of Chicago president Robert Hutchins, thirteen leading liberal intellectuals—including Archibald MacLeish, Reinhold Niebuhr, Charles Merriam, Zechariah Chafee, and Robert Redfield—met to make sense of the complex swirl of changes that had confronted American press freedom over the previous half-century.[6] Hutchins thought that if the commission was to "justify itself, its report must be a landmark in the history of the subject."[7]

The commission's final report, published in 1947, began with a simple question: "Is the freedom of the press in danger?" Its answer was an equally simple "yes." Changes in the economic structure of the press, new forms of censorship, and the growth of a mass democracy meant that "the right of free public expression has lost its earlier reality." The commission's analysis followed Lippmann and Dewey's intellectual moves of the 1920s. The classical theory of free speech was anachronistic (150 years after the drafting of the Bill of Rights, one commissioner declared, "a reconsideration of the principles of freedom underlying the First Amendment has become a matter of urgent concern"). Laissez-faire political philosophy had to be transcended. ("We can dismiss without serious discussion the too simple concept that freedom for the press is complete absence of government control"; "we are all agreed in essence that laissez-faire no longer does the work.") And press philosophy had to be centered on the rights of the reader, rather than those of the speaker. (Philosopher William Hocking, who did much of the conceptual heavy lifting for the group, put it most plainly when he asserted that freedom of the press "is not more the right of editors and reporters to talk than the rights of the public to be informed and instructed.")[8]

The problem was how the rights of the reader could be protected in practice. At first, the commission was enthusiastic about state regulation of the newspaper industry for the good of the public. Early drafts of the commission's report were written by Archibald MacLeish, who continued the liberal crusade against the reactionary press that he had begun in the field of war publicity. Drawing inspiration from the AP antitrust case, MacLeish argued for a robust program of antitrust action in the press: "I would like to see absentee ownership of the press made impossible. I would like to see chains substantially broken down."[9]

But as the commissioners debated the AP matter further, antitrust action began to seem increasingly undesirable. Chafee at first shared in what he called the commission's "general feeling" that its "recommendations would have to rely heavily on the anti-trust laws." "Yet during the long ensuing discussions [of the commission]," Chafee admitted in 1948, "this comprehensive program faded away." He had realized that the AP decision protected the rights only of the publisher, not of the consumer. A focus on reader's rights would have required government intervention in the "contents, performance, and personal attitudes" of papers, journalists, and publishers, and that posed a clear threat to press freedom. Antitrust consent decrees were simply too powerful; Chafee believed them "far more drastic in their potentialities than the sporadic prosecutions of eighteenth century England." As Chafee explained in a private letter to Morris Ernst, protecting classical speech rights had to remain the priority: "We cannot expect the government to employ the anti-trust laws extensively and at the same time to be very sparing in legal actions about sedition and obscenity."[10]

Other commissioners, too, shared Chafee's doubts. John Dickinson, who had headed the Anti-Trust Division of the Justice Department in the mid-1930s before quitting the New Deal administration, shared Chafee's fear that consent decrees would create "a field day for government interference." MacLeish was incredulous. "I haven't the remotest idea what this discussion is about," he interjected in one meeting. "Are these learned gentlemen discussing the question of whether the anti-trust laws apply inside the communications industry? Because if they are discussing that question I don't think it is worth talking about. Of course they apply." But the pendulum had swung away from MacLeish and his aggressive program of statist reform. His draft report was criticized for understating the risk of government censorship and overplaying the dangers of economic concentration. Robert Leigh, director of the commission's staff, took over the drafting of the report. In Reinhold Niebuhr's words, "Leigh took all the animus out of it that MacLeish had in. MacLeish made it appear that this concentration was a terrible thing. Now Leigh reports it and does not say it is a good thing or a bad thing." The commission's final report argued that the antitrust laws should be used "sparingly" to "maintain competition among large units and to prevent the exclusion of any unit from facilities which ought to be open to all; their use to force the breaking-up of large units seems to us undesirable." "At last," Hutchins concluded, "we have come a long way from the Sherman anti-trust act neurosis that we had at the beginning."[11]

The commission retreated to a classical vision of press freedom out of fears that government intervention could open the door to totalitarianism. "Government ownership, government control or government action to break up the greater agencies of mass communication might cure the ills of freedom of the press," the commission opined, "but only at the risk of killing the freedom in the process." Newspapers could not be regulated by the state "because if they are controlled by government we lose our chief safeguard against totalitarianism—and at the same time take a long step toward it."[12]

There still remained the problems that the commission had begun with—the anachronism of classical theories of press freedom, the democratic shortcomings of the mass press, the need to protect the consumer's right to receive adequate information. The commission argued that these problems were best remedied by a reform of professional and moral standards. "The time has come," the commission famously declared, "for the press to assume a new public responsibility." It called on publishers, editors, and journalists to embrace their moral obligations to democracy, and to prioritize the public good over private interest. The commission's reform recommendations favored self-regulation and self-improvement—mutual press criticism, higher standards of professional education, and the establishment of academic and civic agencies to appraise and report on the performance of the press. This came to be known as the "social responsibility" theory of press freedom, and it guided professional ethics throughout the postwar period.[13]

But for a commission that had set out to transcend the classical understanding of press freedom, those were rather limp conclusions. Even in theoretical terms, the commission had found it impossible to develop a philosophy of press freedom that reconciled the negative liberty of self-expression with the positive good of an informed public. Its final report declared that "several factors of an ideal press freedom are to some extent incompatible with one another." It made no attempt to reconcile positive and negative theories. It simply asserted that "press freedom means freedom from *and also* freedom for."[14]

In practice, the commission prioritized protecting negative liberties: the right to speak without government interference would be protected by law, while the right to receive information would be protected only by moral codes. Social responsibility depended entirely on the willing participation of editors, journalists, and, above all, publishers. Less than a decade earlier, press critics like Harold Ickes had argued that "when a publisher has so much wealth and so many investments it would be quixotic to expect him to use his newspaper to advance the general welfare when it conflicts with his personal interest." But now the commission rested its hopes for press freedom on the benevolence of the publisher. To explain social responsibility, Hocking appropriately turned to a feudal metaphor: the duty of the publisher to "assume the burden of giving a rounded presentation of the competing opinions in our community," he elaborated, should be called the "motive of *noblesse oblige.*"[15] The whole theory assumed a hierarchical relationship at the heart of the democratic public sphere. It was a curious move for a group of liberal thinkers.

The theory offered no criticism of the structural problems generated by corporate newspaper monopoly, or any critique of the undemocratic power of the newspaper baron. To ensure that the public would receive a diverse flow of information in the press, the commission meekly suggested that publishers must "be hospitable to ideas and attitudes different to their own, and they must present them to the public as meriting its attention." If Republican publishers would occasionally publish Democrats, and Democratic publishers would return the favor, press freedom would be ensured. Here, at its moment of sanctification—the Federal Communications Commission articulated the fairness doctrine with precisely the same logic two years later—we can see that the demand for "fair and balanced" media is little more than a weak ameliorative to a monopolistic media market.[16] Indeed, the demand that any given newspaper include a diversity of opinions assumes a media market tending toward monopoly. In the traditional democratic theory of press freedom, it would make little sense to try to ensure diversity *within* a newspaper. Diversity was the product of competition *between* individualistic newspapers, each with a discrete and distinct worldview. Now, that hope was gone. And the only alternative offered was the hope that the few individuals who could publish newspapers would occasionally extend an olive branch to their opponents.

So the Hutchins Commission backed itself into a classical and conventional understanding of press freedom. Hutchins himself conceded that its "recommendations are not startling. The most surprising thing about them is that nothing more surprising could be proposed." In fact, the commission's great significance, as one of its members pointed out, was what it did not recommend: no government regulation of press abuses, no antitrust action, no public funding for the media. It counseled resignation to the incorporation of the newspaper industry: "We accept the fact that some concentration must exist in the communications industry if the country is to have the service it needs."[17] Even reform-minded liberals had come to see an industrialized, corporate newspaper market as a necessary cost of a free press.

* * *

After World War II, newspaper diversity continued to decline. Superficially, the industry looked stable after the crises of the interwar years—the decade after World War II even saw a net growth of forty papers in the nation. But newspaper growth was not keeping up with the booming population and economy, and the surface stability was a product of regional redistribution: while new monopoly papers were opening in the south, the west, and the suburbs, papers were declining in the old urban centers of the northeast. The 1950s witnessed the deaths of a number of historic papers: in 1950, Benjamin Day's *Sun,* first of the penny papers, ended 116 years of independence when it merged with the *New York World Telegram;* in 1954, the *Washington Post* bought the *Times-Herald* from McCormick, instantly transforming itself into the second most important paper in the capital; in 1955, the *Brooklyn Eagle* closed; the next year, the *Boston Post* folded; and so on, down the line. As early as 1950, press critic A. J. Liebling complained that "the end of a newspaper story has become one of the commonplaces of our time, and schools of journalism are probably giving courses in how to write one." In 1910, 689 American cities had had competing newspapers; by 1960, only sixty-one still did.[18]

The prospects for diversity and growth in the industry were poor. The rise of suburbia, the car, and the television killed the afternoon editions, because motorists had little use for a paper, and distribution to the far-flung suburbs was possible only when the roads were free of traffic in the early hours of the morning. And advertising revenue flowed only to the most successful paper in a town. In what proved a dangerous spiral, smaller papers were starved of revenue. They could not afford to invest in printing, distribution, and reporting like their flush, larger rivals, and so they could not compete for readers. They couldn't even lower their advertising rates because advertising agencies, which set the rates, were paid a percentage of the contract and had no incentive to lower prices.[19]

Publishers of failing papers were quick to blame their declining profits on the rising costs of printing and distribution equipment, of newsprint, and, particularly, of labor.[20] (Most of the ire would fixate on the unionized printers, but when J. David Stern closed the *Philadelphia Record* in 1947, he blamed the greed of the Newspaper Guild, which was then on strike.)

But the problems really lay with the declining revenue of smaller papers. (Stern's real nemesis was not the guild, but the more successful *Bulletin,* which bought the *Record* to pillage its newsprint and feature contracts and subsequently dominated the Philadelphia newspaper market throughout the 1950s.)[21] Monopoly papers were flourishing, bringing in higher advertising revenues than ever.[22]

But after the Hutchins Commission, there was little political appetite for dealing with the problems of newspaper monopoly. In 1947, Democratic senator James Murray, chairman of the U.S. Senate Small Business Committee, issued a report titled *The Small Newspaper: Democracy's Grass Roots* that worried that the "competitive press is dying" and called for hearings into newspaper economics. But the Republicans had taken over the Senate in 1946, and the hearings were diverted into the less controversial matter of newsprint shortages.[23] Nor was there much antitrust action. There were six antitrust suits brought against the press in the fifteen years after the AP decision, but they concerned a few cases of explicitly anticompetitive advertising discrimination, and only indirectly addressed broader problems of declining diversity. In any case, they generally involved small papers and negligible fines. The most important case of the period was the Justice Department's 1952 prosecution of the Times-Picayune Publishing Company for its requirement that advertisers buy space in both its morning and afternoon papers. This was an effort to cut off revenue from the rival *New Orleans Item,* but the Supreme Court found for Times-Picayune, arguing that there was no evidence that the policy harmed the rival paper. By 1958, the *Item* had been bought by the increasingly wealthy *Times-Picayune,* which subsequently held a complete newspaper monopoly in New Orleans—it immediately increased its advertising rates by 30 percent.[24]

* * *

A broader intellectual failure lay behind these legal and political failings. Press criticism continued after the Hutchins Commission. In fact, it blossomed, for press criticism was a sign of "social responsibility." For three years in the late 1940s, Don Hollenbeck examined press issues on the pioneering *CBS Views the Press*. Between 1947 and 1962, A. J. Liebling did the same in the *New Yorker*'s "Wayward Pressman" column. The *Columbia Journalism Review* was established in 1961. But the new press critics lacked substantive programs for reform. Liebling, for instance, was critical of the corporate control of the press. By declaring that "freedom of the press is guaranteed only to those who own one," he summarized generations of press criticism in one pithy sentence. But he had no solutions to the problem. "The mind turns to regulation," he confessed in 1961, but "public regulation would conflict with the principle of freedom of the press. . . . Men of politics cannot be trusted to regulate the press because the press deals with politics. *Pravda* is even duller than *The Times*." Others, too, had few ideas. In his landmark 1959 study of the role of the press in American politics, Douglass Cater dealt with economic problems in one resigned footnote: "I have deliberately avoided getting into the predominantly one party nature of newspaper ownership. It is a fact of life. Quite frankly, I have no new ideas or information to add on the subject." Even the popular culture depicted a press in inexorable decline. In 1952's *Deadline U.S.A.,* Humphrey Bogart played a crusading old-time editor who successfully cracked a corruption scandal while attempting to keep his paper from merging into a rival. "Without competition there can be no freedom of the press," Bogart declared in an impassioned courtroom speech. The paper was sold anyway.[25]

Those who might have provided constructive criticism were discouraged by the postwar political climate. Hollenbeck's show, for instance, angered some advertisers, who boycotted CBS, and Hollenbeck himself was relentlessly hounded by Red-baiting critics. He was removed from *Views the Press* in 1950, and the program was canceled the next year. In 1954, increasingly isolated, Hollenbeck killed himself. George Seldes, too, tried to continue his interwar press criticism in a newsletter that he published between 1940 and 1950. Dedicated to the "millions who want a free press," and devoted to chronicling the lies and distortions of the corporate press, *In Fact* at one point had a circulation of 176,000. But as Seldes was Red-baited, subscriptions slumped—by 1950, he had only 56,000 subscribers left, and many of them wanted the newsletter sent in plain envelopes to conceal the subscription from nosy neighbors. Seldes gave up the enterprise.[26]

Even the mild-mannered Hutchins report, so worried about totalitarianism, was accused of radicalism. In general, the commission's final report was poorly received. Its self-conscious intellectualism and its lack of empirical research left it open to charges of stuffy academicism from working journalists. And many in the press, predictably, took umbrage when charged with irresponsibility. Criticism of the report often implied that the commission was out of touch with American values, dangerously so given the geopolitical stakes of the postwar moment. Such attitudes sometimes came to the surface, as when Frank Hughes reviewed the book for the *Chicago Tribune* under a typically McCormick headline: "A 'Free Press' (Hitler Style) Sought for US: Totalitarians Tell How It Can Be Done." Even more moderate voices, like Wilbur Forrest, president of the ASNE, thought the report had "whipped up" a "synthetic crisis" under the influence of "European language" and "certain left-wing individuals and groups." Forrest had toured the globe to spread the gospel of the First Amendment, and saw the late 1940s as the wrong time to criticize the press: "We have a right to world leadership in respect to press freedom and freedom of information and I, for one, further deplore any attempt from any quarter to tear down our prestige at a time we seek by our leadership to establish world freedom of information."[27]

* * *

Compared to reform at home, the effort to globalize American press freedom was remarkably uncontroversial. As they debated the postwar global order in the mid-1940s, American journalists, newspaper publishers, and politicians unanimously agreed that the free exchange of news between nations was central to the creation of a more just and peaceful world. Kent Cooper, general manager of the AP and perhaps the leading crusader for a global flow of free information, made speech after speech in which he proclaimed the foundational importance of the issue. "The whole structure of human rights in a world of free men," he asserted in early 1946, "rests upon one basic right—the right to know. . . . World understanding can be achieved only if news flows freely to all countries and may be freely published in them." In July 1944, both the Republican and Democratic Parties had included calls for worldwide freedom of information in their election platforms. Two months later, both houses of Congress unanimously adopted a resolution expressing a "belief in the worldwide right of interchange of news." The resolution had been introduced by two men who agreed on little else about mid-1940s foreign policy: liberal internationalist William J. Fulbright and arch-isolationist Robert Taft. And it was met with international praise. Governments in England, France, China, and Sweden sent messages of approval, and when Hugh Baillie, head of the UP, traveled through Europe later that year, he returned with a "bag of free press pledges."[28]

Bolstered by such apparent political consensus, the campaign for global press freedom moved to the center of efforts to create the postwar global order. In 1946, Harry Truman told the UN General Assembly that "a concerted effort must be made to break down the barriers to a free flow of information among the nations of the world. We regard freedom of expression and freedom to receive information—the right of the people to know—as among the most important of those human rights and fundamental freedoms to which we are pledged under the United Nations charter." By April 1947, a newspaper industry trade journal observed that "few issues have been pressed more earnestly at the UN than freedom of information."[29]

The United Nations soon created an international conference to which it delegated the task of developing the laws and institutions necessary to create a global flow of free information. The Conference on Freedom of Information met in Geneva in the spring of 1948, and over the course of three weeks, participants discussed measures to define, liberalize, and improve the global flow of information. Among other proposals, the conference considered the establishment of an international code of conduct for journalists to be enforced by an international press court with a right to issue and revoke press cards that would accredit foreign correspondents; the international standardization of libel laws; the rights of access, immigration, and deportation of foreign correspondents; legal frameworks for censorship; and the redistribution of the raw materials of journalism such as newsprint and printing presses. Deliberations would center on three practical and important measures. Delegates were asked to debate and approve articles on freedom of information and the press for both the Universal Declaration of Human Rights and the Covenant on Human Rights. And they were asked to draft a UN Convention on Freedom of Information, a binding multilateral treaty to establish concrete, specific laws to remake the international flow of news.[30]

There were good reasons to be optimistic that a new global agreement could be reached, for World War II had wiped away the last remnants of both the practical and moral foundations of the existing international informational order. The international flow of news had once been dominated by a cartel of four wire services: France's Havas, England's Reuters, Germany's Wolff, and the AP. But that system, which had been tottering since the disruptions of World War I, had collapsed during World War II when Wolff and Havas disappeared into the Nazi and Vichy regimes.[31]

And new wartime technologies promised a newly global flow of information: the airplane had shrunk the globe for the traveling journalist, and radio allowed far-flung correspondents to transmit stories back to their newsrooms.[32]

There were also good reasons to be cynical about the U.S. interest in global freedom of information. The American wire services AP and UP had not suffered during World War II, so they were poised to expand into the territory lost by the European services. They also had a new economic incentive to expand their coverage, since the AP antitrust decision had made the domestic market more competitive. When AP head Kent Cooper began to call for global freedom of information, *The Economist* noted sharply that he, "like most big business executives, experiences a peculiar moral glow in finding that his idea of freedom coincides with his commercial advantage."[33]

Both cynics and optimists could sense, though, the important opportunity: for the first time there was both the technological capacity and the political opportunity to create a truly free international flow of information. But by the spring of 1948, when the Geneva Conference on Freedom of Information began to meet, that opportunity, many felt, had already been lost. The conference's president, Carlos Romulo, conceded that it "met in an atmosphere of crisis and some might feel that this was not the most appropriate setting for their deliberations." The U.S. delegation's head, William Benton, reported that Geneva was "thick with pessimism." British and French delegates still held out hope that it "may develop as a political conference of the first order," but thought it just as likely that it "may explode entirely."[34]

Superficially, the earlier optimism was a victim of the Cold War, as hopes for openness and transparency in global communication were replaced by geopolitical confrontation. Tension between the United States and the Soviets was easily expressed in disputes about press freedom. As early as April 1945, U.S. journalists criticized the Soviet practice of throwing up news blockades around territory captured by the Red Army. In 1946 and 1947, American correspondents in Eastern Europe complained about censorship, while Soviet and U.S. officials sparred publicly about the relative freedom of their nation's press. Less than four weeks before the opening of the Geneva conference, U.S. coverage of the Soviet takeover of Czechoslovakia dwelt on the imposition of communist censorship. American delegates to Geneva prepared for a showdown with the Soviets at Geneva, and insisted that the State Department send advisors with expertise on the USSR.[35]

But deeper issues had become intertwined with such geopolitical confrontation. In 1947, observing preliminary debates about international press freedom at the United Nations, journalist William Reed noted that the "considerable divergence between national views on press freedom . . . has been caused chiefly by the degree of emphasis placed on freedom and responsibility . . . [and] there can be no world agreement on freedom unless another is reached on responsibility." The State Department agreed with this assessment, believing that the "fundamental struggle of the [Geneva] conference will develop" around one issue: "While the U.S. will speak of freedom of the press and other information agencies, the USSR and its satellites will insist on the affirmative 'tasks' which the press must perform, including for example the obligation to combat fascist ideology and war mongering."[36]

The prediction was accurate: the modern confusion about the meaning of press freedom was indeed mapped onto postwar geopolitics at Geneva. Foreign nations, particularly those from the Soviet Bloc, criticized the negative liberties of laissez-faire press freedom. One Romanian delegate, for instance, quoted extensively from Morris Ernst, 1930s Newspaper Guild literature, and the work of the Hutchins Commission to argue that international law could not be based on American press freedom because "public opinion in the USA was entirely at the mercy of a small band of unscrupulous newspaper owners and advertisers."[37]

The U.S. delegation, on the other hand, embraced a classically liberal understanding of freedom of the press. The State Department had decided that the United States needed to "exert leadership" by articulating a program of international law inspired by the "classical concept of freedom of information." The conference should aim to ensure that there was "a multiplicity of unfettered sources of information available to the members of the public" by ensuring that monopolies, "particularly those of a government nature," were broken up. The United States would support supplementary, nonlegal measures to improve the performance of the press, such as "self-regulatory codes of ethics," machinery for investigating informational issues, the training and exchange of journalists, and so forth. But it would draw the line at legal measures intending to impose responsibilities. As William Benton put it in his opening address to the conference, "ever since kings confiscated hand-presses . . . ever since medieval times the rulers and exploiters of the people have raised the cry of 'responsibility' when they wished to destroy freedom. . . . Monarchs, dictators and autocrats have always tried to hamstring the press with legal obligations of responsibility."[38]

The U.S. delegation was, at first, successful in writing its vision of classical press freedom into the international infrastructure. A UN subcommittee had prepared a draft statement of the article on press freedom to be included in the Universal Declaration of Human Rights (UDHR), using the language of liberty, not responsibility: "Everyone shall have the right to freedom of thought and expression; this right shall include freedom to hold opinions without interference and to seek, receive and impart information and ideas by any means and regardless of frontiers." The Soviets, predictably, proposed an alternative version, adding the rider that "freedom of speech and freedom of the press shall not be used to advocate fascism or aggression, to sow racial, national or religious hatred, to disseminate false information or to incite the nations to mutual enmity." But the Soviet amendment was voted down, as was a compromise French proposal. The U.S. vision was passed unanimously with Soviet Bloc delegates abstaining in protest.[39] Ultimately, that would prove the most significant debate of the conference, for Article 19 of the UDHR, adopted later that year, would repeat the U.S. vision almost verbatim. A classically liberal vision of press freedom was inscribed into the global rights regime, defining the moral framework for global freedoms of speech and press for the postwar period.

At the time, however, the real prize of the conference was not the article for the UDHR, but the article for the Covenant on Human Rights and the drafting of the international conventions on freedom of information. As the State Department explained to the U.S. delegation, the declaration was "conceived of as a statement of general principles and aspirations [and it] will have no legally binding effect." The covenant, on the other hand, would be a binding legal document, and everyone at Geneva expected the declaration and the covenant to be adopted at roughly the same time. (No one anticipated that it would take almost two decades for a much-revised and debated covenant to finally pass the UN General Assembly, leaving the declaration as the singular centerpiece of the international rights regime.) The real action of the conference thus centered on the drafting of international law, which, as the State Department pointed out, had to be approached with more caution than merely symbolic declarations of rights.[40]

It was relatively easy for all nations to agree, in principle, that freedom of the press was an essential component of world peace. But the consensus fractured over the effort to write specific international laws, particularly when the United States simply repeated its classical vision of liberty and opposed every effort to use the law to regulate the international flow of information. The French delegation, for instance, proposed an international information council at the United Nations, which could issue international press cards to journalists covering foreign affairs, and could retract them in cases of professional misconduct. The United States opposed the French plan because it created a role for government interference with journalism and could "develop into an instrumentality of censorship and control." Instead, the United States favored nonlegal measures to reform press conduct: international exchanges of journalists, private organizations to promote professionalism, and UN fact-finding machinery to explore the problems of international journalism. The United States was also hostile to proposals from poorer nations seeking to equalize the global distribution of newsprint and printing presses, and to efforts by newly independent nations to protect their domestic news-gathering agencies from free-market competition with the well-established AP and UP. Such measures, the United States pointed out somewhat sanctimoniously, would allow the development of nationalistic restrictions on the flow of news. The purpose of the conference "must be to avoid doing anything which would in any way restrict or monopolize that news."[41]

America's self-proclaimed advocacy of "classical liberalism," however, was also strategic and self-interested. One of the central U.S. proposals at Geneva was a multilateral convention that would guarantee international freedom of movement for foreign correspondents. Superficially, this was a straightforward piece of liberal reform, but the draft convention also allowed states to regulate the movement of journalists "in a manner consistent with their respective immigration law and procedures." U.S. immigration law in the late 1940s routinely denied visas to members of the Communist Party or placed serious restrictions on their movements. As an internal State Department memo put it, "The U.S. will have to safeguard its position in limiting the rights of outright communists to enter this country and at the same time endeavor to broaden news coverage throughout the world." That proved an impossible task, and other delegates pointed out the hypocrisy of such concessions to national security from a delegation ostensibly committed to "classical press freedom." Critics also pointed out the obvious fact that the economic might of the

American press would give U.S. news agencies a huge advantage in an unregulated international news market.[42]

As such contradictions piled up, it became impossible for the various delegations to agree to the substance of international law. As the conference closed, it referred draft articles for the UN covenant and declaration back to the General Assembly, as well as three draft international conventions and some forty resolutions outlining the principles of global press freedom. But the conference had simply avoided the difficult questions. No one, including the United States, was entirely happy with the draft article for the covenant, and the three conventions were mutually incompatible. The UDHR, including a protection for free speech, was soon passed by the United Nations, but the covenant and conventions bogged down for decades, and the conventions eventually faded into obscurity. In 1959, one of the founders of the U.S. campaign for a free exchange of news, UP head Hugh Baillie, bitterly summed up the outcome of the Geneva motions: they had been "shipped to the United Nations in New York, where they still molder in some pigeonhole. They have become so loaded with amendments that they would probably damage the cause of Freedom of Information if they were adopted. So let 'em wither. It was a good try."[43]

* * *

The conference was, nevertheless, a significant moment in the development of an American consensus over the meaning of press freedom. The U.S. delegation, comprising leading publishers, editors, State Department officials, and Harry Martin, president of the Newspaper Guild, came together around a classical understanding of the First Amendment and an antistatist vision of press freedom. The American delegation defended corporate monopoly at home by critiquing state monopoly abroad. As the State Department put it, "the American situation may be seen in its most favorable aspects when compared with acknowledged 'monolithic' structure of the USSR press." Chafee agreed: "You don't have to defend what American publishers do but you can channelize the discussion of censorship into government censorship."[44]

Harry Martin was an especially pugnacious spokesperson for this vision of press freedom, and a vitriolic critic of Soviet censorship. One delegate praised Martin for defending "the basic liberties of the press more effectively than any editor or publisher could have done." A decade earlier, the guild had been a leading critic of capitalist domination of the press.

Now, the guild was dismissing that critique as Soviet propaganda. "Any kind of newspaper politics or economic conflict," a meeting of newspaper editors was informed, "definitely stopped at the water's edge."[45]

Moreover, the delegates interpreted the collapse of the Geneva proposals through the lens of the Cold War. U.S. free information advocates throughout the 1940s had assumed the universality of the American vision of press freedom and identified American practices as the embodiment of liberal principles. The U.S. delegation at Geneva, therefore, resisted any compromises with their program. "This is no conference about money or wheat or radio frequencies, where divergent viewpoints must and should be compromised," Benton announced in his first speech to the conference, "this is a conference about principles essential to free men." Confronted with foreign criticism of their proposals, Americans retreated to an even firmer belief in their liberal exceptionalism. Foreign criticism, rather than revealing the imperfections of American press freedom, proved the illiberalism of the rest of the world. Therefore, as the delegation reported, "the search to find common ground in matters of basic principle between the world of freedom and the world of state-control was soon abandoned at Geneva."[46] Under these circumstances, the U.S. quest for global freedom of information would have to be pursued by other means. The U.S. delegation returned from Geneva convinced that their campaign against state propaganda could best be continued by waging their own propaganda campaign, one dedicated to the unilateral export of free information.

In his role as assistant secretary of state after World War II, William Benton had overseen the nation's few postwar propaganda institutions as well as the campaign for free information, and he had long argued that the two practices were complementary. He returned from Geneva more convinced than ever that an aggressive U.S. informational policy was necessary to both the waging of the Cold War and the liberalization of global information. In 1950, Benton, now a senator, introduced a popular resolution that "the international propagation of the democratic creed be made an instrument of supreme national policy—by the development of a Marshall Plan in the field of ideas."[47] The proposal included calls for a global flow of free information.

Harry Martin, too, returned from Geneva convinced of the need for a propaganda campaign. "I find myself in fullest accord," Martin reported to the State Department, "with the theory that it is through "shock treatment" and only such treatment that we can convince the rest of the world of our unwavering support of a press concept that is wholly unfettered and free." The State Department obliged, appointing him as director of Labor Information for the Marshall Plan. Martin took leadership of a propaganda program that produced news features, radio programs, and traveling exhibits to convince Europeans to support the Americanization of the European economy. Continuing his liberal crusade against communism, he deployed what one internal document referred to as an "information panzer force" in his effort to "endow the working people of [Europe] with a faith in the cause of the West." Members of the Newspaper Guild followed their president into service as Cold War propagandists. By 1950, the *Guild Reporter* was boasting that the guild was providing the "bulk of labor information officers": "Springing from the copy desk, the editorial chair, the city hall beat and the sports desk . . . a score of American newspapermen with active backgrounds in organized labor are playing an important role in America's foreign service."[48]

Erwin Canham's experiences at the United Nations similarly convinced him of the need for U.S. propaganda. As recently as 1946, the editor of the *Christian Science Monitor* had opposed press collaboration with a proposed State Department propaganda program. But he returned from Geneva full of praise for the State Department, and he accepted the presidency of the ASNE at the same meeting that the organization voted to support State Department propaganda efforts "for the purpose of disseminating truth through the world." Canham went on to serve on the U.S. Advisory Commission on Information, the policy group responsible for U.S. propaganda in the Cold War.[49] The title of the group was significant. The concepts of information and propaganda had become fused under the pressure of the early Cold War.

Two years later, Truman went to an ASNE convention to announce his response to the "deceit, distortion and lies" of the "crude" propaganda of the communists. On advice from Canham's Advisory Commission on Information, and following the congressional support of Benton's resolution on the "Marshall Plan of Ideas," Truman instructed the State Department to expand propaganda activities. But given that propaganda was a weapon of communism, the United States could not be accused of fighting fire with fire. Instead, Truman declared that propaganda was defined by its falsehood, and announced plans for "a strengthened and more effective national effort to use the great power of truth in working for peace." The United States, he concluded, "must make ourselves known as we really are—not as Communist propaganda pictures us. . . . We must make ourselves heard round the world in a great campaign of truth."[50]

The Campaign of Truth was nonetheless a massive program of international propaganda. It was a direct echo of the "Strategy of Truth" that Archibald MacLeish had outlined to the same organization nine years earlier. And it was the logical outcome of the conflation of U.S. geopolitical interest and liberal universalism that had been implicit in the freedom of information campaign from the beginning. Where once the quest for freedom of information had been seen as a necessary antidote to statist propaganda, now state propaganda was justified as a means to the end of global freedom of information. In the context of the Cold War, an antitotalitarian commitment to classical press freedom easily led to the acceptance of new forms of state power.[51]

* * *

In his address to ASNE, Truman had also lectured the editors on their "tremendous responsibility" in promoting American foreign policy. The notion of liberal responsibilities had moved to the heart of Cold War politics. America's leadership of the free world created a cascading series of obligations and responsibilities: the U.S. state was obliged to protect global freedoms from totalitarianism; citizens were obliged to support the state. The President had concluded his outline of the Truman Doctrine in 1947 by describing these Cold War responsibilities: "The free people of the world look to us for support in maintaining their freedoms. . . . Great responsibilities have been placed upon us by the swift movement of events. I am confident that the Congress will face these responsibilities squarely." And in NSC-68, the foundational planning document of American Cold War strategy, one can find the same logic. "Our position as the center of power in the free world places a heavy responsibility upon the United States for leadership," the report declared. As a result, the freedom of the American citizen had a "counterpart in the positive responsibility to make constructive use of his freedom in the building of a just society."[52] It soon became clear that press freedom did not extend to behavior that irresponsibly threatened Cold War obligations.

The emphasis on responsibilities rather than rights was not uniquely a Cold War phenomenon. Many liberals spoke of responsibilities to the public good in order to mitigate the excesses of individual greed and capitalist self-interest.[53] Press critics in the 1930s had called for a responsible press, and this was the sense in which the Hutchins Commission had called for press responsibilities. Indeed, as the Truman administration began to suppress and regulate domestic radicalism, the commissioners had criticized these policies as interferences with the classical, negative liberties they valued so highly. Zechariah Chafee, for instance, wrote an open letter to Truman opposing the loyalty program, lobbied against the passage of antiradical legislation, and defended Alger Hiss, a former student, from accusations of espionage. And in 1950, Chafee joined with MacLeish and others to launch a Civil Liberties Appeal seeking the repeal of the McCarran Act.[54]

But liberals could not control how the idea of press responsibilities was widely understood. The idea also flowed out of the political culture of World War II, where it had meant the obligation to support the nation. In the Red Scare, the idea that press freedom came with responsibilities was used to justify the policing of radicals in the press. Between 1952 and 1957, more than one hundred journalists were called to testify about their political beliefs before antisubversive congressional committees. Fourteen journalists were fired by their papers as a result of these hearings, usually for taking the Fifth. But Elliot Maraniss of the *Detroit Times* was fired simply because he was named as a suspected communist. And others, such as William Oliver of the *Los Angeles Evening Herald Express* and William Goldman of the *New York Daily Mirror,* resigned upon being named. Working for the Hearst press, they felt that being named made their sacking inevitable.[55]

The firings and investigations were justified as necessary measures to weed out irresponsible radicals and thus preserve American press freedom. Red-baiting senator William Jenner, for instance, argued that communist journalists had to be identified because they could "divert, distract and misguide public opinion" and because "journalists have access to information which never reaches the hands of other citizens." Newspapers justified the firings with the argument that journalists had a unique obligation to gather information from government sources and report honestly and objectively, which communists either could not or would not do. In 1955, for instance, *New York Times* reporter Melvin Barnet testified that he had not been a member of the Communist Party since March 1942, but pleaded the Fifth when asked about his political affiliations while working on the *Brooklyn Eagle* in the late 1930s. The *New York Times* fired him. Arthur Sulzberger's explanation of the decision captured the Cold War logic of press responsibility. All citizens had the legal right to take the Fifth, Sulzberger conceded, but "those whose business it is to edit and report the news have greater responsibilities than those who follow the ordinary walks of life." "What must also be taken into account," he elaborated on another occasion, "is the duty of the newspaper imposed on it by the First Amendment. *That guarantee of a free press carries with it implicitly the conception of responsibility.* Such responsibility demands frankness on the part of the newspaper as well as from all those who are employed in its sensitive departments."[56]

Sulzberger had used calls for responsibility to justify limiting press freedom, rather than expanding it. Others, too, held that journalists had responsibilities that could not be met if they were suspected of communism. In 1955, arbitrators upheld the firing of two journalists in New York, arguing that papers had legitimate interests in policing the politics of reporters who "handle the particularly sensitive position of dealing with foreign news generally" and ensuring that the readership could trust the reporting to be objective and fair. In 1948, the *Washington Evening Star* fired communist journalist Thomas Buchanan because "in good conscience we couldn't have assigned him to get information from government and other sources without telling them he was a communist."[57]

If there was one section of the press that should have protested such practices, it was the Newspaper Guild. It had been founded, after all, to create job security for journalists to improve their freedom to report—and the journalists suspected of communism were suspected largely because of their role in guild politics. But the postwar guild was led by committed anticommunists. Buchanan's local unit refused to file a grievance complaint on his behalf because it considered membership in the Communist Party to be a "just and sufficient cause" for firing. The *New York Times* grievance unit similarly refused to protest Barnet's firing for taking the Fifth, because "every loyal American should cooperate with authorized Government agencies investigating Communism and . . . Barnet's use of the Fifth Amendment showed an indifference to the best welfare of the country." In 1954, the guild even flirted with banning communists from membership, arguing that such a ban was compatible with its commitment to civil liberties because party membership was not a political belief, but participation in an international conspiracy. In the end, the guild thought a ban would only give the guild the difficult job of investigating its members. Rather than police its own communists, the guild left the job to publishers—it would not protest the firing of communist journalists.

As one guild member wrote to the *Guild Reporter,* "I do not believe we should take to ourselves a responsibility that is not primarily ours. The only reason we may have communists in the guild is because the publishers hire them."[58] That was in perfect keeping with the guild's deference to the power of the publisher to hire and fire reporters.

Nor did the guild protest state investigations into the political beliefs of journalists. In 1956, four journalists were convicted of contempt of Congress when they refused to answer questions about their former political affiliations. William Price was fired by the *Daily News,* while the three other journalists, who worked for the *New York Times,* were reassigned while they appealed their case—one of them, longtime guild member and former communist Alden Whitman, ended up at the dreaded obituary section. Whitman wrote to guild leadership for support, arguing that the case had clear implications for press freedom: "Once it has become an unchallenged principle that Congress can establish, even by indirection, standards of newspaper employment, the inner spirit and practical meaning of the First Amendment will be deeply impaired." But the guild leadership declared that there was "no freedom of the press issue involved in this case," and a referendum of members abandoned the case. Suspected communists "must take their own chances," declared one New York guild member, "without dragging us along their murky road." With support from the New York Civil Liberties Union, the four eventually had their convictions overturned in a 1962 Supreme Court decision. In a concurring opinion to an otherwise technical decision, William Douglas held that questioning journalists about political beliefs violated the First Amendment and had a "totalitarian cast." The guild stayed mum throughout. In fact, it protested congressional investigations into press radicalism on only one occasion: it felt that James Eastland's investigations created the "totally false impression" that the guild was riddled with Reds. Eastland merely made some public statements praising the guild's anticommunism, and that ended the matter to the guild's satisfaction. As I. F. Stone observed, the guild had been "shockingly silent on the one big newspaperman's issue that Broun would have fought if he were alive . . . the fight to protect freedom of the press from congressional inquisition."[59]

If the guild did not resist McCarthyism, neither did the rest of the press. As early as 1953, two journalists concluded that "any way you slice it . . . if Joe McCarthy is a political monster, then the press has been his Dr. Frankenstein."[60] The press's role in the construction of the Red Scare can be traced to the problems of press freedom over the previous decades. A number of journalists were themselves committed anticommunists, and were simply continuing the Red-baiting they had begun in the interwar years. As Willard Edwards of the *Chicago Tribune* recalled, "McCarthy just fitted into what we had been saying long before." In fact, Edwards provided McCarthy with much of the material upon which the senator based his famous Wheeling, West Virginia, speech in 1950. Many others, more passively, shared the postwar suspicion of communism. Yet others, sometimes less than willingly, became conduits for McCarthy's accusations. Modern press practices often tied the hands of the press in dealing with McCarthy, because the press was supposed to transmit the news faithfully, and no matter what it was that a senator said, the speech of a senator was news. Thus, by remaining "neutral" and "objective," the press amplified McCarthyite suspicions and accusations. As one newsman of the time recalled, "My own impression was that Joe was a demagogue. But what could I do? I had to report—and quote—McCarthy. . . . The press is supposedly neutral. You write what the man says." The problems of objectivity were particularly accentuated for reporters for the wire services. They provided much of the early coverage of McCarthy's campaign talks. The Wheeling speech, for instance, was reported by one journalist, Frank Desmond of the *Wheeling Intelligencer,* and was then distributed nationally by the AP. As one AP reporter put it later, "It was the most difficult story I ever had to handle. . . . No wire service would have lasted five minutes if we hadn't played it right down the middle."[61]

Moreover, McCarthy was adept at manipulating the news-gathering cycle. He released charges just before deadline, so they could not be cross-checked; he knew, too, that his accusations would make page one, while follow-up stories would be buried on the inside pages. He curried favor with the press by providing them with a regular source of news. And if that failed, McCarthy turned to simple political intimidation to quiet his critics. When criticized by the *Milwaukee Journal,* for instance, McCarthy called for boycotts of the papers by readers and advertisers to exploit, with some effect, the press's dependence on advertising revenue. And when the *New York Post* published a seventeen-part exposé of McCarthy in 1951, its editor was hauled before Congress to answer questions about his youthful political affiliations.[62]

In many ways, then, the state of the modern American press had contributed to McCarthyism: political intimidation, anticommunist publishers and journalists, a passive understanding of objectivity, a reliance on wire services and advertising revenue, and the difficulty of reporting complex issues in daily vignettes. The pressures of antitotalitarianism were warping the concept and practice of press freedom. As Irving Howe put it in 1954, there was a "stampede to . . . trample the concept of liberty in the name of destroying its Enemy." McCarthyism was a sure sign that a classical understanding of press freedom provided no necessary guarantees that America would remain tolerant of diverse points of view.[63]

* * *

The pressures of antitotalitarianism had reaffirmed America's commitment to a classically liberal vision of press freedom while, paradoxically, encouraging widespread resignation to new forms of corporate and state control over the flow of information in the American polity. In the Manichean moral politics of the Cold War, the world could be divided between those who had a free press and those who did not. In 1947, Harry Truman outlined the existence of two ways of life, one that featured "guarantees of individual liberty [and] freedom of speech" and one that featured "a controlled press and radio." By 1953, Julius Ochs Adler, the general manager of the *New York Times,* described the essential difference between American democracy and Soviet totalitarianism: the diverse American press represented "a real marketplace of ideas," whereas the Soviet press was its monolithic "antithesis"—"a kind of mass narcotic." A decade later, the story remained the same. Alan Barth declared that "nothing expresses more clearly the essential differences between a totalitarian society and a free society than the relationship in each of the press to the government."[64] But such a binary understanding of press freedom, and such a formalistic conception of classical speech rights, masked important developments in the press. The corporate consolidation of the newspaper industry, the rise of Cold War propaganda, and the policing of radical journalists were seen as necessary consequences of antitotalitarian political commitments; they were no longer viewed as threats to press freedom.

But as the pressures of the Cold War mounted and fears about domestic subversion escalated, the American state developed a new fixation with keeping information secret in the interests of national security. New interferences with American press freedom became apparent. In October 1948, the chairman of ASNE's World Freedom of Information Committee wrote a memo to his fellow editors, expressing concern that there was an increasing tendency toward secrecy in the United States. "It seems to me," he suggested, that "our responsibility lies in the domestic field as well as the international field." Two years later, the ASNE World Freedom of Information Committee dropped the word "world" from its title, reconstituting itself as the "Freedom of Information Committee." In 1951, Sigma Delta Chi's committee on the advancement of freedom of information likewise shifted its focus from international agreements to domestic problems of secrecy.[65] A new front had opened in the struggle for freedom of the press in America. As the culture of the Cold War bloomed, Americans would engage in a new debate about the problem of access to government secrets.

7

The Rise of State Secrecy

The Elijah Lovejoy award was given for "fearless" journalism in the fight for a free press—it was named for America's "first martyr for freedom of the press." But when he received the inaugural award in 1952, James S. Pope opened his address by declaring that "freedom of the press in our country has become almost an invulnerable institution." In fact, Pope thought that the right to press freedom was "so majestic that for much too long most of us in the newspaper field were blinded by it." Looking for "frontal attacks" on press freedom, Americans had missed a "flanking movement": the decline of access to government information. Classical speech rights, as Walter Lippmann had argued three decades earlier, did not guarantee the stream of news upon which opinions were based. Or, as Pope put it in 1951, "We have hammered for two centuries on the primary theme that the press must be free, that any and every citizen has the right to express his opinion of his government. But of what value are these opinions if they are based on ignorance or on part truths? Lately we have discovered that while we were expounding on freedom of the press, freedom of information was being lost on a major scale by default."[1]

This concern for freedom of information was novel. Pope was chairman of the new Freedom of Information Committee of the ASNE; offering congressional testimony in 1956, he confessed that he "was an old hand in this business of fighting for access to public information and I have been doing it exactly five years." Pope and his colleagues were reacting to the rise of governmental secrecy in the early years of the Cold War, particularly new executive orders that classified government information, and new arguments about the right of the executive branch to keep information from the public. Nobody knows exactly how much information was actually kept secret in America after World War II, but by any estimate it was a staggering amount. When the Pentagon created an Office of Declassification Policy, it estimated that classified material, if piled 2,000 pages to a foot, would stretch out some 3 million feet. That was in 1957; in the same year, it was estimated that over a million people were involved in classifying material. By 2001, when there were 33 million acts of new classification, philosopher of science Peter Galison estimated that there were some 7.5 billion pages being kept secret—a collection roughly the same size as the Library of Congress.[2]

Although it is tempting think of secrecy as a timeless attribute of the state, the American secrecy regime has a short history, having been built in a burst of activity after World War II.[3] In many ways, it was a patchwork of statutes and executive orders. There was little congressional or judicial oversight, and there was no master plan—it evolved in response to Cold War fears and partisan political clashes, and was legitimated by bureaucratic inertia. But it was unprecedented. In 1956, sociologist Edward Shils declared that "the past decade has been the decade of the secret. Never before has the existence of life-controlling secrets been given so much publicity and never before have such exertions been made for the safe-guarding of secrets."[4]

The new secrecy produced a deep paradox in American press freedom: while there were more and more protections for the right to publish without state interference, it became ever more difficult to access information held by the state. This was no accident: the censorship of information was seen as a more palatable method of securing secrets than the antidemocratic censorship of speech or publication. In theory, the secrecy regime helped to protect freedom of the press—it preserved American security in the threatening world of Cold War geopolitics, without contradicting the First Amendment right to speech. But in practice, the rise of secrecy eroded the press's ability to circulate political information to the public and helped to produce the nationalistic and deferential culture of Cold War journalism. Secrecy and the Cold War mutually reinforced each other, producing the McCarthyite obsession with security, the press's participation in the militaristic consensus of Cold War Washington, and the exclusion of the public from the key facts of American foreign policy. There was a backlash to this culture, as journalists, editors, and politicians argued that a free press required access to state secrets. But they only succeeded in passing the Freedom of Information Act (FOIA) of 1966, and that was a superficial response to the new laws of secrecy. The most important trend of the 1950s and 1960s was the decline of press access to information.

* * *

The roots of the national secrecy state could be traced to World War II. In 1958, John Steinbeck argued that "our whole miasmic hysteria about secrecy . . . had its birth" amid the "huge and gassy thing called the War Effort." In the late 1940s, pressure to keep national security information secret continued to mount. In 1946, the Atomic Energy Act declared that much material was "born classified" and introduced mechanisms to regulate the circulation of information about the design, manufacture, and utilization of atomic weapons and nuclear energy. In 1947, the National Security Act created the CIA and specified that the director of the new agency was responsible for protecting intelligence sources and methods from unauthorized disclosure—language that was interpreted expansively to cover any information collected by an intelligence agency, regardless of whether or not the source was open. In the same year, draft rules for a general classification order were leaked from the Security Advisory Board, which had been quietly working on them since 1945. They included provisions that allowed the classification of information that caused "serious administrative embarrassment or difficulty" and, in the face of much public criticism, were quickly retracted. The issue of classification went quiet for a time.[5]

But on September 24, 1951, Harry Truman issued Executive Order 10290, creating, for the first time, a permanent classification regime across all agencies of the government. It featured four levels of classification—Top Secret, Secret, Confidential, and Restricted—and created newly standardized security procedures: information was not to be discussed by phone; methods for destroying classified material were specified. There were even requirements about the kind of safes that could be used for each class of information.[6]

But most significantly, the order explicitly invoked the information disclosure provisions of the Espionage Act to enforce the classification regime. Finally, thirty years after equivalent provisions had been deleted by Woodrow Wilson's Congress, the criminal sanctions of the Espionage Act were being deployed to enforce executive decisions about what information could be released to the public. The order was justified as a necessary response to the increasing amount of information that was vital to national security in the age of total Cold War. For instance, before a company issued stock, the Securities and Exchange Commission collected vast amounts of its financial data, which might include defense contracts; the Departments of Health and Agriculture collected information that could be related to the development of bacteriological weapons. "I am not trying to suppress information," Truman asserted; "I am trying to prevent us from being wiped out."[7]

But the order was criticized by newspaper editors and Republicans, and in 1953, Dwight Eisenhower issued Executive Order 10501, which superseded Truman's order. It made many changes, but two in particular were intended to roll back the classification system: the elimination of the bottom category of classification ("restricted") and the removal of some agencies from the classification system. The reforms turned out to be largely superficial. Authority to classify was removed only from agencies that should never have had it in the first place (such as the American Battle Monuments Commission, or the Committee on Purchases of Blind-Made Products). The classification powers of the Atomic Energy Agency, the CIA and the Departments of State, Defense, Justice, Commerce, and Treasury—responsible for 90 percent of classification—were left untouched. And eliminating the category of "restricted" information had little effect because cautious government employees continued to classify information of marginal security value. They now did so with the more restrictive "confidential" stamp. (Beyond its consequences for democratic deliberation, disgruntled bureaucrats worried that this posed a quite material problem—"restricted" material could be kept in a locked desk, but "confidential" material required the purchase of special filing cabinets.)[8]

In short, Eisenhower's order consolidated rather than reformed Truman's. And between the two, a new regime of classification had been created. Information would now be kept secure by classification at the government source, not by censorship of the press, or even by journalists' self-censorship as in World War II. The system had been coming into view during the 1940s, but with the classification order, the retreat of censorship from the sphere of publication was complete.

The tectonic nature of this shift was not immediately apparent in 1951. During a press conference intended to explain the classification system, Truman struggled to distinguish the new order from the old. In what Arthur Krock described as a "tongue lashing," Truman lectured the press on their duties to deal with national security information, gave examples of improperly published information, and called on editors and journalists "to use good judgment for the safety of the United States." When correspondents pointed out that many of Truman's examples featured information that had been released by the government, the press conference quickly degenerated. Under questioning, Truman did not seem to know whether information should be secured by the press or the state:

> *Q:* Mr. President, recently the Defense Department gave out certain information about the Matador, also on these guided missiles, and so forth. That was published probably in every paper in the land. Was that the publishers' responsibility not to publish that?
>
> *Truman:* I think so, if they want to protect the country.
>
> *Q:* Wouldn't it be better to tighten up over at Defense?
>
> *Truman:* That is what we are doing. I say, that is what we are doing, and that is what you are fussing about.

Throughout the conference, Press Secretary Joe Short had tried by "gestures and a couple of agonizing whispers" to keep Truman on message. But even when given explicit instructions, Truman still garbled the point: "Joe wants me to make it perfectly clear that this order only applies to the officials of the United States Government. My comments, though, apply to everybody who gives away our state secrets." Short had to issue a statement after the conference to clarify the situation: "The recent executive order on classified information does not in any way alter the right of citizens to publish anything."[9]

Truman was still speaking in the language of press responsibility from World War II. But after 1951, the state would not directly interfere with the press's right to publish, or even attempt to inculcate a culture of self-censorship among journalists. In 1948, James Forrestal had met with editors to float the idea of establishing a successor to the Office of Censorship, but nothing came of it. After crises, there would still be calls for the press to act responsibly: shortly after the Bay of Pigs fiasco, JFK asked newspaper publishers to "reexamine their own responsibilities . . . and to heed the duty of self-restraint." But such rhetoric was not institutionally enforced. In the aftermath of the Cuban Missile Crisis, Byron Price had been brought in to talk about drafting a new code of voluntary censorship, but the idea was soon dropped.[10]

And the state certainly did not formally censor press publication of state secrets. The McCarran Act of 1950 tightened the Espionage Act's restrictions on the disclosure of information, but only after Elisha Hanson of ANPA insisted on the inclusion of an explicit guarantee that nothing in the act could be construed "in any way to limit or infringe upon freedom of the press or of speech." Issuing a comprehensive review of the national security apparatus in 1957, Loyd Wright gave an angry address decrying "irresponsible" behavior by the press and calling for "vigorous prosecutions" for the publication of state secrets. But the Wright Commission's proposal of a new law to penalize publication of secrets by "persons outside as well as within the government" was criticized as an undemocratic threat to press freedom, and it quickly died in Congress. In the same year, a Defense Department investigation into the problem of leaks explained that prosecuting journalists made little sense: bringing espionage prosecutions against a journalist risked widening the leak as evidence was disclosed in trial; and such prosecutions risked making a martyr of the journalist. "The real culprit," explained the head of the inquiry, was the "member of our department rather than the reporter."[11] Securing secrets required policing the government employee, not the press. After 1951, the "right of citizens to publish anything" was increasingly sacrosanct.

By focusing on regulating the employee rather than the journalist, classification began to distinguish itself from censorship. In a 1948 debate on government censorship, Tom Wallace of the *Louisville Times* argued that government withholding of information "is not censorship and is not related to censorship." Erwin Canham thought that the best way to reconcile security and press freedom would be to simultaneously "condemn censorship" and "recognize the primary responsibility on the government itself to determine what information it feels should be withheld in the original instance." Joe Short made the same distinction starkly in 1951: "Classification . . . has no realistic relationship to censorship."[12]

In reality, of course, classification was just a different form of censorship, one that was more subtle because it was invisible to the public eye: nobody's speech rights were violated. Censorship now took place within the bureaucracy, with the act of classification. The simple decision that information should be classified triggered a host of consequences: that information was held and transported securely, only certain individuals could know it, and its disclosure became a crime.[13] Government employees decided what to classify within an institutional framework that incentivized the overclassification of documents: a 1956 Defense Department investigation of classification thought that 90 percent of items should not have been classified. Although presidents and government commissions have routinely decried overclassification, there have never been any sanctions against it. As one admiral told a congressional committee in the 1950s, no one had ever been court-martialed for *over*classifying a document.[14] Nor has there ever been a mechanism to encourage transparency at the point of classification. In 1951, William Benton suggested that there should be "a top-ranking advocate of the people's right to know" within the bureaucracy to counterbalance the instinct to classify. But nothing came of it, just as nothing came of proposals that each agency have a public information advocate to argue against classification.[15] At no point have classifiers been instructed to consider the public's right to know when making classification decisions.[16] And not until Clinton's presidency was the classifier required to justify the act of classification—and even then, the classifier simply needed to cite a relevant generic category of classifiable information, hardly an onerous task.[17] Despite these institutional incentives to overclassify, the courts have deferred to the initial act of classification, preferring not to review judgments that are presumably made in the interests of national security.[18]

* * *

The growing desire to keep national security information secret was a product of early Cold War fears about communist espionage. This was distinct from the fears about communist propaganda that justified the period's interferences with free speech: the privately enforced Hollywood Blacklist; university loyalty codes; the criminal conviction of Communist Party leaders for advocating the overthrow of the government, upheld by the Supreme Court in the *Dennis* case of 1951. In fact, government interferences with speech rights were falling out of favor. There was far less federal prosecution of speech during the second Red Scare than there had been during the first. Between 1948 and 1957, the state successfully prosecuted only one hundred speakers under the Smith Act; between 1917 and 1919, using the Espionage Act, it had succeeded close to 1,000 times. And by 1957, the Supreme Court had begun to reverse course on its decision in *Dennis*. It soon conceded that the right to free speech did protect the right to advocate the overthrow of the government. After that, it began to protect an expansive vision of free speech.[19]

The desire to secure state secrets, however, was less controversial. In his ringing dissent in the *Dennis* case, in which he had rearticulated the importance of the free market of ideas, William Douglas had conceded that he "would have no doubts" about the prosecution if "those who claimed protection under the First Amendment were teaching . . . the filching of documents from public files."[20] Fears that communists could steal state secrets helped to legitimize the new loyalty programs, and the theft of documents was a central theme in the signature dramas of the early Cold War: the *Amerasia* editors' possession of hundreds of classified documents; the Rosenbergs' transfer of documents about the bomb; and Whittaker Chambers's sensational revelation of the Pumpkin Papers, the microfilm roll of classified documents that he claimed had come from Alger Hiss. The political impact of the Hiss case shows how broadly respected the classification regime was in postwar America. As Archibald MacLeish later recalled,

> The information that was supposed to be in that bloody pumpkin was the kind of information that any postman in the State Department had. It was of no interest to anybody. Why didn't somebody at some point read it? If you've ever read it, you'd know what I mean. But nobody did, not during the trial; they were so poisoned by McCarthy they thought that anything that had been marked secret must be secret for some reason, not realizing that every bureaucrat in Washington uses that little stamp to protect his own hide![21]

* * *

Ironically, the primary critics of classification and secrecy in the early Cold War were anticommunist Republicans, who were equally committed to keeping state secrets out of the hands of communists. It was just that they didn't believe that the Truman loyalty boards were effectively weeding out communists, and wanted to see the classified raw files for themselves. In March 1948, for instance, the House Un-American Activities Committee subpoenaed the files of the Commerce Department's loyalty board only days after it had cleared Dr. Edward Condon of disloyalty. Secretary of Commerce Averell Harriman refused to turn them over, claiming that revealing the identity of confidential informants would undermine the efficacy of the loyalty program. Shortly thereafter, Truman issued a statement directing all agencies to decline subpoenas for records in order to protect national security, confidential informants, and the reputations of government personnel being subject to unfounded allegations. The House voted 300 to 29 to order the immediate release of the file, but Truman refused to comply, because the vote had not been put to the Senate.[22] The pattern repeated for the remainder of Truman's presidency.

The partisan dynamics of anticommunism thus produced some unlikely advocates of government transparency. In 1951, forty-four Republicans, including Richard Nixon and Joe McCarthy, signed a manifesto declaring that "any attempt to restrain the inherent right of an American to criticize his Government must be resisted by all freedom-loving persons. . . . We shall vigorously resist any attempt to conceal facts from the American people." In 1952, Red-baiting senator William Jenner proposed a sweeping open access bill to make "an initial step in breaking the censorship" of the American state. In a public statement explaining the bill, Jenner criticized the classification order, the rise of propaganda in the New Deal publicity bureaus since 1933, and the Truman administration's limp response to the threat of communist subversion. Jenner's bill was a product of his deeply conservative politics, but it was also a strikingly bold proposal for government transparency. It declared that government records were "public property" and envisioned criminal sanctions for government failure to disclose. Both suggestions were more stringent than the Freedom of Information acts that were ultimately passed in the 1960s and 1970s.[23]

Truman's attorney general made sure that Jenner's bill died in Congress, and the Truman administration repeatedly opposed other efforts to enforce a right to access executive documents. In early 1948, for instance, Truman vetoed a bill that would have allowed Senate review of Atomic Energy Commission appointee files, because it was "an unwarranted encroachment of the legislative upon the executive branch."[24] Presidents had long refused to turn over executive documents, though the limits of the practice were unsettled and the courts had never determined if those refusals were constitutional.[25] But as Truman fought off anticommunist attacks, a newly capacious right to executive secrecy solidified. In 1949, a freelancing Department of Justice attorney, Herman Wolkinson, stitched together the previous incidents of executive denial to argue that there was a clear and settled precedent: the executive had an "uncontrolled discretion to withhold the information and papers in the public interest."[26] Wolkinson's article lacked official imprimatur, but it showed that the executive's right to secrecy was becoming more sharply defined.

The question of executive secrecy and the politics of McCarthyism came to a head at the same moment: the Army-McCarthy hearings of 1954. The army accused McCarthy and his aides of using allegations of communism to gain preferential treatment for a friend in the service; McCarthy alleged that those army accusations were made in bad faith to cover up army ineptitude in rooting out communists. As the hearings unfolded, it became increasingly difficult to evaluate the claims and counterclaims, because the most important evidence was classified. McCarthy had entered as evidence a letter that he claimed was from J. Edgar Hoover to the army, outlining a communist spy ring. It turned out to be a summary of the original, but it did contain classified material, which the attorney general refused to declassify. (He also threatened criminal prosecutions against the leaker, although McCarthy never disclosed his source.) McCarthy also claimed that the army's allegations had been cooked up at a secret meeting of Republican policy heavyweights. One of its attendees, military lawyer John Adams, was called to give testimony. But in a public letter on May 17, Eisenhower ordered that no employees of the Defense Department could offer testimony or provide evidence about conversations, communications, or documents within the executive branch. Eisenhower's letter was accompanied by a memorandum from the attorney general that borrowed liberally from Wolkinson's 1949 article on executive privilege. Eisenhower claimed that "it is essential to efficient and effective administration that employees of the Executive Branch be in a position to be completely candid in advising with each other on official measures." That meant the president had a right to withhold information "whenever he found that what was sought was confidential or its disclosure would be incompatible with the public interest or jeopardize the safety of the nation." Asked in a press conference the next day whether he might modify the order, Eisenhower announced that he had "no intention whatsoever of relaxing or rescinding the order because it is a very moderate and proper statement of the division of powers between the executive and the legislative."[27]

Because the order essentially shut down the Army-McCarthy hearings—devoid of substance, they would continue just long enough for McCarthy to finally, fatally, discredit himself—Ike's action was met with initial praise. As journalist Clark Mollenhoff noted in 1956, "that [Eisenhower] letter won support because it came clothed as a weapon to stop Senator McCarthy." But the order ushered in an unprecedented level of executive secrecy. Executive confidentiality became the norm, not the exception; it was the release of documents that required justification, not their concealment. In 1955, Robert Cutler, former assistant to Eisenhower for national security affairs, declared that "all papers, all considerations, all studies, all intelligence leading to the formulation of national security policy recommendations are the property of the president" and that "only he can dispose of them." "In fact," Cutler continued, "any other concept would lead to chaos." In the threatening shadow of global communism, Cutler believed, those who called for a right to access documents had to prove "that the widespread, public disclosure of our secret projects will make the free world stronger, and the neutral better disposed, will rally the subject people, and will put the Communist regimes at a disadvantage." Both JFK and LBJ took some steps to reduce the use of the privilege from these extremes, but a precedent had been established. When the Johnson administration established a ground rule that agencies were not to transmit to Congress any communication from the White House, Attorney General Ramsey Clark explained that "this is not the establishment of a new policy, but the exercise of a legal privilege in accordance with historical practice of presidents and essential to the separation of powers." Only seven years earlier, a law review article on the privilege had called it "ambiguous and muddled" and an "unresolved constitutional question."[28] The partisan clashes of the McCarthy era had helped to solidify an expansive right of executive secrecy.

* * *

The rise of classification and the rise of executive privilege helped to legitimate a broad culture of secrecy. By 1957, DC reporter Jack Wilson, writing a series on secrecy for the *Des Moines Register,* observed that the laws were important, "but they aren't as significant as the general climate of secrecy in which the agencies operate." Throughout DC, Wilson reported, there was a general sense "that if an item wasn't marked secret, there must have been a mistake." A 1955 questionnaire sent to all agencies found that they had created some thirty categories to keep nonsecurity information from the public, such as "need to know," "for official distribution," "administratively confidential," and "for official use only." In the mid-1950s, a former public relations executive briefly instituted rules in the Commerce and Defense Departments that limited the release of all unclassified information that *might* be inimical to the defense interests of the United States—as one commentator noted, "every telephone book and road map in the country" was in that category. At times, the culture of secrecy took on the air of self-parody. Twelve years after World War II, Harvard continued to store 7,000 feet of military records that its employees lacked clearance to look at. The Department of Labor classified statistics on the army's purchase of peanut butter because enemies might use them to deduce the size of the force—even though the army published monthly reports of its total personnel.[29]

But important information was veiled from the public. A 1953 Atomic Energy Commission report that could have limited the accidental fallout from the 1954 Bikini tests was classified and removed from public knowledge. Congressional efforts to oversee foreign aid expenditures were met with assertions of executive privilege, which obscured aid activities, corruption, and inefficiency in such countries as Laos, Vietnam, Pakistan, Brazil, and Guatemala. In 1959, the General Accounting Office complained that it was being denied information about defense spending and thus denied the opportunity to check for waste, mismanagement, and poor procurement practices. The navy, army, and air force asserted that if internal reports on spending and procurement were to be released, internal inspectors might soften their criticism. The material was therefore not released to protect the "public interest" in "efficient" government.[30]

* * *

The press, too, found it increasingly difficult to gain access to information about government activities. The post–World War II administrations could keep things hidden, or they could strategically disclose them, spinning as they went, or they could provide select journalists with exclusive background information. By the mid-1950s, journalists were criticizing this new set of practices with a new term: "news management."[31] In the broadest sense, of course, there was nothing new about politicians seeking favorable publicity. But there had been two major changes. First, the rise of the administrative state meant that large areas of policy were determined by appointed figures, who did not need publicity for reelection. Second, issues of national security and foreign policy predominated over all others, which encouraged greater secrecy and more strategic communication on behalf of administrators, as well as greater deference on behalf of the press. Thanks to these developments, the rules of the game between journalists and politicians shifted.

The post–World War II administrations, for instance, were far more parsimonious about the information they released through their publicity bureaus. The Presidential Press Conference, continuing its decline after World War II, symbolized the broader trend. Whereas Coolidge, Hoover, and FDR had held around seventy conferences per year, Truman averaged only forty-two, and Ike, JFK, and LBJ held roughly twenty-four per year.[32] This decline in quantity was married to a shift in quality: the press conferences revealed less information and became almost ritualistic. FDR had met the correspondents informally around his desk, but Truman made press conferences more formal, moving them to a newly devoted press room in the old State Department building. JFK chose a cavernous auditorium for his conferences. And with the introduction of television cameras in 1955, the conferences were no longer off the record. Direct quotation of the president became the norm, and newspapers started printing transcripts. Presidents therefore became more cautious and disclosed far less. Eisenhower was infamous for circuitous, rambling answers that consumed time while revealing little. (One journalist quipped that if you asked Ike the time, he would give you a history of clock making.) Adding to the emptiness, large portions of the press conference were used for presidential announcements and set statements, which limited the amount of questions that could be asked in the allotted time.[33]

Handouts, public statements, and press briefings also became increasingly strategic in the early Cold War. Publicity officers within the executive agencies had remained the most important source for political reporting. In 1951, Philip W. Porter of the *Cleveland Plain Dealer* grumbled that press agents "are in the same category as women—they are often puzzling and amazing, but we couldn't get along without them." By the early 1960s, the PR staff of State and Defense alone had grown to some 773 persons. But releases were increasingly crafted simply to maintain the official line. During the Korean War, Truman issued a "gagging order" preventing officials from speaking on foreign policy issues without clearing them through the Department of Defense. Such orders could appear commonsensical—they were a way to handle the strategic imperatives of a Cold War that never bubbled over into total war, and thus never led to the establishment of an heir to the OWI. In the wake of the Cuban Missile Crisis, for instance, JFK explained that there had been an obvious need to speak with one voice and to manage the release of information because all administrative disclosures were simultaneously messages to Moscow. The problem was that times of crisis never ended, and so many areas of the nation's life could be used to make statements to Moscow. In April 1961, for instance, Robert McNamara told the Senate that investigations of the expensive and controversial Zeus missile were publicizing weakness to the Russians: "What we ought to be saying is that we have the most perfect anti-ICBM system the human mind can devise."[34]

Although journalists continued to rely on such official channels as their primary source for news, they increasingly sought out unofficial channels to get a clearer sense of political life than the handouts and briefings could provide. Leaks and background briefings became the order of the day. It is difficult to measure the rise of leaks, but one commentator in the 1940s dated the first "background briefings" to two meetings in November 1942. That date is suspiciously precise, but the statement shows that these briefings were significant new developments, which became more common as secrecy expanded. In 1948, Bruce Catton, who had been a PR officer during World War II, declared that "our particular form of government wouldn't work" without such off-the-record disclosures.[35] The difference between a "leak" and a "background briefing" was entirely political. Both involved the off-the-record disclosure of theoretically confidential information; a leak was simply what one called a background briefing when one disapproved of it.

So although politicians regularly complained about "leaks," and treated them as anarchic and exceptional breaches in security, they were quickly "institutionalized," as Douglass Cater observed in 1959: "Cloaked news has become an institutional practice in the conduct of modern government . . . part of the regular intercourse between government and press." Cater understood that leaks were used by politicians and government officials for a host of reasons: to defuse hostile stories, to float trial balloons, to wage interagency rivalry, to bring pressure to bear on allies in diplomatic negotiation, to manipulate public opinion. And officials in the Cold War were particularly skilled at using leaks to further their own purposes. During the Berlin crisis, plans for a massive defense buildup were leaked, both to create the impression of government activism and to soften the reception for the smaller, but still substantial, increase that was coming. In 1965, Murray Marder of the *Washington Post* was shown a selection of classified diplomatic cables that seemed to support the LBJ administration's assertion that intervention in the Dominican Republic was intended to save American lives. In all, as William S. White put it, "the leak or exclusive story is rarely an example of a reporter's persistence and skill"; leaks occurred because a government official wanted to put the story out.[36]

Beyond their impact on any particular news item, the use of leaks transformed the practice and culture of journalism. Journalists could not do their work unless they cultivated official sources that would speak to them informally. In the 1950s, journalists wined and dined officials, cultivating interpersonal networks to facilitate access to news. The leading journalists were networked with the most powerful and extensive sources—as with the Alsop brothers' lavish Georgetown dinner parties, or their "Sunday Night Suppers" with Chip Bohlen and Frank Wisner, or Drew Pearson's carefully collected files of rumor and gossip. Journalists and officials developed a mutually beneficial system of trust and reciprocity. Only journalists who shared the politician's assumptions would receive the leaks, which reinforced the assumptions, which reinforced the trust, which produced more leaks. The logic of the system was captured in the most superficial of contexts—both correspondents and politicians agreed that sexual indiscretions were not matters of public interest, and the public remained ignorant of them.[37]

But for all the clubby camaraderie, the partnership between the press corps and the politicians was not an equal one. As David Broder of the *Washington Post* later recalled, trust was a form of policing: "One of Kennedy's techniques for dealing with the press was to say things that were so damn candid—to some about sexual things but even his political comments—so that you knew if you printed it, you would be ending your intimate relationship. . . . It was a way of coopting us." The journalist always needed the politician more than the politician needed the journalist. As early as 1951, editor Oxie Reichler complained that journalists were no longer selling "fresh brand new merchandise" but were "accepting more and more of the second hand stuff." Reichler feared that dependence on background briefings was "more serious than the closed door form of censorship." By 1963, Alan Barth believed that the press's greatest failure was "that out of respectable and patriotic motives" it had become "an instrument and partner of the government. . . . Along with newspaper compliance with official secrecy has gone a dangerous tendency to let editorial criticism of the government stop, like politics, at the water's edge."[38]

As a result, without formal censorship or any apparent violation of the First Amendment, the flow of information in the polity was adjusted to state imperatives. Journalists sat on stories to aid the government, as when the *New York Times* kept the Argus atmospheric nuclear tests quiet for six months at the request of the government, or when the Alsops kept quiet what they knew about CIA interventions in Guatemala and Iran. *New York Times* journalists were among those who knew about the secret U2 flights for three years before Gary Powers was shot down over Soviet airspace in 1960, but the paper kept the matter quiet. "We exercised a judgment," Scotty Reston later explained, "that it was not in the national interest for us to print that fact. I still think that is a defensible position." The secrecy of the flights distorted foreign relations and domestic politics. Republicans could not dispel Kennedy's claims that there was a missile gap, because the proof of American military superiority was classified.[39]

The press also sculpted stories to match government policy. Preparations for the Bay of Pigs were well known—JFK's press secretary called it "the least covert military operation in history," and Reston observed that there were "literally hundreds, maybe thousands" of people in Miami who knew about the plans. But key details were kept out of the papers in the lead-up—*New York Times* editors deleted a reference to CIA involvement days before the invasion, and the *Miami Herald* and the *New Republic* had earlier killed stories about preparations in Guatemalan training camps. Far more important than such suppression was the casual approval the papers gave to the invasion. Even after the invasion had come to its dismal conclusion, the press criticized the implementation of the plan, not the underlying questions of ethics or morality. Reflecting the topsy-turvy priorities of midcentury journalism, one reporter even put the blame for the fiasco on the administration's failure to brief the press on the proper way to spin the story: "I believe that if the US had displayed greater trust towards the press and had frankly announced in a background briefing session that the Cuban operation was to be a commando-type mission (which it was) and not a massive invasion, the defeat would not have been interpreted as a humiliating fiasco for Washington."[40]

The state's ability to manipulate the flow of information to the public without relying on formal censorship came to a head in the Vietnam War. The American press had paid little attention to Vietnam throughout the 1950s. When it sent correspondents in the early 1960s, they were responsible for crafting American public opinion about the country for the first time. As American involvement in the conflict escalated under JFK and LBJ, this news was carefully managed. In Vietnam, military briefings to reporters downplayed casualties, while trusted journalists were taken on helicopter tours to the most favorable fronts—one such program was called Operation Maximum Candor. At home, careful releases of information justified increasing involvement. *Time* and *Life* magazine were given selectively leaked Pentagon cables to allow them to write up lurid accounts of the Gulf of Tonkin incident; broader questions about U.S. policy went unasked. The escalation of U.S. troops was deliberately released in a "piecemeal" fashion to mitigate the "crisis atmosphere" that would result from a direct announcement. When U.S. troops began offensive combat operations, General Taylor explained to Dean Rusk that no public announcement should be made, but routine announcements of such activity could be confirmed as they happened: "This low-key treatment will not obviate [all] political and psychological problems . . . but will allow us to handle them undramatically." In a 1963 congressional inquiry into access to government information, James Reston observed that "we are engaged in quite a war in Vietnam and this country hasn't the vaguest idea that it is in a war." In May 1964, almost two-thirds of the public still said they had given little to no thought to Vietnam. In the same month, intensive bombing of Laos began under the cover of secrecy—it would take five years to come to light.[41]

Eventually the public would become far more interested in the war, and as the antiwar movement mobilized, it began to fixate on the secrecy and deceptions of the Johnson administration—what was soon dubbed the "credibility gap." Later, many would attribute the rise of this antiwar movement to the press itself. In reality, press opposition to the war trailed public opposition, and mapped much more closely onto the attitude of official circles. The earliest journalists to criticize the war were a small group of Saigon correspondents, such as David Halberstam and Neil Sheehan. JFK was sufficiently frustrated by them that he tried, in vain, to have the *New York Times* reassign Halberstam. But the Saigon correspondents were mainly critical of the decision to rely on Diem and the South Vietnamese army, not of the broader morality of U.S. involvement. As Neil Sheehan put it, "We were just as interventionist-minded as Joe Alsop; we didn't share any basic differences with Robert McNamara. It was a question of how do you win the war." The Saigon correspondents believed the war would be won with more direct U.S. involvement; they believed that because their sources were military advisors who were dissatisfied with the existing strategy. More broadly, too, the press reflected the range of opinions of those in power—when officials began to question the war, so too did the press. Such a reliance on official sources was natural, explained Peter Lisagor, Washington bureau chief of the *Chicago Daily News,* "because they were supposed to have the facts and you didn't." After leaving the administration, Ted Sorenson reflected on the chasm separating the information available to officials and the public. "In the White House," he recalled, "I felt sorry for those who had to make judgments on the basis of daily newspapers. There's a large difference between reading diplomatic cables and intelligence reports and sitting in your living room reading the papers. Now I'm one of those guys sitting in his living room reading the papers and I'm even more acutely aware of the difference."[42] The press and the public had been cut off from meaningful access to political information.

* * *

Even before the controversy of Vietnam, this secrecy system was criticized. In the 1950s and 1960s, the primary forum for antisecrecy politicking was a Special Subcommittee on Government Information, known by the name of its chairman, John Moss.[43] The Moss Committee was founded in 1955 to explore "the trend in the availability of government information." Over its eleven-year life, it conducted some twenty-four hearings and published fifty-four volumes of reports and transcripts. The vast majority of these hearings were intended to expose secrecy in the government to the light of publicity—a strategy that encouraged government departments to modify or clarify individual information policies. But the committee also helped to promote legislation intended to deal with the problems of secrecy more holistically—particularly the 1966 FOIA.[44]

A particularly powerful lobby of scientists and industrialists used the hearings of the Moss Committee to criticize the way secrecy had compartmentalized knowledge and thus hindered progress in national defense research—these utilitarian arguments did much to undermine the legitimacy of widespread secrecy.[45] The Moss Committee also worked closely with the small group of editors and lawyers who served on a number of committees devoted to accessing federal records, a group that became known as the Freedom of Information (FOI) movement. In innumerable speeches, articles, books, and letters to officials, men such as James Russell Wiggins of the *Washington Post,* Clark Mollenhoff of the *Des Moines*

Register, James Pope of the *Louisville Kentucky Journal,* and Virgil M. Newton of the *Tampa Tribune* both criticized the rise of secrecy and developed strategies to overcome it.[46]

The most important of the FOI movement's many publications was Harold Cross's *The People's Right to Know,* published in 1953. The ASNE's FOI committee commissioned Cross, former counsel for the *New York Herald Tribune,* to undertake a broad survey of access to public information in 1950. He began by noting the simple absence of legal rights to access information held by the federal government. "The dismaying, bewildering fact," Cross announced gloomily, "is that in the absence of a general or a specific act of Congress—and such acts are not numerous—there is no enforceable legal right in public or press to inspect any federal non-judicial record." Others in the FOI movement agreed that access to information depended more "upon official grace than upon legal authority." "Every employee of the government can build his own little dam," James S. Pope complained, "but nobody is empowered to destroy them."[47]

Cross and his allies believed that the obvious solution to the problem was to recognize a legal right to access information. "It is not enough merely to recognize philosophically nor to pay lip service to the important political justification for freedom of information," Cross argued, because "citizens of a self-governing society must have the legal right to examine and investigate the conduct of its affairs." Without that right, Cross concluded, "we have but changed our kings."[48]

The problem was how to ground such a right of access to information. It was unmentioned in the Constitution, little explored in political philosophy, and far from recognized in jurisprudence. Indeed, the whole idea of a "right to know" was a neologism that had emerged from the effort to create global press freedom in the aftermath of World War II. On January 23, 1945, the *New York Times* credited AP head Kent Cooper with coming up with a "good new phrase for an old freedom" when he spoke of the global right to know. Even Pope was forced to concede that "freedom of information is a will-o'-the-wisp among basic liberties."[49]

So FOI advocates became inventive in their efforts to identify a longstanding right to know. Some drew on slim threads of textual evidence to suggest a First Amendment right to information, such as dicta in the 1936 *Grosjean* decision that stated that "it goes to the heart of the natural right of the members of an organized society . . . to impart and *acquire* information about their common interests." Others referred to hints in classical political philosophy, such as Madison's oft-cited claim that a "popular government without popular information or the means to acquire it is but a prologue to a farce, or a tragedy" and John Milton's cry for the "right to know, to utter and to argue freely." "It was not by chance," Pope suggested, "that John Milton had put first the liberty to know."[50]

But most claimed simply that the First Amendment itself implied the right to know, and that the founders had taken this for granted. Lawyer Wallace Parks argued that the founders were "focused on the then current English struggle for a free press which was concerned principally with licensing, taxing, and direct censorship"—and so "could not reasonably have been expected" to discuss access to information explicitly. Pope agreed, arguing that the drafters of the Bill of Rights were thinking of a smaller government than that of the 1950s, and "had spelled out freedom of the press while its twin, freedom of information, they had taken for granted." That was the only explanation, Pope believed, for neither the right to speak nor the right to access information was "self-sufficient"—"if government by and for the people requires the right to speak out and to publish, it requires implicitly the right to know."[51]

In many ways, these intellectual moves were identical to earlier efforts to modernize the First Amendment. But despite the formal similarity between their efforts and the arguments of John Dewey, Archibald MacLeish, the Newspaper Guild, or Felix Frankfurter, the FOI advocates generally believed that they were reestablishing the laissez-faire liberty of the First Amendment, not transcending it. Although they spoke of a positive right to information, they really wanted to roll back what they saw as the state's excessive interference in the marketplace of ideas. Classifying information, after all, required state action. So while it was possible to construct the right to information as a positive right, it was also possible to defend it as a negative right that needed to be protected from state interference.[52] The leading advocates of the right to know certainly saw matters this way, and they were generally critical of *any* government action in the field of the press. J. R. Wiggins, for instance, was opposed both to the NRA effort to regulate the press and the Eastland Commission's investigations of radical journalists. Harold Cross, too, was critical of New Deal efforts to reform the press.[53] And FOI advocates made little use of the language of the AP antitrust decision, in which the case for a First Amendment right to information was stated most explicitly—for that decision encouraged state intervention in newspaper economics.

So although Cross and his allies wanted recognition for a constitutional right to know, their broader political commitments to a laissez-faire vision of press freedom left them isolated. They did not identify the right to know with the other midcentury efforts to articulate a positive vision of press freedom; instead, they thought of themselves as resuscitating a long-dormant aspect of classical press freedom. As Cross put it in 1953, "The issue of the right of the people to know, by means of access to official information, as an essential part of those freedoms [of speech and press] has emerged from its Rip Van Winkle era." Thinking about the problem in those terms, however, forced them to acknowledge that there was little Supreme Court precedent on the issue. And there was little historical evidence to support their gloss on the founders' intent—the Constitutional Convention had met in secret, as did the Senate in its first years. So the case for a right to know had to be stated abstractly: a lack of current jurisprudence "constitutes no bar to recognition" in the future; "the language of the First Amendment was broad enough to embrace" such a right.[54] Those arguments had some rhetorical power, but ultimately the FOI advocates could not embed a right of access within First Amendment jurisprudence.

* * *

Instead, their most significant efforts to counteract the rise of secrecy were legislative. "The time is ripe," Cross declared in 1953, "for an end to ineffectual sputtering about executive refusals of access to official records and for Congress to begin exercising effectually its function to legislate freedom of information for itself, the public, and the press." In what would prove to be the most influential sections of his book, Cross identified two pieces of legislation in need of amendment: the hitherto obscure Housekeeping Statute of 1789, and the Administrative Procedure Act (APA) of 1946. After considerable effort, the FOI movement, working with the Moss Committee, revised both pieces of law—the Housekeeping law in 1958, the APA by the first FOIA in 1966.[55]

The trajectory of the Housekeeping amendment foreshadowed, in miniature, the fate of the FOI bill. The original 1789 statute gave the heads of executive departments the authority to regulate the "custody, use and preservation of the records, papers and property appertaining to it." Cross discovered that the statute, apparently intended to allow for the storage and safekeeping of public records, was increasingly cited as statutory authority to deny access to government records. FOI advocates believed it was the "root" and "fountainhead" of secrecy. "Our feelings about it," James Pope announced giddily in 1951, "are not unlike those of a doctor who has been observing the ravages of some disease, and finally identifies the germ." Despite the opposition of executive agencies, congressional allies of the FOI movement successfully passed a simple one-sentence amendment to clarify that the statute did "not authorize withholding information from the public or limiting the availability of records to the public." But in August 1958, Eisenhower issued a signing statement reiterating that the bill did not alter the constitutional right of executive privilege. FOI advocates soon admitted that the "bill has accomplished precious little, if anything." Government agencies made no changes to their information policies. They simply stopped citing the housekeeping statute as authority to withhold information and, following the logic of Eisenhower's signing statement, fell back on general claims of executive privilege.[56]

Efforts to amend the APA took longer, and had more lasting consequences. The APA, intended to tame and standardize the proliferation of executive agencies in the late New Deal, had a number of provisions intended to improve transparency. But it had become clear that these provisions were so riddled with exemptions that they facilitated secrecy instead. The APA exempted agencies from publishing any information related "solely to the internal management of an agency" or any information concerning "any function of the U.S. requiring secrecy in the public interest." Although the APA required every matter of official record to be made available, it exempted information "held confidential for good cause" and guaranteed a right of access only to "persons properly and directly concerned" with the matter at hand. It was easy to find "good cause" to keep a record secret and the exemption for records relating to "internal management" appeared almost open-ended. In 1961, for instance, the secretary of the navy ruled that telephone directories fell into this category, and could thus be withheld from the public. And the APA provided no remedy for the wrongful withholding of information from citizens—no review process, no appeals process, and no sanctions for official misconduct. Cross was not alone when he declared the public information provisions of the APA to be an "abject failure."[57]

The FOI bill amended the APA in three important ways. First, it allowed all citizens to request access to information, without a need to show "standing." Second, it allowed citizens to appeal to the courts if access to information was withheld, which provided an enforcement mechanism for the public for the first time. And third, whereas the APA's exemptions had been broad, the FOIA created a general presumption of access with specific, and theoretically narrow, exemptions. Cross had originally argued that the act should include only one exemption: material specifically exempted by statute. The 1958 draft bill added to that exemptions for material that was "required to be kept secret in the protection of the national security" and any information that would invade personal privacy. By the time the act was passed, there were nine exemptions to disclosure, including exemptions for trade secrets, intra-agency or interagency memoranda, personnel files, investigatory files, information related to operating and condition reports of financial institutions, and information about oil findings.[58] With each additional exemption, the bill deferred further to the autonomy of government administrators.

Executive opposition to the bill made it easy to water down the language of the exemptions. LBJ's press secretary Bill Moyers later recalled that LBJ "hated the very idea of the Freedom of Information Act." In 1965, it was reported that the president had told House leaders to "scrap" it. Legislative advisors within the administration believed the proposed bill to be an unconstitutional interference with executive branch discretion, a violation of the separation of powers, and an imposition of severe administrative burdens on the heads of the departments and agencies. Agency heads complained that it substituted a "simple, self-executing word formula" for their subtle judgments about what information it was proper to disclose. In March 1964, when a version of the FOI bill passed unanimously through his Senate subcommittee, Edward Long declared, "We should not kid ourselves about the legislation's prospects. There is intense opposition to the bill from virtually every government agency in Washington."[59]

For years, that opposition was enough to ensure that the bill floundered in Congress. But as the public mood began to fixate on the credibility gap and turn against LBJ's secretive administration, pressure began to mount for passage of the act. By February 1965, more than twenty-five members of Congress, from both parties, were sponsoring FOI legislation. Opposition to the bill was becoming politically problematic—Republicans, including a thirty-three-year-old Donald Rumsfeld, began to criticize the administration for its lack of transparency. At the end of 1965, Bill Moyers advised the White House that opposing the bill was a "potential time bomb."[60]

Members of the administration became increasingly inventive as they sought to blunt the bill without putting themselves in what White House counsel Lee C. White called "the awkward position of opposing freedom of information." The Justice Department tried to work with John Moss to redraft the bill. But he would not concede to their changes, for they were so antithetical to transparency that he thought it better to have no bill at all. So the Justice Department made a different offer: Moss could keep the bill as it was, and LBJ would not veto it, but Justice would write the House Report that explained the legislative intent behind the bill. Moss agreed, and on June 21, the bill was quickly passed through Congress, under rules that allowed no more than forty minutes of debate. Compared with the earlier Senate report, the House report weakened the philosophy of the bill and expanded the scope of its exemptions, making it more palatable to the agencies—the National Labor Relations Board (NLRB), for instance, declared that their opposition to the bill "subsided to some extent with the issuance of the House Report." But relying on the report was something of a long shot—as the Department of Defense pointed out, "some of the interpretations by the House Committee find little support in the plain language of the act." So the Department of Defense suggested attaching a signing statement to clarify the limits of the act, as did a number of other agencies. On July 1, LBJ was informed that although the agencies "have been concerned about this bill for years," they "have come around to the view that they can live with it. The agencies are hoping that your signing statement, together with the House Report, will guide the interpretation of the statutory language."[61]

As the bill sat awaiting the president's signature, FOI advocates also hoped for a politically significant signing statement, and urged LBJ to hold a public signing ceremony. Moss argued that if LBJ made an "affirmative" speech on freedom of information, it would help to counter the credibility gap. But such entreaties fell on deaf ears.[62] LBJ signed the bill without ceremony on July 4, the last day before a pocket veto would have kicked in, and his short signing statement, as the agencies had hoped, focused less on access to information than on the exemptions in the bill. Although the opening and closing paragraphs of the statement included some pabulum about "the people's right to know," the bulk of the statement reiterated the instances in which information could not be disclosed: "as long as threats to peace exist, there must be military secrets"; citizens need to be able to confide in their government without fear of being identified; personnel files must be "protected from disclosure"; "officials within government must be able to communicate with one another fully and frankly without publicity." Crucially, LBJ also affirmed his constitutional right to exercise executive privilege: "This bill in no way impairs the president's power under our constitution to provide for confidentiality when the national interest so requires." In fact, LBJ seems to have rewritten the statement himself to further emphasize the need for secrecy. Whereas an early Department of Justice draft of the speech declared that "democracy works best when the people know what their government is doing," LBJ's final version declared only that "democracy works best when the people have all the information that the security of the nation permits."[63]

The final act was, at best, a dubious achievement. The meaning and scope of the nine exemptions was unclear. Frank Wozencraft, head of the Office of Legal Counsel, thought their language so "inartistic" that "it is very difficult to tell what some of them mean." Given the long-standing hostility of the agencies to the bill, it was inevitable that enforcing the act would require further political struggle, and multiple trips to the courtroom.[64] When it came to the foundational question of access to national security information, the act already conceded the central issue by exempting information "specifically required by Executive Order to be kept secret in the interest of the national defense or foreign policy." Such an exemption had been uncontroversial. "None of us," Pope had declared in 1957, "wants security information—genuine security information—revealed." But the exemption opened a potentially large loophole that extended well beyond "genuine security information" and could cover anything that an administration believed to be in the interests of its foreign policy. On only one previous occasion, in 1950's McCarran Act amendment to the Espionage Act, had Congress acknowledged the authority of the president to issue classification orders.[65] But that had come before the creation of the modern classification regime. In 1966, in its *Freedom of Information* Act, Congress did not challenge the legitimacy of the classification system, but acknowledged it.

And on a more foundational level, the act established no general right of access to information. It was a specific piece of legislation, one that created a new mechanism to release prescribed sorts of information from executive agencies. It didn't cover Congress. And it was subject to the whims of future administrations. During JFK's presidency, Assistant Secretary of Defense Arthur Sylvester had told Pierre Salinger that "the citizen's desire to know and be informed is legitimate, but not a constitutional right superior to the security of the United States."[66] After FOIA, there was still no constitutional right to know that could be pitted against the executive right to protect national security.

* * *

Seen in isolation, the passage of the nation's first FOI law seems like an unprecedented breakthrough for transparency. In reality, it was a weak ameliorative to unprecedented levels of secrecy. What is truly significant about FOIA is the fact that American citizens felt they needed such a law for the first time. For the rise of secrecy had been a defining feature of America's Cold War order. Cold War fears of subversion heightened the demand for information security; anticommunist demands for access to executive documents helped legitimize the growth of executive privilege; the desire to secure the nation's secrets produced the excesses of McCarthyism; and the press corps became incorporated in the militaristic consensus of Cold War Washington. It was no accident that the Cold War and the culture of secrecy bloomed together.

But the relatively late development of America's secrecy regime should also be seen as a crucial moment in a broader historical transformation. As First Amendment rights grew in stature, government censorship shifted its logic, and began to focus on the regulation of information, not publication; on the regulation of secrets, not speech. By the late 1960s, American press freedom was marked by deep paradox. A formally free press faced new challenges in accessing basic political information. The drying up of official channels of information had heightened press dependency on unofficial networks of leaks, gossip, and rumor. And a press denied guaranteed access to political news had drawn ever closer to power. "One sometimes has the despairing feeling," journalist Karl Meyer confessed, "that no country has more freedom of the press and uses it less."[67] And then, in 1968, Richard Nixon ascended to the White House.

8

Leaks, Mergers, and Nixon's Assault on the News

In 1972, Tom Wicker declared that the Nixon administration had been "less sensitive to First Amendment rights than any since that of John Adams." He could cite a long list of sins against the press: the attempted suppression of the Pentagon Papers, the issuance of subpoenas to reporters to force them to reveal their confidential sources, the escalation of secrecy in the "most 'closed' administration of modern times," and Vice President Spiro Agnew's much-publicized speeches assaulting the news media. Nixon's assault on press freedom seemed almost preordained, for Nixon's relationship with the media had a strong whiff of the classical tragedy about it. Some of Nixon's greatest successes could be attributed to his manipulation of the news media—the Checkers speech in 1952, the creation of the "New Nixon" image that resuscitated his career and took him to the White House in 1968. But the news media had also unmade Nixon, on more than one occasion, and the sensitive president never forgot it. In 1962, after a failed effort to run for governor of California, Nixon lashed out at a press that he believed had unfairly persecuted him: "For sixteen years, ever since the Hiss case, you've had a lot of fun. . . . Just think of how much you're going to be missing. You won't have Nixon to kick around anymore because gentlemen, this is my last press conference."[1] Nixon returned to politics, of course, which gave the press further opportunity to kick him around—and eventually, after Watergate, an opportunity to help kick him out of office.

But tempting as it is to treat the clash between Nixon and the press as a personal drama, the real story is more complicated. To begin with, as

Tom Wicker noted, the press overwhelmingly supported Nixon's 1972 reelection bid. In general, that could be attributed to the ongoing consolidation of the newspaper industry and the pro-business conservatism of the corporations that dominated the press. The Nixon administration had helped support the business interests of the press in a more specific way as well. In 1970, it had passed a Newspaper Preservation Act that gave newspapers an exemption from antitrust law and allowed them to merge in new ways. The act freed the press from a form of state regulation, but gave the public no guarantees it would be able to rely on a diverse newspaper market to provide them with a variety of political information.

In other ways, too, the clashes between the Nixon administration and the press entrenched the trends of the previous decades. In both the Pentagon Papers affair and the Watergate cover-up, the Nixon administration took unprecedented steps to try to control the flow of information to the public. In neither case was it successful, and the press exercised new rights to publish information hostile to the interests of the administration. But in both cases, the press had relied on exceptional government leaks to get that information. And the backlash against Nixon produced no new rights to access information held by the state. The Pentagon Papers and Watergate moments testified both to the editorial independence of the press and to its practical dependence on leaks from government sources.

In all, the press emerged from the Nixon years with an unprecedented freedom from direct government regulation: it had both a highly protected right to publish what it wanted and a newly protected right to free enterprise in an unregulated media market. The period saw a flourishing of new kinds of journalistic expression. The stars of the period were the New Journalists, who styled themselves as countercultural artists, reinventing press freedom for the revolutionary 1960s. But while the press had new rights to act according to its own self-interest in matters of both business and expression, public rights to access information remained unprotected in law, and faced the ongoing challenges of accelerating press consolidation and entrenched state secrecy. The negative vision of laissez-faire press freedom had never been more highly protected, but ideas about positive rights to the news had withered away.

* * *

During the 1960s, the steady march of newspaper consolidation continued. The overall number of newspapers still held steady—as of 1968, there were 1,749 daily papers in the country, the same number that there had been in 1945. But leading papers in urban centers continued to go under. When the liberal republican *New York Herald Tribune* went out of business in the mid-1960s, the *New York Times* was the last remaining broadsheet in the city. Other urban papers, too, were dying: the *Pittsburgh Sun-Telegraph*, the *Detroit Times*, the *Houston Press*, and others.[2]

The remaining monopoly papers, though, were turning lavish profits. Advertising revenue continued to grow, while publishers used new technologies to lower production costs. Computerized photo-compositing, for instance, was more efficient than the old linotype machines. It also deskilled and automated the job of printing, which helped to break the printing unions and lower labor costs (though only after considerable labor strife, such as the four-month New York newspaper strike of 1962–1963). But with profitability came unexpected costs. The modernization of newspaper plants required new infusions of capital, and the rising value of newspapers imposed high estate taxes on newspaper families seeking to pass a paper to an heir.[3]

So the old family papers either were sold or went public. Before 1967, almost no newspaper stock was traded publicly; by the mid-1970s, thirteen companies, representing 20 percent of national circulation, were listed on the stock exchange. Among them were the *New York Times*, the *Washington Post*, and the Gannett, Knight, and Ridder chains.[4] The papers were increasingly run according to modern management techniques. Modern newspaper owners were not political figures like Hearst but corporate executives like S. I. Newhouse, fixated on returns, profit, and growth. Chains, long a feature of the newspaper industry, grew exponentially. Between 1960 and 1980, 587 papers were sold to newspaper chains. In 1940, only 17 percent of the nation's papers were part of a chain; by 1970, over 50 percent were.[5]

Until the mid-1960s, there was no political effort to respond to the decline of competition in the industry. In 1963, the House Antitrust Subcommittee held a few days of hearings into newspaper concentration, but they were quickly suspended and had no impact—the hearings were not even published. And the Justice Department, continuing to shy away from the tricky AP precedent, made little effort to regulate the consolidation of the industry. At times, it even seemed to encourage it. In 1962, the Chandler and Hearst companies came to an agreement to end competition in the Los Angeles newspaper market: Hearst shut its morning paper, the Chandlers shut their afternoon paper, and both then had a monopoly market. (Given the future dominance of the morning market, the deal would turn out to be a coup for the Chandlers.) But although members of the Antitrust Division thought the deal a "blatant . . . case of willful violation of the antitrust laws," they took no action. A Hearst representative had cleared the deal with higher ups in the Justice Department before its consummation.[6]

In January 1965, however, the Justice Department brought antitrust charges against two Tucson papers, the *Citizen* and the *Star,* which had pooled profits and jointly set subscription and advertising rates in what was called a Joint Operating Agreement (JOA). JOAs existed in over twenty cities and dated back to 1933, but their legality had never been tested in court. The Tucson agreement provided the Justice Department with an ideal case, for in 1965 the *Citizen* had bought out the *Star,* creating traditional antitrust questions that could be pursued alongside the JOA issue. And the consolidation of the newspaper industry in the 1960s called for new antitrust action, because it threatened a new wave of highly visible JOAs in major markets. In San Francisco, for instance, Hearst's *Examiner* was joining with the independent *Chronicle.* Antitrust experts in the Justice Department hoped the Tucson case would produce a precedent that "could result in the widespread renewal of newspaper competition."[7]

The Justice Department won the case, and its victory was upheld by the Supreme Court. The Tucson papers had argued that they were exempted from antitrust laws because they were "failing companies," but the courts found that this seldom-used defense did not apply in the case because the papers had not exhausted all other business strategies before merging (the exemption allowed merger only if failure was so inevitable that competition could not be preserved any other way). While the outcome might have portended more robust antitrust action, it was actually a narrow decision. The papers were ordered to sever their advertising and circulation departments, but the final consent decree allowed the continuation of the JOA, the combination of mechanical facilities and business departments, and the publication of a joint Sunday edition.[8]

Even this moderate approach to antitrust action was not to be. As the Tucson matter was proceeding through the courts, Congress was moving to protect newspaper combinations from antitrust prosecution. In March 1967, Arizona senator Carl Hayden introduced a bill that would formally exempt "failing newspapers" from antitrust laws. The bill defined failure loosely, and it grandfathered in all existing JOAs and opened the door to future mergers. Its ostensible purpose was to advance "the public interest of maintaining a newspaper press editorially and reportorially independent and competitive in all parts of the U.S."[9]

It was a controversial piece of legislation. Publishers of chain and large metropolitan papers generally supported it. (Arthur Hanson, Elisha's son, had inherited the family business and testified for the bill on behalf of ANPA.) Proponents of the bill said that the exemption was necessary to maintain newspaper diversity when smaller papers were going out of business. As Jack R. Howard of the Scripps-Howard chain put it, to apply antitrust laws to JOAs "would be to ignore and subvert what seems to me to be the very purpose of such laws by pronouncing the death sentence on a failing newspaper." Opponents of the bill—especially the Newspaper Guild, smaller publishers, and the Department of Justice—argued that antitrust laws had sufficient flexibility to allow JOAs where needed, and that a blanket exemption would erode competition by legitimizing a new round of mergers. Leading the congressional charge against the bill was Philip Hart, who thought the proposed exemption nothing more than the granting of "special favors" to newspaper publishers and the offer of a "shelter . . . to reap monopoly profits." On one occasion, he suggested it could be called the "millionaire-crybabies-publishers' bill." As debate dragged on into the Nixon years, even the new administration was divided. The FTC and the Justice Department opposed the bill because it "would mean less, not more competition," while the Commerce Department favored it to preserve the "independence of the press and diversity of reporting."[10]

But by the middle of 1969, momentum was building for the passage of the bill, newly re-titled the Newspaper Preservation Act. The Supreme Court's decision against the Tucson papers was widely misrepresented as a sweeping decision against all JOAs—one that would threaten even the entirely uncontroversial combination of printing plants. Two days after the decision was handed down, twenty-five senators reintroduced the bill in the Senate; by May, over one hundred representatives were sponsoring the bill in the House. Behind the scenes, the newspaper industry exercised its political clout, conducting what one reporter called "some of the most intensive lobbying ever seen on Capitol Hill," comparable only to the newspaper industry's lobbying against the NRA in the 1930s. "Not many senators," complained Newspaper Guild member Jim Cesnik, "have any great desire to take on big publishers in public." In private correspondence with Richard Nixon, Richard Berlin of the Hearst papers made it clear how important the bill was to the publishers and how important the publishers were to a president eager for reelection in 1972. By May, Emmanuel Celler was referring to an "avalanche of opinion in favor of the bill." The bill passed easily through Congress, and Nixon signed it into law at the end of July. A quarter of a century after the AP case, newspapers finally had their antitrust exemption.[11]

In the end, the press would make little use of its newfound right to form JOAs—only eight were created as a result of the act. Amid the accelerating consolidation of the industry, they were not a desirable option. They took a long time to create, during which time one had to lose money. They were no guarantee of success; a number of papers collapsed even while in a JOA. And there were ever fewer places that even had competitive papers that could enter into a JOA, let alone two papers that were willing to bind themselves to a rival in a long-term contract.[12]

The real significance of the 1970 act was symbolic—it abandoned even the pretense of antitrust regulation in the newspaper industry. The law was a tangle of contradictions, united only by its deference to the economic prerogatives of the newspaper industry. To preserve diversity, it sanctioned new forms of monopoly. The 1970s saw some constitutional challenges on this front, as smaller papers argued that their right to compete was undermined by the existence of a JOA in their market. But the arguments went nowhere, as courts found that the Newspaper Preservation Act (NPA) was a simple adjustment in the antitrust laws, not a form of state interference in the press. In fact, the law did open the door to new forms of government regulation. To qualify for the failing newspaper exemption, papers had to be approved by the attorney general. In 1988, there were rumors that the *Detroit Free Press* had ordered its cartoonists to lay off the attorney general while the paper's JOA application was being considered.[13]

In any case, during the 1970s and 1980s, newspaper diversity continued to decline. Once-powerful newspapers closed their doors: the *Philadelphia Bulletin,* the *Washington Star,* and the *Cleveland Press.* By 1986, only twenty-eight American cities still had competing daily papers, and the remaining monopoly papers were cogs in ever-expanding chains. By the mid-1980s, the ten largest chains controlled 45 percent of the nation's circulation. As recently as 1960, there had been two independently owned papers for every one paper in a chain; a quarter of a century later, that ratio had been reversed.[14]

There was no antitrust response. Of the forty-five antitrust actions brought in the newspaper field in the 1980s, only one was brought by the

Department of Justice. The rest were brought by private interests, particularly advertisers complaining about rate discrimination. The interests of the reader in a diverse newspaper market had never found a legal grounding in antitrust law, and simply fell by the wayside as the corporate economics of the 1980s pushed ever onward.[15]

* * *

In the late 1960s, there was a final effort to legally protect the public interest in a diverse press. In 1967, George Washington law professor Jerome Barron argued, in familiar terms, that the First Amendment theory of a marketplace of ideas was "romantic" and out of date. Because the ability to print a newspaper was now held by such a restricted class, Barron argued that there should be a legally enforceable right of "access to the press" that would allow citizens to force their voices into the pages of the newspaper. (He called it a "twentieth century interpretation of the First Amendment which will impose an affirmative responsibility on the monopoly newspaper to act as a sounding board for new ideas and old grievances.") In the early 1970s, Barron took this argument to the Supreme Court when he represented a political candidate who had been editorially attacked by the *Miami Herald.* The candidate claimed a right to publish a rebuttal to the charges based on an obscure clause in the 1913 Florida Electoral Code. The *Herald,* predictably, argued that such a law violated its First Amendment freedom to publish without government interference. But the Florida Supreme Court, drawing on the precedent of the AP decision, argued that a right of reply enhanced "freedom of the press in its true meaning—that is, the right of the reader to the whole story rather than half of it." Barron's victory was short-lived. On appeal, the U.S. Supreme Court unanimously held the right of reply law to be unconstitutional. Reiterating the logic of the Hutchins Commission, and quoting from the work of Zechariah Chafee, Chief Justice Burger opined that "a responsible press is an undoubtedly desirable goal, but press responsibility is not mandated by the constitution and like many other virtues it cannot be legislated." The classical understanding of press freedom continued to hold sway: the interests of the reader were sacrificed to protect the First Amendment rights of the publisher.[16]

In the 1980s, this laissez-faire vision of the First Amendment would be extended to the broadcast media. Since World War II, broadcast media had been more highly regulated than the press. As the Supreme Court repeatedly held throughout the period, the limited nature of the spectrum meant that a laissez-faire attitude to speech rights was inappropriate to broadcasting: there were national caps on the number of radio and TV stations that an individual could own, the granting of licenses to broadcast turned on an assessment of public responsibility, and, in 1969, the Supreme Court had unanimously upheld the constitutionality of a right of access to broadcast media. There were also limits on cross-media ownership. In 1978, a unanimous Supreme Court had dismissed newspaper industry arguments that a new ban on newspaper-broadcast partnerships violated their First Amendment rights and harmed economic solvency in tough times. Broadcasting, the court asserted, remained a privilege and not a right. But in the 1980s and 1990s, arguments first developed by the newspaper industry succeeded in deregulating broadcast media. In the first place, with the rise of cable and digital media, the technological limitations of the spectrum disappeared, and with them went the argument for distinguishing broadcast media from the laissez-faire vision of speech rights that had protected the press from economic regulation since the New Deal. Second, media lobbyists argued that radio stations were failing enterprises. Like the proponents of the NPA in the 1960s, the lobbyists argued that new forms of merger and acquisition were necessary to preserve even a modicum of media diversity. In the increasingly deregulated media economy at the end of the twentieth century, newspaper chains would become parts of vast media enterprises.[17]

* * *

Since the 1930s, proponents of the laissez-faire vision of press freedom had asserted that a financially strong and independent press was foundational to a robust and critical press. With financial growth, the argument ran, came resources for reporting, and with financial independence came an ability to confidently criticize the government. (Publisher John Cowles expressed the point most bluntly in 1951. "Fewer newspapers," he declared, "means better newspapers.") The media monoliths that were emerging in the 1970s justified their contribution to press freedom by suggesting they now had the requisite size and financial strength to act as a counterweight to the state.[18] How successful, then, was the press in combating the secretive state that had emerged since World War II?

There were reasons to think that the press was asserting its independence from the state in new ways. On June 13, 1971, the *New York Times* carried a front-page article based on a hitherto secret official history of the war in Vietnam. The "Pentagon Papers" had been prepared within the Defense Department, and in 7,000 pages, they documented the buildup of the war behind the veil of official denial. They were uniformly classified "Top Secret," and only fifteen copies of them were produced. One of the copies was read by Daniel Ellsberg, a Defense Department employee. Ellsberg had been a consummate Cold War insider—Harvard educated, a former Marine, an academic specialist in game theory and geopolitical strategy. But he had become disillusioned with the war, begun to move in antiwar circles, and decided that leaking the papers "might, just might, forestall the secretly prepared and threatened escalation" of the war. At first Ellsberg tried to convince war skeptics in Congress to read them into the public record while protected by congressional immunity. When that failed, Ellsberg turned to *New York Times* journalist Neil Sheehan, whom he had met in Vietnam and who had recently established his antiwar bona fides in a lengthy review of thirty-three books on the war. After considerable internal debate, the paper began publication of articles based on the leaked documents in June 1971.[19]

For a very brief moment, it seemed there might be no government response, for Nixon hoped that the release of such historical documents would discredit only the Democrats. But Henry Kissinger argued that a reputation for leaks would scuttle secret negotiations with the Chinese, and Nixon quickly decided to block further publication of the papers. On Monday, June 14, William Rehnquist in the Office of Legal Counsel reviewed the *Near v. Minnesota* decision from 1931, and prepared a memo arguing that the prior restraint of newspaper stories could be justified when their publication harmed national security. The next day, a district court judge temporarily enjoined the *New York Times* from publishing material from the papers while the matter worked its way through the courts. But the government was losing control of the situation. Ellsberg leaked the papers to the *Washington Post,* which began publishing them on June 18; a government effort to enjoin the *Post* was denied in court. And Ellsberg had gone into hiding and begun leaking the reports to a wide variety of newspapers. Given the confusion, both the *New York Times* and the government appealed to the Supreme Court.[20]

Less than two weeks after the first publication of the papers, the Supreme Court heard arguments about the matter. The importance of the case justified the unusual urgency. The temporary injunction of the *Times* marked the first use of prior restraint in the history of the federal government. And the case also promised to force the long-awaited judicial clarification of the relationship between the classification system and the public right to know. At first, sweeping arguments were offered to the lower courts. Justice Department lawyers generally rested their case for suppression on the simple fact of classification. They did not try to show particular harms that would follow from particular leaks of information, but argued that courts should simply defer to executive judgments about what material should be held secret. And civil liberties groups argued in amicus briefs that the public had a right to know even classified material. In one brief, the National Emergency Civil Liberties Committee, representing Noam Chomsky, Howard Zinn, Carl Schorske, and others, argued "that the right of a free press guaranteed by the First Amendment is a right not only of the publisher but also of those who would read the material published." They challenged the constitutionality of both the Espionage Act and the Eisenhower executive order establishing the classification system.[21]

The arguments presented to the Supreme Court were narrower than either of these two broad positions. Government failure in the lower courts, combined with the extra time to review the documents, led Solicitor-General Erwin Griswold to abandon the effort to rely simply on the fact of classification to justify suppression. Instead he argued that prior restraint of this particular information was necessary to prevent harm to the nation—he focused particularly on vague but potentially grave harms to diplomatic relations and future intelligence gathering. The lawyer for the *New York Times,* constitutional scholar Alexander Bickel, conceded that classification and even some forms of prior restraint were constitutional, but insisted that the government had to meet a high bar of proof: it had to show that harm would be "direct and immediate and visible" as well as "grave." It fell to the court to decide which of these standards was required to justify prior restraint.[22]

When the justices handed down their decision, just four days later, a majority found that the newspapers had the right to publish the papers because the government had not met the burden of proof to justify restraint. But the six-to-three decision, outlined in a bland and terse per curiam opinion, was far from straightforward. The judges had issued nine individual opinions, and agreed on very little. In part this was a product of the speed of the process, which prevented discussion, compromise, and redrafting. But it also reflected ongoing confusion about the relationship between the classification scheme and the First Amendment as well as deep uncertainty about how the law should manage the tension between national security and press freedom.

Five of the justices resolved that tension by straightforwardly prioritizing either First Amendment rights or the national security prerogatives of the state. First Amendment absolutists Hugo Black and William Douglas argued simply that prior restraint was unacceptable under all circumstances. In what proved to be his final decision, the aging Black declared that any prior censorship would "make a shambles of the First Amendment" and undermine the constitutional duty of the press to "bare the secrets of the government and inform the people." On the other side of the spectrum, Justice Harlan and Justice Blackmun asserted in dissenting opinions that the executive had wide discretion in the field of foreign affairs, and that First Amendment claims had little purchase on the classification system—Harlan favored judicial deference to executive decisions about what should be kept secret. Although Chief Justice Burger refused to decide on the merits of the case as a protest against its "unseemly" and "frenetic haste," he was sympathetic to government arguments and referred dismissively to the *New York Times'* claims of an "alleged 'right to know.' "[23]

That left a rump of four judges to determine the matter. In an idiosyncratic opinion, Thurgood Marshall decided for the press on the grounds that there was no statutory authority to justify prior restraint. So the outcome came down to the opinions of Justices White, Stewart, and Brennan. All three decided that the government had not met the necessary standard of harm to justify a prior restraint of the press. Glossing the *Near* decision, Brennan argued "that publication must inevitably, directly, and immediately cause the occurrence of an event kindred to imperiling the safety of a transport already at sea" to justify even a temporary injunction. Stewart asserted that disclosure would have to "surely result in direct, immediate, and irreparable damage to our Nation or its people" to justify a prior restraint.[24]

In the short term, the decision freed the *Times* and the *Post* to resume publication of the articles. Large portions of the Pentagon Papers were soon published in three different book editions. In the longer term, Stewart, White, and Brennan's establishment of such a high burden of proof essentially ended the viability of prior restraint as a mechanism for securing secrets. On only one subsequent occasion, when the *Progressive* attempted to publish an article outlining the science of the H-bomb, did the state even attempt to enjoin the publication of national security information.

Even that effort was soon dropped, and the *Progressive* published its article in November 1979.[25]

But although the decision seemed a straightforward victory for the press's right to publish without government interference, an important uncertainty remained. The majority of the justices had found that prior restraint, a particularly objectionable form of censorship, was unjustified. But were the papers guilty of violating the Espionage Act? Justices White and Stewart, who had protected the press from prior restraint, practically encouraged the state to pursue a criminal prosecution. Stewart declared that there were laws on the books to protect the classification system, and that "several of them are of very colorable relevance to the apparent circumstances of these cases." In passages that won praise from Burger, White went further, quoting from the 1941 *Gorin* decision and vast sections of the Espionage Act to outline a theory of criminal liability for publishing state secrets. "Failure by the government to justify prior restraints," he intoned, "does not measure its constitutional entitlement to a conviction for criminal publication. That the government mistakenly chose to proceed by injunction does not mean that it could not successfully proceed in another way."[26]

One can only wonder what the decision would have been had the government initiated an Espionage Act prosecution in the first place. And even after initial victory, it remained entirely unclear whether the *Post* and *Times,* having been freed to publish the Pentagon Papers, would now face criminal prosecution for that act. In April 1972, the deputy assistant attorney general for internal security, Kevin Maroney, warned a meeting of newspaper editors that publication of classified documents would be met with Espionage Act prosecutions.[27]

In the end, there were no prosecutions, and the case was hailed as a great victory for freedom of the press. The *Boston Globe* declared the decision "a beautiful day for America" and "as great in many ways as the acquittal of John Peter Zenger in 1735." What stayed the hand of the Justice Department remains unclear, though it seems probable that prosecuting the press in an election year was politically unpalatable. And a decision to prosecute the press to protect state secrets would have bucked the logic of post–World War II classification. The Pentagon Papers decision capped the retreat of censorship from the sphere of publication. In fact, it was entirely appropriate that those seeking to block publication of the papers continued to invoke the responsibilities of the press to preserve national security. In an internal memo, Nixon criticized the *New*

York Times for "irresponsibility and recklessness in deliberately printing classified documents without regard to the national interest." Justice Blackmun, too, lectured the press on its nationalist obligations: "I strongly urge and sincerely hope that these two newspapers will be fully aware of their ultimate responsibilities to the United States of America."[28] But such talk of responsibility was a holdover from World War II and the early Cold War. It seemed antidemocratic and repressive in the context of the early 1970s. After the Pentagon Papers decision, the press would be free to publish state secrets and to act as irresponsibly as it desired.

If freedom to publish represented one half of the logic of classification, the other side of the coin was the policing of government employees who leaked information. In 1971, Daniel Ellsberg and fellow RAND employee-turned-whistleblower Anthony Russo were indicted on numerous charges of stealing government documents and violating the Espionage Act. But the Nixon administration was not content to wait on the slow progress of the justice system. In July, Nixon created a small group within the White House to solve the problem of leaks. The group was soon known as the plumbers, and on September 3, 1971, they broke into the office of Ellsberg's psychiatrist in an effort to find incriminating evidence about the leaker. Eighteen months later, after this break-in as well as other illegal government activities came to light during the Watergate scandal, all charges against Ellsberg and Russo were dismissed.[29]

In the short term, the result was a clear victory for Ellsberg and Russo, and a clear defeat for the Nixon administration. But the deeper issues of the case had not been resolved: Was it legal for government employees to leak classified documents to the press? Under what circumstances? How could one square the Espionage Act's penalties for disclosure with First Amendment rights? As the *Boston Globe* astutely put it the day after the charges were dropped, the outcome was a "triumph for our system of justice," but "was it also a victory for the people's right to know? This question, going to the heart of the case, remains to be answered." It is impossible to know how the matter would have ended if the Nixon administration had suppressed its worst inclinations and allowed the trial to play out. In the immediate aftermath of the dismissal, there were reports that a majority of the jurors were intending to decide for the defendants. If that decision had survived what would have been a drawn-out process, it might have done much to scuttle the Espionage Act.[30] On the other hand, the logic of Espionage Act and First Amendment jurisprudence since World War II suggested that the corollary to the Supreme Court's decision to allow the publication of the papers was the state's right to prosecute leakers. Because of the plumbers, no final decision was reached, and the drama of the Pentagon Papers further muddied the jurisprudence of the Espionage Act. In the immediate case, the right of the public to know state secrets was protected, and Ellsberg and Russo went free, but the underlying theory of the law was left, again, in limbo.

* * *

In the medium term, the creation of the plumbers during the Pentagon Papers affair was a crucial turning point in the trajectory of modern American political history. On June 17, 1972, five of these plumbers broke into Democratic Party headquarters at the Watergate in DC. Exactly what they were up to remains something of a mystery, but they were easily discovered by a night security guard and arrested in the early hours of the morning.[31] The Nixon administration's concern with leaks begat the plumbers. The plumbers' break-in at the Watergate begat a political mystery that would ultimately, two years later, end the Nixon administration. The press's role in that process has been condensed into a myth about the triumph of the adversarial press; the dethroning of Nixon has become an object lesson in the freedom of America's press from state control. In reality, the press played a far more ambiguous role in uncovering Watergate.

To begin with, much of the press ignored the story. Of the 433 Washington correspondents in 1972, only about fifteen of them worked full-time on the Watergate story in its first five months, and a number of them did so only briefly. Most early coverage fixated on the humorous side of the bungled break-in, dubbing it the "Watergate caper." Between the break-in and the election, the DC press corps asked Nixon only three questions about the matter. He fielded the first with textbook legalese—"The White House has had no involvement in this particular incident"—and was asked no follow-up questions. Cynical and disinterested, the press corps didn't pursue the issue; their job was just to attend the briefings. As late as October 1972, a Gallup Poll revealed that 48 percent of the public was unfamiliar with the term "Watergate."[32]

A slightly more accurate version of the Watergate myth attributes the fall of Nixon to two young journalists on the *Washington Post,* Carl Bernstein and Bob Woodward, whose role was glamorized in the blockbuster book and film *All The President's Men.* (Warner Brothers marketed the film as the "story of the two young reporters who cracked the Watergate conspiracy . . . [and] solved the greatest detective story in American history.") The two certainly broke many important stories. On August 1, they were the first to connect the burglars to Nixon's reelection committee (CREEP) when they reported that a check from a Nixon fund-raiser had ended up in the Miami bank account of one of the burglars. And in a sequence of stories in September and October, the pair exposed a secret CREEP fund that was used to finance campaign "intelligence activities," including the Watergate break-in, as well as an array of dirty tricks intended to sabotage the Democratic presidential campaign.[33]

But other journalists also played important roles in breaking the story. On June 18, it was the AP that first identified that Watergate burglar James McCord worked for Nixon's reelection committee—the *Post* had identified him simply as a former CIA man. In mid-July, Woodward and Bernstein's reporting had stalled, and the story threatened to die: Bernstein had returned to the Virginia political beat and Woodward had gone on vacation. But on July 25, Walter Rugaber in the *New York Times* reported a number of telephone calls between the lead Watergate burglar and CREEP in the lead-up to the break-in. That story encouraged the *Post* to expand their efforts, which led to the breakthrough story on August 1.[34]

Other news organizations continued to advance the story throughout the fall. On October 15, *Time* magazine more conclusively established a link between a Nixon aide and a field operative; Woodward and Bernstein conceded that "*Time*'s story was better than the *Post*'s in some respects." The *Los Angeles Times,* trying to match the *Post*'s coverage despite the fact that they were on the other side of the country, gained the first exclusive interview with Alfred Baldwin, a former FBI agent who had assisted in the break-in—the story helped to personalize the scandal. In January 1973, Seymour Hersh, recently hired by the *New York Times* to improve its Watergate coverage, was the first to report that the burglars were being paid to keep quiet during their trial. *Time* had further details on the hush money a day later. The *Post,* having received a similar tip, had sat on the story.[35]

Neither the press as a whole nor Woodward and Bernstein alone were responsible for pushing the story. Rather, a small group of reporters covered the scandal. The group was united by the fact that all were able to cultivate official sources who would speak to them "off the record." Official channels of political news were blocked. "It took less than 48 hours," declared one *New York Times* reporter, "for the authorities to clamp a fairly tight lid on things. Much of the information that emerged afterward, even on the most pedestrian points, was unofficial or leaked by unnamed sources." An ability to cultivate leaks was thus the key to covering Watergate. *Time*'s reporting was handled by Sandy Smith, the veteran investigative reporter who had extensive contacts within the FBI and the Justice Department. The *New York Times*' early coverage of the Watergate affair, by contrast, was hamstrung because reporter Robert M. Smith, who had handled the Justice Department and FBI beats, had quit the paper to go to law school.[36]

The youthful Woodward and Bernstein were particularly adept at cultivating such insider sources. They were not typical DC correspondents, but they were networked into the important lower levels of the bureaucracy. *All the President's Men* is a remarkable catalogue of contacts with off-the-record sources: "The reporters checked regularly with a half-dozen persons in the Justice Department and FBI who were sometimes willing to confirm information"; "Bernstein made one of his regular calls to the former administration official." Bernstein made contact with a crucial source within CREEP because he noticed the name of "someone he had once met" on CREEP's payroll. Trying to work out whether he could trust an informant, Bernstein realized that he and the source had a "mutual acquaintance" who could vouch for the source. And their stories in the *Post* were littered with vague references to "sources close to the investigation" or "sources of varied political persuasions and at all levels of the investigation."[37]

The most crucial individual source in the story—Deep Throat—also developed out of the reporters' social networks. Nicknamed ironically after the popular porn movie because he provided information only on "deep background," Deep Throat was the highly secretive source that provided Woodward with important context, tips, and guidance throughout 1972. We now know that Deep Throat was Mark Felt, a career FBI agent who by the early 1970s had risen to the third-highest post in the agency. Felt had ambitions for the directorship, but when J. Edgar Hoover died, he was passed over in favor of a political appointment—Nixon installed Patrick Gray in an effort to bring the agency under White House control. Embittered, and apparently motivated to undermine Gray and protect FBI autonomy from the White House, Felt leaked information about the Watergate investigation to Woodward. Felt had befriended the younger Woodward, then in the navy, when they had met in a waiting room in the White House in the summer of 1969.[38]

In general, therefore, the press's coverage of Watergate revealed how dependent journalists had become on leaks from official sources. All of the newspaper stories were based largely on the confidential investigations of the FBI and federal prosecutors looking into the case. A March 1975 memo from within the FBI explained that "in essence" Woodward and Bernstein "were interviewing the same people we had interviewed but subsequent to our interviews and often after the interviewee had testified before the grand jury." Prosecutors had discovered the CREEP money trail by late June, a month before Woodward and Bernstein's breakthrough story on August 1. By the time Bernstein interviewed CREEP bookkeeper Judy Hoback, the FBI had already interviewed her several times. As Sandy Smith put it, "There's a myth that the press did all this, uncovered all the crimes. . . . It's bunk. The press didn't do it. People forget that the government was investigating all the time. In my material there was less than two percent that was truly original investigation. There was an investigation being carried out here. It may have been blocked, bent, botched or whatever, but it was proceeding. The government investigators found the stuff and gave us something to expose."[39]

Bringing the investigation to light was important, of course. But as journalists tried to replicate the findings of investigations through leaked pieces of information, they could not accurately depict the affair to the public. Mistakes crept in. At one point, Woodward and Bernstein incorrectly named three individuals as recipients of information gleaned from the Watergate bugs, tarnishing their names. In late October, they incorrectly reported that H. R. Haldeman, Nixon's chief of staff, had been named to a grand jury for campaign finance improprieties. And journalists, dependent on the agenda of the leaker, simply could not know what was not being leaked to them. Mark Felt, for instance, was aware of the White House's effort to use the CIA to stall the FBI's investigation.[40] But this fact, which was what ultimately brought down Nixon, would not become public for almost two years.

In fact, the press was unable to piece the story together before Nixon's easy reelection in November. By late October, *Post* editor Barry Sussman acknowledged, the paper "ran out of gas" on Watergate. Woodward and Bernstein referred to the final stretch of the campaign as "the most frustrating period they had encountered since June 17. . . . Little new information was developed." After the election, the pair would have even less success in uncovering the story. By March 1973, Woodward and Bernstein "were well aware that they would have far less to do with events than before. Much bigger forces were firmly in charge. Government investigations were underway." By May, they had "gotten lazy" and had "begun to rely on a relatively easy access to the Senate committee's staff investigators and attorneys." Appropriately, the book version of *All the President's Men* lacks a dramatic resolution. At the end of the story, Nixon is still in power, and the protagonists matter less and less (the film appended a montage of Nixon's fall to try to get around this problem). They had become minor characters in a major drama. By 1973, as *Post* editor Howard Simons observed, the journalists "were really reacting more than we were acting."[41]

The real actors were the various government authorities investigating and prosecuting the break-in. In 1973, it was these state actors that cracked the defensive denials of the White House and produced the evidence that brought down the president. In February and March, evidence of White House interference in the FBI's investigation of the break-in came to light during hearings on Patrick Gray's confirmation as FBI director. In March, it was the pressure of a criminal trial that led Watergate burglar James McCord to write a letter to Judge Sirica, implicating the White House in the original break-in as well as attempts to cover up their involvement by pressuring the burglars to perjure themselves. In June, it was the Ervin Committee hearings that provided White House counsel John Dean an opportunity to offer lengthy testimony on his role in the cover-up. And it was Ervin Committee interrogation of a former Haldeman aide in late July that uncovered the existence of a secret White House taping system.[42]

Richard Nixon was shocked that the taping system had come to light. Only a few staffers knew about it, and he believed they should have claimed executive privilege rather than concede its existence. The final year of the Watergate crisis thus boiled down to a dispute about access to information held by the executive. Again and again, special prosecutors and Senate committees called for access to information and charged the administration with abusing executive privilege. And again and again, Nixon asserted a broad right to keep presidential information confidential. In August 1973, in a televised address to the nation, Nixon reiterated the need to maintain presidential confidentiality, and argued that turning over the tapes would "set a precedent that would cripple all future Presidents by inhibiting conversations between them and those they look to for advice." But his various, and increasingly desperate, tactics to keep the tapes secret could not put the matter to bed. In 1974, after Nixon had invoked executive privilege to quash yet another subpoena, the issue went to the Supreme Court.[43]

For the first time, the Supreme Court considered the constitutionality of executive privilege. The court unanimously rejected Nixon's claims of an "absolute, unqualified privilege of immunity from judicial process under all circumstances." Instead, it argued that while there was a "presumptive privilege" that was "fundamental to the operation of government and inextricably rooted in the separation of powers under the Constitution," such a privilege needed to be balanced against the right to know. In this case, the court found, the right to know trumped the right to secrecy. Although Nixon lost the case, the decision did not amount to an unqualified victory for government transparency. For the first time, the Supreme Court recognized a right to executive privilege—in fact, it was willing to concede that "the interest in preserving confidentiality is weighty indeed and entitled to great respect." Only two decades earlier, a "right" to executive privilege was an uncertain legal invention, articulated by Justice Department lawyers during the turmoil of the second Red Scare. Now, it ascended to constitutional jurisprudence. And the court also took pains to reiterate that "utmost deference" should be shown to claims of confidentiality in the area of "military and diplomatic secrets." In general, the *U.S. v. Nixon* decision clarified that the Office of the President had broad rights to secrecy. It was just that this particular president did not have a right to keep these particular secrets. On August 5, Nixon was forced to release a run of secret tapes. They included the smoking gun tape of June 23, 1972, in which Nixon ordered the cover-up of the Watergate break-in. On August 9, the president resigned.[44]

* * *

If the Pentagon Papers and Watergate affairs were victories for the rights of the press over the state, then, they were delimited and ambivalent victories. In both cases, the press had exercised its right to publish information that was hostile to the interests of the Nixon administration. In both cases, that meant that the public's right to know about the secret affairs of the state had been protected in practice. But the publication of the Pentagon Papers and the details of the Watergate scandal depended on leaks of information from government employees, and in neither affair were there any guarantees that such leaks were legal, let alone legally protected.

In the Pentagon Papers case, Ellsberg had gone free, but only because the entire matter had been thrown out of court. And in the Watergate affair, the Supreme Court had explicitly recognized the rights of the executive to keep information secret. The press's much-hallowed role in publicizing the excesses of the Nixon administration rested on the existence of government employees willing to supply the press with otherwise secret information. And while the press emerged from the scandals of the early 1970s with a clearly protected right to publish state secrets, there was no such constitutional protection for the sources that provided those secrets to the press.

In the aftermath of the Nixon administration, this uneasy situation would be embraced as a positive contribution to press freedom. Constitutional scholar Alexander Bickel, who had represented the *New York Times* in the Pentagon Papers case, made the most explicit case for the desirability of this state of affairs. Bickel argued that democracies had competing interests in both secrecy and transparency. A democracy could not simply prioritize either the state's right to police secrecy or the press's right to publish government information: "If we should let the government censor as well as withhold, that would be too much dangerous power, and too much privacy. If we should allow the government neither to censor nor withhold, that would provide for too little privacy of decision-making and too much power in the press and in Congress." So Bickel proposed a balancing act: the state had a right to withhold secrets and the press had a right to publish whatever information it could get hold of. It was a procedural resolution to a normative problem—Bickel called it the "game theory of the First Amendment." In hoping that the rough-and-tumble of democratic politics would produce positive outcomes that abstract theorizing could not, Bickel legitimized the theory of classification that had emerged after World War II. And he bid final farewell to the theory of press responsibility that had been midwife to the new order of national security censorship: "The presumptive duty of the press is to publish, not to guard security or to be concerned with the morals of its sources." "Those responsibilities," he concluded, "rest chiefly elsewhere"; the "chief responsibility of the press . . . is to play its role in the contest."[45]

In the 1970s and 1980s, this distinction found repeated expression in law. Courts upheld the constitutionality of nondisclosure agreements that prevented present and former state employees from releasing information that they learned through their employment. In 1980, for instance, the Supreme Court found that a former CIA operative had no right to publish information about his former activities; he first had to submit even unclassified material to the CIA for clearance. In 1985, Samuel Loring Morison, a naval intelligence analyst, leaked information about Soviet naval power to *Jane's Fighting Ships,* and became the first leaker to serve jail time under the Espionage Act. The Fourth Circuit Court of Appeals explicitly dismissed the claim that Morison had a First Amendment right to leak the material, and the Supreme Court declined to hear an appeal of the matter.[46]

If leakers had few First Amendment rights, newspapers continued to have a well-protected right to publish information however it was obtained. In a unanimous decision in 1978, the Supreme Court upheld the rights of a Virginia paper to publish confidential information from a hearing into judicial misconduct. Although the court conceded that there was a public interest in such confidential hearings, it argued that one could not protect such an interest by interfering with First Amendment rights. Rather, the harm from disclosure could "be eliminated through careful internal procedures to protect the confidentiality of Commission proceedings." The same distinction found expression in the 1982 Intelligence Identities Protection Act, which prohibited government employees from revealing the names of covert intelligence agents but was drafted to ensure that reporters would be protected from prosecution.[47]

In the abstract, this balancing test made some sense. The law sees an interest in secrecy and security and an interest in disclosure and debate, and it appears to balance them. But in reality, the balancing act is weighted in favor of the government right to secrecy. Although the rights of the press and the rights of the state are treated as autonomous rights, the press cannot publish information it has not been able to pry from the state. The rights of the state to secure information are prior to the rights of the press to publish, so the press's right to publish secret information is entirely dependent on an action that the state is regulating. Given the sprawl of the classification regime and the illegality of disclosing classified information, the press is often dependent on individual employees to break the law to provide the public with information. The threat of jail time plus the rupturing of professional and cultural norms and the loss of security clearances and employment are powerful disincentives militating against any decision to blow the whistle on state misconduct.[48]

Because all leaks were issued in the shadow of such retribution, the majority of leaks were made with at least the tacit blessing of the administration. Leaks certainly blossomed in the 1970s and 1980s—by the mid-1980s, according to one study, 42 percent of federal policy-making officials had leaked information to reporters. But they tended to come from the top of the administration, and the leaks primarily served as a tool for the conduct of administrative politics by other means. Even if institutional and partisan politicking therefore meant that some otherwise secret information was reaching the public, relying on leaks underprotected the public right to information in several ways. To protect the leaker, the use of anonymous sources became common. One 1974 study found that 54 percent of stories in the *Washington Post* and *New York Times* used at least one anonymous source. That made it very difficult for the reader to parse the accuracy of the information, let alone to assess the motives of the leaker (and it was still possible to selectively leak for self-interested reasons). As journalists continued to rely on anonymous leaks to conduct their trade—Max Frankel called leaked secrets the "coin" of the journalistic realm—they continued to depend on their sources for information, undermining the likelihood of aggressive watchdog journalism. And in some bureaucracies, and on some issues, consensus was sufficiently strong to preclude any leaks of information. The FBI's COINTELPRO program, which illegally monitored and intimidated the civil rights and antiwar movements over a period of decades, came to light only when a group of antiwar activists broke into an FBI office in Media, Pennsylvania, and stole internal FBI documents (even this extreme action was only sufficient to uncover the name of the operation; it took several years in court before FOIA requests unearthed the details and scope of the FBI's activity). In the context of ongoing overclassification, in short, it seemed inadequate to rely on leaks to inform the public.[49]

But after Nixon, there was little effort to create a more secure public right to access information. There was no foundational reform of the classification system, even though the Pentagon Papers affair had revealed that too much information was being classified: Nixon's secretary of defense believed that 98 percent of the papers did not need to be classified, and all could see that the nation did not collapse when the papers were released. Between 1972 and 1975, there were seventeen congressional hearings on a number of bills that bore titles such as the "Free Flow of Information Act." But these were limited laws that would have done nothing to reform the foundations of the secrecy regime. They simply sought to exempt reporters from being forced to name their sources in criminal trials. Their advocates, including Alexander Bickel, argued that by protecting the anonymity of leakers such a "reporter's privilege" would encourage a greater flow of information to the public. But it created no new rights of access and did nothing to lessen the sanctions on leaking; it just impeded the government's ability to prosecute leakers. In any case, the law was never passed, and in 1974 a divided Supreme Court ruled that the First Amendment implied no such privilege. Over the coming decades, the Justice Department's internal guidelines tightly restricted the actual issuing of subpoenas to journalists, while lawyers for the newspaper industry were able to massage the ambiguities of the Supreme Court decision to convince a number of lower courts that a privilege did exist. But they were building on shaky precedent.[50] And when whistle-blowing protections were passed in the 1970s and 1980s to help encourage employee disclosure of government illegality or impropriety, they exempted the national security and intelligence agencies, and provided little protection to those disclosing classified information.[51]

* * *

The only area of meaningful post-Watergate reform was the revision of the FOIA in 1974. Implementation of the 1966 act had revealed a number of problems. Ralph Nader thought FOIA was being "undercut by a riptide of agency ingenuity"; a congressional committee agreed that it had "been hindered by five years of foot-dragging by the federal bureaucracy." Agencies had considerable discretion to delay their response to requests, particularly when denials were challenged in court—it took, on average, 167 days for a FOIA case to come to resolution. The agencies could charge prohibitive finding fees and dismiss requests they considered to be imprecise. They relied heavily on the statutory exemptions to disclosure, and the courts were deferential to such claims if the material was classified. In 1974, the Supreme Court ruled that such deference was required.[52]

The process frustrated researchers. When one requestor, Harrison Wellford, tried to access reports on pesticides filed with the Department of Agriculture, he was at first denied because he had not identified them clearly enough. Upon asking for indexes to help him identify the reports, he was denied this request because the indexes were interagency memoranda and thus exempt from disclosure. Wellford took the case to court, where, two years later, he won access to the reports. But then the department announced that it would cost $91,840 to remove confidential information from the reports and prepare them for public release. "At that point," Wellford recalled, "we decided to try to find other means to get the information." Such problems made the law next to useless for reporters working to deadline. A 1971 survey of 123 AP managing editors found that only 16 had used the law or even threatened to do so. FOIA was more valuable to corporations and private law firms, who could afford the costs and time delays if it allowed them to access commercially valuable information such as investigatory processes, or the details of successful contract bids.[53]

In early 1973, bills to reform FOIA were introduced in both the Senate and the House. Despite unanimous agency opposition to the bills during hearings, both were reported favorably out of committee and went to conference for final drafting. The bills, in slightly different ways, made a number of changes to remedy the problems with FOIA: they established hard time limits within which agencies had to respond to FOIA requests, they allowed federal courts to award court and attorney costs to prevailing plaintiffs, they tightened the exemption on investigatory files, and they prevented agencies from withholding whole documents if they contained one piece of exempt information under a new principle that "reasonably segregable portions" of documents had to be disclosed once the exempt sections were deleted. Both bills also explicitly authorized judicial review of classification decisions to overturn the Supreme Court interpretation of the law. The Senate bill even tried to put teeth into FOIA by allowing the court to order the suspension of any federal official who had improperly withheld information.[54]

As the conference committee hammered out a compromise bill, President Ford sent it a letter expressing his concern that the new bill imposed unreasonable requirements on the agencies, that the proposed penalty for employees was too harsh, and that the law undermined the classification system. To calm the president, and ward off a potential veto, some changes were made to the final bill. Most significantly, the potential sanction of suspension was abandoned, replaced with a watered-down provision that if the court believed the employee had acted "arbitrarily or capriciously" in withholding documents, it could order the Civil Service Commission to determine whether disciplinary action was warranted. And although the final language of the new national security exemption did make clear that courts had authority to review the act of classification, the conference report instructed future courts to "accord substantial weight" to agency representations about the need to keep classified information secret. Ford tried to veto even this watered-down bill. But it was not a propitious moment for a president to oppose a freedom of information law. Nixon had stepped down as the conference committee was in session, and Ford's veto came a little over a month after his controversial pardon of the former president. In November, both the House and the Senate voted to override the veto, and the FOIA was amended.[55]

The new FOIA was an improvement over its predecessor. After it went into effect in early 1975, FOIA requests quadrupled, and individuals began to have greater success accessing information. The ACLU, the AP, and the National Security Archive have been dogged in their use of the law. And whereas administrators had once been generally opposed to disclosure, a new generation of government employees came up in a climate more hospitable to transparency. In 1980, a number of FOIA personnel formed the American Society of Access Professionals (going by the clever acronym of ASAP) that worked to forge a culture of disclosure across agencies and between the government and FOIA requestors.[56]

But problems remained. Delays were common, rendering FOIA less than helpful for reporters on deadline. While FOIA became an important tool for patient researchers, historians, and investigative journalists, it remained unwieldy. It was difficult to pry information loose from many agencies, and many a long-awaited document arrived heavily redacted, having fallen under one of the exemptions. By the early 2000s, only 6 percent of FOIA requests came from the media; 61 percent came from commercial interests. More fundamentally, FOIA remained a specific and delimited statute, subject to the expansion and contraction of classification with changing administrations. In 1994, the Clinton administration unilaterally declared that the National Security Council was not an agency, but a part of the presidency, and therefore immune from FOIA requests. One of FOIA's exemptions, moreover, applied to all material that was declared secret in another statute—in essence, the exemption could expand, accordion like, to cover more and more material. In 1984, the CIA Information Act exempted CIA operational files from FOIA; by 2003, the Department of Justice was citing 140 statutes as specific authority to withhold records under the exemption.[57] And courts remained deferential to state secrecy when asked to adjudicate on FOIA requests. By 1985, the Supreme Court had ruled in favor of disclosure in only two of the nineteen FOIA cases that had come before it. Agencies had developed two powerful new arguments to justify withholding information: they claimed that some material was so secret that even acknowledging its existence would harm national security, and they argued that even harmless pieces of information could be pieced together to form a mosaic picture that would aid enemies of the nation. As judges were asked to engage in speculation about potentially unknowable dangers, they deferred to claims of secrecy.[58]

More broadly, the response to the excesses of the Nixon administration did not produce new rights to access information. The mid-1970s did see a brief flurry of jurisprudential and intellectual activity centered on the meaning of the press clause. In November 1974, Supreme Court justice Potter Stewart gave a famous address at the Yale Law School in which he argued that the existence of the press clause had to imply that the institutional press possessed greater First Amendment rights than the speech rights that were held by the general public. Superficially, Stewart's arguments seemed to suggest that he was the intellectual heir to Lippmann and Dewey, and that he was attempting to outline a positive notion of press freedom to complement the negative right to free speech. But in reality, Stewart was arguing that the press clause guaranteed the institutional press even greater autonomy from the state than the speech clause. He argued that the press could not be regulated like any other industry, that it could not be censored, that it should be protected from warrants and subpoenas. In 1973, Stewart had gone so far as to argue that an antidiscrimination statute that banned gender-specific job ads violated the First Amendment. (Stewart was part of a four-judge minority that nearly carried the day on this issue.) Stewart, in other words, continued to conceptualize press freedom in classical terms. He thought that guaranteeing a positive right to information would involve the state in the news-gathering process, and he joined majority decisions in the mid-1970s that found that the First Amendment did not grant the press a special right of access to prisons. In the 1970s, press freedom meant protection from government interference. Such protection was unprecedented, and the Supreme Court increasingly meant that the First Amendment guaranteed absolute autonomy, and nothing less than that, to all speakers, including the press. But the Supreme Court was also increasingly adamant that press freedom meant nothing more than the right to free speech.[59]

* * *

The era did produce real gains for freedom of expression. In 1964, a unanimous Supreme Court radically expanded First Amendment protections against libel claims. The particulars of the case emerged from the civil rights struggle—Alabama had brought libel claims against the *New York*

Times in an effort to squelch criticism of its resistance to desegregation—but the decision was a sweeping affirmation of what the court called a "profound national commitment to the principle that debate on public issues should be uninhibited, robust and wide-open." (The court even went so far as to declare the 1798 Sedition Act unconstitutional for the first time.) Freed from fears of libel, the press was newly liberated to investigate and critique public officials. Civil libertarian Alexander Meiklejohn called the decision an occasion for "dancing in the street."[60] More broadly, too, the court was extending unprecedented First Amendment protections to forms of speech that had previously been subject to regulation: movies, sexually explicit culture, advocacy of violence, and obscene and offensive language.[61] Such First Amendment absolutism was a boon to individual rights. But on the coattails of the rising civil libertarianism came signs of a new deference to economic freedoms. In 1976, the Supreme Court recognized commercial speech and advertising as protected First Amendment speech for the first time. In the same year, it struck down limits on campaign expenditures, holding that money was speech and that such regulations therefore violated First Amendment rights. Two years later, the court ruled that corporations had a First Amendment right to express their opinions through campaign contributions.[62]

The new jurisprudential emphasis on uninhibited rights to individual free speech was reflected in theoretical considerations of the First Amendment. The leading theorist of the First Amendment in the 1960s was Yale law professor Thomas Emerson, who argued in 1966 that the "right to freedom of expression is justified first of all as the right of an individual purely in his capacity as an individual." Emerson's emphasis on the importance of free speech to "self-fulfillment," as well as his redefinition of the right to speech as a general right to "expression," stood in stark contrast to the arguments of Alexander Meiklejohn, the leading First Amendment theorist of the previous generation. In 1948, at the height of efforts to think about the public obligations of the press, Meiklejohn had argued that the right to free speech was primarily justified not as an individual freedom but as an essential component of public governance. More important than self-expression, Meiklejohn asserted, was the right to hear a diversity of opinions: "What is essential is not that everyone shall speak, but that everything worth saying shall be said." To that end, Meiklejohn had extended an absolute right to free speech only to political speech; private speech, commercial speech, and artistic expression had lesser constitutional rights. In 1948, this was an expansive vision of the First

Amendment—Meiklejohn was attempting to carve out at least one area in which there were unlimited rights to free speech. By the early 1970s, things had moved so quickly that Meiklejohn's distinction between protected public speech and unprotected private speech had become a conservative position. When Robert Bork borrowed Meiklejohn's arguments in 1971, he did so to argue against the ongoing expansion of individual speech rights. After the 1970s, it was Emerson's position that won out: the First Amendment protected individual speech, all of it.[63]

* * *

In journalism, too, the 1960s and 1970s saw a new glorification of the right to free expression. The stars of the period were the so-called New Journalists, who expanded the scope, style, and substance of reporting by fusing the techniques of journalism and fiction writing. Although the New Journalism was largely published in magazines, its early practitioners tended to come from the newsrooms of the nation's papers: Tom Wolfe had been a reporter for the *Springfield Union* and the *Washington Post* and the *New York Herald Tribune;* Gay Talese had worked for the *New York Times;* Hunter S. Thompson had bounced around the lower echelons of the journalism profession in a sequence of short reporting gigs. The New Journalists were an important symbol of the cultural changes roiling journalism in the late 1960s, and the public controversy they engendered spilled out to ensnare broader debates about journalism. "Neither of us is an advocate of the New Journalism in general," Bob Woodward was forced to clarify, but one aspect of it appealed: "writing about your own personal experiences, getting close to your own feelings and reactions. That's what we tried to do in our book." In such ways did the New Journalists reflect and inspire a new sensibility among aspiring reporters.[64]

The New Journalism was a reaction against what its practitioners felt to be the stultifying norms of Cold War journalism. It was a repudiation of the doctrines of objectivity and responsibility that had guided postwar journalism and were now cracking under the pressures of Vietnam, political protest, and official deception. *Village Voice* journalist Jack Newfield argued that monopoly ownership, professional norms, advertising influence, and government news manipulation had created a press that was not really objective; what journalists called objectivity was really a uniform belief in "welfare capitalism, God, the West, Puritanism, the Law, the family, property, the two party system, and perhaps most crucially, in the notion that violence is only defensible when employed by the state." Those beliefs blinded the "Old Journalism" to important realities about American behavior in the Cold War, and about the structure of power at home. And they turned journalists into agents of the status quo: "through a desire to be the 'responsible' fourth branch of government," the press both censored itself and automatically reproduced the "press releases and white papers of the government without any note of skepticism." Fresh from his stint as White House press secretary, Bill Moyers declared in 1968 that the myth of objectivity was being discarded. Moyers predicted a "major development in the history of journalism in this country because there really is no such thing, in journalism, as an innocent bystander."[65]

The New Journalism was thus an effort to produce journalism more appropriate to the political realities of 1960s America. Norman Mailer's coverage of the 1960 Democratic convention, entitled "Superman Comes to the Supermarket," was the first to self-consciously embrace this program.[66] Mailer had begun his career as a novelist—he was one of the few to arrive at New Journalism by starting from fiction rather than journalism—but the opening sentence of the article announced his desire to challenge the norms of political journalism: "For once let us try to think about a political convention without losing ourselves in housing projects of fact and issue." What followed was an extensive meditation on the experience of the convention and the cultural meaning of Kennedy's ascension. It was a piece of analysis and reflection and opinion much more than a piece of straight reporting. And it was tied together by Mailer's subjective experiences in Los Angeles. As Mailer later put it, he had created an "enormously personalized journalism in which the character of the narrator was one of the elements in the way the reader would finally assess the experience. I had felt that I had some dim intuitive feeling that what was wrong with all journalism is that the reporter tended to be objective and that that was one of the great lies of all time." For proponents of New Journalism, this was a form of liberation. Writing in the *Atlantic* in 1966, Dan Wakefield declared that Mailer had presented the facts "in a full instead of a naked manner, brought out the sights, sounds and feel surrounding those facts . . . [given] greater depth and dimension to the facts."[67]

All of the New Journalists were trying to transcend existing journalism in order to give fuller expression to the facts. Tom Wolfe, who gave the various experiments in journalism the common name "New Journalism," did so through stylistic experimentation. He argued that the facts could be expressed only through the use of literary techniques that had previously been shunned by journalists: the use of scenic construction, the reproduction of extended dialogue, and the use of the third-person narration to document the subjectivity of characters. Gay Talese borrowed the fictional techniques of John O'Hara and Irwin Shaw because he felt he "couldn't tell through the old journalism the whole story." Others tried to reimagine journalism by involving themselves directly in the story, rupturing the professional obligations of neutrality. Norman Mailer and Hunter S. Thompson were masters of this technique. Mailer's extended coverage of the March on the Pentagon, which fused fiction, reportage, and introspection, won widespread praise. Nat Hentoff declared that the book "could hardly be more personal and yet it simultaneously digs more deeply into the essence—and some of the putrescences—of the way we live now than the total wordage moved by AP and UPI during the past year." Thompson, too, was the star of his drug-fueled explorations of the decadent byways of American culture. In a repudiation of Cold War journalism's embrace of professional responsibility, Thompson declared his account of the Kentucky Derby "a shitty article, a classic of irresponsible journalism."[68]

On one level, the preoccupations of New Journalism were a return to the concerns of the Newspaper Guild. Both the early guild and the New Journalists rejected professional norms; both sought to reimagine the labor of journalism in order to improve the flow of information to the public. The early 1970s even saw some short-lived efforts to democratize the management of the newsroom. In 1972, working journalists organized a counter-convention to protest the annual publisher's meeting, and their manifesto echoed the guild's labor theory of press freedom: "Thousands of men and women capable of giving their communities the kind of enlightened tough-minded reporting they deserve are daily demeaned by the feckless institutions for which they work. . . . Journalists must be as free from censorship and arbitrary interference by management as management is free from censorship and interference by government."[69]

Unlike the guild, however, the New Journalists eschewed collective political action. Their vision of freedom was distinctly individualistic. The guild had rejected the professional ethos of journalism in favor of an identity as proletarian workers, but the New Journalists rejected the professional ethos of the journalist in favor of an identity as individual artists. "We want to pursue writing as an art form," declared Talese; "I think that is wonderful: the reporter as the artist." Whereas the Newspaper Guild had sought to dispel the romantic myth of the bohemian, alcoholic reporter, Thompson more than embraced it, proudly turning his binges into feats of participatory journalism—the drugs, the booze, and the scabrous paranoia reromanticized the figure of the journalist for the late 1960s. And Tom Wolfe, in his own way, also romanticized the act of writing as the discovery of a unique voice—the founding myth of Wolfe's New Journalism period concerned the night he overcame a severe case of writer's block and inadvertently unleashed a new style full of run-on sentences, self-consciously scholarly metaphors, enthusiastic punctuation, and gee-whizz exuberance.[70] In the 1930s, progressive writers had produced fiction that drew on the tropes of journalism; in the 1960s, progressive writers produced journalism that drew on the tropes of fiction. Fact was being displaced by expression.

Above all, the New Journalism was a celebration of the individual genius of a handful of idiosyncratic writers. The emphases on personal reporting, on participation, and on formal innovation all centered on the figure of the writer. The New Journalism was an "'I' writing for an 'I' Time," declared one commentator—"a personal writing for an age of personalism." An emphasis on the instincts of the journalist was an understandable reaction to the widespread sense that preexisting social norms were hopelessly intertwined with a corrupt status quo. The New Journalist, declared Jack Newfield, "does not call the anonymous source . . . he does not try to speak for an institution, only for his own conscience. He does not take into account 'the national interest' but only what he sees and thinks." At first, there was something refreshing about that self-centeredness. Turning the lens of journalism back on the act of reporting did much to expose the shortcomings of journalism as it was being practiced. In Thompson's *Fear and Loathing on the Campaign Trail* and Timothy Crouse's *The Boys on the Bus,* New Journalism produced two of the classics of campaign literature in 1972. Combined, the two did much to shatter myths about politicians, elections, and the press corps. When meaningful access to political life shut down, self-criticism, insider gossip, and satirical denunciation were appropriate responses. But that was a trick that could only be played so many times, and it didn't, in any case, do much to open up new channels of information from within the black box of politics.[71]

Much of the New Journalism, moreover, was far less political. Talese and Wolfe focused their skills on celebrity profiles and cultural trend-pieces. As Talese put it, he focused on old culture, whereas Wolfe focused on the new. So Talese's pieces focused on aging stars, and decline, and failure—they were stories of struggling boxers, and New York, and Broadway; of Joe DiMaggio, and Frank Sinatra, and Peter O'Toole. Wolfe's were stories of novelty and success and youth—custom cars, Vegas, Phil Spector, fashion. But while their stories provided wonderful insight into the cultural mores of the late 1960s—and Talese's stories, in particular, have aged beautifully—the work as a whole tended to bracket politics. Wolfe focused his discerning eye on questions of style and play, not work and power. And Talese focused on individual struggles, with politics retreating into the distant background. In 1966, Talese wrote a lovely study of the *New York Times* obituary writer Alden Whitman, using the profile to explore celebrity, mortality, and the work of journalism. But Talese made no mention of the fact that Whitman had only been assigned to obituary writing as punishment for his impertinent responses to the Eastland inquiry into Newspaper Guild activity a decade earlier. Talese treated Whitman's role in the politics of the guild and McCarthyism in a single, bland sentence.[72]

The fatal flaw of the New Journalism, however, turned out to be economic. For all that the New Journalists lionized the individual writer, they depended on the ongoing financial support of editors and publishers. New Journalism took time. The New Journalists employed what Wolfe called "saturation reporting": "The New Journalism involves a depth of reporting and an attention to the most minute facts and details that most newspapermen, even the most experienced, have never dreamed of. To pull it off you casually have to stay with the people you are writing about for long stretches." In a panel in 1970, Talese and Wolfe dwelt on the fact that they would wait weeks or months till they felt they had the scenes and insight they needed. Talese's masterpiece was "Frank Sinatra Has a Cold," a profile that was vastly improved by the fact that Talese was unable to interview Sinatra, and had to content himself with observing Sinatra's entourage, his habits, and his experiences. Such observation ended up telling the reader much more about Sinatra than a canned interview. In that sense, the Sinatra piece summed up the innovative nature of the New Journalism: when traditional channels of information dried up, the New Journalists hit upon new techniques that could provide their readers with a glimpse of reality anyway. But it took Talese six weeks to complete the reporting for the story.[73]

So the New Journalists were expensive—they required the support of institutions willing to pay for long periods of reporting for relatively infrequent articles. But the New Journalism was born at the very moment that the journalistic institutions that could provide such support were going under in increasing numbers. In fact, the New Journalists were inspired by the wreckage of the institutional press, and saw freelancing as a form of freedom. Talese, safely ensconced in the *New York Times* in the early 1960s, looked on the journalists at the failing *Herald Tribune* with jealousy. "A dying newspaper," he declared in 1973, "is a place where the troops, the members of the staff, have a great amount of fun, freedom." And many of the New Journalists, including Wolfe and Talese, began freelancing while their regular papers were shut during the 1962–1963 newspaper strike. "The freedom that came of that strike," confessed Talese years later, "made me, for the first time, know what it was like to be a writer rather than a reporter whose life was owned by the *Times*."[74] In the late 1960s, the magazine *New York* was the institutional home for a great deal of New Journalism. It had started as a supplement to the *New York Herald Tribune,* but when the paper had gone under, it had been revived as a stand-alone magazine.

That brief moment of chaotic freedom, however, did not last. In 1976, *New York* was bought out by Rupert Murdoch, and evolved into an upper-class lifestyle magazine. Except for a handful of the superstar journalists, money for innovative long-form journalism began to dry up throughout the media. Absent the support for serious reporting, the New Journalism was little more than a series of stylistic tricks and the glorification of distinctive voices and opinions. Without funding, all that was left was a new form of expression.[75]

* * *

The cultural ferment that gave rise to the New Journalism produced a number of other significant developments in the press. Correspondents asked more direct and aggressively adversarial questions at presidential press conferences.[76] Election coverage became more critical of the candidates—so much so that people were soon complaining about the rise of negativity in the news. News stories became more analytical, contextual, and interpretive—journalists began explaining the significance of the facts to the reader. In the late 1960s and early 1970s, there was even a brief resurgence of investigative reporting, though it remained too expensive to become a mainstay of a press that continued to watch its bottom line. A more successful venture was the rise of the op-ed page. Although there had been a few earlier experiments with such a page of commentary, the "opposite the editorial" page that the *New York Times* established in 1970 relied less on the paper's columnists than on outside writers. Like the New Journalists, the contributors were freelancers, paid to express their opinions—the more "highly individualistic, opinionated and pungent" the better, one contributor was instructed. It was a self-conscious effort to expand the range of voices in a press that risked becoming more homogenous as it became more monopolistic (when the *Herald Tribune* collapsed in 1966, Harrison Salisbury argued that the *Times* needed to consider "providing a platform for responsible conservative opinion" because "a very serious responsibility has been thrust upon us by the death of the Tribune"). It certainly didn't hurt that the op-ed page was profitable, cheap, and easy to produce—within two years, both the *Chicago Tribune* and the *Boston Globe* had created one.[77]

All of these trends revealed that norms of midcentury reporting were being rejected in favor of a new posture of adversarial, aggressive, and opinionated journalism. These developments were an improvement from the deferential journalism that had characterized the press of the high Cold War, and in the last decades of the twentieth century, newspapers featured longer stories and more analysis.[78] Even the economics of the press looked good. By the 1980s, the remaining monopoly papers were turning lavish profits as advertising dollars poured in. The *Chicago Tribune,* for instance, tripled its profit margins, and the number of journalists in the nation's newsrooms expanded from 39,000 in 1971 to 62,000 in 1992. Not even the widely noted and apparently irreversible collapse of circulation was necessarily a cause for concern—some papers were able to charge higher advertising rates when they lost less affluent subscribers, for advertisers were happy to pay more to reach a wealthy slice of the population.[79]

But deeper problems persisted. The extraordinary profits of the 1980s were hard to maintain, but they had become expected, and were required to maintain stock prices and to service debts taken on in the earlier rush to expand. It was difficult to measure the impact of these commercial pressures on the nation's journalism—the quality of the press is a subject not easily measured with the quantitative tools of communications scholarship, and the new practices were transforming newspapers whose quality under old family owners was uneven. But as costs were cut in the 1990s, the number of journalists in the nation declined by 5 percent, which meant that more had to be done with less. And there was plenty of anecdotal evidence, at least, that the desire to maintain advertising revenues had begun to dismantle the firewall separating the business and editorial side of the papers. According to one survey in 2000, roughly one in five journalists had faced criticism or pressure from their bosses for producing a story that was seen to harm the company's financial interests. While it is impossible to know what sorts of stories didn't make it into the papers, "advertorials" became more common, and boosterish real estate, business, and automobile sections were carefully edited to avoid displeasing advertisers. In 1980, a study of a single issue of the *Wall Street Journal* found fifty-three stories based solely on corporate press releases. Thirty-two of them were almost verbatim.[80]

Journalists also continued to rely on government sources for access to political information, which continued to be tightly managed in the Reagan years. Communications strategists in the White House managed the public image of the administration, while reforms to the classification system and FOIA expanded state secrecy. That meant that independent reporting on issues of national security and foreign policy remained difficult. From Libya to Nicaragua to Grenada, the press continued to reflect the foreign policy assumptions of the governing elite. And despite the glorification of investigative journalism after Watergate, the press did not follow up on early evidence of the Iran-Contra affair, which first broke via a news story in a Lebanese weekly newspaper. "For all the shouting across the White House lawn and the hardball questions," reflected journalist Eleanor Randolph, "the news establishment has been a lot softer and more malleable than it appears." Soon, Ben Bradlee was complaining of a "return to deference" in the coverage of the Reagan administration.[81]

While the new adversarialism was therefore an important shift in cultural values, it was uneven. And it was not accompanied by structural reforms that would have truly transformed the flow of information to the public. Compared with the state of the press in the 1950s and 1960s, there were certainly improvements—but it sometimes seemed that press independence was a matter of tone, style, and form as much as substance. Post-Nixon journalism, in short, was marked by deep tensions. Take, for instance, the much-noted rise in "soft news." Sports, lifestyle, and celebrity coverage grew remarkably in the period—one study found an increase from 30 percent of the news in 1980 to 50 percent in 1998. On the one hand, the trend could be seen as an expansion of the range of subjects about which the public might wish to be informed, particularly when contrasted with the dry and deferential stenography that characterized so much of the "hard news" of the 1950s and 1960s. But it also seemed a clear dereliction of the press's duty to inform the public rather than amuse or distract them.[82]

Such ambivalence also characterized the much-noted rise of scandal journalism. From Gary Hart to Bill Clinton, aggressive reporting on the personal indiscretions of politicians was a significant feature of late twentieth-century journalism. It had a number of causes—round-the-clock news networks, distrust of the government after Watergate and Vietnam, the politicization of personal life in the wake of the 1960s, a fixation on questions of morality during the culture wars. But the rise of scandal journalism can also be seen as a product of a tension between modern journalists' self-conception as antiestablishment watchdogs and the structural limitations on their ability to play that role. Scandal journalism took the form of investigative, adversarial journalism. Reporters got to ask tough questions of politicians, and exposing political hypocrisy was a way to bring new information to the public (and compared to the clubby elitism of Cold War journalism, it was certainly a democratizing development). But exposing a personal scandal didn't require access to classified government information, or the time and financial support to probe and parse complex policy issues. In fact, one needed to know very little to hold a strong opinion about a politician's suitability to govern. The complexities of government could be reduced to a simple moral question: did the politician commit the indiscretion or not? And from the point of view of the editor and the publisher, as scandals unfolded in real time, they produced a steady stream of breaking headlines and press conferences and disclosures. They produced plenty of copy, and sold plenty of papers.[83]

* * *

In the years after Nixon, then, the press seemed to be riding high. The newly streamlined newspaper industry was profitable and prosperous. The reaction to the excesses of the Nixon years and the high Cold War had produced a cultural shift in the press, which sought to be more aggressive, more opinionated, and more informative. Journalism had even become glamorous. Journalism school enrollments were increasing rapidly, and Woodward and Bernstein's accounts of the fall of Nixon turned the investigative journalist into a folk hero. In April 1976, the pair topped both hardback and paperback bestselling lists, and a stylish film version of their exploits was the nation's number one movie.[84] Beneath the surface, however, the press was facing deep crises. State secrecy continued to grow, and press reliance on leaks was a fragile guarantee of the public's right to know. The political culture of journalism was precariously poised between a new desire to challenge authority and the structural constraints that confronted reporters. And as the consolidation of the press accelerated, press diversity continued to decline. America's free press had emerged from Nixon's assaults with greater freedom to express itself, to publish what it wanted, and to conduct its business according to its own self-interest. The era had been less kind to the public's right to the news.

9

Sprawling Secrecy and Dying Newsrooms

Superficially, the Internet changed everything. In one sense, it seemed to suggest a rebirth of press freedom. Blogging and social media created new possibilities for expression for all citizens; a trove of new information, from all over the world, was instantly accessible. But press freedom had never been a pure expression of technological capacity. It also depended on economic, political, and legal practices. And on these fronts, the legacy of the twentieth century shaped the state of press freedom at the new online frontier. The Internet certainly helped Americans to express their opinions, but their rights to information remained imperiled. Facing rapid economic decline, newspapers slashed their reporting budgets. And government secrecy continued to expand. In 2012, exploring the "unexpected crisis" of the news industry, media scholar Paul Starr rediscovered the old distinction between freedom of speech and press freedom. "The digital revolution," Starr declared, "has been good for freedom of expression because it has increased the diversity of voices in the public sphere"—"but it has not been as good for freedom of the press."[1] The transformations ushered in by the rise of the Internet reopened old questions about the meaning of press freedom. By rethinking our current crises through the lens of the distinction between the right to speech and the right to the news, and in light of the history of the twentieth century, we can come to a clearer understanding of our present moment, and gain a more accurate sense of the strengths and deficiencies of American press freedom.

* * *

The right to express one's opinion without government interference has never been as widely protected as it is today. In the last two decades, the Supreme Court has found that Americans have a constitutionally protected right to all sorts of speech. The First Amendment has even protected rights to self-expression that a majority of Americans find distasteful: cross-burning, videos of dog-fighting, "outrageous" and emotionally offensive religious picketing at military funerals. The right to free speech also has a broad cultural power. The right to express one's opinion has been elevated to something of a trump card in political disputes: in 2013, one could find arguments circulating that open-carry gun protests were a form of constitutionally protected speech. Significantly, even when national security concerns were heightened in the immediate aftermath of 9/11, the federal government eschewed limiting speech rights. The PATRIOT Act raised many civil liberties concerns because it expanded the surveillance and detention powers of the state. Civil liberties activists, with good reason, pointed out that these powers created a climate of suspicion that chilled speech. But it was noteworthy that even at the height of the War on Terror, there was no frontal assault on general speech rights.[2]

The laissez-faire vision of the First Amendment that protects free expression has also become a powerful tool for broader antistatist politics. In 2010, the Supreme Court's infamous *Citizens United* decision overturned a federal limit on corporate campaign expenditure as a violation of the speech rights of corporations.[3] And as the production and exchange of information has become a leading sector of the economy, the First Amendment has been deployed as a way to block state regulation of business. In 2008, for instance, the Supreme Court overturned a privacy law that restricted the sale of health records to a pharmaceutical marketing firm because the law interfered with the First Amendment right to exchange information. Commentators and legal scholars have begun to explore the "corporate takeover of the First Amendment," but its origins lie deeper in the past than their analyses suggest—they can be traced to Elisha Hanson's assault on New Deal press reform in the 1930s.[4]

The Internet's emergence as a peerless space for self-expression, on the other hand, was a significant new development. Unlike the broadcast media, the Internet is a deregulated medium. Throughout the twentieth century, federal regulation of the media had developed on a two-track path. The broadcast media were regulated in the public interest. Because the spectrum was limited, the ability to broadcast was treated as a privilege, not a right. The print media were subject to no such regulations because they were not scarce in the same sense—one could start a new paper without limiting the technical capacity of a rival paper to reach their audience. In 1996, the Supreme Court ruled that the Internet was legally akin to the print media rather than the broadcast media, for the medium was not limited. The classically liberal law of press freedom that had developed in the print industry over the twentieth century became the regulatory framework for the Internet.[5]

Unlike the midcentury press, however, the Internet has also provided Americans with the practical ability to express their opinions through a mass medium. While printing was never a technologically scarce medium like the early radio spectrum, the modern mass press was highly concentrated in the hands of a small class of producers. The Internet has radically democratized the costs of producing and distributing media content—all one needs is a computer with an Internet connection. The old distinction between the producer and consumer of media content has been blurred—according to one account, roughly one in ten online news consumers have submitted their own content to news websites or blogs. And the rise of social media has provided both another platform for expression and a collective mechanism for filtering and distributing information. Where once a distant editor decided the range of content one saw in the day's paper, now the consumer shares that task with peers, friends, and like-minded strangers. And where once the news media were local or national in scope, it is now possible to communicate easily across national borders, and to read stories published far away from one's hometown. One need not exaggerate the democratization of the new medium: the ability to express one's opinion provides no guarantees that one will be heard; Internet traffic is dominated by legacy media organizations; and popular blogs continue to be overwhelmingly produced by the same elite minorities that provided the majority of old-media content.[6] Nevertheless, it is now easier than ever to find a platform to express one's opinion, and to participate in discussions about a seemingly endless range of subjects.

* * *

The Internet has been less hospitable, however, to the task of reporting. Much online activity makes no claim to be producing new information; it is commentary, expression, or criticism. But even online news sources have struggled to produce new content. A study of the news cycle in

Baltimore in 2009, for instance, found that online news providers largely reproduced stories generated by the traditional media. Only 17 percent of all stories in the news cycle featured any new information; 95 percent of them were in traditional media sources. As the Federal Communications Commission put it in 2011, "An abundance of media outlets does not translate into an abundance of reporting."[7]

In fact, the proliferation of media channels has coincided with a steep decline in reporting. Between 2006 and 2009, daily newspapers cut their editorial spending by more than a quarter; by 2011, newsroom employment had fallen 25 percent from 2006 levels. At least 13,400 reporters lost their jobs between 2007 and 2011. The *Raleigh News and Observer* had 205 reporters on staff in 2005, but only 103 by 2011; in 2008, the *Newark Star Ledger* reduced its staff by 45 percent. Whole beats began to disappear: statehouse reporting, science, education. And even though the *Baltimore Sun* remained a central source of all information in Baltimore's news cycle, it was producing less information: in 2009, it produced 32 percent fewer stories than in 1999 and 73 percent fewer stories than it had in 1991.[8]

What is often called the death of the daily newspaper should more accurately be called the death of reportorial labor. If the death of the newspaper was simply the end of a costly, environmentally damaging, and economically centralized industrial product, there would be little reason for concern. But the contemporary crisis of the newspaper industry marks the collapse of the old funding model for the labor of reporting.[9] The daily newspaper had relied on advertising revenues to fund reporting, and the rise of the Internet eliminated the newspaper's monopoly over advertising space. At the same time, it dispersed readers into a series of niche audiences and media content into niche products.[10] Advertisers had little interest in expensive ads going to the newspaper's undifferentiated audience, and they had a new host of inexpensive media channels seeking advertising dollars. Newspaper ad revenue fell by more than 50 percent from 2003 to 2012; for every $15 of print advertising that was lost in 2012, only a dollar of digital advertising was brought in.[11] As recently as 1985, Warren Buffett had asserted that "the economics of a dominant newspaper are excellent, among the very best in the business world." All that mattered was market dominance, Buffett explained: "While first-class newspapers make excellent profits, the profits of third-rate papers are as good or better." By 2009, Buffett declared that he would not buy newspapers at "any price."[12]

In many ways, the economic collapse of the newspaper industry is a product of their unregulated development over the course of the twentieth century. As monopoly papers became immensely profitable, publicly listed businesses, they necessarily fixated upon maintaining profits. Even when they were earning money in the 1990s, newspapers were cutting reportorial costs. So when economic crisis hit, and revenues slumped, they slashed costs to try to maintain profits. That made perfect sense if one thought about the paper only as a business like any other. But if newspapers had been treated as a unique industry earlier in their development, as a business with a unique obligation to provide diverse information to the public, they might have behaved differently. If the Newspaper Guild had established more control over newspaper economics in the 1930s, reporting might not have been first on the newspaper chopping block—media CEO salaries kept growing even as the industry cut jobs.[13] And if antitrust laws had been applied more vigorously to stop mergers and advertising rate combinations, then it is possible that a more diverse newspaper industry would have become accustomed to lower rates of profit, or developed different and more adaptable business models to support journalism.

As the twentieth century unfolded, however, the newspaper industry became dependent on one business model: the maximization of monopoly profits. It did so, in large part, because of fears that interference with the economics of the industry would undermine the freedom of the press. But when the economics of the industry shifted, and the existing business model broke, the industry struggled to adapt. Amid falling revenues and severe cutbacks to newsrooms, newspapers have begun experimenting with various sorts of pay-walls to ask consumers to subsidize more of the cost of news production. The *New York Times,* for instance, has recently invested in the Dutch company Blendle, which provides a digital kiosk in which readers make a micro-payment for the stories they read rather than paying a lump sum to one news organization. It is too soon to tell how that model will work, but there is some evidence that more traditional pay-walls are producing new revenue streams. In 2012, for instance, the *New York Times* received higher revenues from circulation than from advertising for the first time in the paper's history. But that reflected the collapse of advertising revenues as much as the rise in circulation. Despite job cuts and aggressive digital advertising efforts, the paper's profits continued to decline in 2014. And while elite newspapers like the *Times* and the *Wall Street Journal* may be able to rely on revenues from an elite class of increasingly transnational readers, it remains unclear whether pay-walls are viable for smaller newspapers.[14]

Meanwhile, the digital economy is producing some innovative efforts to fund reporting. As of 2014 some surprising websites, including BuzzFeed and Mashable, have begun sinking money into reporting. And ProPublica provides an intriguing a model of nonprofit, philanthropically endowed investigative reporting. But as of 2014, philanthropic and capital investment combined account for only 1 percent of newspaper industry revenue; while editorial spending dropped $1.6 billion per year, foundations contributed only $180 million over a five-year period.[15]

By and large, the Web remains a place for commentary and expression rather than original news reporting. As ProPublica puts it, in terms that are strikingly similar to those that Walter Lippmann developed a century ago, "we face a situation in which sources of opinion are proliferating, but sources of facts on which those opinions are based are shrinking."[16]

* * *

A significant countertrend is the new ability to host vast amounts of information online, which allows citizens direct access to government documents that were previously inaccessible. The state itself is taking advantage of this capacity. One day after taking office, President Barack Obama called for an "unprecedented level of openness" in his administration. His ensuing open government policies have led to the online availability of large amounts of government data.[17] Some private organizations, too, are experimenting with new ways of presenting and analyzing unprecedented amounts of government information. Many news organizations have devoted themselves to "big data" journalism, and the nonprofit Sunlight Foundation relies on crowd-sourcing and other forms of modern communication to improve government transparency and accountability. Most famously, WikiLeaks used the Internet's capacity for anonymous transactions and its boundless size to transmit classified government information to the public in 2010: the "collateral murder" video of U.S. gunship violence in Iraq; Afghan and Iraq War logs; and State Department–Embassy cables. Government contractor Edward Snowden, too, relied on encrypted email and digital storage devices to transfer vast amounts of classified information about the National Security Agency (NSA) to journalists.[18]

But the most important limit on government transparency was never technological capacity. It was the classification system and the laws and practices of secrecy. And on this front, the trends of the twentieth century have continued—the state right to secrecy is prioritized, not the public right to know. When Obama called for openness on his second day in office, he clarified that "this memorandum is not intended to, and does not, create any right or benefit, substantive or procedural, enforceable at law or in equity."[19] In fact, the Obama administration has prosecuted leakers with greater vigor than any previous administration. It has charged seven individuals with violating the Espionage Act by illegally releasing classified information. All previous administrations combined had charged only four individuals. During the Obama administration, leakers have faced severe consequences: Chelsea Manning, the soldier responsible for the leaks to WikiLeaks, was sentenced to thirty-five years in jail for violating the Espionage Act; Shamai Leibowitz received twenty months for leaking five documents to a blogger; John Kiriakou, who leaked information about the CIA, pled guilty to lesser charges and received thirty months in jail. Even failed leak prosecutions, such as the effort to prosecute NSA whistleblower Thomas Drake, have sent a clear message—Drake was subject to many years of investigation, and faced with severe criminal charges, before the prosecution crumbled and he pled guilty to the minor misdemeanor of misusing a work computer.[20]

Pressure to police leaks is not a new phenomenon, and some of the recent prosecutions were inherited from the tail end of the Bush years.[21] But the current fixation on leaks is distinctive. In an October 2011 executive order, Obama established an "Insider Threat Task Force" to develop programs for "deterring, detecting and mitigating insider threats, including the safeguarding of classified information from exploitation, compromise or other unauthorized disclosure." In June 2012, the director of national intelligence announced that during routine polygraph examinations, employees of all sixteen intelligence agencies would be asked if they had ever leaked information. In November 2012, new programs were implemented throughout the government asking employees to monitor each other's activity, watching for indicators that a colleague might be a security risk.[22]

This clampdown on leaks is the culmination of the shifting logic of censorship over the past century. Censorship of the government source of information has tightened as it became the only viable tool for the enforcement of state secrecy. Even after the state focused its censorship powers on employees rather than journalists, even after it had abandoned formal efforts to enjoin publication of state secrets, it could still rely on informal networks of authority to keep leaked information from being distributed widely. Journalists dependent on access to the state for information were unlikely to burn bridges to future disclosures by publishing leaked information when they had been told not to. On request from the government, for instance, the *New York Times* sat for a year on leaked information that the NSA was conducting warrantless wiretaps. Although the *Washington Post* was not deterred from publishing information about the existence of secret "black site" prisons in 2005, it did not publish the names of countries hosting those sites at the request of U.S. officials. But it is now possible to bypass journalists and distribute leaks directly online. After the WikiLeaks disclosures in 2010, the organization found itself under attack—it was starved of donations and kicked from servers as private companies, responding to public and political outrage, denied their services to the organization. But the WikiLeaks website and its content were replicated across the Web.[23]

The recent uproar over leaks represents, in part, official discomfort with the potential of the new world of unregulated distribution. Fixation on the character of the leakers—on Manning's gender identity, on Snowden's limited education, his "narcissism," and his alleged representation of an "asocial" generation—was an effort to come to terms with the fact that the "responsible" journalists who had previously acted as a safety net for the classification regime seemed to have become unnecessary.[24] In reality, neither the Manning nor Snowden leaks represented a break with the pattern of Daniel Ellsberg's leak four decades earlier. Ellsberg, too, had been the subject of pop psychological speculation—hence the plumber's break-in at his psychiatrist's office. Injunction of the *New York Times* had not been effective in 1971—Ellsberg simply leaked the Pentagon Papers to other newspapers. And the twenty-first-century leaks did not cut journalists out of the loop entirely, either, despite claims that leakers had "dumped" information. Manning turned the information over to WikiLeaks, which then collaborated with traditional news media such as the *Guardian,* the *New York Times,* and *Der Spiegel* to edit and prepare the releases, as well as redact sensitive information.[25] Snowden turned his information over to journalists Glenn Greenwald and Laura Poitras, who, collaborating with other newspapers, have released it slowly after further research.[26]

At times, in fact, the pressure to prosecute leakers has produced new problems for the press. In 2005, Judith Miller spent eighty-five days in jail while refusing to turn over to federal investigators the source that had leaked the name of CIA agent Valerie Plame. It was not an ideal test case for the journalist's right to keep the identity of leakers secret—Plame's name had been leaked in an effort to discredit her husband, Joseph Wilson, who had publicly criticized the case for the war in Iraq. But although the leaker in this instance was a powerful member of the administration, not a classic whistleblower, the legal decisions in the case reiterated the 1972 Supreme Court ruling that there was no reporter's privilege, making it clear that journalists could not rely on the First Amendment to protect their sources from subpoena. In 2008, the Bush administration subpoenaed *New York Times* journalist James Risen to identify the source of his information about a failed CIA operation in Iran (the *Times* had sat on the story, but Risen published it in a book). For seven years, Risen fought the subpoena in court with no success, and it appeared he would go to jail to protect his source. Meanwhile, in 2013, the Obama administration seized AP phone records in an effort to trace a leak. Journalists understandably challenged such practices as an interference with their press freedom—in 2014, Risen called Obama "the greatest enemy of press freedom in a generation." In the end, prosecutors did not force Risen to reveal his sources, and the Department of Justice tightened internal guidelines to restrict their use of subpoenas in cases involving the press.[27]

It is worth remembering, though, that the right of journalists to protect their sources is really only one, limited, mechanism to block prosecutions of the leaker. (Even without Risen's testimony, the leak in that case was successfully prosecuted when Jeffrey Sterling was found guilty of violating the Espionage Act.)[28] Either respecting or ignoring such a reporter's privilege does nothing to change the underlying balancing act of modern censorship: the state cannot police the publication of secrets, but it can police the source. Despite pressure from some conservatives to prosecute the press, that balancing act has continued to hold true in recent years. Julian Assange, head of WikiLeaks, has proven something of a liminal case in this regard. On any functional analysis, Assange played the role of a journalist in the Manning leaks. He published secrets that had been leaked to him, just as the newspaper journalists who collaborated with Assange did. But Assange's radical transparency agenda led to calls to prosecute him under the Espionage Act (and even some suggestions that he should be assassinated). In order to avoid unrelated rape and sexual assault charges in Sweden, Assange has been granted political asylum by Ecuador, and has spent nearly three years in the Ecuadorian embassy in

London to avoid extradition. Assange and his supporters believe that if he faces the Swedish charges he will be extradited to the United States, where he could face Espionage Act charges. If that happened, it would represent a major reversal of censorship practices dating back to World War II.[29]

At present, however, the general principles of modern press freedom hold: publication is protected by the First Amendment, while leaking secrets is not. It is significant, for instance, that Glenn Greenwald signs freelance contracts with all the foreign papers with whom he shares the NSA leaks, so that his journalistic activity protects him from Espionage Act charges of sharing classified information with unauthorized foreign nationals. Publication remains free, but the leaks upon which publication depends are met with severe penalty. While the *New York Times,* the *Guardian,* and *Der Spiegel* sold papers based on Manning's leaks, the twenty-three-year-old Manning sat in jail, having spent almost a year in solitary conditions that the UN Special Rapporteur on Torture called "cruel, inhuman and degrading." The *Guardian* and the *Washington Post* won a Pulitzer Prize for their stories on the NSA; Snowden has gone into exile in Russia to avoid facing Espionage Act prosecutions. According to DC correspondents, the visible prosecution of leakers is having a deterrent effect, and the correspondents are finding it increasingly difficult to cultivate leaks and inside sources.[30]

Meanwhile, six decades after its creation, the classification system continues to expand. In a 2003 executive order, George W. Bush allowed the reclassification of previously declassified information and established that a classifier should presume that all material relating to foreign governments should be kept secret. In 2005, twice as many documents were classified as in 2001—some 15.6 million documents, or 125 every minute of the year. Simultaneously, steps were taken to undermine the effectiveness of the FOIA. The White House instructed federal agencies to withhold "sensitive but unclassified information," and the Homeland Security Act formally exempted a broad category of "critical infrastructure information" from FOIA disclosure. Attorney General John Ashcroft instructed all federal agencies that the Department of Justice would defend decisions to withhold information from FOIA requests "unless they lack a sound legal basis." Such strict legalism reversed the presumption of disclosure that had been introduced under Bill Clinton, and narrowed the power of FOIA: in September 2003, one-third of federal FOI officers said they were less likely to make discretionary disclosures of information than they had been before the memo. And the Bush administration expanded its use of the state secrets doctrine, using it to dismiss entire legal cases brought in the fields of warrantless surveillance, extraordinary rendition, and torture.[31]

Secrecy continued to grow under Obama. There were, to be sure, some areas of improvement. The Ashcroft memo on FOIA was rescinded, and agencies were instructed to institute a "presumption of disclosure." Obama's executive order on classification made reclassification more difficult, and began to rein in the authority to classify. But classification nevertheless continued to balloon. In 2013, there were some 80 million decisions to classify a document, and the classification system cost the government at least $11.63 billion, up from $6.5 billion ten years earlier. Less than 1 percent of that budget was spent on declassification. Some 4.2 million Americans required security clearances. And the Obama administration continued to make extensive use of the state secrets privilege, and continued to carefully manage the flow of information from within the administration. "This is the most closed, control freak administration I've ever covered," declared *New York Times* DC correspondent David E. Sanger.[32]

Such widespread secrecy continues to distort the flow of information in the polity. It grants the government power to screen activities from public scrutiny, but it also allows them to selectively leak information to shape public attitudes. The prime example of this process came in the lead-up to the Iraq War in 2003. In the fall of 2002, the Bush White House began a public relations campaign to convince the public of the necessity and moral virtue of the war. ("From a marketing point of view," explained White House Chief of Staff Andrew H. Card, "you don't introduce new products in August.") Central to that campaign was the selective declassification of secret intelligence reports and strategic leaks to journalists—both made the case for war look stronger than it was. On the second Sunday in September, for instance, Vice President Dick Cheney told the audience of *Meet the Press* that Iraq's intentions to build atomic weapons could be seen in its purchase of aluminum tubes. The claim was dubious—classified intelligence reports questioned whether they could be used for such a purpose—but Cheney buttressed the assertion by citing as evidence a story in the *New York Times* that had been written by Judith Miller. But that story was not independent proof of Cheney's claims; it was a selective leak from the administration, now being used to reinforce another misrepresentation of the case. Throughout the lead-up to the war, the press would continue to depend on tips and leaks from official sources and Iraqi informants, whose insider information was reproduced uncritically. The *New York Times* later called its own reporting overly "credulous," but the damage had been done. The public had little ability to assess the sourcing of such stories or the veracity of the claims made by officials. One study later found that members of the administration made 935 false statements to the public in the run-up to the war.[33]

* * *

Combined, the decline of reporting and the rise of secrecy pose ongoing challenges to the free flow of information in the American polity. Formally, the public sphere retains its autonomy. Awash with opinion, argument, and expression, the American press seems to be conducting a vibrant democratic debate. But the debate rests on shoddy foundations. Fewer journalists are asked to produce more stories to fill the news-hole, and they increasingly turn, of necessity, to official handouts or corporate press releases to provide the bulk of information. In Pew's study of the Baltimore news cycle, the vast majority of stories had begun with official sources or press releases. An increasing amount of publicly circulating material is prepared by PR agents rather than journalists: in 1960, there was less than one PR agent for every journalist; by 2011, there were four PR agents for every journalist. Desperate for both cheap content and revenue, news organizations are even turning to "native advertising"—stories prepared by advertising firms. And they increasingly rely on opinion pieces, which are cheaper to produce than original reporting. Supreme Court watching, for instance, is a reliable stream of content—legal scholars from afar can endlessly parse the meaning of important decisions, arguing about their likely implications for the future. Such opinion pieces are also easier to market as distinctive content—the *New York Times* has recently expanded its opinion section and rolled it out as a discrete, pay-walled app. And more broadly, one finds the Internet full of criticism, speculation, and commentary—it is easier to criticize the spin of officials, or the commentary of other organizations, than it is to produce decisive new information on an issue.[34]

It is hard to shake the sense that something is amiss in the state of public opinion. Americans do poorly when answering factual questions about basic public issues. The lead up to the Iraq War provides the most pointed example. Despite a lack of censorship and a plethora of ways to access the news, the majority of Americans believed demonstrably false things about Iraq's alleged role in the 9/11 attacks. Low levels of political knowledge are not a new phenomenon, and the problem clearly has complex causes. But given the rapid expansion of First Amendment protections in the second half of the twentieth century, as well as the supposed ease of access to online information, it is sobering that Americans in 2007 did no better on public knowledge tests than their ancestors did in 1959 or 1989.[35] In part, this is a product of public disinterest in the news. Where once the public read papers fleetingly, skimming the headlines or focusing on the funny pages and box scores, today the public turns away from consuming the news altogether. By 2009, some 17 percent of Americans said they had not looked at the news at all in the day prior to the poll, and the trend is more pronounced among young people. Political scientist Markus Prior has argued that this is a function of the proliferation of media channels, which allows audiences to tailor their news consumption. Those who enjoy the news now do better on public knowledge tests than they did before the rise of cable and the Internet; those who dislike the news now do worse.[36] It is therefore tempting to blame the poor state of public knowledge on public taste and political apathy (this was one of Walter Lippmann's arguments in the 1920s). Perhaps more importantly, broader social conditions clearly play an important role in the turn away from the news. Long hours of work, inadequate levels of education, and a general disenchantment with public life and the institutions of government all discourage engagement with the news.

But the actual state of the news also plays a role, for people turn away not from the news in the abstract, but from the news as they know it. According to one survey, 31 percent of the public say they have deserted a news outlet because it no longer provides them with the information they were accustomed to receiving. Such sentiments are understandable. Even leaving to one side the online explosion of clickbait, listicles, and light content (kittens, mainly), many of the modern news media are more easily characterized as forms of expression than anything else. The blogosphere is highly polarized on partisan lines—conservative blogs link primarily to other conservative blogs, liberal blogs to other liberals. In the performative crossfire, real arguments rarely take place. There is endless critique of the other side, but rarely a final reckoning with the accuracy of an opinion. In the 2012 election campaign, even the definition of the "facts" became the subject of partisan dispute. "We're not going to let our campaign be dictated by fact-checkers," declared Romney pollster

Neil Newhouse—by which he meant that the fact-checkers were themselves simply expressing biased opinions. The statement captured the triumph of argument and spin, as well as the mainstreaming of postmodernist skepticism about truth—but it was made effective by the lack of any trusted public mechanism that could provide accurate information against which spin could be judged. And although social media provides an unprecedented mechanism for circulating and aggregating news in a democratized manner, it is particularly adept at providing an easy avenue for self-expression: Twitter, between staccato bursts of smug criticism and witty rejoinder, descends into wildfires of moral outrage; Facebook allows one to endlessly express one's "like" (but not one's "dislike") for the opinions of others. The traditional theory of democratic opinion assumed that self-expression would lead to truth, but only after truth and falsehood had clashed. It requires the clash—the serious consideration, the assessment of claims. Today, this moment rarely arrives. The act of expression, alone, seems to have become the essence of political life.[37]

* * *

What, if anything, can be done to improve the flow of information in the American polity? The history of press freedom in the twentieth century helped to produce a vibrant right to free speech. We now need to find protections for the public's right to the news. It is tempting to identify a forgotten moment, a lost opportunity, or an untraveled road and to propose, based on it, a holistic solution to present problems. But the problem of press freedom cannot be "solved" in that way. The problem of adequately informing the public is the foundational problem for democracy. And the concept of a free press captures two desires that are distinct and difficult to reconcile. Americans committed to press freedom want both a diverse and unregulated marketplace of ideas, speech, and opinion and a guaranteed right to access information of a high quality, diversity, and accuracy.[38] The challenge today is to find ways to improve practical rights to the news without interfering with rights to free speech. How do contemporary reform proposals look in this light? And what are the most urgent problems?

* * *

Finding a way to fund independent, quality journalism remains difficult. Our theories of press freedom have long assumed that market forces and advertising dollars would subsidize the flow of information to the public. As the history of press freedom reminds us, this was always a problematic assumption, and the crises of newspaper industry are an opportunity to reimagine the funding structures for journalism. But that doesn't mean, as some more optimistic commentators seem to think, that digital disruption and entrepreneurial innovation will automatically produce a more democratic press.[39] The Internet has certainly democratized the possibilities for expression—but the challenge of guaranteeing the public's right to the news remains.

Although there has been little serious public discussion of this issue, a small group of media scholars and reformers, inspired by New Deal theories of press freedom, have begun to imagine policy solutions. Drawn to the AP antitrust case and the early drafts of the Hutchins Commission, they argue that the state should play a role in creating a more democratic flow of information in the polity. These critics are heirs to the long-running effort to imagine a positive vision of press liberty alongside the laissez-faire theory.[40] Their analysis of our current predicament is important, and some of their proposals make a great deal of sense. But there are reasons to be skeptical that the policy approaches of the past are the best guide to the present problems of the press.

Take, for instance, the question of antitrust. Antitrust activity is primarily good at creating diversity in conditions of market monopoly. Eighty years ago, to be sure, such policies could have created a more diverse newspaper industry and provided readers of monopoly papers with access to a more diverse range of perspectives. But the Internet has done a great deal to accomplish that task on its own. The challenge today is not to break apart profitable newspaper monopolies, but to prop up original, independent journalism. So while antitrust may have a role to play in diversifying telecommunications or broadcast industries, and while tightening cross-media ownership laws is important, it is hard to see how policies intended to improve diversity would help produce quality in the already diversified ecology of journalism.

Direct state funding of the press, on the other hand, is one obvious way to provide financial support for journalism. In the United States, the idea of publicly funded media often produces both unrealistic hopes and unnecessary fears. The experiences of Australia, the United Kingdom, and many other nations—as well as the more limited history of public broadcasting in America—reveal that public funding of the media is neither an automatic death-knell for democracy nor a necessary guarantee of a more informed public opinion.[41] Clear models exist for creating relatively autonomous governmental media entities, and there is no reason to think that something similar to the BBC could not be created by the United States, or that a more diverse set of grants could not produce a number of small, high-quality newsrooms.

But while such public funding should be part of a solution to the problem of the press, it is far from a cure-all. Publicly funded media are not purely independent entities. They are dependent on state funds, and will be as independent as the state allows them to be. Which means that public funding is most important as a way to diversify homogenously commercial media: dependent on different revenues, and organized on a different logic, public media can counterbalance commercial biases and create content that the market will not support. At the same time, in theory at least, the independence of commercial media helps to check or counterbalance any state manipulation of public media. All of which is to say that public funding of a small set of newspapers might help to diversify the media, but it is no automatic guarantee of quality. And the democratic legitimacy of public funding depends on the existence of an otherwise vibrant and independent press. It is not, of itself, a way to create such a press.

Rather than creating a small group of state-funded newspapers, some have therefore suggested broader policy initiatives that would subsidize commercial newsrooms to help make them financially viable. These range from calls for tax credits to offset the salaries of journalists, to proposals for direct subsidies on the model of Scandinavian or French newspapers, to adjustments to nonprofit law that would allow newspapers to incorporate as low-profit firms. A particularly intriguing proposal has been developed by Robert McChesney and John Nichols, who call for the funding of news through citizen vouchers: every citizen would receive a voucher from the state, which they would be free to distribute to whichever news medium they wished, creating a directly democratic method of funding the press. McChesney and Nichols suggest that such a positive state role in the press is in keeping with a long American tradition—they emphasize particularly the nineteenth-century postal subsidy to newspapers—and promise that such policies would necessitate no violation of First Amendment rights to free expression. Alternatively, in a model that mirrors private-sector experimentation with micropayments, Bruce Ackerman has suggested that such funds could be allocated according to the number of "votes" that readers cast by clicking a box on stories they like.[42]

Such proposals are worth serious consideration, but they raise many difficult questions. Creating benefits for the press necessarily involves the state in a discretionary activity, for it has to decide who would qualify for the benefit. Who gets to decide? And on what criteria would they decide what counts as reporting worthy of public support? If the state polices the conditions for qualifying for a benefit, which would require some supervision of the newsrooms receiving it, it would open the door to two forms of potential abuse. The first, which is perhaps the most likely, is that the existing newspaper industry will "capture" such programs to the exclusion of more innovative forms of journalism. As the history of New Deal newspaper reform and the Newspaper Preservation Act reminds us, the newspaper industry is a powerful lobby—and there is little reason to think that current American politics are immune to corporate influence. Using scarce public dollars to prop up the business models of monopoly papers seems an unlikely way to improve the quality of information flowing to the public. At the same time, it is hard to believe that the American state would long remain completely neutral in allowing the distribution of benefits. How, for instance, might politicians, or the American press itself, react if citizens used such vouchers for Arabic news organizations? It is troubling that the more effective such government funds became in propping up journalism, the more threatening such viewpoint discrimination would become to the diversity of the American press.[43]

It is possible, in theory at least, that the state could maintain strict neutrality in providing the benefit to all-comers.[44] While this would preserve the independence of the press, it would raise a number of practical problems—such as fraudulent claims to the vouchers, to take a basic example. And it would obviously blunt the efficacy of such funding as a means of press reform. Many of the funds would likely flow to forms of journalism that simply exacerbate existing trends away from news and toward expression. In principle, that is a completely acceptable and possibly even a desirable state of affairs. Letting the public experiment with funding new forms of journalism would likely also produce interesting new ventures. Whether it is the most practical and effective use of scarce public dollars is a more difficult question.

So while public funds have some role to play in supporting independent journalism, it would be better to direct them to discrete public entities competing with an otherwise independent press. This is the case for practical, financial reasons—it is likely to be cheaper—and also because such delimited programs of spending raise fewer concerns about government tampering with the general independence of the press. Even then, of course, public funding won't be a magic bullet. But combined with other forms of experimentation in the private and nonprofit sectors, it might begin to prop up independent journalism.

* * *

More broadly, there are good reasons to be exceedingly cautious when outlining any program of press reform. The more ambitious and sweeping any state program of press reform, the greater the risk it would pose to classical press freedom. It is hard to promote positive rights without interfering with negative rights. Modern-day admirers of the AP decision like to cite Hugo Black's dicta, because of his First Amendment absolutism, but their vision of a positive right to the news more closely follows Felix Frankfurter's concurrence, and he was happy to regulate speech for the public good. And history suggests that it is a rather short step from state efforts to promote press freedom to state repression of minority speech. While postal subsidies were crucial to the development of the nineteenth-century press, that power led to widespread censorship of birth-control information, as well as feminist, pacifist, and radical sentiments from the late nineteenth century through to World War I. We should remember, moreover, that the absolutism of the modern American First Amendment *is* exceptional. Nations that see fit to fund the news also embrace regulations of speech that would be unconstitutional in the United States—bans on hate speech, for instance, or lesser press protections from libel claims.[45]

Perhaps some readers might be willing to give up First Amendment protections for hate speech in exchange for a broad program of publicly funded media. Given the increasingly baroque use of the First Amendment as an antiregulatory tool, renewed skepticism of First Amendment absolutism is appropriate. Some reconsideration of the types of activity that First Amendment jurisprudence recognizes as speech might be necessary, but it would be a serious mistake to underestimate the importance of the unprecedented speech protections of the modern First Amendment.

This book has argued that First Amendment speech rights are insufficient for the production of press freedom. But they are nevertheless necessary. This was the paradox of press reform in the twentieth century. The consolidation of the newspaper market and the division between the press and the public meant that speech rights were, in practice, unequally distributed. Most media policy is an effort to grapple with that problem—the rights and obligations of speakers and media producers are regulated to protect the rights of the readers. Twentieth-century media reform therefore tried to adjust First Amendment theory in response to a social reality marked by a high degree of media concentration and by deep inequalities between producers and consumers of news.

Today, however, conditions have changed, and such trade-offs between First Amendment rights are less necessary. The Internet has diversified the channels for speech and eroded the distinction between news producers and news consumers. It is now possible to conceive of citizens playing a more active role in producing and distributing information—the Pro-Am journalism movement, the proliferation of video footage of police brutality, and the crowd-sourcing of big-data projects all testify to this potential. More importantly, the Internet has lowered the cost of funding skilled, full-time journalists. Even at their height, modern monopoly newspapers devoted only about 10 to 20 percent of their operating budgets to news gathering; the bulk of expenditures were for printing plants, newsprint, ink, mechanical labor, and delivery trucks.[46] When one doesn't need the capital for a printing press or a distribution network, let alone guaranteed returns to stockholders, or competitive salaries for CEOs and ad-men, it is far easier to get into the journalism business. It is now possible, for instance, to imagine small consumer-funded news organizations—the sorts of labor and funding structures of such organizations would more closely approximate the early Newspaper Guild's vision of independent journalism than anything heretofore possible. And while pay-walls and foundation donations and public grants may never bring in as much revenue as midcentury advertising, they don't need to. Far lower levels of expenditure, if carefully targeted at news gathering and reporting, could actually produce a great deal of quality journalism.

All of this makes it possible that a diverse news ecology will be cobbled together that will provide an adequate flow of information to the public: pay-walled legacy newspapers alongside philanthropically endowed newsrooms; publicly endowed websites alongside consumer-funded investigative reports. The best policy solutions will seek to promote this diversity on multiple fronts: some public funding, some adjustments to nonprofit law, the continued enforcement of cross-media ownership limits, and so forth. That will keep alive the possibility that high-quality journalism will emerge within a diverse and unregulated marketplace of ideas.

It is exceedingly difficult to realize this potential, of course. But the ultimate challenge is not to create new types of news organizations dedicated to independent reporting, or to seek tricks to fund them, but to make them essential to the American public. When the public is turning away from even reading the news, is there any hope that they will demand high-quality journalism, let alone help to fund it (either through subscriptions or publicly funded vouchers)? This has always been a difficult proposition. Because news is a public good, it is always tempting for consumers to free ride. As early as 1922, Walter Lippmann complained that the modern citizen "expects the fountains of truth to bubble, but he enters into no contract, legal or moral, involving any risk, cost or trouble to himself"; "it would be regarded as an outrage to have to pay openly the price of a good ice cream soda for all the news of world."[47] In tough economic times, and amid the dysfunctional cynicism of American politics, it is even less likely that citizens will find the time or resources to involve themselves in the careful consumption of news—let alone producing or funding it.

Such problems of citizen engagement cannot be remedied by press reform alone, and it would be a mistake to try to grapple with them by adjusting our theory of rights. They are problems of social and political citizenship—of providing citizens with education and economic security and incentives to participate in public life. Confronting social inequality and civic engagement are daunting problems, obviously, and they lie beyond the scope of this book. But that doesn't mean that nothing can be done to address them. If we want to improve the quality of information in the news, the problem will ultimately need to be addressed on this level. Media policy can be used to democratize and diversify the structures of the press, but any policy effort to improve the quality of the news would open the door to statist interferences with speech rights. If reform is aimed at society, however, it might be possible to simultaneously enhance the right to speak and the right to receive information. It might, at long last, be possible to adjust our social conditions to bring them into line with the equal marketplace of ideas presumed by First Amendment theory. After all, as Harold Laski put it in 1938, "a free press, in any sense of the word that has meaning, is only possible in an equal society."[48]

* * *

In the meantime, there are concrete steps that can be taken to solve the problems of state secrecy. The unwieldy sprawl of the secrecy system has already inspired several proposals for reform. There have been renewed calls for Congress to pass a journalism shield law that would allow reporters to protect their confidential sources from prosecutors—one such "Free Flow of Information" bill passed the Senate Judiciary Committee in late 2013. Congress has also debated legislation intended to enhance FOIA, particularly by limiting the ability of agencies to withhold internal deliberations. And there have been proposals to improve whistleblower protections. In 2014, for instance, Yochai Benkler proposed that Congress pass a statute protecting leakers from criminal prosecutions if they leaked information with a reasonable belief that they were exposing wrongdoing to the public.[49] Improvements to the law in these areas would certainly improve the flow of information to the public.

But as long as the classification system remains unreformed, such measures will never be as effective as they could be. Because FOIA exempts national security information and the Espionage Act criminalizes leaks of classified information, existing channels for public access to information are blocked by the root problem of the current system: it is classifying too much information. Officials familiar with the system have been criticizing overclassification since the 1950s. In 2004, the 9/11 Commission chairman, Thomas Kean, told Congress that 75 percent of the classified information reviewed by the commission should have been open to the public. But overclassification is the inevitable outcome of the patchwork institutional structure of the classification regime. Legislation that grants access to information acknowledges, and defers to, the classification rules established by executive order—but the classification rules do not defer to access rights of the public. As a result, bureaucratic inertia has produced a sprawling classification system, with severely limited rights of access granted in subsidiary statutes.[50]

In the past, politicians and reformers have suggested that the easiest way to fix this problem would be to codify the existing access and secrecy laws in one overarching statute. Such a reform would have clear benefits. It would establish classification on a statutory basis, thus stabilizing a system currently subject to rapid reversals at the whims of shifting administrations—while Carter-era employees were instructed to err on the side of openness in classification decisions, for instance, Reagan-era employees were instructed to err on the side of secrecy.[51] Incorporating FOIA, whistleblowing, and journalist protections into the same act would also emphasize that the principle of access is at least as important as the principle of secrecy. And it would provide a long-overdue opportunity to redraft the vague Espionage Act prohibitions on disclosing information.[52]

To be truly effective, however, such legislation would also need to check the bureaucratic presumption in favor of classification at the point of initial review—this is the motor that drives overclassification. Obama's executive order, for instance, asks classifiers only to consider if a document's "unauthorized disclosure could reasonably be expected to cause identifiable or describable damage to the national security." This could be amended: classifiers could be required, for instance, to consider whether such harms outweigh a public interest in disclosure. The exact language to be used would need to be carefully drawn, obviously, but part of the benefit of developing such instructions via statute rather than executive order is to open up such drafting to the democratic process. The ideal would be to create a positive, legal duty on the classifier to consider the public interest before declaring information secret.[53]

Any such instructions would, of course, have to be institutionally enforced. One current proposal, for instance, suggests that incorporating classification costs into agency budget lines might reduce overclassification. But the easiest way to ensure enforcement is to embody the conflicting interests in secrecy and transparency in competing organizations. The government's right to secrecy is embodied in the classification system, and there are bureaucratic penalties for underclassification. Critics in the 1950s and 1970s occasionally called for an independent office, committed to transparency, to balance that imperative to secrecy. In 1978, in fact, Jimmy Carter did establish an Information Oversight Office to provide some supervision of the classification system, but it lacks the ability to audit individual classification decisions and penalize overclassification. A more robust Office of Public Knowledge, with those powers, would help check the tendency to overclassification. Such an office would limit the growth of the expensive classification scheme, so it could be defended on budgetary grounds. And while it would not be a panacea—oversight of national security often devolves into rubber-stamping—creating at least some procedural check on classification would improve the current system.[54]

When posed abstractly, the trade-offs between secrecy and transparency can seem like intractable problems of democracy. But secrecy, as currently practiced by the U.S. government, is not an ahistorical abstraction; it is a set of institutional practices that developed in a haphazard and counterproductive way.[55] Reforming them would do a great deal to improve the flow of information to the public.

* * *

In all, the problem of press freedom remains difficult. Its resolution eluded some of the finest minds of the twentieth century. As the current transformations of the news media continue, we should neither mourn the passing of a golden age nor pin our hopes on a utopian future. The problems caused by state secrecy and the economics of the newspaper industry have been with us for a long time, and they will not disappear without a deliberate program of reform. Current First Amendment orthodoxy, however, provides little guide in navigating these changes. Over the course of the twentieth century, Americans prioritized their right to speech, not their right to the news. They did so for particular, and understandable, historical reasons—largely because they sought to protect liberty from totalitarianism. But looking back over the complex history of press freedom, we can see that the contemporary American ideal of a free press is partial and incomplete. What FDR referred to as the "freedom of the news" cannot be produced simply by protecting the right to speak without government interference. By acknowledging that fact, perhaps a new generation can begin to reimagine and revitalize what Walter Lippmann once called the "highway of liberty": the free flow of information to the public.[56]

ABBREVIATIONS

APP	Gerhard Peters and John T. Woolley, The American Presidency Project, online at www.presidency.ucsb.edu/
CJR	*Columbia Journalism Review*
CT	*Chicago Tribune*
EP	*Editor and Publisher*
GR	*Guild Reporter*
HC	Commission on Freedom of the Press Records, Special Collections Research Center, University of Chicago Library, Chicago, IL
HZ	Howard Zinn Papers, TAM 542, Tamiment Library, New York University, NY
JQ	*Journalism Quarterly*
NG	Newspaper Guild Collection, Part II, Accession 401, Archives of Labor and Urban Affairs, Walter P. Reuther Library, Wayne State University, MI
NGNY	Newspaper Guild of New York Collection, Wagner 125, Tamiment Library, New York University, NY
NR	*Nieman Reports*
NYT	*New York Times*
OF 375	FDR Official File 375: Tugwell 1933–1935, Franklin Delano Roosevelt Library, Hyde Park, NY
OF 466	FDR Official File 466: NRA 1933–1935, Franklin Delano Roosevelt Library, Hyde Park, NY
RC	Papers of Ramsey Clark, Lyndon B. Johnson Library, Austin, TX

RG 9	Record Group 9: Records of the National Recovery Administration, National Archives and Records Administration II, College Park, MD
RG 43	Record Group 43: Records of International Conferences, Commissions and Expositions, National Archives and Records Administration II, College Park, MD
RG 51	Bureau of the Budget Series 41.3, War Records Section, Record Group 51: Records of the Office of Management and Budget, National Archives and Records Administration II, College Park, MD
RG 208	Record Group 208: Records of the Office of War Information, National Archives and Records Administration II, College Park, MD
RG 216	Record Group 216: Records of the Office of Censorship, National Archives and Records Administration II, College Park, MD
RG 267	Record Group 267, Records of the Supreme Court of the United States, National Archives and Records Administration, Washington, DC
RT	Rexford G. Tugwell Papers, Franklin Delano Roosevelt Library, Hyde Park, NY
Truman OF	Truman Official File, Harry S. Truman Library, Independence, MO
WHCF	White House Central File, Lyndon B. Johnson Library, Austin, TX
WP	*Washington Post*

NOTES

Prologue

1. Franklin D. Roosevelt, "Letter of Congratulations to the St. Louis Post-Dispatch," November 2, 1938, APP.

2. Willard Grosvenor Bleyer, "Freedom of the Press and the New Deal," *JQ* 11 (1934): 22; St. Louis Post-Dispatch, *St. Louis Post-Dispatch Symposium on Freedom of the Press: Expressions by 120 Representative Americans,* reprinted from December 13 to December 25, 1938 issues (no publication details, 1938); Summary of Discussion, July 7–9, 1946, Doc. 108b, p. 53, box 8, folder 4, HC.

3. On the importance of the totalitarian moment to American political culture and American political development, see Edward A. Purcell Jr., *The Crisis of Democratic Theory: Scientific Naturalism and the Problem of Value* (Lexington: University Press of Kentucky, 1973); Benjamin L. Alpers, *Dictators, Democracy, and American Public Culture: Envisioning the Totalitarian Enemy, 1920s–1950s* (Chapel Hill: University of North Carolina Press, 2003); David Ciepley, *Liberalism in the Shadow of Totalitarianism* (Cambridge, MA: Harvard University Press, 2006); Ira Katznelson, *Fear Itself: The New Deal and the Origins of Our Time* (New York: Liveright, 2013); Richard A. Primus, "A Brooding Omnipotence: Totalitarianism in Postwar Constitutional Thought," *Yale Law Journal* 106 (1996): 423–457. Of course, the "totalitarianism" that did work in American political culture was an ideological construct that filtered American perceptions of distinct European dictatorships—see Abbott Gleason, *Totalitarianism: The Inner History of the Cold War* (New York: Oxford University Press, 1995); Les K. Adler and Thomas G. Paterson, "Red Fascism: The Merger of Nazi Germany and Soviet Russia in the American Image of Totalitarianism, 1930's–1950's," *American Historical Review* 75 (1970): 1046–1064; Tomas R. Maddux, "Red Fascism, Brown Bolshevism: The American Image of Totalitarianism in the 1930s," *Historian* 40 (1977): 85–103.

4. Raymond Clapper, "A Free Press Needs Discriminating Public Criticism," in *Freedom of the Press Today: A Clinical Examination by 28 Specialists,* ed. Harold L. Ickes (New York: Vanguard, 1941), 86.

5. Thomas I. Emerson, *The System of Freedom of Expression* (New York: Random House, 1970), 5.

6. In thinking about the unintended consequences of reform movements, I have been inspired by Thomas Bender, ed., *The Antislavery Debate: Capitalism and Abolitionism as a Problem in Historical Interpretation* (Berkeley: University of California Press, 1992); T. J. Jackson Lears, *No Place of Grace: Antimodernism and the Transformation of American Culture, 1880–1920* (Chicago: University of Chicago Press, 1994).

7. For introductions to the vast historiography of speech rights, see Geoffrey R. Stone, "Reflections on the First Amendment: The Evolution of the American Jurisprudence of Free Expression," *Proceedings of the American Philosophical Society* 131 (1987): 251–260; Geoffrey R. Stone, *Perilous Times: Free Speech in Wartime: From the Sedition Act of 1798 to the War on Terrorism* (New York: W. W. Norton, 2004); Christopher Finan, *From the Palmer Raids to the Patriot Act: A History of the Fight for Free Speech in America* (Boston: Beacon Press, 2007); Anthony Lewis, *Freedom for the Thought We Hate: A Biography of the First Amendment* (New York: Basic Books, 2007). Works that tell a more critical story while still focusing on speech rights include Mark A. Graber, *Transforming Free Speech: The Ambiguous Legacy of Civil Libertarianism* (Berkeley: University of California Press, 1991); David Yassky "Eras of the First Amendment," *Columbia Law Review* 91 (1991): 1699–1755.

8. John Stuart Mill, *On Liberty and Other Essays* (Oxford: Oxford University Press, 1998), 16–20; Paul Starr, *The Creation of the Media: Political Origins of Modern Communications* (New York: Basic Books, 2004), 74.

9. Lee C. Bollinger, *Uninhibited, Robust, and Wide-Open: A Free Press for a New Century* (New York: Oxford University Press, 2010), 8–10.

10. Press Release, February 22, 1945, box 922, folder: Speeches Price 1944, entry 1, RG 216; "Press Held Keeper of Bill of Rights," *NYT,* February 22, 1945, 32.

11. William Novak recently called for a "true philosophical and political history of the American present" in William J. Novak, "The Myth of the 'Weak' American State," *American Historical Review* 113 (2008): 752. Press freedom provides an important lens through which to begin to write such a history.

12. Much of the work on the press and politics in the twentieth century has worked on a smaller scale, focusing on the role of particular press institutions and individuals, or the coverage of individual events. My debts to this scholarship can be found throughout the references in this book. Works covering broader time periods have tended to follow a technological teleology, devoting much of their analysis of midcentury to the new media of radio, cinema, and television. See Starr, *Creation of the Media* and Mark Lloyd, *Prologue to a Farce: Communication and Democracy in America* (Urbana: University of Illinois Press, 2006). The law and politics of the press, however, remained distinct from those of the broadcast media throughout the period. And they have again returned to the fore in the age of the

Internet and media deregulation. See Lee Bollinger, *Images of a Free Press* (Chicago: University of Chicago Press, 1991).

13. Philip Schuyler, "Government News Gag Press Freedom Problem," *EP*, April 8, 1944, 7.

1. The Inadequacy of Speech Rights

1. Thomas Healy, *The Great Dissent: How Oliver Wendell Holmes Changed His Mind—and Changed the History of Free Speech in America* (New York: Metropolitan Books, 2013), 61; Walter Lippmann, *Liberty and the News* (Princeton, NJ: Princeton University Press, 2008), 11, 41.

2. Lippmann, *Liberty and the News*, 12.

3. Paul Starr, *The Creation of the Media: Political Origins of Modern Communications* (New York: Basic Books, 2004), 58–62; Bernard Bailyn, *The Ideological Origins of the American Revolution* (Cambridge, MA: Belknap Press of Harvard University Press, 1992), 35–37; David A. Anderson, "The Origins of the Press Clause," *UCLA Law Review* 30 (1983): 491–492; Leonard W. Levy, *The Emergence of a Free Press* (New York: Oxford University Press, 1985), 37–45, 113, 124–135; James Alexander, "Free Speech Is a Pillar of Free Government," in *Freedom of the Press: From Zenger to Jefferson; Early American Libertarian Theories*, ed. Leonard W. Levy (Indianapolis, IN: Bobbs-Merrill, 1966), 61–62; Margaret A. Blanchard, "Freedom of the Press: 1600–1804," in *The Media in America: A History*, ed. Wm. David Sloan and James D. Startt (Northport, AL: Vision, 1999), 98–102; Wm. David Sloan and Julie Hedgepeth Williams, *The Early American Press, 1690–1783* (Westport, CT: Greenwood, 1994), 81–91.

4. Starr, *Creation of the Media*, 65–68; Richard Buel Jr., "Freedom of the Press in Revolutionary America: The Evolution of Libertarianism, 1760–1820," in *The Press and the American Revolution*, ed. Bernard Bailyn and John B. Hench (Boston: Northeastern University Press, 1980), 59–98; David Waldstreicher, "Rites of Rebellion, Rites of Assent: Celebrations, Print Culture, and the Origins of American Nationalism," *Journal of American History* 82 (1995): 37–61.

5. I include Vermont, though it would not join the union until 1791. Anderson, "Origins of the Press Clause," 463–465; Levy, *Emergence of a Free Press*, 183–189.

6. Contrary to modern mythology, nothing should be read into the primacy of this "First Amendment"—it had been intended as the Third Amendment and ascended to its current position only when amendments clarifying the election and compensation of congressmen were rejected by the states. See Anderson, "Origins of the Press Clause," 486.

7. There has been a great deal of debate about what precisely the founders meant by press freedom, but it remains unsettled—the evidentiary record does not support a fine-grained parsing of their press philosophy, and there was no single theory held by a philosophically diverse and politically fractious generation. See Levy, *Emergence of a Free Press;* David M. Rabban, "The Ahistorical Historian: Leonard Levy on Freedom of Expression in Early American History," *Stanford Law Review* 37 (1985): 795–856; Thomas I. Emerson, "Colonial Intentions and Current Realities

of the First Amendment," *University of Pennsylvania Law Review* 125 (1977): 737–738.

8. James Madison, "Report on the Virginia Resolutions," January 7, 1800, in *Selected Writings of James Madison,* ed. Ralph Ketcham (Indianapolis, IN: Hackett, 2006), 259; Thomas Jefferson to Edward Carrington, January 16, 1787, in Levy, *Freedom of the Press,* 333. See more broadly Richard D. Brown, *The Strength of a People: The Idea of an Informed Citizenry in America, 1650–1870* (Chapel Hill: University of North Carolina Press, 1996).

9. Thomas Jefferson to Edward Carrington, January 16, 1787, in Levy, *Freedom of the Press,* 333.

10. John Milton, *Areopagitica: A Speech of Mr. John Milton, for the liberty of unlicens'd printing, to the Parliament of England, first published in the year 1644* (London, 1738), Eighteenth Century Collections Online, Gale, George Mason University, 33, 42, 51.

11. Mill argued that trade could be subject to more regulations than speech. John Stuart Mill, *On Liberty and Other Essays* (Oxford: Oxford University Press, 1998), 105–106.

12. *Cato's Letters; or, Essays on Liberty, Civil and Religious, and other important subjects,* 3rd ed., 1733 (New York: Russell and Russell, 1969), vol. 1, 96, vol. 2, 266, vol. 3, 295. On the relationship between capitalism and ideas about liberal public opinion, see the much-debated Jürgen Habermas, *The Structural Transformation of the Public Sphere: An Inquiry into a Category of Bourgeois Society,* trans. Thomas Burger and Frederick Lawrence (Cambridge, MA: MIT Press, 1991); Craig Calhoun, ed., *Habermas and the Public Sphere* (Cambridge, MA: MIT Press, 1992).

13. Jeffrey A. Smith, *War and Press Freedom: The Problem of Prerogative Power* (New York: Oxford University Press, 1999), 32.

14. James Madison, "Public Opinion," in Ketcham, *Selected Writings of James Madison,* 208.

15. Tunis Wortman, *A Treatise Concerning Political Enquiry, and the Liberty of the Press* (New York: Printed by George Forman, 1800), cited from HathiTrust, 121; Levy, *Emergence of a Free Press,* 327–332.

16. Wortman, *A Treatise Concerning Political Enquiry,* 46, 140.

17. Anthony Smith, *The Newspaper: An International History* (London: Thames and Hudson, 1979), 7–11, 17–45; Starr, *Creation of the Media,* 23–46; Brian Winston, *Messages: Free Expression, Media and the West from Gutenberg to Google* (London: Routledge, 2005), 31–65; Asa Briggs and Peter Burke, *A Social History of the Media: From Gutenberg to the Internet,* 2nd ed. (Cambridge: Polity Press, 2005), 61–87; David Zaret, *Origins of Democratic Culture: Printing, Petitions, and the Public Sphere in Early-Modern England* (Princeton, NJ: Princeton University Press, 2000), 120.

18. Frank Luther Mott, *American Journalism: A History of Newspapers in the United States through 250 Years, 1690–1940* (New York: Macmillan, 1962), 56–59; Starr, *Creation of the Media,* 86; Steven J. Shaw, "Colonial Newspaper Advertising: A Step toward Freedom of the Press," *Business History Review* 33 (1959): 409–420; Charles E. Clark, *The Public Prints: The Newspaper in Anglo-American Culture, 1665–1740* (New York: Oxford University Press, 1994).

19. Jeffrey A. Smith, *Printers and Press Freedom: The Ideology of Early American Journalism* (New York: Oxford University Press, 1988), 19.

20. Starr, *Creation of the Media,* 84–94; Richard R. John, *Spreading the News: The American Postal System from Franklin to Morse* (Cambridge, MA: Harvard University Press, 1995).

21. Alexis de Tocqueville, *Democracy in America,* trans. and ed. Harvey C. Mansfield and Delba Winthrop (Chicago: University of Chicago Press, 2000), 494.

22. See Jeffrey L. Pasley, *The Tyranny of Printers: Newspaper Politics in the Early American Republic* (Charlottesville: University of Virginia Press), 2001; Mott, *American Journalism,* 167–180.

23. William Livingston, "Of the Use, Abuse, and Liberty of the Press," in Levy, *Freedom of the Press,* 79–81; Buel, "Freedom of the Press," 70; Levy, *Emergence of a Free Press,* 98, 173–177, 251; Jan C. Robbins, "Jefferson and the Press: Resolution of an Antinomy," *JQ* 48 (1971): 421–430, 465; Lippmann, *Liberty and the News,* 16–19; John Nerone, *Violence against the Press: Policing the Public Sphere in U.S. History* (New York: Oxford University Press, 1994), 18–52.

24. Levy, *Emergence of a Free Press,* 307; Anderson, "Origins of the Press Clause," 507; David Yassky, "Eras of the First Amendment," *Columbia Law Review* 91 (1991): 1712. There are stronger and weaker versions of this argument. See Walter Berns, "Freedom of the Press and the Alien and Sedition Laws: A Reappraisal," *Supreme Court Review,* 1970, 109–159; Michael Kent Curtis, *Free Speech, The People's Darling Privilege: Struggles for Freedom of Expression in American History* (Durham, NC: Duke University Press, 2000), 105–106.

25. Levy, *Emergence of a Free Press,* 258–262; Anderson, "Origins of the Press Clause," 483; Akhil Reed Amar, *The Bill of Rights: Creation and Reconstruction* (New Haven, CT: Yale University Press, 1998), 22.

26. Margaret A. Blanchard, "Filling in the Void: Speech and Press in the State Courts Prior to Gitlow," in *The First Amendment Reconsidered: New Perspectives on the Meaning of Freedom of Speech and Press,* ed. Bill F. Chamberlin and Charlene J. Brown (New York: Longman, 1982), 18, 27; Smith, *Printers and Press Freedom,* 154; Linda Cobb-Reiley, "Aliens and Alien Ideas: The Suppression of Anarchists and the Anarchist Press in America, 1901–1914," *Journalism History* 15 (1988): 50–59; Smith, *War and Press Freedom,* 38–39; Yassky, "Eras of the First Amendment," 1713; Alfred H. Kelly, "Constitutional Liberty and the Law of Libel: A Historian's View," *American Historical Review* 74 (1968): 439–440; Pasley, *Tyranny of Printers,* 278–279; Curtis, *Free Speech, the People's Darling;* William J. Novak, *The People's Welfare: Law and Regulation in Nineteenth Century America* (Chapel Hill: University of North Carolina Press, 1996); Gary Gerstle, "The Resilient Power of the States across the Long Nineteenth Century: An Inquiry into a Pattern of American Governance," in *The Unsustainable American State,* ed. Lawrence Jacobs and Desmond King (Oxford: Oxford University Press, 2009), 61–87.

27. Joseph Story, *Commentaries on the Constitution of the United States* (Boston: Hilliard, Gray, 1833), 703, cited from HathiTrust; Starr, *Creation of the Media,* 235–250, 267–295; David M. Rabban, *Free Speech in Its Forgotten Years* (Cambridge: Cambridge University Press, 1997), 27–41, 248–298; Geoffrey R. Stone, *Perilous Times: Free Speech in Wartime: From the Sedition Act of 1798 to the War*

on Terrorism (New York: W. W. Norton, 2004), 135–234; Stephen Vaughn, *Holding Fast the Inner Lines: Democracy, Nationalism and the Committee on Public Information* (Chapel Hill: University of North Carolina Press, 1980); Christopher Capozzola, *Uncle Sam Wants You: World War I and the Making of the Modern American Citizen* (New York: Oxford University Press, 2008), 144–172; Paul L. Murphy, *World War I and the Origin of Civil Liberties in the United States* (New York: W. W. Norton, 1979).

28. Schenck v. United States, 249 U.S. 47 (1919); Frohwerk v. United States, 249 U.S. 204, at 208–209 (1919); Debs v. United States, 249 U.S. 211 (1919).

29. Patterson v. Colorado, 205 U.S. 454 (1907); Fox v. Washington, 236 U.S. 273 (1915); G. Edward White, *Justice Oliver Wendell Holmes: Law and the Inner Self* (New York: Oxford University Press, 1993), 425; Healy, *Great Dissent,* 24, 56.

30. Zechariah Chafee Jr., "Freedom of Speech," *New Republic,* November 16, 1918, 66–69; Ernst Freund, "The Debs Case and Freedom of Speech," *New Republic,* May 3, 1919, 13–15; Zechariah Chafee Jr., "Freedom of Speech in War Time," *Harvard Law Review* 32 (1919): 932–973; Rabban, *Free Speech in Its Forgotten Years,* 316–335; Fred D. Ragan, "Justice Oliver Wendell Holmes, Jr., Zechariah Chafee, Jr. and the Clear and Present Danger Test for Free Speech: The First Year, 1919," *Journal of American History* 58 (1971): 24–45; Healy, *Great Dissent.*

31. Abrams v. United States, 250 U.S. 616, at 630 (1919) (my emphasis). On Mill's influence on Holmes, see Liva Baker, *The Justice from Beacon Hill: The Life and Times of Oliver Wendell Holmes* (New York: HarperCollins, 1991), 176, 180, 192, 519; White, *Justice Oliver Wendell Holmes,* 94–98; Healy, *Great Dissent,* 98–99, 205–206; Vincent Blasi, "Holmes and the Marketplace of Ideas," *Supreme Court Review,* 2004, 19.

32. Richard Polenberg, *Fighting Faiths: The Abrams Case, the Supreme Court, and Free Speech* (New York: Viking, 1987), 241; Felix Frankfurter to Oliver Wendell Holmes Jr., November 26, 1919, in *Holmes and Frankfurter: Their Correspondence, 1912–1934,* ed. Robert M. Mennel and Christine L. Compston (Hanover, NH: University Press of New England, 1996), 76.

33. On the "marketplace of ideas" as a guiding jurisprudential metaphor, see Geoffrey R. Stone, "Reflections on the First Amendment: The Evolution of the American Jurisprudence of Free Expression," *Proceedings of the American Philosophical Society* 131 (1987): 259; Stanley Ingber, "The Marketplace of Ideas: A Legitimizing Myth," *Duke Law Journal* 1984 (1984): 1–91; Haig Bosmajian, *Metaphor and Reason in Judicial Opinions* (Carbondale: Southern Illinois University Press, 1992), 49–72.

On the novelty of the "marketplace of ideas" metaphor, see John Durham Peters, "'The Marketplace of Ideas': A History of the Concept," in *Toward a Political Economy of the Culture: Capitalism and Communication in the Twenty-First Century,* ed. Andrew Calabrese and Colin Sparks (Lanham, MD: Rowman and Littlefield, 2004), 65–82; Blasi, "Holmes and the Marketplace of Ideas." Both Peters and Blasi date its first use to 1935; earlier uses can be found in T. V. Smith, "Review," *International Journal of Ethics* 38 (1928): 480–482; Tully Nettleton, "The Philosophy of Justice Holmes on Freedom of Speech," *Southwestern Political Science Quarterly* 3 (1923): 287–305 (referring to a "market of ideas"). The casual use of the phrase in both cases suggest that it was already circulating.

34. Summary of Meeting, September 17–19, 1945, document 75, box 3, folder 10, p. 47, HC; Fred S. Siebert, Theodore Peterson, and Wilbur Schram, *Four Theories of the Press: The Authoritarian, Libertarian, Social Responsibility, and Soviet Communist Concepts of What the Press Should Be and Do* (Urbana: University of Illinois Press, 1956), 70.

35. Healy, *Great Dissent,* 109; White, *Justice Oliver Wendell Holmes,* 515.

36. Rather than treat either the penny press of the 1830s or the yellow press of the 1890s as *the* founding moment of the modern newspaper, it makes more sense to see the nineteenth century as a long process of commercial transformation and industrialization in the press. Michael Schudson, *Discovering the News: A Social History of American Newspapers* (New York: Basic Books, 1978); Dan Schiller, *Objectivity and the News: The Public and the Rise of Commercial Journalism* (Philadelphia: University of Pennsylvania Press, 1981); Alexander Saxton, "Problems of Class and Race in the Origins of the Mass Circulation Press," *American Quarterly* 36 (1984): 211–234; John C. Nerone, "The Mythology of the Penny Press," *Critical Studies in Mass Communications* 4 (1987): 376–404; W. Joseph Campbell, *Yellow Journalism: Puncturing the Myths, Defining the Legacies* (Westport, CT: Praeger, 2001); W. Joseph Campbell, *The Year That Defined American Journalism: 1897 and the Clash of Paradigms* (New York: Routledge, 2006); David R. Spencer, *The Yellow Journalism: The Press and America's Emergence as a World Power* (Evanston, IL: Northwestern University Press, 2007); Gerald J. Baldasty, *The Commercialization of the News in the Nineteenth Century* (Madison: University of Wisconsin, 1992), 86.

37. Starr, *Creation of the Media,* 251–253; Schudson, *Discovering the News,* 31–35.

38. Baldasty, *Commercialization of the News,* 5, 59, 84, 137; James T. Hamilton, *All the News That's Fit to Sell: How the Market Transforms Information into News* (Princeton, NJ: Princeton University Press, 2004), 48.

39. Determining the exact number of papers in the nation at any point in time is tricky: newspaper censuses were conducted by industry groups, and were notoriously imprecise. In 1942, for instance, one scholar put the total number of papers at the 1909 peak at 2,600; in 1954, another scholar put the peak at 2,202. The overall trend remains clear. In this book, I use the figures that were widely accepted at the time. Alfred McClung Lee, "The Basic Newspaper Pattern," *Annals of the American Academy of Political and Social Science* 219 (January 1942): 46; Raymond B. Nixon, "Trends in Daily Newspaper Ownership since 1945," *JQ* 31 (Winter 1954): 7; Morris Ernst, *The First Freedom* (New York: Macmillan, 1946), 56.

40. Starr, *Creation of the Media,* 252; Raymond B. Nixon and Jean Ward, "Trends in Newspaper Ownership and Inter-Media Competition," *JQ* 38 (1961): 5; Margaret A. Blanchard, "Press Criticism and National Reform Movements: The Progressive Era and the New Deal," *Journalism History* 5 (1978): 33; A. J. Liebling, *The Press,* 2nd ed. (New York: Pantheon Books, 1975), 16.

41. Baldasty, *Commercialization of the News,* 129; Starr, *Creation of the Media,* 174–175, 183–187; Richard L. Kaplan, "From Partisanship to Professionalism: The Transformation of the Daily Press," and Michael Schudson, "The Persistence of Vision: Partisan Journalism in the Mainstream Press," in *A History of the Book in*

America, vol. 4, ed. Carl F. Kaestle and Janice A. Radway (Chapel Hill: University of North Carolina Press, 2009), 116–146; Michael Schudson, "The Emergence of the Objectivity Norm in American Journalism," in *Social Norms,* ed. Michael Hechter and Karl-Dieter Opp (New York: Russell Sage Foundation, 2001), 165–185.

42. The Commission on Freedom of the Press, *A Free and Responsible Press: A General Report on Mass Communication: Newspapers, Radio, Motion Pictures, Magazines, and Books* (Chicago: University of Chicago Press, 1947), 14.

43. Rob Kroes and Robert W. Rydell, *Buffalo Bill in Bologna: The Americanization of the World, 1869–1922* (Chicago: University of Chicago Press, 2005), 104.

44. Linda Lawson, *Truth in Publishing: Federal Regulation of the Press's Business Practices, 1880–1920* (Carbondale: Southern Illinois University Press, 1993), 15, 69–70.

45. Henry George, *The Menace of Privilege,* New York 1906, excerpted in *Our Unfree Press: 100 Years of Radical Media Criticism,* ed. Robert McChesney and Ben Scott (New York: New Press, 2004), 88; Blanchard, "Press Criticism and National Reform Movements."

46. Will Irwin, *The American Newspaper,* commentary by Clifford F. Weigle and David G. Clark (Ames: Iowa State University Press, 1969), 51, first published in *Collier's* in 1911; Will Irwin, *The Making of a Reporter* (New York: G. P. Putnam's Sons, 1942), 164–165.

47. Irwin, *The American Newspaper,* 69.

48. Charles Edward Russell, "The Keeping of the Kept Press," *Pearson's Magazine* 31 (1914): 33–44, http://books.google.com/books?id=0ZQkAQAAIAAJ.

49. Upton Sinclair, *The Brass Check: A Study of American Journalism* (Pasadena, CA: printed by author, 1920), 224.

50. For introductions to a large field, see John Dewey, *Liberalism and Social Action,* in *The Later Works, 1925–1953,* vol. 11, *1935–1937,* ed. Jo Ann Boydston (Carbondale: Southern Illinois University Press, 1981–1990); John Gray, *Liberalism* (Minneapolis: University of Minnesota Press, 1986), 26–37; Gary Gerstle, "The Protean Character of American Liberalism," *American Historical Review* 99 (1994): 1043–1073.

51. If drawn crudely, the distinction between positive and negative liberties can create analytic problems. But it remains a conceptually useful distinction, not least because so many of the actors in this history relied on it. See Emily J. Zackin, *Looking for Rights in All the Wrong Places: Why State Constitutions Contain America's Positive Rights* (Princeton, NJ: Princeton University Press, 2013), 36–47.

52. Thomas L. Haskell, "The Curious Persistence of Rights Talk in the 'Age of Interpretation,'" *Journal of American History* 74 (1987): 984–1012; John Fabian Witt, "Crystal Eastman and the Internationalist Beginnings of American Civil Liberties," *Duke Law Journal* 54 (2004): 705–763; Laura Weinrib, "The Liberal Compromise: Civil Liberties, Labor, and the Limits of State Power, 1917–1940," (Ph.D. diss., Princeton University, 2011); Chafee, "Freedom of Speech in War Time," 957.

53. Chafee, "Freedom of Speech in War Time," 957–959. Mark Graber is correct that Chafee's theory of speech bracketed economic questions; but whereas Graber attributes this fact to Chafee's pragmatism and sociological jurisprudence,

I think it is because of Chafee's unreconstructed classical liberalism. See Mark A. Graber, *Transforming Free Speech: The Ambiguous Legacy of Civil Libertarianism* (Berkeley: University of California Press, 1991), 122–164; Charles L. Barzun, "Politics or Principle? Zechariah Chafee and the Social Interest in Free Speech," *Brigham Young University Law Review*, 2007, 259–326.

54. On Smith, see Thomas Healy, "The Justice Who Changed His Mind: Oliver Wendell Holmes Jr., and the Story behind Abrams v United States," *Journal of Supreme Court History* 39 (2014): 45. On Holmes's fatalism, see Durham Peters, "'Marketplace of Ideas'"; Louis Menand, *Metaphysical Club: A Story of Ideas in America* (New York: Farrar, Straus and Giroux, 2001), 65; White, *Justice Oliver Wendell Holmes;* Blasi, "Holmes and the Marketplace of Ideas."

55. Whitney v. California, 274 U.S. 357 (1927); Vincent Blasi, "The First Amendment and the Ideal of Civic Courage: The Brandeis Opinion in Whitney v California," *William and Mary Law Review* 29 (1988): 653–697; Melvin Urofsky, *Louis D. Brandeis: A Life* (New York: Pantheon Books, 2009), 359–360, 637–638.

56. Weinrib, "Liberal Compromise," 371.

57. Beginning in the 1980s, Dewey and Lippmann's work was dubbed a "debate," and a simplistic narrative of that conflict was constructed in which Lippmann straightforwardly rejected democracy and Dewey defended it. In recent years, Michael Schudson, Sue Curry Jansen, and others have revisited the original texts, finding far more nuance and subtlety in Lippmann's work and far more overlap with Dewey. In the analysis that follows, I trace an evolving disagreement between Dewey and Lippmann, as the latter's critique of theories of democratic public opinion grew more severe. See Sue Curry Jansen, "Phantom Conflict: Lippmann, Dewey and the Fate of the Public in Modern Society," *Communication and Critical/Cultural Studies* 6 (September 2009): 221–245; Michael Schudson, "The 'Lippmann-Dewey Debate' and the Invention of Walter Lippmann as an Anti-Democrat, 1986–1996," *International Journal of Communications* 2 (2008): 1031–1042.

58. After decades of neglect, the book was reissued in 2008 and again in 2010, and has begun to receive more attention. Sean Wilentz, "General Editors Introduction," in Lippmann, *Liberty and the News* (2008), vii; Walter Lippmann, *Liberty and the News* (Mineola, NY: Dover Publications, 2010); Michael Schudson, "Political Observatories, Databases and News in the Emerging Ecology of Public Information," *Daedalus* 139 (Spring 2010): 100–109; Sue Curry Jansen, *Walter Lippmann: A Critical Introduction to Media and Communication Theory* (New York: Peter Lang, 2012), 86–94, 152–154.

59. Lippmann, *Liberty and the News* (2008), 2, 33; Walter Lippmann and Charles Merz, "A Test of News," *New Republic,* August 4, 1920, supplement.

60. Lippmann, *Liberty and the News* (2008), 37–41 (my emphasis).

61. Lippmann, *Liberty and the News* (2008), 37; Walter Lippmann, *Public Opinion* (Miami: BN Publishing, 2007), 100.

62. Lippmann, *Liberty and the News* (2008), 5–7, 22, 40.

63. Ibid., 40–61.

64. Ibid., 2–3, 7.

65. Ibid., 33; Lippmann, *Public Opinion,* 15, 113.

66. Lippmann, *Public Opinion,* 111, 113.

67. Ibid., 15, 65, 81; Schudson, "Lippmann-Dewey Debate," 1033.

68. Walter Lippmann, *The Phantom Public: A Sequel to "Public Opinion"* (New York: Macmillan, 1927), 20, 25, 39, 61, 155.

69. "Practical Democracy," *New Republic,* December 2, 1925, 52; Ronald Steel, *Walter Lippmann and the American Century* (New York: Vintage Books, 1981), 216–218.

70. John Dewey, *The Public and Its Problems* (New York: Henry Holt, 1927), 116–117.

71. Robert B. Westbrook, *John Dewey and American Democracy* (Ithaca, NY: Cornell University Press, 1991), xiii.

72. Dewey, *Public and Its Problems,* 126–127, 146, 168.

73. Dewey agreed with Lippmann that "it would be a mistake to identify the conditions which limit free communication and circulation of facts and ideas . . . merely with overt forces which are obstructive." Dewey, *Public and Its Problems,* 168–169, 182.

74. John Dewey, "Public Opinion," *New Republic,* May 3, 1922, 288.

75. Dewey, *Public and Its Problems,* 146, 166, 182, 184.

76. Ibid., 184.

77. Rabban, *Free Speech in Its Forgotten Years,* 299–335.

78. Lippmann, *Liberty and the News,* 44–45.

79. Steel, *Walter Lippmann,* 314–315, 584–585; Barry D. Riccio, *Walter Lippmann: Odyssey of a Liberal* (New Brunswick, NJ: Transaction Publishers, 1994), 100, 195–198.

80. John Dewey, *Liberalism and Social Action,* in *Later Works,* vol. 11, 48; John Dewey, "Justice Holmes and the Liberal Mind," *New Republic,* January 11, 1928, 210–212.

81. John Dewey, *Ethics,* in *The Later Works, 1925–1953,* vol. 7, *1932,* ed. Jo Ann Boydston (Carbondale: Southern Illinois University Press, 1981–1990), 358.

82. John Dewey, "Meaning of Liberalism," 1935, and John Dewey, "Democracy Is Radical," January 1937, both in *Later Works,* vol. 11, 299, 367.

83. John Dewey, "Freedom," in *Later Works,* vol. 11, 253–255.

84. Such vagueness about institutional practices was typical of Dewey's political philosophy, and perhaps unavoidable. See Alan Ryan, *John Dewey and the High Tide of American Liberalism* (New York: W. W. Norton, 1995), 309–311, 319–324.

85. Sinclair, *Brass Check,* 409, 413, 421.

86. John Dewey, "Our Un-free Press," in *Later Works,* vol. 11, 269–273.

87. Lippmann, *Liberty and the News* (2008), 45.

2. Interwar Threats to Press Freedom

1. "Ickes and Gannett Debate Free Press," *NYT,* January 13, 1939, 14.

2. Frank Knox, "What Price Freedom," in *Freedom of the Press Today: A Clinical Examination by 28 Specialists,* ed. Harold L. Ickes (New York: Vanguard, 1941),

163; Marlen Pew, "Shop Talk at 30," *EP,* September 9, 1933, 36; *St. Louis Post-Dispatch, St. Louis Post-Dispatch Symposium on Freedom of the Press: Expressions by 120 Representative Americans,* reprinted from December 13 to December 25, 1938 issues (no publication details, 1938), 47.

3. Edward A. Purcell, *The Crisis of Democratic Theory: Scientific Naturalism and the Problem of Value* (Lexington: University Press of Kentucky, 1973), 95–113, 126, 132; John P. Diggins, "Flirtation with Fascism: American Pragmatic Liberals and Mussolini's Italy," *American Historical Review* 71 (1966): 487–506; Benjamin L. Alpers, *Dictators, Democracy, and American Public Culture: Envisioning the Totalitarian Enemy, 1920s–1950s* (Chapel Hill: University of North Carolina Press, 2003), 15–58; Eric Hobsbawm, *The Age of Extremes: A History of the World, 1914–1991* (New York: Vintage Books, 1994), 109–141; Ira Katznelson, *Fear Itself: The New Deal and the Origins of Our Time* (New York: Liveright, 2013).

4. Frederic A. Ogg, "Does America Need a Dictator?" *Current History* 36 (1932): 641–649; "Wanted: A Dictator! A Solution to the National Difficulty," *Vanity Fair,* June 1932, 32, 66; Ronald Steel, *Walter Lippmann and the American Century* (New York: Vintage Books, 1981), 299; David M. Kennedy, *Freedom from Fear: The American People in Depression and War, 1929–1945* (New York: Oxford University Press, 1999), 111; Alpers, *Dictators, Democracy, and American Public Culture,* 29–32; Mordaunt Hall, "Gabriel over the White House," *NYT,* April 9, 1933, X3.

5. Michaela Hoenicke Moore, *Know Your Enemy: The American Debate on Nazism, 1933–1945* (Cambridge: Cambridge University Press, 2010), 41–77; George Bernard Herrmann, "American Journalistic Perceptions of the Death of Weimar Germany: January 1932–March 1933" (Ph.D. diss., Carnegie Mellon University, 1979), 165–202.

6. "Reich Gags Press, End Prussian Diet," *NYT,* February 7, 1933, 1; "Hitler Suspends Reich Guarantees; Left Press Banned," *NYT,* March 1, 1933, 1; Robert Desmond, "200 Dailies Are Suppressed by Hitler," *EP,* April 1, 1933, 8; "Editorial: Censorship Terror," *EP,* April 1, 1933, 24; Mark Ethridge, "Reich Press Defeat Held 'Degrading,'" *EP,* April 22, 1933, 13; "Editorial: Utter Degradation," *EP,* January 6, 1934, 20.

7. Abbott Gleason, *Totalitarianism: The Inner History of the Cold War* (New York: Oxford University Press, 1995), 19; Sidney B. Fay, "The Nazi 'Totalitarian' State," *Current History* 38 (1933): 610–611; Prince Hubertus Loewenstein, "The Totalitarian State in Germany and the Individual," *Annals of the American Academy of Political and Social Science* 189 (1935): 28; Alpers, *Dictators, Democracy, and American Public Culture,* 144; Richard Gid Powers, *Not without Honor: The History of American Anticommunism* (New York: Free Press, 1995), 144–145, 452–457; Carlton J. H. Hayes, "The Challenge of Totalitarianism," *Public Opinion Quarterly* 2 (1938): 23.

8. "The Future of Democracy," *University of Chicago Roundtable* 21 (August 7, 1938): 6; Julius Yourman, "Propaganda Techniques within Nazi Germany," *Journal of Educational Sociology* 13 (1939): 148.

9. Franklin D. Roosevelt, "Greeting to the Institute of Human Relations," August 20, 1937, APP; "The Future of Democracy," *University of Chicago Roundtable,* 21 (August 7, 1938), 6–7.

10. *St. Louis Post-Dispatch Symposium on Freedom of the Press,* 35–36, 69; Rexford Tugwell, "Return to Democracy, Speech before American Society of Newspaper Editors," April 21, 1934, box 55, folder: Return to Democracy, RT; Oswald Garrison Villard, "Freedom of the Press," *Public Opinion Quarterly* 2 (1938): 58–59.

11. The gag law had been designed to deal with the pro-temperance newspaper *Ripsaw,* but attempts to enjoin *Ripsaw* became moot when the publisher of the newspaper passed away. Fred W. Friendly, *Minnesota Rag: Corruption, Yellow Journalism, and the Case That Saved Freedom of the Press* (Minneapolis: University of Minnesota Press, 1981), 3–53; Near v. Minnesota, 283 U.S. 697 (1931); John E. Hartmann, "The Minnesota Gag Law and the Fourteenth Amendment," *Minnesota History* 37 (1960): 161–173.

12. Friendly, *Minnesota Rag,* 50–53, 61–63; Hartmann, "Minnesota Gag Law," 168.

13. Gilbert v. Minnesota, 254 U.S. 325 (1920); "Anti-war Speech False, Court Rules," *WP,* December 14, 1920, 13; Paul L. Murphy, *The Constitution in Crisis Times, 1918–1969* (New York: Harper, 1972), 58–60.

14. Friendly, *Minnesota Rag,* 38, 61, 64.

15. Ibid., 70, 76–77, 90–91 106; "History of 2300 Years Cited in 'Gag' Law Brief," *CT,* March 29, 1929, 9; "Minnesota Joins the Monkey States," *CT,* March 28, 1929, 14; Paul L. Murphy, "Near v. Minnesota in the Context of Historical Developments," *Minnesota Law Review* 66 (1981): 96, 148–149; "A Vicious Law," *NYT,* April 26, 1929, 17; Richard Norton Smith, *The Colonel: The Life and Legend of Robert T. McCormick, 1880–1955* (Boston: Houghton Mifflin, 1997), 278–285; "Chandler to Head News Publishers," *NYT,* April 26, 1930, 4.

16. Argued after *Near,* but handed down two weeks before, the court's decision in Stromberg v. California was technically the first decision to uphold a free speech claim against a state law. But the decision was far less sweeping and categorical than *Near,* and it "attracted far less popular attention." Stromberg v. California, 283 U.S. 359 (1931); George Foster Jr., "The 1931 Personal Liberties Cases," *New York University Law Quarterly Review* 64 (1931): 64, 66; Christopher M. Finan, *From the Palmer Raids to the Patriot Act: A History of the Fight for Free Speech in America* (Boston: Beacon Press, 2007), 109–128.

17. Gitlow v. New York, 268 U.S. 652 (1925); Fiske v. Kansas, 274 U.S. 380 (1927); Foster, "1931 Personal Liberties Cases," 64; Murphy, *Constitution in Crisis Times,* 83–87.

18. "A Vicious Law," *NYT,* April 26, 1929, 17; on the legal briefs, see Friendly, *Minnesota Rag,* 59–60; Murphy, "Near v. Minnesota," 150–151; Harry Shulman, "The Supreme Court's Attitude toward Liberty of Contract and Freedom of Speech," *Yale Law Journal* 41 (1931): 269.

19. *Near,* 283 U.S. at 708, 713, 720.

20. *Near,* 283 U.S. at 723–724, 732.

21. Smith, *Colonel,* 284.

22. *Near,* 283 U.S. at 716; "Recent Cases," *Minnesota Law Review* 16 (1931): 98; Jeffrey A. Smith, *War and Press Freedom: The Problem of Prerogative Power* (New York: Oxford University Press, 1999), 50–55.

23. "Press Heartily Acclaims Decision Vindicating Freedom Principle," *EP*, June 6, 1931, 17; "Decision Ends Gag on Press," *CT*, June 2, 1931, 1; Arthur Sears Henning, "Supreme Court Liberalized in Recent Months," *CT*, June 3, 1931, 4; Pendleton Howard, "The Supreme Court and State Action Challenged under the Fourteenth Amendment, 1930–1931," *University of Pennsylvania Law Review* 80 (1932): 504–505; Maurice S. Culp, "Constitutional Law—Freedom of the Press—Restraints on Publication," *Michigan Law Review* 30 (1931): 279–281.

24. "Previous Restraints upon Freedom of Speech," *Columbia Law Review* 31 (1931): 1148–1149; "Ruling on Free Speech Praised," *Los Angeles Times*, June 3, 1931, A2.

25. "Press Heartily Acclaims Decision Vindicating Freedom Principle," *EP*, June 6, 1931, 17; "Press Freedom Celebration Set for Monticello," *CT*, October 13, 1931, 21; John Herrick, "Laud Jefferson as Champion of a Free Press," *CT*, October 21, 1931, 6; Friendly, *Minnesota Rag*, 161.

26. Gerald W. Johnson, "Freedom of the Newspaper Press," *Annals of the American Academy of Political and Social Science* 200 (1938): 64–65; "Press vs. Public," *New Republic*, March 17, 1937, 190.

27. "Sees Ballyhoo to Lift Stocks," *Wall Street Journal*, April 27, 1932, 11; "La Guardia Charges Pools Paid Writers to 'Ballyhoo' Stock," *NYT*, April 27, 1932, 1.

28. George Seldes, *Freedom of the Press* (1935; repr., New York: Da Capo, 1971), 78; Carl D. Thompson, *Confessions of the Power Trust* (New York: E. P. Dutton, 1932), vii–viii.

29. John W. Perry, "Utilities Abandon Propaganda Work," *EP*, February 18, 1933, 7; Seldes, *Freedom of the Press*, 82–96; Thompson, *Confessions of the Power Trust*, 269–329.

30. Seldes, *Freedom of the Press*, 85; Harold L. Ickes, *America's House of Lords: An Inquiry into Freedom of the Press* (New York: Harcourt, Brace, 1939), 21–27.

31. Thompson, *Confessions of the Power Trust*, 285–287.

32. Alfred McClung Lee, "The Basic Newspaper Pattern," *Annals of the American Academy of Political and Social Science* 219 (1942): 46.

33. Ickes, *America's House of Lords*, 14.

34. "Affidavit of Alfred McClung Lee," May 10, 1943, Appellate Case Files 57 02 1944, folder 1, box 3844, RG 267; Census data from www.census.gov/popest/data/national/totals/pre-1980/tables/popclockest.txt.

35. Robert McChesney and John Nichols, *The Death and Life of American Journalism: The Media Revolution That Will Begin the World Again* (Philadelphia, PA: Nation Books, 2010), 31–33.

36. Saul Nelson, "The Newspaper Industry," November 11, 1933, box 1943, file: Reports, Studies and Surveys, entry 25, RG 9.

37. Alfred McClung Lee, "Recent Developments in the Newspaper Industry," *Public Opinion Quarterly* 2 (1938): 133; Lee, "Basic Newspaper Pattern," 49; Alfred McClung Lee, "Trends Affecting the Daily Newspapers," *Public Opinion Quarterly* 3 (1939): 497–502.

38. Arthur Robb, "Newspaper Groups Doubled in Decade," *EP*, February 17, 1934, 11; Lee, "Basic Newspaper Pattern," 49; Lee, "Trends Affecting the Daily

Newspapers," 497–502; William Weinfeld, "The Growth of Daily Newspaper Chains in the United States: 1923, 1926–1935," *JQ* 13 (December 1936): 357–380.

39. Irving Brant, "The Press for Willkie Club," in Ickes, *Freedom of the Press Today,* 52; *St. Louis Post-Dispatch Symposium on Freedom of the Press,* 64.

40. Ickes, *America's House of Lords,* 17–18; Seldes, *Freedom of the Press,* 123; Vernon McKenzie, "A Newspaper Should Be Accurate, Fair and Make Money," in Ickes, *Freedom of the Press Today,* 195–202 (emphasis in original).

41. Bruce Bliven, "Balance Sheet for American Journalism," in Ickes, *Freedom of the Press Today,* 34; Sinclair Lewis, *It Can't Happen Here* (New York: Signet Classics, 2005), 288; Stephen L. Tanner, "Sinclair Lewis and Fascism," *Studies in the Novel* 22 (1990): 57–66.

42. *Mr. Smith Goes to Washington,* directed by Frank Capra (Starry Night Studio, 1939) streamed on Amazon, www.amazon.com/Mr-Smith-Goes-Washington-Unavailable/dp/B00N17PYZA/ref=sr_1_cc_1?s=aps&ie=UTF8&qid=1437745194&sr=1-1-catcorr&keywords=mr+smith+goes+to+washington; *Meet John Doe,* directed by Frank Capra (Echelon Studios, 1941), streamed on Amazon, www.amazon.com/Meet-John-Doe-Frank-Capra/dp/B002KVX7JI/ref=sr_1_2?ie=UTF8&qid=1437744880&sr=8-2&keywords=meet+john+doe; Glenn Alan Phelps, "The 'Populist' Films of Frank Capra," *Journal of American Studies* 13 (1979): 377–392; "Mr. Capra Goes to Washington," *Representations* 85 (2003): 213–248.

43. The *Fortune* figure ignored Hearst's considerable debts, which were not public knowledge until the late 1930s. David Nasaw, *The Chief: The Life of William Randolph Hearst* (Boston: Houghton Mifflin, 2000), 405, 508; Betty Houchin Winfield, *FDR and the News Media* (Urbana: University of Illinois Press, 1990), 21; George Seldes, *Lords of the Press* (New York: Blue Ribbon Books, 1941), 234; "Challenges Court over Hearst Suit," *NYT,* March 27, 1936, 6.

44. "15,000 Here Object to Rift with Reds," *NYT,* February 26, 1935, 8; "Antiwar Protest Defies Police Ban," *NYT,* April 7 1935, 81; "Educators Assail Hearst 'Influence,' " *NYT,* February 25, 1935, 18; Nasaw, *Chief,* 507; Los Angeles League Against Yellow Journalism Report, November 1935, box 89, folder: League Against Yellow Journalism, Record Group 233: Records of the US House of Representatives, National Archives and Records Administration, Washington, DC; "Work Plan Irks Thomas," *NYT,* January 7, 1935, 31; W. A. Swanberg, *Citizen Hearst* (New York: Scribner, 1961), 523–531, 565; Raymond Gram Swing, *Forerunners of American Fascism* (New York: Julian Messner, 1935), 134–152.

45. Winfield, *FDR and the News Media,* 127–128.

46. The limited effects theory of media influence on voting broke through with Paul Lazarsfeld, Bernard Berelson, and Hazel Gaudet, *The People's Choice: How the Voter Makes Up His Mind in a President Campaign* (New York: Columbia University Press, 1944). It was foreshadowed in "Conclusions," *New Republic,* March 17, 1937, 188; J. Roscoe Drummond, "Public Duty of a Free Press," *Public Opinion Quarterly* 2 (1938): 60; B. P. Garnett, "Press," *Public Opinion Quarterly* 5 (1941): 119–121.

47. Irving Brant, "The Press for Willkie Club," in Ickes, *Freedom of the Press Today,* 59–60.

48. William Allen White, "How Free Is Our Press?" *Nation,* June 18, 1938, 693–695; Seldes, *Lords of the Press,* 19; "Ickes and Gannett Debate Free Press," *NYT,* January 13, 1939, 14.

49. J. David Stern, "The Newspaper Publisher Moves across the Railroad," in Ickes, *Freedom of the Press Today,* 245; Herbert Agar, "Rights Are Responsibilities," in Ickes, *Freedom of the Press Today,* 22.

50. Bryant Putney, "Federal Publicity," *Editorial Research Reports,* March 18, 1940, 203.

51. Paul Starr, *The Creation of the Media: Political Origins of Modern Communications* (New York: Basic Books, 2005), 374.

52. Putney, "Federal Publicity," 210.

53. Leo C. Rosten, *The Washington Correspondents* (New York: Harcourt, Brace, 1937), 67–71.

54. Putney, "Federal Publicity," 210–211; James L. McCamy, *Government Publicity: Its Practice in Federal Administration* (Chicago: University of Chicago Press, 1939), 138, 144; Cedric Larson, "How Much Federal Publicity Is There?" *Public Opinion Quarterly* 2 (1934): 636–644.

55. Putney, "Federal Publicity," 209; Delbert Clark, *Washington Dateline* (New York: Frederick A. Stokes, 1941), 130–138; George Michael, *Handout* (New York: G. P. Putnam's Sons, 1935), 219–232; Rosten, *Washington Correspondents,* 70; Elisha Hanson, "Official Propaganda and the New Deal," *Annals of the American Academy of Political and Social Science* 179 (1935): 176, 180; McCamy, *Government Publicity,* 206–209; E. Pendleton Herring, "Official Publicity under the New Deal," *Annals of the American Academy of Political and Social Science* 179 (1935): 168.

56. Donald A. Ritchie, *Press Gallery: Congress and the Washington Correspondents* (Cambridge, MA: Harvard University Press, 1991); Donald A. Ritchie, *Reporting from Washington: The History of the Washington Press Corps* (Oxford: Oxford University Press, 2005), xv, 8; Winfield, *FDR and the News Media,* 79.

57. Rosten, *Washington Correspondents,* 19–51, 62–63; Clark, *Washington Dateline,* 80–89, 142–164; Douglass Cater, *The Fourth Branch of Government* (Cambridge, MA: Houghton Mifflin, 1959), 142–155; Graham J. White, *FDR and the Press* (Chicago: University of Chicago Press, 1979), 5–24.

58. Putney, "Federal Publicity," 208, 216; Mordecai Lee, *Congress vs. the Bureaucracy: Muzzling Agency Public Relations* (Norman: University of Oklahoma Press, 2011); Arthur Krock, "The Press and Government," *Annals of the American Academy of Political and Social Science* 180 (1935): 162–167; David Lloyd Jones, "The US Office of War Information and American Public Opinion During World War II" (Ph.D. diss., SUNY-Binghamton, 1976), 41; Mordecai Lee, "Government Public Relations during Herbert Hoover's Presidency," *Public Relations Review* 36 (2010): 56–58; J. Frederick Essary, "Uncle Sam's Ballyhoo Men," *American Mercury,* August 1931, 419–428.

59. Rosten, *Washington Correspondents,* 8; Harold W. Stoke, "Executive Leadership and the Growth of Propaganda," *American Political Science Review* 35 (1941): 490–500; Herring, "Official Publicity under the New Deal," 174; Putney, "Federal Publicity," 218; McCamy, *Government Publicity,* 15–19.

60. Mark W. Summers, *The Press Gang: Newspapers and Politics, 1865–1878* (Chapel Hill: University of North Carolina Press, 1994); Culver H. Smith, *The Press, Politics and Patronage: The American Government's Use of Newspapers, 1789–1875* (Athens: University of Georgia Press, 1977); Ted Curtis Smythe, *The Gilded Age Press, 1865–1900* (Westport, CT: Praeger, 2003), 204; Ritchie, *Press Gallery,* 182; Michael Schudson, "The Persistence of Vision: Partisan Journalism in the Mainstream Press," in *A History of the Book in America,* vol. 4, ed. Carl F. Kaestle and Janice A. Radway (Chapel Hill: University of North Carolina Press, 2009): 143–145.

61. Sidney M. Milkis, *The President and the Parties: The Transformation of the American Party System since the New Deal* (New York: Oxford University Press, 1993).

62. Richard Polenberg, *Reorganizing Roosevelt's Government: The Controversy over Executive Reorganization, 1936–1939* (Cambridge, MA: Harvard University Press, 1966), 31–39, 64–65, 149; Lee, *Congress vs. the Bureaucracy,* 206–214; Milkis, *President and the Parties,* 120–121.

63. Michael, *Handout,* vii–ix, 3–4; "Legislator Finds Hornets Nest of Publicity Offices," *WP,* April 11, 1938, x2; McCamy, *Government Publicity,* 15; "Dewey Denounces 'Propaganda' Cost," *NYT,* February 17, 1940, 7; Arthur Evans, "New Deal Propaganda Hit," *CT,* February 17, 1940, 1.

64. Elmer Davis, "The New Deal's Uses of Publicity: Review of Handout," *NYT,* May 19, 1935, BR5; McCamy, *Government Publicity,* 110, 263–264; Mordecai Lee, "Herman Beyle and James McCamy: Founders of the Study of Public Relations in Public Administration, 1928–1939," *Public Voices* 11 (2010): 34; "McCamy Named Farm Aide," *Christian Science Monitor,* January 27, 1939, 9.

65. McCamy, *Government Publicity,* 28–29, 246, 263–264; Lee, *Congress vs. the Bureaucracy,* 147; "Dickinson of Iowa Asks Senate Quiz of New Deal Press," *CT,* May 8, 1935, 7; "Roosevelt Praises Radio, Raps Press," *Broadcasting,* May 15, 1939, 9; Franklin D. Roosevelt: "Radio Interview on Government Reporting to the People," May 9, 1939, APP.

66. Clark, *Washington Dateline,* 102; Putney, "Federal Publicity," 218; McCamy, *Government Publicity,* 32.

3. A New Deal for the Corporate Press?

1. "Free Press Crisis Stressed as Leaders Celebrate John Zenger's Triumph," *EP,* November 4, 1933, 3; "Zenger, Free Press Defender, Honored," *Wall Street Journal,* October 30, 1933, 10.

2. Frank Knox, "What Price Freedom," in *Freedom of the Press Today: A Clinical Examination by 28 Specialists,* ed. Harold L. Ickes (New York: Vanguard, 1941), 164.

3. J. B. S. Hardman, "The Newspaper Industry and Freedom of Press," in Ickes, *Freedom of the Press Today,* 128–130.

4. "Press: Newsboy Labor," *Time,* June 25, 1934, 68; "Elisha Hanson Sees Signs of Reaction to 'Over-Regulation,' " *Baltimore Sun,* March 5, 1939, 2; Elisha Hanson,

"Official Propaganda and the New Deal," *Annals of the American Academy of Political and Social Science* 179 (1935): 180; Elisha Hanson, "Life, Liberty and Property: The Need for a Free Press," *Vital Speeches of the Day*, February 1, 1938, 254–256; "Publishers' Counsel Warns of Press Peril," *Los Angeles Times*, January 16, 1938, 16; "Two Warn of Peril in Curbs on Press," *NYT*, October 14, 1936, 22; Elisha Hanson, "Says AP Ruling will Lead to Regulation of the Press," *EP*, November 13, 1943, 8; Edwin Emery, *History of the American Newspaper Publishers Association* (Minneapolis: University of Minnesota Press, 1950), 218–247.

5. "Roosevelt Hails Goal: He Calls Recovery Act Most Sweeping Law in Nation's History," *NYT*, June 17, 1933, 1; Ellis Hawley, *The New Deal and the Problem of Monopoly: A Study in Economic Ambivalence* (Princeton, NJ: Princeton University Press, 1966), 19–146; David M. Kennedy, *Freedom from Fear: The American People in Depression and War, 1929–1945* (New York: Oxford University Press, 1999), 150, 177–189.

6. John W. Perry, "US Press Organizes Nucleus Group under Provisions of Industry Act," *EP*, June 17, 1933, 6; "Milwaukee Journal Scores ANPA Bulletin on Recovery Act," *EP*, July 29, 1933, 6; "Editorial: Trying to Fit the Shoe," *EP*, July 15, 1933, 20; Margaret Blanchard, "Press Freedom and the Newspaper Code," *JQ* 54 (1977): 40–49.

7. "Milwaukee Journal Scores ANPA Bulletin on Recovery Act," *EP*, July 29, 1933, 6; "Editorial: They Should Have It," *EP*, October 28, 1933, 22; Lindsay Rogers, "If Dailies Want Free Press Code Clause, They Should Have It Rogers Says," *EP*, October 28, 1933, 5.

8. "Editorial: Trying to Fit the Shoe," *EP*, July 15, 1933, 20; "Editorial: Surplusage," *EP*, September 30, 1933, 32; "Editorial: Recovery," *EP*, June 24, 1933, 26; Kennedy, *Freedom from Fear*, 183; George A. Brandenburg, "NRA Can't License Press—Johnson," *EP*, November 11, 1933, 7; "Editorial: Getting Rough," *EP*, November 11, 1933, 24.

9. "Editors Supporting New Deal Legislation: Feel Newspapers Are Not Affected," *EP*, June 24, 1933, 5; Albert W. Bates, to Hugh Johnson, November 18, 1933, Code of Fair Competition for Daily Newspaper Publishing Business, vol. B, pt. 1, box 203, entry 20, RG 9; "Editorial: They Should Have It," *EP*, October 28, 1933, 22; "Editorial: Groping Forward," *EP*, July 22, 1933, 24.

10. George Manning, "Free Press and Open Shop Protection in Substitute Newspaper Code," *EP*, August 19, 1933, 5; "Revised Newspaper Code Approved," *EP*, August 19, 1933, 7; Daniel J. Leab, *A Union of Individuals: The Formation of the American Newspaper Guild, 1933–1936* (New York: Columbia University Press, 1970), 35–39; Alfred McClung Lee, *The Daily Newspaper in America: The Evolution of a Social Instrument* (New York: Macmillan, 1937), 242–246.

11. Testimony of Elisha Hanson, Hearing on Code of Fair Practices and Competition Presented by Newspaper Publishing Industry, September 22, 1933, box 95, entry 44, RG 9; A. H. Kirchhofer to FDR, November 13 1933, Code of Fair Competition for Daily Newspaper Publishing Business, vol. B, pt. 1, box 203, entry 20, RG 9.

12. Memo on Fair Competition and Newspaper Industry, n.d., OF 466; Testimony of Elisha Hanson, and Testimony of Harry Von Horn, both in Hearing on

Code of Fair Practices and Competition Presented by Newspaper Publishing Industry, September 22, 1933, box 95, entry 44, RG 9.

13. Memo on Fair Competition and Newspaper Industry, n.d., OF 466; Suffolk News Company Inc., to General Hugh S. Johnson, August 7, 1933, box 203, Code of Fair Competition for Daily Newspaper Publishing Business, vol. B, pt. 1, entry 20, RG 9; Newspaper and Publisher-Printing Industry of Pennsylvania, "Suggested Code of Fair Competition," August 17, 1933, box 1930, file: Documents for Code Approval, entry 25, RG 9; H. Doorly to Hugh S. Johnson, December 11, 1933, box 203, Code of Fair Competition for Daily Newspaper Publishing Business: vol. B, pt. 1, entry 20, RG 9; John H. Payne to Francis M. Robinson, November 20, 1933, Code of Fair Competition for Daily Newspaper Publishing Business, vol. B, pt. 1, box 203, entry 20, RG 9; Testimony of E. E. Keister and Testimony of John Fahey, Hearing on Code of Fair Practices and Competition Presented by Newspaper Publishing Industry, September 22, 1933, 1462, 1492–1495, box 95, entry 44, RG 9.

14. Deryl J. Case, *A History of the Code of Fair Competition for the Daily Newspaper Publishing Business,* December 27, 1935, box 48, Records of the Review Division, RG 9; George H. Manning, "Weekend Talks May Settle Code Disputes between Press and NRA," *EP,* December 2, 1933, 4; Memo on December 9 Code 1933, n.d., OF 466; "Newspaper Code Guards Freedom of Press Ideal," *CT,* February 29, 1934, 8; "Press Freedom Is Guaranteed by News Code," *WP,* February 20, 1934, 3.

15. Warren L. Bassett, "President's Remarks Draw Press Fire," *EP,* February 24, 1934, 5; George H. Manning, "President's Approval of Dailies Code Raises New Questions for Publishers," *EP,* February 24, 1934, 3; Franklin D. Roosevelt, "Executive Order," February 17, 1934, OF 466.

16. Homer Cummings to Stephen Early, June 19, 1934, OF 466; Hugh S. Johnson, *The Blue Eagle from Egg to Earth* (Garden City, NJ: Doubleday, 1935), 309; Frederick I. Thompson to Hugh Johnson, n.d., box 1943, file: Trade Practices, entry 25, RG 9; Frederick I. Thompson to Colonel W. T. Chantland, FTC, May 20, 1933, box 1943, file: Trade Practices, entry 25, RG 9; S. M. Williams to Walter Webb, April 27, 1934, box 1928, file: Complaints A–F, entry 25, RG 9; Payson Irwin to Harold M. Stephens, February 10, 1934, box 1943, file: Trade Practices, entry 25, RG 9.

17. Testimony of W. G. Campbell, Hearing on Code of Fair Practices and Competition Presented by Newspaper Publishing Industry, September 22, 1933, 1485–1489, box 95, entry 44, RG 9; Press Release, n.d., OF 375; Inger L. Stole, *Advertising on Trial: Consumer Activism and Corporate Public Relations in the 1930s* (Urbana: University of Illinois Press, 2006), 26, 44, 53; James Rorty, "The Business Nobody Knows," in *Our Unfree Press: 100 Years of Radical Media Criticism,* ed. Robert McChesney and Ben Scott (New York: New Press, 2004), 135; George Seldes, *Freedom of the Press* (1935; repr., New York: Da Capo, 1971), 75.

18. Stole, *Advertising on Trial,* 50–51; "Trade Board Loses Advertising Case," *NYT,* May 26, 1931, 24; Richard S. Tedlow, "From Competitor to Consumer: The Changing Focus of Federal Regulation of Advertising, 1914–1938," *Business History Review* 55 (1981): 48–51; Tugwell to FDR, January 26, 1934, OF 375.

19. Draft Bill cited from a Henry Wallace Circular Letter, June 1, 1933, OF 375; Rexford G. Tugwell, "Tugwell Defends Food and Drug Bill; Holds Sweeping Powers Necessary," *EP,* September 16, 1933, 5; Tugwell to FDR, June 1, 1933, OF 375; Stole, *Advertising on Trial,* 57.

20. "Opinion Is Divided on Tugwell Bill," *EP,* September 23, 1933, 9; "Wallace Seeks Control of Drug Output and Ads," *CT,* June 3, 1933, 3; Bernard Sternsher, *Rexford Tugwell and the New Deal* (New Brunswick, NJ: Rutgers University Press, 1964), 223, 239–240; "Bill to Strengthen Food Act Weighed," *Wall Street Journal,* May 18, 1933, 2; "N.Y. Trade Body Attacks Drug and Food Bill," *CT,* June 2, 1934, 4; "President Says He Still Wants Food-Drug Bill," *CT,* May 2, 1936, 15; 74 Cong. Rec. H10677–10680 (June 20, 1936); David F. Cavers, "The Food, Drug and Cosmetic Act of 1938: Its Legislative History and Substantive Provisions," *Law and Contemporary Problems* 6 (1939): 17.

21. *Food, Drugs and Cosmetics: Hearings before a Subcommittee of the Committee on Commerce on S.1944,* 73rd Cong., 2nd Sess. (December 7–8, 1933) (Statement of Walter G. Campbell) (Statement of Elisha Hanson), 69, 456–458; George H. Manning, "New Food and Drug Bill Strictly Regulates Advertising Copy," *EP,* June 10, 1933, 38.

22. In 1942, a unanimous Supreme Court would explicitly deny First Amendment protections to commercial speech in Valentine v. Chrestensen, 316 U.S. 52 (1942). Truthful advertising would be granted First Amendment protections in VA Board of Pharmacy v. VA Citizens Consumer Council, 425 U.S. 748 (1976).

23. *Food, Drugs and Cosmetics: Hearings before a Subcommittee of the Committee on Commerce on S.1944,* 73rd Cong., 2nd Sess. (December 7–8, 1933) (Statement of Elisha Hanson), 456–458.

24. "Hearing Feb 27 on New Copeland Bill," *EP,* February 17, 1934, 9; Amon Carter to Marvin McIntyre, May 18, 1934, OF 375; *Business Week,* October 28, 1933, cited in Rexford Tugwell, A New Deal Memoir, n.d., 127, box 42, file: A New Deal Memoir, chap. 4, RT; Wesley E. Disney to FDR, January 26, 1934, OF 375.

25. R. Karger to FDR, June 15, 1938, OF 375; Cavers, "Food, Drug and Cosmetic Act," 5; Leo C. Rosten, *The Washington Correspondents* (New York: Harcourt, Brace, 1937), 217–218, 229, 287; Harold L. Ickes, *America's House of Lords: An Inquiry into the Freedom of the Press* (New York: Harcourt, Brace, 1939), 33–34.

26. "Hearing Feb 27 on New Copeland Bill," *EP,* February 17, 1934, 9; George H. Manning, "Many Changes in Tugwell Bill as Rewritten by Copeland," *EP,* January 13, 1934, 10; Tugwell to FDR, February 21, 1934, OF 375; Loda Mae Davis to FDR, February 20, 1934, OF 375; Warren P. Munsell, Theatre Guild, to FDR, June 8, 1934, OF 375.

27. Cavers, "Food, Drug and Cosmetic Act of 1938," 22; Stole, *Advertising on Trial,* 145, 155–156; Tedlow, "From Competitor to Consumer," 57; Elisha Hanson, "The Guaranty of a Free Press," *Vital Speeches of the Day,* April 15, 1940, 435; "Free Press Peril Seen," *Los Angeles Times,* October 18, 1934, A16.

28. Rexford G. Tugwell, The Tugwell Bill Becomes Un-American, n.d., box 31, folder: Diary June 1933–1934, RT; George Seldes, *Lords of the Press* (New York: Blue Ribbon Books, 1941), 12; James L. McCamy, *Government Publicity: Its*

Practice in Federal Administration (Chicago: University of Chicago Press, 1939), 25–26, 31, 110.

29. U.S. District Court for the Southern District of New York, "Findings of Fact and Conclusions of Law," Civil Action no. 19–163, box 2842, folder 3, Appellate Case files, 57 O.T. 194, RG 267; Paul Starr, *The Creation of the Media: Political Origins of Modern Communications* (New York: Basic Books, 2004), 174–175, 183–187; Margaret A. Blanchard, "The Associated Press Antitrust Suit: A Philosophical Clash over Ownership of First Amendment Rights," *Business History Review* 61 (1987): 44–50; Department of Justice, Press Release, August 28, 1942, box 60, folder: Associated Press, Thurman Wesley Arnold Papers, Collection Number 00627, American Heritage Center, University of Wyoming, WY (hereafter, Arnold Papers).

30. Upton Sinclair, *The Brass Check: A Study of American Journalism* (Pasadena, CA: printed by author, 1920), 353–376; Oswald Garrison Villard, *The Disappearing Daily: Chapters in American Newspaper Evolution* (New York: A. A. Knopf, 1944), 40–57; Walter Lippmann and Charles Merz, "A Test of News," *New Republic,* August 4, 1920, supplement, 24, 26, 35; Seldes, *Freedom of the Press,* 173, 177, 184, 192.

31. Blanchard, "Associated Press Antitrust Suit," 49–52.

32. Marshall Field to Francis Biddle, February 5, 1942, exhibit 1, and "Affidavit of Marshall Field," May 13, 1943, Appellate Case Files, 57 02 1944, box 3844, folder 1, RG 267; "Affidavit of Alfred McLung Lee," May 20, 1943, Appellate Case Files, 57 02 1944, box 3844, folder 1, RG 267; Department of Justice, Press Release, August 28 1942, box 60, folder: Associated Press, Arnold Papers; Walter E. Schneider, "3-Judge Court Hears Opening Argument in Suit against AP," *EP,* July 10, 1943, 5.

33. "AP Brief Sees Free Press as Main Issue in Case," *EP,* July 10, 1943, 7; "AP Assails Indirect Approach to Control," *EP,* December 2, 1944, 12.

34. "Affidavit of Robert Rutherford McCormick," June 19, 1943, Appellate Case Files, 57 02 1944, box 3844, folder 1, RG 267; Brief on behalf of *Chicago Times,* amicus curiae, Brief of the American Newspaper Publishers Association as amicus curiae, both in box 3845, folder 57 OT 1944, RG 267.

35. United States v. Associated Press, 52 F. Supp. 362 at 372 (1943).

36. Ibid.; Biddle, AG, Memorandum for the President, October 13, 1943, Franklin D. Roosevelt Official File 172: Associated Press, Franklin Delano Roosevelt Library, Hyde Park, NY; "Lewin Says U.S. won AP Case; Biddle Satisfied," *EP,* October 16, 1943, 16.

37. George A. Brandenburg, "AP Members Vote to Fight Federal Control of News," *EP,* April 29, 1944, 13; Robert Jackson recused himself because he had been attorney general when the Justice Department was preparing its case. "Questions from Bench Enliven Debate on AP," *EP,* December 9, 1944, 9; "Supreme Court Rules against AP 5–3," *EP,* June 23, 1945, 5.

38. This balancing act was made explicit in the famous footnote 4 in Justice Harlan Stone's decision in United States v. Carolene Products Co., 304 U.S. 144 (1938); David Yassky, "Eras of the First Amendment," *Columbia Law Review* 91 (1991): 1729–1738; William E. Leuchtenburg, *The Supreme Court Reborn: The*

Constitutional Revolution in the Age of Roosevelt (New York: Oxford University Press, 1995), 213–258. In Associated Press v. Labor Board, 301 U.S. 103 (1937), discussed in Chapter 4, the court had held that the First Amendment did not automatically exempt the press from general economic legislation. But the case had come before the court's new balancing theory was fully articulated, and it dealt only with the Wagner Act.

39. AP v. U.S., 326 U.S. at 48 (1945), 28–29.

40. Paul L. Murphy, *The Constitution in Crisis Times: 1918–1969* (New York: Harper Torchbooks, 1972), 191–194; Hawley, *Problem of Monopoly*, 284.

41. W. Wallace Kirkpatrick, "Justice Black and Antitrust," *UCLA Law Review* 14 (1967): 475–500; "Justice Black and First Amendment 'Absolutes:' A Public Interview," *NYU Law Review* 37 (1962): 549–563.

42. AP v. U.S., 326 U.S. at 18–19.

43. AP v. U.S., 326 U.S. at 13–14.

44. AP v. U.S., 326 U.S. at 20.

45. U.S. v. AP, 52 F. Supp. at 374–375.

46. Keith Roberts, "Antitrust Problems in the Newspaper Industry," *Harvard Law Review* 82 (1968): 332; Richard A. Schwarzlose, "Trends in U.S. Newspapers' Services Resources, 1934–1966," *JQ* 43 (1966): 627–638; Randy Brubaker, "The Newspaper Preservation Act: How It Affects Diversity in the Newspaper Industry," *Journal of Communication Inquiry* 7 (1982): 100.

47. Zechariah Chafee Jr., *Government and Mass Communications: A Report from the Commission on Freedom of the Press* (Chicago: University of Chicago Press, 1947), 628, 633, 643.

48. AP v. U.S., 326 U.S. at 23, 58.

49. St. Louis Post-Dispatch, *St. Louis Post-Dispatch Symposium on Freedom of the Press: Expressions by 120 Representative Americans*. Reprinted from December 13, to December 25, 1938 issues (no publication details, 1938), 50; Tom Wallace, "The Press Is Free, Not Faultless," in Ickes, *Freedom of the Press Today*, 254.

50. Elisha Hanson, "Says AP Ruling Will Lead to Regulation of the Press," *EP*, November 13, 1943, 8; "The Text of Grenville Clark's Address on the Rights of the Press," *NYT*, April 28, 1938, 13; Grenville Clark, "Conservatism and Civil Liberties," *American Bar Association Journal* 24 (1938): 640–644; Laura Weinrib, "The Liberal Compromise: Civil Liberties, Labor, and the Limits of State Power, 1917–1940" (Ph.D. diss., Princeton University, 2011), 382–389; Murphy, *Constitution in Crisis Times*, 175–176; Donald L. Smith, *Zechariah Chafee, Jr.: Defender of Liberty and Law* (Cambridge, MA: Harvard University Press, 1986), 195; Jeremy K. Kessler, "The Civil Libertarian Conditions of Conscription" (paper presented at the Annual Meeting of the American Society for Legal History, November 8, 2013), 9–17; Jeremy K. Kessler, "The Early Years of First Amendment Lochnerism," draft article. My thanks to Jeremy for sharing his excellent work with me while his article was in draft form.

51. Elisha Hanson, "The Guaranty of a Free Press," *Vital Speeches of the Day*, April 15, 1940, 435; Virginius Dabney, "The Press and the Election," *Public Opinion Quarterly* 1 (1937): 124; Rosten, *Washington Correspondents*, 217; "Whose Freedom of the Press?" *New Republic*, July 14, 1937, 266.

52. Grosjean v. American Press Co., Inc., 297 U.S. 233 (1936); Richard C. Cortner, *The Kingfish and the Constitution: Huey Long, the First Amendment and the Emergence of Modern Press Freedom in America* (Westport, CT: Greenwood, 1996), 164; Samuel R. Olken, "The Business of Expression: Economic Liberty, Political Factions and the Forgotten First Amendment Jurisprudence of Justice George Sutherland," *William and Mary Bill Rights Journal* 10 (2002): 281–308; Editorial, *The Nation,* April 3, 1935, 374; Editorial, *The Nation,* February 26, 1936, 234.

53. Richard L. Wilson, "Freedom of the Press: Its Practical Meaning," in Ickes, *Freedom of the Press Today,* 301; Freda Kirchwey, "How to Get a Free Press," in Ickes, *Freedom of the Press Today,* 155–162.

54. Wilson, "Freedom of the Press," 301.

4. Dependent Journalists, Independent Journalism?

1. Jonathan Eddy to International Executive Board, January 21, 1938, box 63, folder 10, NG; Press Release, March 26, 1940, box 5, folder 16, NGNY; "The Press: Showdown," *Time,* December 19, 1938, 33; "Hearst Gives Gangsterism New Boost," *GR,* January 3, 1939, 3; "Hearst Gets Sweeping Writ," *GR,* February 15, 1939, 1.

2. As a result of loose internal bookkeeping, early membership figures were imprecise—according to some accounts the guild had up to 20,000 members in 1940. "Collective Bargaining by the American Newspaper Guild," *Monthly Labor Review* 50 (1940): 826; Summary Highlights of Officers' Report to 1955 ANG convention, n.d., folder 1: ANG Convention 1955 (1), box 70, NGNY; Sam Kuczun, "History of the American Newspaper Guild" (Ph.D. diss., University of Minnesota, 1970), 225, 229, 363; Louis Stark, "Labor News in the Secular Press," in *Freedom of the Press Today: A Clinical Examination by 28 Specialists,* ed. Harold L. Ickes (New York: Vanguard, 1941), 238; "Free Press Status Weighed at Herald Tribune Forum," *EP,* October 9, 1937, 13.

3. "Free Press Status Weighed at Herald Tribune Forum," *EP,* October 9, 1937, 13.

4. Joseph S. Myers, "What Have the Schools Done?" *Journalism Bulletin* 2 (1925): 1–2; Will Irwin, *The American Newspaper* (Ames: Iowa State University Press, 1969), 40. On the rise of the waged journalist, see Henry King, "The Pay and Rank of Journalists," *Forum* 18 (1895): 587–596; Ted Curtis Smythe, "The Reporter 1880–1900: Working Conditions and Their Influence on the News," *Journalism History* 7 (1980): 1–10; William E. Huntzicker, *The Popular Press, 1833–1865* (Westport, CT: Greenwood, 1999): 165–168; Marianne Salcetti, "The Emergence of the Reporter," in *Newsworkers: Toward a History of the Rank and File,* ed. Hanno Hardt and Bonnie Brennan (Minneapolis: University of Minnesota Press, 1995), 48–74; Michael Schudson, *Discovering the News: A Social History of American Newspapers* (New York: Basic Books, 1978), 61–87; Michael Schudson, "Question Authority: A History of the News Interview," in *The Power of the News* (Cambridge, MA: Harvard University Press, 1995): 72–93; Gerald J. Baldasty, *The Commercialization of the News in the Nineteenth Century* (Madison: University of Wisconsin Press, 1992), 88–97.

5. For competing, but not necessarily mutually exclusive, accounts of the rise of objectivity, see Michael Schudson, "The Emergence of the Objectivity Norm in American Journalism," in *Social Norms,* ed. Michael Hechter and Karl-Dieter Opp (New York: Russell Sage Foundation, 2001), 165–185; Jeffrey Rutenbeck, "Toward a History of the Ideologies of Partisanship and Independence in American Journalism," *Journal of Communication Inquiry* 15 (1991): 126–139; Donald L. Shaw, "News Bias and the Telegraph: A Study of Historical Change," *JQ* 44 (1967): 3–12; Richard L. Kaplan, "From Partisanship to Professionalism: The Transformation of the Daily Press," in *A History of the Book in America,* vol. 4, ed. Carl F. Kaestle and Janice A. Radway (Chapel Hill: University of North Carolina Press, 2009), 116–139; Richard Streckfuss, "Objectivity in Journalism: A Search and a Reassessment," *JQ* 67 (1990): 973–983.

6. In conceptualizing the journalistic profession as a field of policed jurisdiction over a task, I follow John Soloski, "News Reporting and Professionalism: Some Constraints on the Reporting of the News," *Media, Culture and Society* 11 (1989): 210; Michael Schudson and Chris Anderson, "Objectivity, Professionalism and Truth-Seeking in Journalism," in *The Handbook of Journalism Studies,* ed. Karin Wahl-Jorgensen and Thomas Hanitzsch (New York: Routledge, 2009), 88–101; Silvio Waisbord, *Reinventing Professionalism: Journalism and News in Global Perspective* (Cambridge: Polity, 2013); Andrew Abbott, *The System of Professions: An Essay on the Division of Expert Labor* (Chicago: University of Chicago Press, 1988), 225.

7. Maurice DeBlowitz, "Journalism as a Profession," *Contemporary Review,* January 23, 1893, 37–46.

8. "Man Nobody Knows," *GR,* April 1934, 5; Leon Nelson Flint, *The Conscience of the Newspaper: A Case Book in the Principles and Problems of Journalism* (New York: D. Appleton, 1925), 260; Walter Avenel, "Journalism as a Profession," *Forum* 21 (1898): 368; James Weber Linn, "Working for Hearst," in *The Chicagoan: A Lost Magazine of the Jazz Age,* ed. Neil Harris and Teri J. Edelstein (Chicago: University of Chicago Press, 2008), 301–303; Hamilton Holt, *Commercialism and Journalism* (Boston: Houghton Mifflin, 1909), 343–344; Silas Bent, *Ballyhoo: The Voice of the Press* (New York: Boni and Liveright, 1927), 117–120.

9. Albert Alton Sutton, *Education for Journalism in the United States from Its Beginning to 1940* (Evanston, IL: Northwestern University, 1945), 18; Marion Tuttle Marzolf, *Civilizing Voices: American Press Criticism 1880–1950* (New York: Longman, 1991), 64–66, 98–100; Hazel Dicken-Garcia, *Journalistic Standards in Nineteenth Century America* (Madison: University of Wisconsin Press, 1989); Stephen J. A. Ward, *Invention of Journalism Ethics: The Path to Objectivity and Beyond* (Montreal: McGill-Queens University Press, 2004).

10. Sutton, *Education for Journalism,* 12; David R. Davies, *The Postwar Decline of American Newspapers, 1945–1965* (Westport, CT: Praeger 2006), 22; Glenn Frank, "The Profession of Journalism," *Journalism Bulletin* 2 (1926): 6; R. Justin Miller, "The Professional Spirit," *Journalism Bulletin* 1 (1924): 5; Flint, *Conscience of the Newspaper,* 262; "Official Notices: Principles and Standards of Education for Journalism," *Journalism Bulletin* 1 (1924): 30; "Editorial: National Bulwark," *EP,* February 18, 1933, 22; Leo C. Rosten, *The Washington Correspondents* (New

York: Harcourt, Brace, 1937), 159; Francis Prugger, "Social Composition and Training of Milwaukee Journal News Staff," *JQ* 18 (1941): 231–244; Testimony of Stanley Walker, Hearing on Daily Newspaper Publishing Industry Amendment, December 5 1934, 739–741, box 95, entry 44, RG 9.

11. Brad Asher, "The Professional Vision: Conflicts Over Journalism Education, 1900–1955," *American Journalism* 11 (1994): 304–320; Ward, *Invention of Journalism Ethics,* 205–206; John E. Drewry, "Is Journalism a Profession?" *Sewanee Review* 38 (1930): 197.

12. Warren L. Bassett, "President's Remarks Draw Press Fire," *EP,* February 24, 1934, 5; Irwin, *American Newspaper,* 40; Walter Lippmann, *Liberty and the News* (Princeton, NJ: Princeton University Press, 2008), 47; "Ackerman Answers Critics of the Press," *EP,* May 6, 1933, 9.

13. United States Bureau of Labor Statistics, "Salaries and Conditions of Newspaper Editorial Employees," *Monthly Labor Review* 40 (1935): 1137–1148; Bureau of Labor Statistics, "History of Wages in the United States from Colonial Times to 1928," Bulletin No. 604: Revision of Bulletin No. 499 with Supplement, 1929–1933 (Washington, DC: Government Printing Office, 1934), 529; David J. Brown and Spencer H. Reed, "Editorial Employees: Comparison of American Newspaper Publishers Association and Guild Data," November 1934, box 95, entry 44, RG 9.

14. "Salaries and Conditions of Newspaper Editorial Employees," 1142; "Hours, Wages Bad in Texas Capital," *GR,* May 1934, 2; "Editorial Guilds," *EP,* November 4, 1933, 20; "Bargaining Policy up at Guild Meet," *EP,* April 7, 1934, 11; Illegible to Oliver Pilat, October 24, 1963, box 18, folder 18, Daniel Leab Papers, Archives of Labor and Urban Affairs, Walter P. Reuther Library, Wayne State University, MI (hereafter, Leab Papers); "Newspapers Issuing Scrip to Staff" and "Ames IA, Employees Placed 100% on Scrip," *EP,* March 13, 1933, 10; Donald A. Ritchie, *Press Gallery: Congress and the Washington Correspondents* (Cambridge, MA: Harvard University Press, 1991), 219; Herbert E. Langendorff, Preliminary Report on Wisconsin News, n.d., box 62, folder 14, NG; Saul Nelson, "The Newspaper Industry," Division of Economic Research and Planning, November 11, 1933, box 1943, file: Reports, Studies and Surveys, entry 25, RG 9; A. J. Liebling, *The Press,* 2nd ed. (New York: Pantheon Books, 1975), 17; Sol Jacobson, "The Fourth Estate: A Study of the American Newspaper Guild" (Ph.D. diss., New School for Social Research, 1960), 12; Newspaper Guild of New York, The Guild Story, n.d., folder: Newspaper Guild of New York, Tamiment Vertical Trade Union Files, Tamiment Library, New York University, NY; Gavin Payne to Hugh Johnson, August 12, 1933, box 1937, folder 4, Consolidated Approved Code Industry File, entry 25, RG 9.

15. "Why a Guild," *Bridgeport Guildsman,* August 2, 1936, box 3, folder 42, Alden Whitman Papers, New York Public Library; F. von Falkenberg to FDR, November 18, 1934, box 1937, folder 2, RG 9.

16. B. F. James to FDR, November 10, 1934, box 1937, folder 3, RG 9.

17. Ibid.

18. "President Signs the Newspaper Code, but 'Conditionally,' " *CT,* February 19, 1934, 6; Daniel J. Leab, *A Union of Individuals: The Formation of the American Newspaper Guild, 1933–1936* (New York: Columbia University Press, 1970), 120–121; Kuczun, "History of the American Newspaper Guild," 67–70; "Texts of

Order and Letter by President on New Code for Newspapers," *NYT,* February 20, 1934, 8.

19. Charles Fisher, *The Columnists* (New York: Howell, Soskin, 1944), 11–12; Richard O'Connor, *Heywood Broun: A Biography* (New York: Putnam, 1975).

20. Heywood Broun, "A Union of Reporters," in *The Collected Edition of Heywood Broun,* comp. Heywood Hale Broun (New York: Harcourt, Brace, 1941), 295–297.

21. Emmett Crozier to Daniel Leab, July 21, 1966, box 9, folder 9, Leab Papers; Lewis Gannett to Daniel Leab, January 5, 1965, box 9, folder 13, Leab Papers; Leab, *Union of Individuals,* 12–23, 48–49, 67–68, 92–102; Jacobson, "Fourth Estate," 6–12; Upton Sinclair, *The Brass Check: A Study of American Journalism* (Pasadena, CA: printed by author, 1920), 413, 421; Newspaper Guild of New York, The Guild—Time Style: A History of the Newspaper Guild at Time Incorporated, n.d., folder: Newspaper Guild of New York, Tamiment Vertical Trade Union Files; "Broun to Organize Editorial Workers," *EP,* August 12, 1933, 4; "National Guild Meeting Scheduled," *EP,* November 4, 1933, 7; "Reporters Draw Code under NRA Law," *EP,* August 19, 1933, 6.

22. An important exception was liberal Philadelphia publisher J. David Stern, who signed the first contract with the guild on April 8, 1934. Leab, *Union of Individuals,* 117, 176–177; Kuczun, "History of the American Newspaper Guild," 7–34; John Eddy Memo to All Guild Officers, March 12, 1934, box 62, folder 13, NG; 1935 Convention: Executive Secretary's Draft Report, June 2, 1935 to June 8, 1935, box 1, folder 18, Leab Papers; Jacobson, "Fourth Estate," 42–44; John W. Perry, "New York Writers Organize," *EP,* September 23, 1933, 7; "Contract Provisions Are Suggested for Guidance of Newspaper Guilds," *EP,* June 16, 1934, 41.

23. The guild had come close to affiliating the year before, when a convention vote to join the AFL fell just short of the necessary two-thirds affirmation in a members referendum. "AFL Affiliation Is Vetoed by Guild," *EP,* October 19, 1935, 16; "Guild Votes to Become a Labor Union," *EP,* June 6, 1936, 7; 1935 Convention: Executive Secretary's Draft Report, June 2, 1935 to June 8, 1935, box 1, folder 18, Leab Papers; "ANG Supports CIO; Spurns AFL Parley," *EP,* May 29, 1937, 32; Minutes of Meeting of International Executive Board, September 11, 1937, box 60, folder 6, NG.

24. "Editorial: The Newspaper Code," *EP,* August 12, 1933, 18; "Editorial Unions," *EP,* August 26, 1933, 20; "New York Guild," *EP,* September 23, 1933, 24; Arthur Robb, "Standardization Is Foe of Press," *EP,* April 17, 1937, 20; "Editorial: Breaking Up," *EP,* October 6, 1934, 24; Marlen Pew, "Professional v. Trade Union News Departments," November 8, 1934, box 8, folder 42, Leab Papers; "An Editors Case against the Guild," *EP,* June 26, 1937, 48; see also "NY World Telegram Ends Parleys with Guild for Contract," *EP,* August 1, 1936, 4.

25. Bice Clemow, "Unparalleled Strike May Lead to Discontinuance of P-I," *EP,* August 29, 1936, 1; "Seattle Guild Strike Settled," *EP,* November 28, 1936, 12; "Editorial Writers Uphold P.I. Fight against Radical Unions," *EP,* September 5, 1936, 7–8; "Strike Condemned as Undemocratic," *EP,* September 19, 1936, 42.

26. Jim Kieran, "Freedom of Press Statement," July 24, 1937, box 1, folder 52, Leab Papers (my emphasis); "American Newspaper Guild Votes to Affiliate with

AFL," *EP,* June 6, 1936, 8; "Broun Is Arrested in Guild Strike," *EP,* March 28, 1936, 10; "Only 1 Industry Outyields Press," *GR,* September 1934, 1.

27. George Seldes, *Lords of the Press* (New York: Blue Ribbon Books, 1941), 18.

28. "Guild and Capitalistic Ownership Called Free Press Threats," *EP,* March 21, 1936, 14; "Guild Members to Act on Affiliation," *EP,* June 8, 1935, 5; Bruce Catton, "Brief for Guild Shop," April 6, 1938, box 78, folder 28, NG.

29. "Four Little Publishers," n.d., box 82, folder 18, NG.

30. Clipping from Publishers Service Magazine, "Broun to Go West in Organizing of News Guilds," May 3, 1934, 12, box 2, folder 3, Leab Papers; Testimony of Heywood Broun and Testimony of Joseph Lilly, Hearing on Code of Fair Practices and Competition Presented by Newspaper Publishing Industry, September 22, 1933, 1371–1374, box 95, entry 44, RG 9.

31. Kuczun, "History of the American Newspaper Guild," 33.

32. Bruce Catton, Brief for Guild Shop, April 6, 1938, box 78, folder 28, NG; "A Good Beginning," *GR,* April 1934, 4; "Editorial Workers in Cleveland Organize under Recovery Act," *EP,* August 26, 1933, 6; "NY Daily News Signs Guild Contract," *EP,* December 5, 1936, 5; Broun Radio Address, August 1 1934, box 2, folder 5, Leab Papers; Seymour Glazer, "Three Mansions," Term Paper for Journalism 192: Ethics of Journalism, April 1941, box 8, folder 44, Leab Papers.

33. "Contract Provisions Are Suggested for Guidance of Newspaper Guilds," *EP,* June 16, 1934, 41; "Fail to End Strike on Newark Ledger," *NYT,* November 20, 1934, 7; memo on collective bargaining for local guilds, October 30, 1936, box 62, folder 14, NG; "Herald Tribune Denies Guild Demands," *EP,* February 2, 1935, 9; "'No Contract' NY Herald Tribune Tells Newspaper Guild," *EP,* March 2, 1935, 11; "Re: Guild Closed Shop," *EP,* March 20, 1937, 26; Roper Commercial Survey, August 1938. Retrieved May 7, 2014 from the iPOLL Databank, The Roper Center for Public Opinion Research, University of Connecticut.

34. Associated Press v. Labor Board, 301 U.S. 103 (1937); Jacobson, "Fourth Estate," 73.

35. Associated Press v. Labor Board, 301 U.S. at 132, 137–138, 140 (1937); Samuel R. Olken, "The Business of Expression: Economic Liberty, Political Factions and the Forgotten First Amendment Jurisprudence of Justice George Sutherland," *William & Mary Bill Rights Journal* 10 (2002): 308–327.

36. "Daily Newspapers Mobilize to Meet Guild's Closed Shop Demand," *EP,* June 19, 1937, 1; "Firm Stand against Guild Closed Shop Voted by Eleven Newspaper Groups," *EP,* July 3, 1937, 1; "Editorial: Press and Workers," *EP,* June 19, 1937, 28; "Contract Provisions Are Suggested for Guidance of Newspaper Guilds," *EP,* June 16, 1934, 41; "Publishers Are Standing Firm against Guild Closed Shop," *EP,* April 30, 1938, 17; "Crawford Tells Guild Attitude on Closed Shop," *GR,* March 3, 1940, 4; Bruce Catton, "Brief for Guild Shop," April 6, 1938, box 78, folder 28, NG; "Collective Bargaining by the American Newspaper Guild," *Monthly Labor Review* 50 (1940): 827; Marianne Salcetti, "Competing for Control of Newsworkers: Definitional Battles between the Newspaper Guild and the American Newspaper Publishers Association, 1937–1938" (Ph.D. diss., University of Iowa, 1992), 197–261, quote at 235; "Crawford Denies 'Guild Shop' Threat to Freedom

of the Press," *Boston Globe,* February 23, 1940, 3; Dale Benjamin Scott, "Labor's New Deal for Journalism—the Newspaper Guild in the 1930s" (Ph.D. diss., University of Illinois, Urbana-Champaign, 2009), 255; Kuczun, "History of the American Newspaper Guild," 173, 229.

37. Salcetti, "Competing for Control of Newsworkers," 202; "Cleveland Editorial Group Denies Newswriting Is a Profession," *EP,* September 23, 1933, 6; Editorial Employees of Spokane to Lindsay Rogers, October 3, 1933, in Code of Fair Competition for Daily Newspaper Business, vol. B, pt. 1, box 203, entry 20, RG 9; Arthur Robb, "Union Calls ANPA Code 'Inadequate to Effect NRA Purposes,' " *EP,* September 30, 1933, 14; Testimony of Doris Fleeson, Hearing on Code of Fair Practices and Competition Presented by Newspaper Publishing Industry, September 22, 1933, 1366, box 95, entry 44, RG 9.

38. An Editor's Case against the Guild," *EP,* June 26, 1937, 12; "Divided Loyalty Called Impossible," *EP,* April 28, 1934, 26; "Editorial: Guild Bargaining," *EP,* February 10, 1934, 26; Circular to Chicago NG Members on Chicago Daily Times Staff, January 2 1937, box 63, folder 4, NG; Bruce Catton, Brief for Guild Shop, April 6 1938, box 78, folder 28, NG; "Where Are the Guilds Heading?" *EP,* April 28, 1934, 60.

39. "Equal Pay for Women Urged by Resolution," *GR,* June 15, 1934, 1; Greta Palmer, "Maedchen in City Room," *GR,* February 23, 1934, 5; "Salaries and Conditions of Newspaper Editorial Employees," *Monthly Labor Review* 40 (May 1935): 1138–1139; Christine Stansell, *The Feminist Promise: 1792 to the Present* (New York: Modern Library, 2010), 300–304; Katherine Turk, "Equality on Trial: Women and Work in the Age of Title VII" (Ph.D. diss., University of Chicago, 2011), 121–182.

40. Leonard Teel, *The Public Press, 1900–1945: A History of American Journalism* (Westport, CT: Praeger, 2006), 136, 174; Susan E. Tifft and Alex S. Jones, *The Trust: The Private and Powerful Family Behind the New York Times* (Boston: Little, Brown, 1999), 276; IEB Minutes, October 1–4, 1956, folder 18: IEB 1955–56, box 72, NGNY; Jacobson, "Fourth Estate," 295.

41. "Guild Will Vote on Affiliation in September; Broun Re-elected," *EP,* June 15, 1935, 20; "American Newspaper Guild Votes to Affiliate with AFL," *EP,* June 6, 1936, 8; Arthur Robb, "Guild Votes to Join CIO, Opens Ranks to Unorganized Newspaper Employees," *EP,* June 12, 1937, 1; Resolution Passed at Meeting and Released April 4, IEB Minutes, March 26–27, 1938, box 60, folder 6, NG; IEB Minutes, September 20, 1939, box 60, folder 8, NG; Resolution, n.d., box 59, folder 14, NG; Legislative Report to the IEB of the ANG, April 28, 1940, box 8, folder 9, NGNY; "Out of Politics!," *EP,* May 20, 1940, 20; IEB Minutes, January 8–9, 1937, box 60, folder 6, NG.

42. Gary Gerstle, *Working-Class Americanism: The Politics of Labor in a Textile City, 1914–1960* (Cambridge: Cambridge University Press, 1989); Michael Denning, *The Cultural Front: The Laboring of American Culture in the Twentieth Century* (London: Verso, 1996).

43. Bruce Catton, Brief for Guild Shop, April 6, 1938, box 78, folder 28, NG; Glazer, "Three Mansions," box 8, folder 44, Leab Papers; Hollywood Citizen News-Striker, n.d., box 93, folder: Unions (1 of 3), Record Group 233: Records of the US

House of Representatives, National Archives and Records Administration, Washington, DC.

44. "Guild Votes to Join CIO, Opens Ranks to Unorganized Newspaper Employees," *EP,* June 12, 1937, 1; IEB Minutes, September 11, 1937, box 60, folder 6, NG; Resolution, n.d., box 63, folder 4, NG; "3,000 Give Leider a Hero's Funeral at Carnegie Hall," *New York Post,* August 19, 1939, Memorial Service Honors Ben Leider, *New York World Telegram,* August 18, 1938, both in box 1, folder 4, Benjamin Leider Papers, ALBA Collection, Tamiment Library, NYU; Ione Boulenger to Ben Leider Memorial Committee, November 3, 1938, box 1, folder 1a, Leider Papers.

45. "Outside Interests of Guild Attacked," *EP,* July 10, 1937, 14.

46. Marlen Pew, "Professional v. Trade Union News Departments," November 8, 1934, box 8, folder 42, Leab Papers; "Editorial: Sharing Wealth," *EP,* July 13, 1935, 28; "Editorial Men Form Independent Group," *EP,* July 17, 1937, 4; "American Press Society Modeled along the Lines of British Institute," *EP,* July 17, 1937, 12; "Anti-CIO Guildsmen Form AFL Union in Chicago for Newsmen Only," *EP,* July 24, 1937, 1; Jacobson, "Fourth Estate," 96–100; "Anti-CIO Guildsmen Form AFL Union in Chicago for Newsmen Only," *EP,* July 24, 1937, 1, 13.

47. "Rank and File Fights to Oust Left-Wing Leaders of Guild," *EP,* June 15, 1940, 11; "Guildsmen Squaring Off for Opening of Controversial Memphis Convention," *PM,* July 7, 1940, "Guild Convention Opens in Memphis," *PM,* July 9, 1940, "Crawford May Run for News Guild Post," *PM,* July 11, 1940, all clippings in box 1, folder 22, NGNY; Jacobson, "Fourth Estate," 130–131; Sullivan, Kaufman and Pasche Circular to Membership, October 9, 1940, box 4, folder 13, NGNY; "Both 'isms' Motions Carry," *GR,* March 1, 1941, 1.

48. Lewis Gannett recalled that "everybody in the New York Guild knew that the Eagle unit was Communist-dominated; Nat Einhorn did nothing to conceal his Communist Party loyalties," Lewis Gannett to Ralph B. Novak, July 26, 1955, box 8, folder 10, Leab Papers.

49. "CP Opposition Gains Strength in News Guild," *Labor Leader,* May 19, 1941, box 3, folder 3, NGNY; Stephen J. Monchak, "Rank and File Fights to Oust Left-Wing Leaders of Guild," *EP,* June 15, 1940, 11; Stephen J. Monchak, "Uninstructed Delegates to Dominate ANG Meet," *EP,* July 6, 1940, 8; Harry Read to Paul Weber, 1940, box 8, folder 10, Leab Papers; Ferdinand Lundberg to John Hohenberg, March 1941, box 8, folder 14, NGNY; General Membership Meeting, September 19, 1941, box 1, folder 21, Newspaper Guild of Detroit Collection, Archives of Labor and Urban Affairs, Walter P. Reuther Library, Wayne State University, MI (hereafter, NG of Detroit Collection).

50. "The Candidates, the Issues," n.d., box 3, folder 2a, NGNY; Harry Raymond, "Opposition Loses Ground at Guild Convention," *Daily Worker,* July 10, 1940, box 1, folder 22, NGNY; Seattle Newspaper Guild Publicity Committee, June 4, 1940, box 1, folder 29, NGNY; Report of Publications and Labor Press Committee, 1940, box 1, folder 29, NGNY; Reuben Meury to Milton Kaufman, November 15, 1938, box 17, folder 9, NGNY; "The New York Elections," *Guild Progressive,* January 30, 1940, box 12, folder 27, NGNY; Report of the Committee

to Investigate the Guild American Committee, December 17, 1940, box 4, folder 13, NGNY.

51. "The Man on the Flying Trapeze," flyer, box 3, folder 3, NGNY; Kenneth Crouse to All Guild Locals, May 1940, box 1, folder 29, NGNY; "The Anti-Red Slate: Vote It Straight," box 12, folder 16, NGNY; "Officers Link Guild to Many Stalin Fronts," *Guild Progressive,* March 30, 1940, box 12, folder 27, NGNY; *Are Their Faces Red!,* box 12, folder 27, NGNY.

52. "Murray-Eubanks Slate Sweeps All Offices in National Election," *GR,* October 17, 1941, 1; "New IEB Fires Three, Hires Two," *GR,* November 15, 1941, 2; IEB Minutes, November 1–2, 1941, box 60, folder 10, NG.

53. Judith Crist, "Gentleman and Scholars of the Press," *Columbia University Forum,* Winter 1959, 42.

54. Election Flyer, 1941, file: The Newspaper Guild of New York, Tamiment Trade Union Vertical File, Tamiment Library, New York University, NY; I. L. Kenen and William J. Farson, Statement, June 12, 1940, box 1, folder 29, NGNY; An Appeal to All Guild Members, flyer, n.d., box 3, folder 3, NGNY; "4 Million in Wage Increases for 11,000 in 65 Contracts," *GR,* February 8, 1946, 1, 8; "Report on Wage Program," *GR,* July 9, 1948, 8; "Collective Bargaining by the ANG," *Monthly Labor Review* 50 (April 1940): 839; Jacobson, "Fourth Estate," 3; Kuczun, "History of American Newspaper Guild," 249–272; constant dollars calculated on BLS CPI inflation calculator, http://data.bls.gov/cgi-bin/cpicalc.pl?cost1=160.00&year1=1964&year2=1940.

55. "Murray Cites Guild Goals at Convention of US Editors," *GR,* April 25, 1947, 3; Report of the Committee to Investigate the Guild American Committee, December 17, 1940, box 4, folder 13, NGNY; "The ANG National Wage Program," *GR,* November 8, 1946; "Stern Refused to Bargain, Sold out for Profit, Guild Charges," *GR,* February 14, 1947, 1.

56. "Queries and Answers on Project X Referendum," *GR,* August 25, 1950, 2; Harry Martin, "The Thinking Behind Project X," *GR,* August 25, 1950, 7; "Project X Fund Is Snowed Under," *GR,* September 22, 1950, 1; IEB minutes, July 2–5, 10, 1952, folder 15: IEB 1952, box 72, NGNY; William J. Farson to IEB Members, December 27, 1954, folder 17: IEB 1954, box 72, NGNY Records; Jacobson, "Fourth Estate," 223.

57. Minutes of the Executive Committee Meeting, August 17, 1937, box 1, folder 9, NG of Detroit Collection; F. Lundberg to Harry Read, n.d., box 8, folder 10, Leab Papers; "Letters Page," *GR,* September 26, 1947, 6; Edward Alwood, *Dark Days in the Newsroom: McCarthyism Aimed at the Press* (Philadelphia: Temple University Press, 2007), 45; "Letters Page," *GR,* October 10, 1947, 7; "Report of the Committee to Investigate the 'Guild American Committee,'" December 17, 1940, box 4, folder 13, NGNY.

58. Theodore Peterson, "Changing Role of Journalism Schools," *JQ* 37 (1960): 579–585; "Harvard Proffers Study to Newsmen," *NYT,* January 11, 1938, 25; Eric Odendahl, "College Backgrounds of Staffs of American Daily Newspapers," *JQ* 42 (1965): 463; The Commission on Freedom of the Press, *A Free and Responsible Press: A General Report on Mass Communication: Newspapers, Radio, Motion*

Pictures, Magazines, and Books (Chicago: University of Chicago Press, 1947), 21, 77.

59. Warren Breed, "Social Control in the Newsroom: A Functional Analysis," *Social Forces* 33 (1955): 326–335; Liebling, *Press,* 32.

60. "A Statement," *GR,* November 15, 1941, 12; Milton Murray, "We Have a Duty," *GR,* December 15, 1941, 1; "Rodgers Gives War Victory Pledge," *GR,* January 15, 1943, 5; "Strong Guild Needed in War," *GR,* January 1, 1942, 9; "Guild's War Course is Charted," *GR,* January 15, 1942, 1; Edward Hunter, "Newsmen Can Win Jap Word War in Orient," *GR,* January 15, 1942, 3; "Murray Keynotes Guild's Role in Wartime," *GR,* July 4, 1942, 3; Jacobson, "Fourth Estate," 150–153.

61. "Ship Named for Broun," *GR,* August 1, 1943, 1; "SS Broun Did Good War Job," *GR,* September 14, 1945, 4.

5. The Weapon of Information in the Good War

1. "Press Has Dual Obligation in War Effort," *EP,* December 12, 1942, 6; "Editorial: Vindication," *EP,* August 22, 1942, 18; Arthur Robb, "Shop Talk at 30," *EP,* March 22, 1941, 44; Mathew Gordon, *News Is a Weapon* (New York: A. A. Knopf, 1942); "California Publishers Unanimous in Backing Defense Program," *EP,* January 25, 1941, 5; Admiral R. P. McCullough, "Documentary Security," May 26, 1944, box 1, folder: Documentary Security Committee, entry 12, RG 208; Carl J. Friedrich, "Issues of Informational Strategy," *Public Opinion Quarterly* 7 (1943): 77–89; Franklin D. Roosevelt, "Annual Message to Congress on the State of the Union," January 6, 1941, APP; Franklin D. Roosevelt, "Radio Address on the 150th Anniversary of the Ratification of the Bill of Rights," December 15, 1941, APP.

2. Richard W. Steele, *Free Speech in the Good War* (New York: St. Martin's, 1999), 284; Geoffrey R. Stone, *Perilous Times: Free Speech in Wartime; from the Sedition Act of 1798 to the War on Terrorism* (New York: W. W. Norton, 2004), 235–310; Patrick Scott Washburn, *A Question of Sedition: The Federal Government's Investigation of the Black Press during World War II* (New York: Oxford University Press, 1986); Hartzel v. United States, 322 U.S. 680 (1944).

3. Scholars used to assume that World War II proved how "thin" and liberal American state nationalism was. See Robert B. Westbrook, "'I Want a Girl, Just Like the Girl That Married Harry James': American Women and the Problem of Political Obligation in World War II," *American Quarterly* 42 (1990): 587–614; Mark H. Leff, "The Politics of Sacrifice on the American Home Front in World War II," *Journal of American History* 77 (1991): 1296–1318. I follow more recent scholarship on the growth of central authority: James T. Sparrow, *Warfare State: World War II Americans and the Age of Big Government* (New York: Oxford University Press, 2011); Wendy A. Wall, *Inventing the American Way: The Politics of Consensus from the New Deal to the Civil Rights Movement* (New York: Oxford University Press, 2011). My thinking about shifting modes of regulation is influenced by Michel Foucault, *Discipline and Punish: The Birth of the Prison* (New York: Vintage Books, 1995).

4. Allan M. Winkler, *The Politics of Propaganda: The Office of War Information, 1942–1945* (New Haven, CT: Yale University Press, 1978), 21–22; David Lloyd Jones, "The US Office of War Information and American Public Opinion during World War II" (Ph.D. diss., SUNY-Binghamton, 1976), 49–50, 69–74; Edward P. Lilly, "A History of the Office of War Information," box 3, folder: OWI History Chs1–2, entry 6H, RG 208. Harold F. Gosnell, "Division of Information of the Office for Emergency Management," April 18, 1944, box 15; Harold F. Gosnell, "Office of Facts and Figures," September 23, 1943, pp. 7–11, box 16; Harold F. Gosnell, "The Framing of the OWI Executive Order," December 29, 1944, p. 4, box 15. All three Gosnell reports in RG 51; "President Forms Top News Agency," *NYT*, June 14, 1942, 1; Franklin D. Roosevelt, "Executive Order 9182 Establishing the Office of War Information," June 13, 1942, APP; Lester G. Hawkins Jr. and George S. Pettee, "OWI Organization," February 12 1943, p. 9, box 1, folder: Outline of OWI Organization, entry 6H, RG 208.

5. Meetings of June 19–20, 1944, doc.18, p. 2, box 1, folder 7, HC; Archibald MacLeish to Council for Democracy, December 30, 1941, box 12, folder: OFF History, entry 6E, RG 208; Jones, "US Office of War Information," 112–113; Gosnell, "Office of Facts and Figures."

6. Bernard A. Drabek, ed., *Archibald MacLeish: Reflections* (Amherst: University of Massachusetts Press, 1986), 149–150; Jones, "US Office of War Information," 112; Sydney Weinberg, "What to Tell America: The Writers' Quarrel in the Office of War Information," *Journal of American History* 55 (1968): 76; Winkler, *Politics of Propaganda,* 23–24; Gosnell, "Office of Facts and Figures."

7. Scott Donaldson, *Archibald MacLeish: An American Life* (Boston: Houghton Mifflin, 1992), 350–351; John Morton Blum, "Archibald MacLeish: Art for Action," in *Liberty, Justice, Order: Essays on Past Politics* (New York: W. W. Norton, 1993), 227–260; Archibald MacLeish, "Freedom to End Freedom," in *A Time to Speak* (Cambridge, MA: Riverside Press, 1940), 138.

8. Archibald MacLeish, "The Irresponsibles," in *A Time to Speak,* 103–121; Archibald MacLeish, "The Communists, the Writers and the Spanish War," in *A Time to Speak* (my emphasis).

9. Archibald MacLeish, *A Time to Act: Selected Addresses* (Freeport, NY: Books for Libraries Press, 1970), 9–31.

10. Francis Biddle, "Symposium on Civil Liberties," *American Law School Review* 9 (1941): 895; John Morton Blum, *V Was for Victory: Politics and American Culture during World War II* (New York: Harcourt, Brace, 1976), 26–27; Judith E. Smith, *Visions of Belonging: Family Stories, Popular Culture, and Postwar Democracy, 1940–1960* (New York: Columbia University Press, 2004), 22.

11. "Statement by Elmer Davis on Aims and Functions of the OWI—September 1942," n.d., box 3, folder: OWI Histories, entry 6H, RG 208; Harold F. Gosnell, "Domestic Pamphleteers in World War II," June 1, 1946, p. 1, box 15, RG 51; "A History of the Domestic News Bureau," n.d., pp. 10–11, box 1, folder: News Bureau, entry 6H, RG 208; Wall, *Inventing the American Way,* 114; Weinberg, "What to Tell America."

12. "Grafters and Skulkers Find a Friend," *CT,* April 19, 1942, 16; "Poet Essays to Crack Down on Newspapers," *CT,* May 16, 1942, 3; "OWI Publication of

'Victory' Stirs Storm in Congress," *NYT,* February 13, 1943, 1; "18 Agencies Voted Nearly 3 Billions," *WP,* June 19, 1943, 1; "Race Issue Politics Seen Behind Moves to Scuttle War Effort on Home Front," *Chicago Defender,* June 26, 1943, 20; Gosnell, "Domestic Pamphleteers," 30; "New OWI Magazine Irks Congressional Groups," *NYT,* February 14, 1943, E3; "Tax Abatement Foe Quits Conferences," *NYT,* May 20, 1943, 22; Jones, "US Office of War Information," 453, 523–524; Summary of Meeting, September 17–19 1945, p. 43, doc. 75, box 3, folder 10, HC; Elmer Davis, "Report to the President: Office of War Information: 13 June 1942–15 September 1945," pp. 57–58, box 13, folder: Davis Final Report, entry 6E, RG 208; Wall, *Inventing the American Way,* 106–121; Blum, *V Was for Victory,* 21–44.

13. "OWI Quitting Pamphlet War on the Home Front, Hoyt Says," *CT,* July 7, 1943, 3; Jones, "US Office of War Information," 468; "Final Report of the Domestic News Bureau, Office of War Information," box 1, folder: Domestic News Bureau, 1942–1945, entry 6A, RG 208; "What the News Bureau Does," February 3, 1945, p. 6, box 1, folder: News Bureau, RG 208; "A History of the Domestic News Bureau"; Statement of Elmer Davis, House Appropriations Committee, April 19, 1944, p. 2, box 13, folder: Davis Final Report, entry 6E, RG 208.

14. "Final Report of the Domestic News Bureau, OWI"; Davis, "Report to the President," 59; Gosnell, "Domestic Pamphleteers," 34.

15. Frank W. Fox, *Madison Avenue Goes to War: The Strange Military Career of American Advertising, 1941–1945,* Charles E. Merrill Monograph Series in the Humanities and Social Sciences 4, no. 1, June 1975; Robert Griffith, "The Selling of America: The Advertising Council and American Politics, 1942–1960," *Business History Review* 57 (1983): 389–391; Inger Stole, *Advertising at War: Business, Consumers and Government in the 1940s* (Urbana: University of Illinois Press, 2012).

16. Richard W. Steele, "News of the 'Good War': World War II News Management," *JQ* 62 (1985): 709; Eben Ayers Diary, March 28, 1942, box 18, Eben A. Ayers Papers, Harry S. Truman Library, Independence, MO.

17. George H. Roeder, *The Censored War: American Visual Experience during World War II* (New Haven, CT: Yale University Press, 1993), 10–16; Steele, "News of the 'Good War,'" 712; "A History of the OC," vol. 2, p. 43, box 1, entry 4, RG 216; David M. Kennedy, *Freedom from Fear: The American People in Depression and War, 1929–1945* (New York: Oxford University Press, 1999), 618; Second Meeting of Security Advisory Board, May 12, 1943, p. 3, box 1, folder: Security Advisory Board Minutes 1, entry 11, RG 208; Jones, "US Office of War Information," 477–478.

18. Franklin D. Roosevelt: "Executive Order 8985 Establishing the Office of Censorship," December 19, 1941, APP; "A History of the OC," vol. 1, 33–34, box 1, entry 4, RG 216; Michael S. Sweeney, *Secrets of Victory: The Office of Censorship and the American Press and Radio in World War II* (Chapel Hill: University of North Carolina Press, 2001), 34–36; Byron Price, "War Censorship," in *War Information and Censorship,* ed. Elmer Davis and Byron Price (Washington, DC: American Council on Public Affairs, n.d.), 65.

19. Sweeney, *Secrets of Victory,* 23–26; "Knox Requests Voluntary Censorship," *EP,* January 18, 1941, 36; "Voluntary Censorship Broadened," *EP,* May 31, 1941,

12; "Knox Restricts Naval Construction News," *EP,* June 7, 1941, 34; Walter E. Schneider, "Malaya Story First Real Test of Voluntary Censorship Plan," *EP,* April 12, 1941, 7; "Army, Navy Press Chiefs Declare No Censorship Is Wanted," *EP,* April 26, 1941, 114.

20. Code of Wartime Practices, January 15, 1942, in "History of the OC," vol. 1, Exhibit J-1.

21. "History of the OC," vol. 2, 32; Edward N. Doan, "The Organization and Operation of the Office of Censorship," *JQ* 21 (1944): 208; Price, "War Censorship," 66; "Transcript of OC Meeting," April 14, 1942, 20, box 109, folder: Training, entry 1, RG 216; Jones, "US Office of War Information," 284; "Marvin Says War Brings Editors into Their Own," *EP,* April 18, 1942, 10.

22. "Office of Censorship's Newspaper Division," *EP,* April 4, 1942, 5; "History of the OC," vol. 1, 40; "History of the OC," vol. 2, 32–33; Theodore F. Koop, *Weapon of Silence* (Chicago: University of Chicago Press, 1946), 172.

23. "History of the OC," vol. 2, 4; A. D. Surles to Byron Price, August 29, 1942, box 109, folder: New York, entry 1, RG 216; "Explanatory Material on Censorship Issued," *EP,* December 12, 1942, 56; "History of the OC," vol. 2, 115; "Long Vacation in Price's Plans," *EP,* August 18, 1945, 14; Koop, *Weapon of Silence,* 175.

24. "History of the OC," vol. 1, 33–36, vol. 2, 8; Koop, *Weapon of Silence,* 174–175; "Editorial: Sense in Censorship," *EP,* March 21, 1942, 22; Roscoe Ellard to Byron Price, July 28, 1942, box 108, folder: Schools of Journalism, entry 1, RG 216; Harold F. Gosnell, "Selected Personnel Problems in the War Information Field," May 7, 1945, 8, box 16, Bureau of the Budget Series 41.3, RG 51; "Editorial: Press Agent Army," *EP,* October 25, 1941, 24.

25. Doan, "Organization of the Office of Censorship," 208; "Publishers Represented in Censors Office," *EP,* January 31, 1942, 6; N. R. Howard to Cranston Williams, November 7, 1942, box 109, folder: New York, entry 1, RG 216.

26. Grace E. Ray to Bill Stevens, n.d., N. R. Howard to Professor A. L. Higginbotham, August 27, 1942, Theodore Koop to Earl English, August 10, 1942, all in box 108, folder: Schools of Journalism, entry 1, RG 216; N. R. Howard to Robert Newcomb, August 25, 1942, box 108, folder: Industrial Publications, entry 1, RG 216; John Sorrels to William F. Swindler, June 24, 1942, box 109, folder: Mylander's Trip, entry 1, RG 216; "Transcript of OC Meeting," April 14, 1942, 3–4; G. W. Marble to N. R. Howard, November 29, 1942, box 108, folder: Conferences, entry 1, RG 216; N. R. Howard to William F. Swindler, December 23, 1942, box 109, folder: Idaho, entry 1, RG 216; Doan, "Organization of the Office of Censorship," 208.

27. Tom Keene to L. E. Lambert, September 9, 1942, Tom H. Keene to N. R. Howard, January 7, 1943, Tom H. Keene Memo, January 1, 1943, N. R. Howard to Tom Keene, May 24, 1943, all in box 109, folder: Indiana, entry 1, RG 216; Tom Keene to N. R. Howard, November 20, 1942, box 108, folder: Conferences, entry 1, RG 216; George A. Brandenburg, "Censorship, Delivery Problems Discussed at Inland Meeting," *EP,* May 23, 1942, 5; "Transcript of OC Meeting," April 14, 1942, 5; Koop, *Weapon of Silence,* 173.

28. "History of the OC," vol. 2, 35, 72, 127; "Press Praised by White House," *EP,* January 3, 1942, 7; "Editorial: Censorship Rules," *EP,* January 24, 1942, 18;

"Mrs. Roosevelt Gets Letter from the Censor," *EP*, August 22, 1942, 27; Koop, *Weapon of Silence*, 207–208, 216; Sweeney, *Secrets of Victory*, 100–104, 108–112; N. R. Howard to Keats Speed, May 13, 1942, box 554, folder: Misc General re Press, entry 1, RG 216; Meetings of June 19–20, 1944, 24, doc. 18, box 1, folder 7, HC; "Editorial: Official Secrets," *EP*, February 28, 1942, 22.

29. Koop, *Weapon of Silence*, 27; "Transcript of OC Meeting," April 14, 1942, 3; John H. Sorrels to Colonel Ralph Lovett, April 23, 1942, Edward J. Rakes to Office of Censorship, n.d., box 554, folder: Miscellaneous Press, entry 1, RG 216; Bulletin on Censorship no. 22, December 14, 1943, box 109, folder: New York, entry 1, RG 216.

30. "History of the OC," vol. 1, 14–20; George Creel, "The Plight of the Last Censor," *Colliers*, May 24, 1941, 13, 34; "Creel Repeats Plea for Radio, Cable Censorship," *EP*, August 23, 1941, 12; George Creel, *How We Advertised America: The First Telling of the Amazing Story of the Committee on Public Information That Carried the Gospel of Americanism to Every Corner of the Globe* (New York: Harper and Brothers, 1920), 16–27; Paul L. Murphy, *World War I and the Origin of Civil Liberties in the United States* (New York: W. W. Norton, 1979), 109.

31. Sally M. Miller, "Introduction," in *The Ethnic Press in the United States: A Historical Analysis and Handbook*, ed. Sally M. Miller (New York: Greenwood, 1987), xvii–xviii; Brett Gary, *Nervous Liberals: Propaganda Anxieties from World War I to the Cold War* (New York: Columbia University Press, 1999), 175–242; Washburn, *Question of Sedition*.

32. "History of the OC," vol. 1, 20; Meeting minutes, March 31 to April 2, 1946, 39, doc. 94, box 5, folder 4, HC.

33. "History of the OC," vol. 2, 14; James Russell Wiggins, *Freedom or Secrecy* (New York: Oxford University Press, 1956), 98.

34. Davis, "Report to the President," 16; Arvin S. Quist, *Security Classification of Information*, vol. 1, 2002, 14–23, www.fas.org/sgp/library/quist/14–23; Harold Edgar and Benno C. Schmidt Jr., "The Espionage Statutes and Publication of Defense Information," *Columbia Law Review* 73 (1973): 1002–1005; Harold C. Relyea, "The Evolution of Government Information Security Classification Policy: A Brief Overview (1775–1973)," in *Government Secrecy, Hearings before the Subcommittee on Intergovernmental Relations of the Committee on Government Operations*, 93d Cong. 846–857 (1974); Arthur M. Schlesinger Jr., *The Imperial Presidency* (Boston: Mariner Books, 2004), 339; "History of the OC," vol. 1, chap. 8; "Army Censors Story of Shooting at USO Party," *EP*, July 29, 1944, 53; "Newark Reporter Jailed Attempting to Get Port Pass," *EP*, March 14, 1942, 12; "Iceland Writers Busy Chasing Hats and 5 Censors," *EP*, April 11, 1942, 44; Jim A. Richstad, "The Press under Martial Law: The Hawaiian Experience," *Journalism Monographs* 17 (1970): 1–41; Lauren Kessler, "Fettered Freedoms: The Journalism of WWII Japanese Internment Camps," *Journalism History* 15 (1988): 70–79; Takeya Mizuno, "Journalism under Military Guards and Searchlights: Newspaper Censorship at Japanese American Assembly Camps during World War II," *Journalism History* 29 (2003): 98–106; Elmer Davis, "OWI Regulation 4," September 29, 1942, box 969, folder: OWI Regulations, entry 175, RG 208.

35. Donald A. Ritchie, *Press Gallery: Congress and the Washington Correspondents* (Cambridge, MA: Harvard University Press, 1991), 90–91, 163–178; Smith, *War and Press Freedom,* 31; Frank Luther Mott, *American Journalism: A History of Newspapers in the United States through 250 Years, 1690–1940* (New York: Macmillan, 1962), 173; Timothy L. Ericson, "Building Our Own 'Iron Curtain': The Emergence of Secrecy in American Government," *The American Archivist* 68 (2005): 27; Anna Kasten Nelson, "Secret Agents and Security Leaks: President Polk and the Mexican War," *JQ* 52 (1975): 9–14, 98; Everette E. Dennis, "Stolen Peace Treaties and the Press: Two Case Studies," *Journalism History* 2 (1975): 6–14; Rahul Sagar, *Secrets and Leaks: The Dilemma of State Secrecy* (Princeton, NJ: Princeton University Press, 2013), 35; "History of Security Office and Security Advisory Board, OWI," n.d., p. 1, box 2, folder: Security Advisory Board, entry 6H, RG 208; Relyea, "Evolution of Government Information Security," 855; "Talk of Lieutenant Commander Theodore Gould to Trainees at the Office of Economic Warfare," n.d., box 5, folder: Miscellaneous, entry 12, RG 208; "Security Indoctrination Programs for Civilian Employees of Nonmilitary Federal War Agencies," n.d., box 2, folder: Secret Indoctrinations, entry 12, RG 208.

36. Third Meeting of SAB, May 19, 1943, 6–8, Fourth Meeting of SAB, May 26, 1943, 3, both in box 1, folder: Security Advisory Board Minutes 1, entry 11, RG 208; "History of Security Office and Security Advisory Board, OWI," 23–28; "Common Violations of Security," n.d., box 5, folder: Miscellaneous, entry 12, RG 208; "Security of Classified Documents," February 21, 1944; "Security Training," April 11, 1944; "Removal of Classified Documents from Official Place of Storage," April 26, 1944, all three in box 1, folder: SAB Memoranda, entry 11, RG 208.

37. Jeffrey A. Smith, *Printers and Press Freedom: The Ideology of Early American Journalism* (New York: Oxford University Press, 1988), 156–161; James Tagg, *Benjamin Franklin Bache and the Philadelphia Aurora* (Philadelphia: University of Pennsylvania Press, 1991), 246–247, 342, 366–394; Dennis, "Stolen Peace Treaties," 7–9; Stone, *Perilous Times,* 126; Quist, *Security Classification of Information,* 13; Smith, *War and Press Freedom,* 99–116; James G. Randall, "The Newspaper Problem in Its Bearing upon Military Secrecy during the Civil War," *American Historical Review* 23 (1918): 303–323; Harold Holzer, *Lincoln and the Power of the Press: The War for Public Opinion* (New York: Simon and Schuster, 2014).

38. Stone, *Perilous Times,* 147; Edgar and Schmidt, "Espionage Statutes," 947–957.

39. Ericson, "Building Our Own 'Iron Curtain,'" 32; Stone, *Perilous Times,* 146–152; Daniel Patrick Moynihan, *Secrecy: The American Experience* (New Haven, CT: Yale University Press, 1998), 95; United States Commission on Government Security, *Report of the Commission on Government Security,* S.doc.64 (Washington, DC: Government Printing Office, 1957), 617; Steven I. Vladeck, "Inchoate Liability and the Espionage Act: The Statutory Framework and the Freedom of the Press," *Harvard Law and Policy Review* 1 (2007): 219–237.

40. Edgar and Schmidt, "Espionage Statutes," 1001, 1008–1009; Relyea, "Evolution of Government Information Security," 852.

41. George H. Manning, "Press Gag Averted in 'Secrets' Bill," *EP,* April 8, 1933, 7; "Editorial," *EP,* April 8, 1933, 20; "New Bill Eliminates Press Censorship," *EP,*

April 15, 1933, 8; Buel W. Patch, "Protection of Official Secrets," *Editorial Research Reports* February 25, 1948, 133.

42. "Biddle Proposes Law to Tighten Censorship," *EP*, February 21, 1942, 6; "White House Writers Hit Justice Bill," *EP*, February 28, 1942, 3; Editorial, *EP*, February 29, 1942, 22; Patch, "Protection of Official Secrets," 134; Richard L. Worsnop, "Secrecy in Government," *Editorial Research Reports*, August 18, 1971, 642.

43. "Two 'Spies' Guilty in Trial on Coast," *NYT*, March 11, 1939, 9; "Russian Spies Sentenced," *NYT*, March 21, 1939, 10; "Spy Law Is Upheld by Supreme Court," *NYT*, January 14, 1941, 12; Gorin v. United States, 312 U.S. 19 (1941).

44. Dina Goren, "Communication Intelligence and the Freedom of the Press: The Chicago Tribune's Battle of Midway Dispatch and the Breaking of the Japanese Naval Code," *Journal of Contemporary History* 16 (1981): 663–690; Oliver S. Cox, "Criminal Liability for Newspaper Publication of Naval Secrets," June 16, 1942, in *Supplemental Opinions of the Office of Legal Counsel of the US Department of Justice*, vol. 1, ed. Nathan A. Forrester (Washington, DC, 2013), 93–101, www.justice.gov/olc/file/477221/download.

45. "Flier Says Heine Bought Army Data," *NYT*, September 19, 1941, 10; "Nazi Spying Charges Denied by 2 Accused," *NYT*, July 26, 1941, 6; "Defendant Admits Alias at Spy Trial,' *NYT*, October 30, 1941, 10; "33 in Spy Ring Get Heavy Sentences," *NYT*, January 3, 1942, 1; United States v. Heine, 151 F.2d 813 (2nd Cir. 1945); Edgar and Schmidt, "Espionage Statutes," 981–986.

46. United States v. Heine, 151 F.2d 813 (1945); "Ruling Is Refused in Espionage Case," *NYT*, April 30, 1946, 10.

47. Winters Memo to Robert Harris, September 4, 1944, box 5, folder: Wall Street Journal Story, entry 12, RG 208; Meeting of SAB, July 26, 1944, 5–7; Meeting of SAB, September 20, 1944, 6, both in box 1, folder: SAB Minutes 3, entry 11, RG 208; "Laws Applicable to Officers or Employees of the Government Giving Out Information or Copies of Papers or Results of Investigations which are of a Confidential Character," n.d., box 2, folder: SAB Memo 7, entry 12, RG 208; Meeting of SAB, July 26, 1944, 2–3, box 1, folder: SAB Minutes 3, entry 11, RG 208; Relyea, "Evolution of Government Information Security," 855.

48. "History of the OC," vol. 1, 117–119; ibid., vol. 2, 112–131; Walter Schneider, "35 US Newsmen at New Front in Africa with American Army," *EP*, November 14, 1942, 5; "Another Swell Job by Press, Says Censor," *EP*, January 30, 1943, 3; S. J. Monchak, "Record Allied Press Corps Covering Invasion of Sicily," *EP*, July 17, 1943, 5; "Editorial: We Can Keep Secrets," *EP*, July 17, 1943, 26; Jones, "US Office of War Information," 177.

49. Byron Price, Confidential Note to Editors and Publishers, June 25, 1943, box 146, folder: Notes to Editors, June 1943, entry 1, RG 216; Patrick S. Washburn, "The Office of Censorship's Attempt to Control Press Coverage of the Atomic Bomb during World War II," *Journalism Monographs* 120 (1990): 1–43.

50. Koop, *Weapon of Silence*, 272; Sweeney, *Secrets of Victory*, 195–209; "Knoxville Sat on Atomic News Bombshell," *EP*, August 11, 1945, 59.

51. "Eye Witness Account Atomic Bomb Mission over Nagasaki, War Dept Bureau of Public Relations, Press Branch Release," September 9, 1945, box 5, folder: Atomic Bomb, 2 of 4, Ayers Papers, Truman Library.

52. Ibid.; Beverly Ann Deepe Keever, "Top Secret: Censoring the First Rough Drafts of History," *Media History* 14 (2008): 185–204; William L. Laurence, "U.S. Atom Bomb Site Belies Tokyo Tales," *NYT,* September 12, 1945, 1; "War Department Called Times Reporter to Explain Bomb's Intricacy to Public," *NYT,* August 7, 1945, 5; "William Laurence of the Times Dies," *NYT,* March 19, 1977, 1.

53. Price, "War Censorship," 78; "Byron Price Decorated," *NYT,* January 16, 1946, 23; "Winner for Novel Long in Business," *NYT,* May 2, 1944, 16; Koop, *Weapon of Silence,* 17; "Biggest Secret," *EP,* August 11, 1945, 40; "Religious Leaders Hail Free Press," *EP,* October 2, 1943, 14; "History of the OC," vol. 1, chap.17.

54. Franklin D. Roosevelt, "Fireside Chat 19: On the War with Japan," December 9, 1941, http://millercenter.org/president/speeches/speech-3325; Walter F. Schneider, "Editors Suggest Improvements in Voluntary Censorship Plan," *EP,* May 3, 1941, 3; Press Release, February 22, 1945, box 922, folder: Speeches Price 1944, entry 1, RG 216.

55. "Danger in Failure of Voluntary Censorship," *EP,* March 14, 1942, 9; Meetings of June 19–20, 1944, 24–34, doc. 18, box 1, folder 7, HC.

56. Harry S. Truman, Statement to the Newspapers of the Nation, September 7, 1945, box 172, folder: 82 Press, President's Personal File, Truman Library; Donaldson, *MacLeish,* 379–388; "Price, Wartime Censor Named Assistant Secretary of UN by Lie," *NYT,* February 20, 1947, 1.

6. The Cold War Dilemma of a Free Press

1. William Reed, "UN Freedom Body Sets up 48 Conference in Europe," *EP,* May 24, 1946, 5; Donald L. Smith, *Zechariah Chafee, Jr.: Defender of Liberty and Law* (Cambridge, MA: Harvard University Press, 1986).

2. Elizabeth Borgwardt, *A New Deal for the World: America's Vision for Human Rights* (Cambridge, MA: Belknap Press of Harvard University Press, 2007); Robert Latham, *The Liberal Moment: Modernity, Security and the Making of Postwar International Order* (New York: Columbia University Press, 1997).

3. "Free Press Can End War, Says Warren," *NYT,* November 28, 1946, 25; "Free Press Obstacles," *EP,* November 16, 1946, 42; "A Free and Responsible Press," *University of Chicago Roundtable,* no. 472, April 6, 1947, 3–4; "US Press Hailed as Best in the World," *NYT,* April 7, 1947, 25.

4. "Ramsey Calls for a World Free Press," *EP,* April 22, 1944, 34; "US Press Aids Post-War Peace Says Welles," *EP,* December 25, 1943, 45; Arthur Robb, "Shop Talk at 30," *EP,* May 1, 1943, 48; "Free Press Held World Peace Key," *NYT,* February 24, 1946, 16; "Atom Bomb Makes News Essential to Civilization—Hoyt," *EP,* August 11, 1945, 7; "Hoyt Calls on Editors to Spur Freedom Fight," *EP,* May 11, 1946, 10; "Sees Obligation to Extend Free Press Around World," *EP,* May 22, 1943, 9.

5. "Free Press Crisis Is Termed in Past," *NYT,* February 22, 1945, 32; *Full Report of ASNE Committee on Freedom of Information,* 5, reprinted as supplement to *EP,* June 18, 1945; Jerry Walker, "Forrest Sees World Press as Fighting for Treaty Clause," *EP,* May 5, 1945, 10.

6. Morris Ernst, *The First Freedom* (New York: Macmillan, 1946), xi–xii, 268–271; Henry Luce, "The American Century," *Diplomatic History* 23 (1999): 160; Elie Abel, "Hutchins Revisited: Thirty-Five Years of Social Responsibility Theory," in *The Responsibilities of Journalism,* ed. Robert Schmuhl (Notre Dame, IN: University of Notre Dame Press, 1984), 39; "New Commission to Study Press Freedom," *EP,* March 4, 1944, 22.

7. Jerilyn S. McIntyre, "Repositioning a Landmark: The Hutchins Commission and Freedom of the Press," *Critical Studies in Mass Communication* 4 (1987): 136.

8. The Commission on Freedom of the Press, *A Free and Responsible Press: A General Report on Mass Communication: Newspapers, Radio, Motion Pictures, Magazines, and Books* (Chicago: University of Chicago Press, 1947), 1, 15; Draft Report—Commission on Freedom of the Press, First Revision, doc. 34, 1–2, box 2, folder 2, HC; Summary of Discussions, June 5–6, 1945, doc. 66, 49, box 3, folder 3, HC; First Draft of Commission's Report, doc. 20a, 1–3, box 1, folder 8, HC; Synopsis of Committee Meeting of March 21, 1944, doc. 14, 5, box 1, folder 3, HC; William E Hocking, "Definition and Scope of the General Problems before the Group," doc.1, 10, box 1, folder 1, HC.

9. "Draft Report—Commission on Freedom of the Press: First Revision," doc. 34, 151, box 2, folder 4, HC; Summary of Discussion and Action for Meetings, January 27–29, 1946, doc. 90, 9, box 4, folder 9, HC.

10. Zechariah Chafee Jr., *Government and Mass Communications: A Report from the Commission on Freedom of the Press* (Chicago: University of Chicago Press, 1947), 674; Smith, *Zechariah Chafee, Jr.,* 107.

11. Summary of Discussion, July 7–9, 1946, doc. 108c, 146, 150, 161, box 8, folder 5, HC; Meeting Minutes, March 31 to April 2, 1946, doc. 94, 21–24, box 5, folder 4, HC; *Free and Responsible Press,* 83–85; George L. Haskins, "John Dickinson: 1894–1952," *University of Pennsylvania Law Review* 101 (1952): 1–25.

12. *Free and Responsible Press,* 2–5.

13. Ibid., 17; Theodore Peterson, "The Social Responsibility Theory of the Press," in *Four Theories of the Press: The Authoritarian, Libertarian, Social Responsibility, and Soviet Communist Concepts of What the Press Should Be and Do,* Fred S. Siebert, Theodore Peterson, and Wilbur Schram (Urbana: University of Illinois Press, 1956), 73–103; Abel, "Hutchins Revisited," 39–48.

14. *Free and Responsible Press,* 128–131 (my emphasis).

15. Harold L. Ickes, *America's House of Lords: An Inquiry into Freedom of the Press* (New York: Harcourt, Brace, 1939), 18; Summary of Discussion and Action for Meetings January 27–29, 1946, doc. 90, 39, box 4, folder 9, HC.

16. *Free and Responsible Press,* 93; Victor Pickard, *America's Battle for Media Democracy: The Triumph of Corporate Libertarianism and the Future of Media Reform* (New York: Cambridge University Press, 2015), 98–123.

17. *Free and Responsible Press,* viii, 83; George Shuster in "A Free and Responsible Press," *University of Chicago Roundtable,* no. 472, April 6, 1947, 5.

18. "World-Telegram Acquires the Sun," *NYT,* January 5, 1950, 1; "Brooklyn Eagle Put up for Sale," *NYT,* April 13, 1955, 13; "Boston Post Stops Publishing," *NYT,* July 7 1956, 13; "Hearst Sells Detroit Times to News," *NYT,* November 8, 1960, 24; "Washington Post Purchases Rival," *NYT,* March 18, 1954, 33;

David Halberstam, *The Powers That Be* (New York: Knopf, 1979), 302–303; A. J. Liebling, *The Press* (New York: Pantheon Books, 1975), 60; Raymond B. Nixon, "Trends in Daily Newspaper Ownership since 1945," *JQ* 31 (1954): 13; Raymond B. Nixon, "Who Will Own the Press in 1975," *JQ* 32 (1955): 10–16; Raymond B. Nixon and Jean Ward, "Trends in Newspaper Ownership and Inter-Media Competition," *JQ* 38 (1961): 5.

19. "Big Newspapers Hit by Move from Cities to Suburbs," *Business Week*, May 27, 1961, box 116a, folder 4: Monopoly and the Newspaper Crisis, NGNY; Halberstam, *Powers That Be*, 291–292; James L. Baughman, *The Republic of Mass Culture: Journalism, Film-Making and Broadcasting in America since 1941*, 3rd ed. (Baltimore, MD: Johns Hopkins University Press, 2006), 60–65; "Local Monopoly in the Daily Newspaper Industry," *Yale Law Journal* 61 (1952): 948–1009; Royal H. Ray, "Economic Forces as Factors in Daily Newspaper Concentration," *JQ* 29 (1952): 31–42; Nixon and Ward, "Trends in Newspaper Ownership," 9.

20. Of increased costs, newsprint seems to have been more important than labor. Charles V. Kinter, "The Changing Patterns of the Newspaper Publishing Industry," *American Journal of Economics and Sociology* 5 (1945): 43–63; James N. Rosse, "The Decline of Direct Newspaper Competition," *Journal of Communication* (Spring 1980): 65–71; David R. Davies, *The Postwar Decline of American Newspapers, 1945–1965* (Westport, CT: Praeger, 2006), 160n6; James E. Pollard, "Spiraling Newspaper Costs Outrun Revenues, 1939–1949," *JQ* 26 (1949): 270–276.

21. "Stern's 3 Papers Sold to Bulletin," *NYT*, February 1, 1947, 1; "Monopoly's Other Foot," *Christian Science Monitor*, February 15, 1947, 18; "Radicals Devour Their Child," *CT*, February 3, 1947, 18; "Philadelphia Bulletin Order for Presses May Be Record," *Wall Street Journal*, April 3, 1953, 5; Philadelphia Hails New Bulletin Plant," *NYT*, June 2, 1955, 32; Peter Binzen, ed., *Nearly Everybody Read It: Snapshots of the Philadelphia Bulletin* (Philadelphia: Camino Books, 1998), 1–16; Robert E. L. Taylor, *Robert McLean's Bulletin and a Look at Our Free Press in 1987* (Bryn Mawr, PA: Dorrance, 1988), 12–23, 57.

22. Davies, *Postwar Decline*, 3, 166n10; Benjamin M. Compaine, *Papers and Profits: A Special Report on the Newspaper Business* (White Plains, NY: Knowledge Industry Productions, 1971), 11, 40; Jon G. Udell, *Economics of the American Newspaper* (New York: Hastings House, 1978), 69–71; 112–115; Robert G. Picard, "U.S. Newspaper Ad Revenue Shows Consistent Growth," *Newspaper Research Journal* 23 (2002): 21–33.

23. Chairman of Special Committee to Study Problems of American Small Business, United States Senate, *Survival of a Free, Competitive Press: The Small Newspaper: Democracy's Grass Roots*, January 2, 1947, Senate committee print no. 17, 80th Cong., 1st Sess. (Washington, DC: Government Printing Office, 1947), 5; "Monopoly Strangling Free Press, Senate Report Says," *GR*, February 14, 1947, 5; Davies, *Postwar Decline*, 25.

24. Times-Picayune Publishing Co. v. United States, 345 U.S. 594 (1953); Keith Roberts, "Antitrust Problems in the Newspaper Industry," *Harvard Law Review* 82 (1968): 341, 354; "Kansas City Star Indicted as Trust," *NYT*, January 7, 1953, 29; "2-paper Ad Rule Held Trust Law Violation," *NYT*, May 28, 1952, 27;

"Times-Picayune Co. Wins on Unit Ads," *NYT,* May 26, 1953, 26; "Local Monopoly in the Daily Newspaper Industry," 1007; "Item Bowing Out in New Orleans," *NYT,* September 14, 1958, 76; William E. Lee, "Antitrust Enforcement, Freedom of the Press and the 'Open Market': The Supreme Court on the Structure and Conduct of Mass Media," *Vanderbilt Law Review* 32 (1979): 1254–1278; Richard J. Barber, "Newspaper Monopoly in New Orleans: The Lessons for Antitrust Policy," *Louisiana Law Review* 24 (1964): 503–554; Stephen R. Barnett, "Newspaper Monopoly and the Law," *Journal of Communication* 30 (1980): 72–77.

25. Liebling, *Press,* 8, 32; Douglass Cater, *The Fourth Branch of Government* (Cambridge, MA: Houghton Mifflin, 1959), 171; *Deadline U.S.A.,* written and directed by Richard Brooks (1952; Henderson, NV: TVS Home Video, Margate Entertainment, 2010), DVD.

26. Loren Ghiglione, *CBS's Don Hollenbeck: An Honest Reporter in the Age of McCarthyism* (New York: Columbia University Press, 2008); George Seldes Interview with Howard Zinn, n.d., box 64, folder 16, HZ; Pamela A. Brown, "George Seldes and the Winter Soldier Brigade: The Press Criticism of *In Fact,* 1940–1950," *American Journalism* 6 (1989): 85–102.

27. Robert W. Desmond, "Of a Free and Responsible Press," *JQ* 24 (1947): 188–192; Andie L. Knutsen, "The Commission versus the Press," *Public Opinion Quarterly* 12 (1948): 130–135; Frank Tripp, "The Movies Join the Press," *EP,* March 29, 1947, 9; "Editorial: Press Is Indicted," *EP,* March 29, 1947, 38; Margaret A. Blanchard, "The Hutchins Commission, the Press and the Responsibility Concept," *Journalism Monographs* 49 (May 1977): 29–50; Wilbur Forrest, "Forrest Says Report Helps Destroy Prestige of Press," *EP,* March 29, 1947, 11.

28. "Cooper Regrets Delay in UNO Press Action," *EP,* February 16, 1946, 18; Robert U. Brown, "Democrats Endorse World Press Freedom in Platform," *EP,* July 22, 1944, 7; Robert U. Brown, "GOP Endorses Principle of International Free Press," *EP,* July 1, 1944, 7; "Congress Adopts World Free News Resolution," *EP,* September 23, 1944, 12; "Editorial: World Free Press and Dumbarton Oaks," *EP,* September 16, 1944, 36; "Baillie Back with Bag of Free Press Pledges," *EP,* November 4, 1944, 8.

29. "Freedom of Information," *EP,* October 26, 1946, 84; "Step by Step Progress in UN," *EP,* April 12, 1947, 13.

30. "World Information Parley Voted," *EP,* December 21, 1946, 11; Margaret A. Blanchard, *Exporting the First Amendment: The Press-Government Crusade of 1945–1952* (New York: Longman, 1986).

31. See Daniel R. Headrick, *The Invisible Weapon: Telecommunications and International Politics, 1851–1945* (New York: Oxford University Press, 1991); Jonathan Fenby, *The International News Services* (New York: Schocken Books, 1986), 23–58; Anthony Smith, *The Geopolitics of Information: How Western Culture Dominates the World* (London: Faber and Faber, 1980), 74–82.

32. "Planes Change World Coverage," *EP,* January 5, 1946, 7; Raymond Clapper, "World Will Be a 'City Beat Desk' after the War, Clapper Predicts," *EP,* May 23, 1942, 6.

33. Herbert I. Schiller, *Communication and Cultural Domination* (White Plains, NY: M. E. Sharpe, 1976), 29.

34. Summary Record of First Meeting, UN Doc e/conf.6/sr.1, box 3, folder: FOI Summary Records, RG 43; William Benton, Confidential Report, n.d., box 2, folder: FOI Reports, RG 43; Benton to Lovett, March 20, 1948, box 5, folder: Freedom of Information, RG 43.

35. "Writers Protest Soviet Blackout; Spain Opens Up," *EP,* April 21, 1945, 18; "Russian Blackout," *EP,* May 19, 1945, 36; "Byrnes, Molotov Clash on Free Press Ideal," *EP,* August 10, 1946, 8; "Binder Held by Russians Then Freed," *EP,* September 28, 1946, 20; "Eastern Europe Nations Expel US Writers," *EP,* November 8, 1947, 10; Richard S. Clark, "Reds Grab Czechoslovakia after Gagging Press, Radio," *EP,* February 28, 1948, 7; "Soviet Editor Pays with Life for Deviating from Policy," *EP,* February 7, 1948, 9; "Soviet Press," *EP,* February 14, 1948, 40; Dawson to Allen, Evaluation of Work of US Delegation, April 30 1948; Benton to Jack Hickerson, February 18, 1948, both in box 4, folder: FOI File, RG 43; Lloyd Free to Howland Sargeant, February 24, 1948, Benton to Howland Sargeant and Lloyd Free, February 16, 1948, both in box 1, folder 1, RG 43.

36. William Reed, "Censorship, Propaganda on Freedom Parley Agenda," *EP,* May 31, 1947, 7; Conference on Freedom of Information Annotated Agenda, March 4, 1948, 6, box 2, folder: Delegate's File, RG 43.

37. Summary Record of the Fourth Meeting of Committee III, UN Doc e/conf.6 /c.3/sr/4, box 4, RG 43.

38. Howland Sargeant to Lloyd Free, March 6, 1948, box 1, folder: US Delegation File, RG 43; Under Secretary of State to William Benton, March 11, 1948, box 250, folder 2, William Benton Papers, Special Collections Research Center, University of Chicago Library, Chicago, IL; Conference on Freedom of Information Annotated Agenda, March 4, 1948, 10–12, box 2, folder: Delegate's File, RG 43; Press Release of Benton's Address at Geneva, March 25, 1948, box 2, folder: US Delegate Documents, RG 43.

39. Summary Record of the Tenth Meeting of Committee IV, UN Doc e/conf.6 /c.4/sr/10, box 4, RG 43; Minutes of US Delegation Meeting, April 15, 1948, box 2, folder: US Delegates Documents, RG 43; US Delegates Report, May 7, 1948, box 2, folder: FOI Reports, RG 43.

40. Conference on Freedom of Information Annotated Agenda, March 4, 1948, 1, box 2, folder: Delegate's File, RG 43; Minutes of US Delegation Meeting, March 15, 1948, box 2, folder: US Delegate Documents, RG 43.

41. William Reed, "French Submit Plans for Press Freedom," *EP,* March 22, 1947, 11; Summary Record of the Eleventh Meeting of Committee I, e/conf.6/c.1/ sr/11, box 3, RG 43; Conference on Freedom of Information Annotated Agenda, March 4, 1948, 32, box 2, folder: Delegate's File, RG 43; Views on the US on Measures for Combating False or Distorted Reports, UN Doc e/conf.6/6 add.6, box 3, folder: FOI Summary records, RG 43; Sevellon Brown Speech Excerpts, April 7, 1948, box 2, folder: US Delegation Files, RG 43.

42. William Benton, Address on Convention on the Gathering and Transmission of News, April 19, 1948, box 2, folder: US Delegation Files, RG 43; Convention on the Gathering and International Transmission of News, n.d., box 2, folder: US Delegation Files, RG 43; Mr. Hendrick to Mr. Bohlen, Confidential Memo on UN Conference on Freedom of Information, March 22, 1948, box 5, folder: Freedom of

Information, RG 43; Summary Record of the Fifth Meeting of Committee II, UN Doc e/conf.6/c.2/sr/5, box 4, RG 43; Summary Record of the Thirteenth Meeting of Committee 1, UN Doc e/conf.6/c.1/sr13, box 3, RG 43; Summary Record of the Second Meeting of Committee I, UN Doc e/conf.6/c.1/sr2, box 3, RG 43. On visa policy, see David Caute, *The Great Fear: The Anti-Communist Purge under Truman and Eisenhower* (New York: Simon and Shuster, 1978), 251–260.

43. Lloyd Free to Harry Martin, December 10, 1948, box 1, folder: US Delegation (2), RG 43; Kenneth Cmiel, "Human Rights, Freedom of Information and the Origins of Third-World Solidarity," in *Truth Claims: Representation and Human Rights,* ed. Mark Philip Bradley and Patrice Petro (New Brunswick, NJ: Rutgers University Press, 2002), 107–130; Hugh Baillie, *High Tension: The Recollections of Hugh Baillie* (New York: Harper and Brothers, 1959), 286–287.

44. Conference on Freedom of Information Annotated Agenda, March 4, 1948, 20, box 2, folder: Delegate's File, RG 43; Minutes of US Delegation Meeting, March 26, 1948, box 2, folder: US Delegates Documents, RG 43.

45. Remarks of Harry C. Martin, March 29, 1948, Harry C. Martin Memo to US Delegation, April 21, 1948, both in box 2, folder: US Delegates Documents, RG 43; World News Roundup, March 31, 1948, box 4, folder: FOI File, RG 43; Erwin Canham, Report of Committee on Freedom of Information, ASNE, April 16, 1948, box 4, folder: FOI File, RG 43; Bert Andrews, "State Department Bars Anti-Red Chief of News Guild," newsclipping, n.d., box 1, folder: US Delegation 2, RG 43; CGR to President, Memo Re Membership of American Delegation, March 11, 1948, box 535, folder 85GG: UN Freedom of Information conference, Truman OF.

46. Press Release of Benton's Address at Geneva, March 25, 1948, box 2, folder: US Delegate Documents, RG 43; Report of the US Delegates, May 7, 1948, box 2, folder: US delegates report, RG 43.

47. William Benton, Confidential Report, n.d., box 2, file: FOI Reports, RG 43; Nicholas Cull, *The Cold War and the United States Information Agency: American Propaganda and Public Diplomacy, 1945–1989* (Cambridge: Cambridge University Press, 2008), 53–54.

48. William Benton, Confidential Report, Appendix II: Harry Martin memo, n.d., box 2, file: FOI Reports, RG 43; ECA's Overseas Labor Information Program for 1951, Confidential, February 5, 1951, box 12, folder: Harry Martin's File, ECA Office of Information, Office of the Director Subject Files, Record Group 469: Records of US Foreign Assistance Agencies, 1948–1961, National Archives and Records Administration II, College Park, MD; Brian Angus McKenzie, *Remaking France: Americanization, Public Diplomacy and the Marshall Plan* (New York: Berghahn Books, 2005), 147–192; "Newspapermen Have Vital ECA Role," *GR,* June 23, 1950, 8.

49. Arthur W. MacMahon, *Memorandum on the Postwar International Information Program of the United States,* Dept. of State Publication 2438 (Washington, DC: Government Printing Office, 1945); Blanchard, *Exporting the First Amendment,* 109; "AP Board to Hear Benton, UP Studies His Arguments," *EP,* January 26, 1946, 7; Government News Service Justified, ASNE Unit Says," *EP,* December 14, 1946, 11; Canham Report, April 16, 1948, box 4, folder: FOI File, RG 43; *Problems of Journalism: Proceedings of the 1948 Convention American Society of Newspaper*

Editors, April 15–18, 1948, 260; Robert U. Brown, "ASNE Urges AP, UP Service for Government Newscasts," *EP,* April 24, 1948, 17; "Erwin Canham, Long Time Editor of Christian Science Monitor, Dies," *NYT,* January 4, 1982, B10.

50. Harry S. Truman, "Address on Foreign Policy at the Luncheon of ASNE," April 20, 1950, APP.

51. Edward W. Barrett, *Truth Is Our Weapon* (New York: Funk and Wagnalls, 1953), 73–76.

52. Harry S. Truman: "Special Message to the Congress on Greece and Turkey: The Truman Doctrine," March 12, 1947, APP; "A Report to the National Security Council—NSC-68," April 14, 1950, www.trumanlibrary.org/whistlestop/study_collections/coldwar/documents/pdf/10–1.pdf.

53. Carl Becker, *Freedom and Responsibility in the American Way of Life* (New York: Vintage, 1955).

54. *Free and Responsible Press,* 88; Zechariah Chafee Jr., Erwin M. Griswold, Milton Katz, and Austin W. Scott, "The Loyalty Order," *NYT,* April 13, 1947, 110; Smith, *Zechariah Chafee, Jr.,* 246–262.

55. Edward Alwood, *Dark Days in the Newsroom: McCarthyism Aimed at the Press* (Philadelphia: Temple University Press, 2007), 3, 58–60, 119, 130; "Comrades of the Press," *Newsweek,* July 25, 1955, 52, box 91, folder 1: Eastland Committee Hearings, NGNY; Joanne Lisa Kenen, "White Collars and Red-Baiters: Communism and Anti-Communism in the American Newspaper Guild, 1933–1956" (BA honors thesis, Radcliffe College, March 1980), 141–145. My thanks to Ellen Schrecker for sharing this thesis with me.

56. "Jenner Warns Press of Communist Tactics," *EP,* March 3, 1956, 42, box 91, folder 1: Eastland Committee Hearings, NGNY; "Jenner Criticizes Times Editorial," *NYT,* February 28, 1956, 13; Alwood, *Dark Days in the Newsroom,* 101–106; "NY Times Discharges Fifth Amendment Pleader," *EP,* July 16, 1955, 11, box 91, folder 1: Eastland Committee Hearings, NGNY (my emphasis); "Press and Constitution: An Exchange of Letters about the 5th Amendment and Newspapermen Men," *NYT,* July 22, 1955, 10.

57. Edward P. Corsi, Award of Arbitration, Newspaper Guild of New York and New York Times Company, June 19, 1956, box 83a, folder 15: Communist Affiliation Dismissal, NGNY; Burton B. Turkus, Opinion and Award in the Matter of the Arbitration between American Newspaper Guild and New York Mirror Division—the Hearst Corporation, November 13, 1956, box 83a, folder 15: Communist Affiliation Dismissal, NGNY; Alwood, *Dark Days in the Newsroom,* 49–50.

58. "Actions That Shape Policies of ANG," *GR,* June 28, 1946, 13; "ANG Convention Resolutions," *GR,* July 25, 1947, 6; "Resolutions Adopted by the Convention," *GR,* July 18, 1949, 12; "Board Resolution Censures Murray," *GR,* April 25, 1947, 6; "Locals Called on to Fight Firings Based Solely on Political Beliefs," *GR,* July 9, 1948, 5; "Washington Ponders Case of Reporter Fired for Communist Party Membership," *GR,* June 11, 1948, 1; Alwood, *Dark Days in the Newsroom,* 100–103; Bill Farson to IEB Members, April 29, 1955, Fritz Irwin to New York delegates to ANG Convention, June 1, 1955, both in box 70, folder 1: ANG Convention 1955 (1), NGNY; "Says Publishers, Not Guild, Created Communist Problem," *GR,* March 11, 1955, 6.

59. Alden Whitman to Irving Dilliard, May 24, 1956, box 5, folder 71, Alden Whitman Papers, New York Public Library (hereafter, Whitman Papers); Charles A. Perlik to Alden Whitman, February 28, 1957, box 4, folder 61, Whitman Papers; Minutes of Representative Assembly Meeting, January 30, 1957, box 154, folder 9: RA Minutes, 1956–1957, NGNY; Alden Whitman to George Rundquist, NYCLU, May 24, 1962, George Rundquist to Alden Whitman, June 12, 1962, both in box 4, folder 50, Whitman Papers; Brief for New York Civil Liberties Union, Amicus Curiae, Gerhard P. Van Arkel and George Kauffmann, Brief for the Petitioner, Alden Whitman v. USA, box 5, folder 83, Whitman Papers; Russell v. U.S., 369 U.S. 749, at 779 (1962); Alwood, *Dark Days in the Newsroom,* 100, 121–127; Ralph B. Novak to James O. Eastland, July 20, 1955, William J. Farson to IEB, July 25, 1955, both in box 94, folder 5: Executive Board 1955, NGNY; James Aronson, *The Press and the Cold War* (New York: Monthly Review Press, 1990), 134–135; "Red Stand Cleared, News Guild Feels," *NYT,* July 28, 1955, 7; I. F. Stone letter, February 20, 1957, box 4, folder 61, Whitman Papers.

60. Jack Anderson and Ronald W. May, *McCarthy: The Man, the Senator, the "Ism"* (Boston: Beacon Press, 1952), 267; Ellen Schrecker, *Many Are the Crimes: McCarthyism in America* (Boston: Little, Brown, 1998), 67, 243, 263; Richard H. Rovere, *Senator Joe McCarthy* (New York: Harcourt, Brace, 1959), 166.

61. David M. Oshinsky, *A Conspiracy So Immense: The World of Joe McCarthy* (New York: Free Press, 1983), 108, 182, 186; Edwin R. Bayley, *Joe McCarthy and the Press* (Madison: University of Wisconsin Press, 1981), 15–19, 24–25, 67; Aronson, *Press and the Cold War,* 65–86.

62. Marquis Childs, "What Signs Threaten a Free Press?" *NR,* July 1951, 8; Geoffrey R. Stone, *Perilous Times: Free Speech in Wartime: From the Sedition Act of 1798 to the War on Terrorism* (New York: W. W. Norton, 2004), 379; Alwood, *Dark Days in the Newsroom,* 69–73; Full Text of ASNE Report on Wechsler-McCarthy Case, *NR,* October 1953, 27–35; Bayley, *Joe McCarthy and the Press,* 142–145.

63. Stone, *Perilous Times,* 313; Cater, *Fourth Branch of Government,* 71, 73; Dozier C. Cade, "Witch-Hunting, 1952: The Role of the Press," *JQ* 29 (1952): 396–407.

64. Truman, "Special Message to the Congress on Greece and Turkey"; "Press Called Key to Reds' Tyranny," *NYT,* August 15, 1953, 3; William Hachten, "The Press as Reporter and Critic of Government," *JQ* 40 (1963): 17.

65. Davies, *Postwar Decline of American Newspapers,* 34–35; Harold L. Cross, *The People's Right to Know: Legal Access to Public Records and Proceedings* (New York: Columbia University Press, 1953), xiv; George Penn Kennedy, "Advocates of Openness: The Freedom of Information Movement" (Ph.D. diss., University of Missouri–Columbia, 1978), 23, 29.

7. The Rise of State Secrecy

1. James S. Pope, "The Cult of Secrecy," *NR,* October 1951, 8; James S. Pope, "Freedom Is Indivisible," *NR,* January 1953, 30–31; "Award Honors Abolitionist

Editor Lovejoy," *Chicago Defender,* September 6, 1952, 3; "JS Pope Gets Lovejoy Award," *NYT,* October 5, 1952, 39.

2. *Availability of Information from Federal Departments and Agencies, Part 1: Panel Discussion with Editors, Hearings before a Subcommittee of the Committee on Government Relations,* 84th Cong. 4 (1955) (Statement of James S. Pope); "Defense Department Lifts Secrecy Curtain Slightly," *EP,* July 27, 1957, 9; Wallace Parks, "Secrecy and the Public Interest in Military Affairs," *George Washington Law Review* 26 (1957): 60; Peter Galison, "Removing Knowledge," *Critical Inquiry* 31 (2004): 229–231.

3. Weber, for instance, famously noted that "every bureaucracy seeks to increase the superiority of the professionally informed by keeping their knowledge and intentions secret. Bureaucratic administration always tends to be an administration of 'secret sessions.'" See H. H. Gerth and C. Wright Mills, eds., *From Max Weber: Essays in Sociology* (New York: Oxford University Press, 1946), 233–235.

4. Edward Shils, *The Torment of Secrecy: The Background and Consequences of American Security Policies* (Glencoe, IL: Free Press, 1956), 36.

5. John Steinbeck, *Once There Was a War* (New York: Viking, 1958), xi–xii; Timothy L. Ericson, "Building Our Own 'Iron Curtain': The Emergence of Secrecy in American Government," *The American Archivist* 68 (2005): 41; Arvin S. Quist, *Security Classification of Information,* vol. 1, 2002, 44, www.fas.org/sgp/library/quist; "A Recurrent Effort to Control the News," *NYT,* October 24, 1947, 22; "Secrecy Modified on U.S. Material," *NYT,* October 29, 1947, 56.

6. "New Order Due Soon on Federal Secrets," *NYT,* September 9, 1951, 70; "Editors Object to Order," *NYT,* September 26, 1951, 17; Harry S. Truman, "Executive Order 10290," September 24, 1951, APP.

7. United States Commission on Government Security, *Report of the Commission on Government Security,* S.doc.64, at 155 (1957); Executive Order 10290; Anthony Leviero, "Yale Men 'Acting Like Spies,' Bared Grave Security Leaks," *NYT,* October 14, 1951, 1; President's News Conference, October 4, 1951, APP. The invocation of the Espionage Act in Executive Order 10290 and Executive Order 10501 was somewhat circuitous, adding to the general imprecision of secrecy law. See Harold Edgar and Benno C. Schmidt Jr., "The Espionage Statutes and Publication of Defense Information," *Columbia Law Review* 73 (1973): 1052–1054.

8. "Editors Denounce Truman News Ban," *NYT,* September 30, 1951, 39; "New Policy Is Due on Agencies Data," *NYT,* June 14, 1953, 60; David Greenberg, "The Tale of the Upside-Down Recipe Cake: Harry Truman, the Press, and Executive Confidentiality in the Cold War Years," in *Civil Liberties and the Legacy of Harry S. Truman,* ed. Richard S. Kirkendall (Kirksville, MO: Truman State University Press, 2013), 101–112; Dwight D. Eisenhower, "Executive Order 10501," November 5, 1953, APP; Anthony Leviero, "Security Revision Raises Problems," *NYT,* June 20, 1953, 5; "Eisenhower Issues New Security Code," *NYT,* November 7, 1953, 1; *Report of the Commission on Government Security,* 162; David H. Morrissey, "Disclosure and Secrecy: Security Classification Executive Orders," *Journalism and Mass Communication Monographs* (February 1997): 14–17.

9. Arthur Krock, "Truman's Press Views Mystify the Capital," *NYT,* October 7, 1951, 157; "Text of Truman Security Statement and Transcript of Discussion," *NYT,* October 5, 1951, 12; President's News Conference, October 4, 1951, APP.

10. James Russell Wiggins, *Freedom or Secrecy* (New York: Oxford University Press, 1956), 100; John F. Kennedy, "The President and the Press: Address before ANPA," April 27, 1961, www.jfklibrary.org/Research/Research-Aids/JFK-Speeches/American-Newspaper-Publishers-Association_19610427.aspx; Creed C. Black to Pierre Salinger, July 31, 1963, folder: Freedom of Information 3b, box 143, Pierre Salinger Papers, John F. Kennedy Library, Boston; *Government Information Plans and Policies, Part 1: Hearings before a Subcommittee of the Committee on Government Operations,* 88th Cong. 9 (1963).

11. Edgar and Schmidt, "Espionage Statutes," 1026–1027; *Report of the Commission on Government Security,* 1, xxiii, 687–688; "Wright, Moss Expound Views on 'Leak' Law," *EP,* July 13, 1957, 10; "Text of Wright's Statement on Journalists and U.S. Security," *NYT,* July 1, 1957, 14; 85 Cong. Rec. A5155 (June 27, 1957); "2 in House Score Leak Proposals," *NYT,* June 24, 1957, 12; "Editorial," *EP,* June 29, 1957, 6; William A. Korns, "Secrecy and Security," *Editorial Research Reports,* August 7, 1957, 571; *Availability of Information from Federal Departments and Agencies, Part 8: Hearings before a Subcommittee of the Committee on Government Operations,* 85th Cong., 2044–2045 (1957); Committee on Classified Information, U.S. Department of Defense, *Report to the Secretary of Defense* (Washington, DC: Government Printing Office, 1957).

12. *Problems of Journalism: Proceedings of the 1948 Convention American Society of Newspaper Editors,* April 15–18, 1948, 241–242; Joseph Short to Maclean Patterson, November 5, 1951, folder: Executive Order Re Classified Information, 285-M, misc., box 928, Truman OF.

13. *Report of the Commission on Protecting and Reducing Government Secrecy,* S.Doc 105–2, at xxvi, 4, 35 (1997); Quist, *Security Classification of Information,* 6; Galison, "Removing Knowledge," 237.

14. *Government Information Plans and Policies, Part 1: Hearings before a Subcommittee of the Committee on Government Operations,* 88th Cong. 64 (1963); Arthur M. Schlesinger Jr., *The Imperial Presidency* (Boston: Mariner Books, 2004), 343; "Defense Department Lifts Secrecy Curtain Slightly," *EP,* July 27, 1957, 9; "Adm. Hoskins Given Job of Declassifying Secrets," *WP,* May 22, 1957, B11; Jason Ross Arnold, *Secrecy in the Sunshine Era: The Promise and Failure of US Open Government Laws* (Lawrence: University Press of Kansas, 2014), 21–22.

15. 82 Cong. Rec. S12508 (October 3, 1951); "Press Groups Ask Congress to Stem the Tide of Secrecy," *EP,* February 8, 1958, 9; James S. Pope to Joseph Short, copied to Benton, n.d., folder: Executive Order Re Classified Information, 285-M, miscel., box 928, Truman OF; Arthur Krock, "The New Checks on Government Information," *NYT,* September 28, 1951, 28; "Security and News," *NYT,* October 6, 1951, 13.

16. According to the executive orders issued by Jimmy Carter, Bill Clinton, George W. Bush, and Barack Obama, the public interest in disclosure was to be considered when making declassification decisions, but not in the initial classification

decision. While Carter, Clinton, and Obama all encouraged classifiers to err on the side of openness when in doubt about whether to classify, they did not require positive weighing of a public interest in disclosure. See Executive Order 12065, Executive Order 12958, Executive Order 13292, and Executive Order 13526, all at APP.

17. *Report of the Commission on Protecting and Reducing Government Secrecy* (1997), 30.

18. Robert P. Deyling, "Judicial Deference and De Novo Review in Litigation over National Security Information under the Freedom of Information Act," *Villanova Law Review* 37 (1992): 67–112.

19. Geoffrey R. Stone, *Perilous Times: Free Speech in Wartime: From the Sedition Act of 1798 to the War on Terrorism* (New York: W. W. Norton, 2004), 312–426; Robert Justin Goldstein, *Political Repression in Modern America: From 1870 to the Present* (Cambridge, MA: Schenkman, 1978), 285–369; John W. Caughey, "McCarthyism Rampant," in *The Pulse of Freedom: American Liberties: 1920–1970s,* ed. Alan Reitman (New York: W. W. Norton, 1975), 154–210.

20. Dennis v. U.S., 341 U.S. 494, at 581 (1951).

21. Bernard A. Drabek, ed., *Archibald MacLeish: Reflections* (Amherst: University of Massachusetts Press, 1986), 165.

22. William S. White, "Files of Condon Loyalty Test Demanded by House Inquiry," *NYT,* March 3, 1948, 1; "Subpoena Seeks Data on Dr Condon," *NYT,* March 4, 1948, 8; "Harriman Holds up Report on Condon," *NYT,* March 5, 1948, 1; "President Orders Agencies to Bar Data on Loyalty," *NYT,* March 16, 1948, 1; Samuel A. Tower, "Atomic Committee Takes Up Charges against Dr Condon," *NYT,* March 7, 1948, 1; "House Bids Truman Yield Condon File; He Defies Demand," *NYT,* April 23, 1948, 1; "Memorandum Reviewing Inquiries by the Legislative Branch during the Period 1948–1953 Concerning the Decision Making Process and Documents of the Executive Branch," n.d., pp. 10–17, box 88, file: Executive Privilege 2, RC; James Reston, "Loyalty File Request Puts Hard Decision up to Truman," *NYT,* March 14, 1950, 4; "McCarthy Asserts Truman Is 'Afraid' to Release Files," *NYT,* April 10, 1950, 1; "President Opens 81 Loyalty Files to Senate Inquiry," *NYT,* May 5, 1950, 1.

23. 82 Cong. Rec. S12853 (October 9, 1951); "Legislator Scores Truman Gag Order," *NYT,* October 7, 1951, 82; "Bricker Deplores Order on Security," *NYT,* October 3, 1951, 4; *Individual Views of Mr. Jenner in Respect to the Report of the Committee on Rules and Administration Relative to the Maryland Senatorial Election of 1950,* S.Doc. 81 (1951); 82 Cong. Rec. S12933 (October 11, 1951); "Memorandum Reviewing Inquiries by the Legislative Branch during the Period 1948–1953," 102–108.

24. Samuel A. Tower, "President Upheld by Senate on Veto of Atom Inquiry Bill," *NYT,* May 22, 1948, 1.

25. While there were instances of withholding before the 1940s, they were different in scope, frequency, and character to what became codified as "executive privilege" after World War II. For an introduction to the historical debate about them, see Mark J. Rozell, *Executive Privilege: Presidential Power, Secrecy and Accountability,* 3rd ed. (Lawrence: University Press of Kansas, 2010); Raoul Berger, *Executive Privilege: A Constitutional Myth* (New York: Bantam, 1974).

26. Schlesinger, *Imperial Presidency,* 40–47, 155; Herman Wolkinson, "Demands of Congressional Committees for Executive Papers," *Federal Bar Journal* 10 (1948–1949): 103–150, 223–259, 319–350.

27. "Senator Is Irate: President Orders Aides Not to Disclose Details at Top-Level Meeting," *NYT,* May 18, 1954, 1; "Texts of Eisenhower Letter and Brownell Memorandum," *NYT,* May 18, 1954, 24; "Transcript of Presidential Press Conference," *NYT,* May 20, 1954, 18; Robert Kramer and Herman Marcuse, "Executive Privilege: A Study of the Period 1953–1960," *George Washington Law Review* 29 (1961): 669–687.

28. Clark Mollenhoff, "A Precedent the Press Should Examine," *NR*, January 1956, 31; "Unnecessary Suspense," *NYT,* May 18, 1954, 28; "Presidential Discretion," *WP,* May 18, 1954, 14; Kramer and Marcuse, "Executive Privilege," 827–916; JFK to John Moss, March 7, 1962, folder: Executive Privilege, box 22, Office Files of Harry McPherson, Lyndon B. Johnson Library, Austin, TX; Theodore C. Sorensen to Attorney General, March 30, 1962, folder: Executive Privilege 2, box 88, RC; Joseph W. Bishop Jr., "The Executive's Right of Privacy: An Unresolved Constitutional Question," *Yale Law Journal* 66 (1957): 477–491; Ramsey Clark, "Memorandum for the President," December 9, 1964, file FE 14–1, box 25, WHCF.

29. "Shop Talk at Thirty," *EP,* September 21, 1957, 124; "New Labels Bar Public Data," *WP,* November 3, 1955, 26; "Moss Committee Vital to Public Information," *EP,* January 26, 1957, 62; "Ex-Pentagon Aide Defends Secrecy," *NYT,* January 14, 1956, 4; William T. Stone, "Secrecy in Government," *Editorial Research Reports,* December 21, 1955, 906–907; "Industry Warned to Restrict Data," *NYT,* September 17, 1955, 9; "Harvard Quandary Aired," *Christian Science Monitor,* June 3, 1957, 10; "APME Again Demands White House Rescind Secrecy Rule," *EP,* November 23, 1957, 11, 62, 64; *Freedom of Information and Secrecy in Government, Part 2: Hearing before the Subcommittee on Constitutional Rights of the Committee on the Judiciary,* 85th Cong. 550 (1958).

30. "Scientist Says Secrecy Hides Fallout Threat," *EP,* August 9, 1958, 53; Kramer and Marcuse, "Executive Privilege," 848–853; "GAO Says Three Agencies Thwart Will of Congress on Vital Data," *WP,* May 14, 1959, A11; "Navy Policy Called Curb on GAO Reviews," *WP,* April 22, 1959, A2; *Availability of Information from Federal Departments and Agencies, Part 17: Hearings before a Subcommittee of the Committee on Government Operations,* 86th Cong., 3926, 3974, 4111, 4124 (1959).

31. "Reston Sees No Conspiracy to Seal News," *EP,* January 3, 1959, 45; "PR Releases Called Worse than Secrecy," *EP,* April 9, 1960, 70; Michael Schudson, *Discovering the News: A Social History of American Newspapers* (New York: Basic Books, 1978), 170.

32. Gerhard Peters, "Presidential News Conferences," APP, www.presidency.ucsb.edu/data/newsconferences.php.

33. Douglass Cater, *The Fourth Branch of Government* (Cambridge, MA: Houghton Mifflin, 1959), 39–41; William S. White, "Analyzing the 'Adversary' Relationship," in *The Presidency and the Press,* ed. Hoyt Purvis (Austin: University of Texas, 1976), 10–12; "Presidential Press Parley Changes Advocated in Memo," *EP,* December 3, 1960, 9; "Shop Talk at Thirty," *EP,* February 25, 1961, 68.

34. David R. Davies, *The Postwar Decline of American Newspapers* (Westport, CT: Praeger, 2006), 37; Steven Casey, *Selling the Korean War: Propaganda, Politics, and Public Opinion in the United States, 1950–1953* (New York: Oxford University Press, 2008), 218; John F. Kennedy, "President's News Conference," November 20, 1962, APP; "Background Outline: Recent Developments in Government Information Control Procedures," n.d., box 142, folder: Freedom of Information 2a, Salinger Papers, JFK Library; *Government Information Plans and Policies, Part 1: Hearings before a Subcommittee of the Committee on Government Operations,* 88th Cong. 6–8, 25, 93 (1963).

35. Leon V. Sigal, *Reporters and Officials: The Organization and Politics of Newsmaking* (Lexington, MA: D.C. Heath, 1973); Dan C. Nimmo, *Newsgathering in Washington: A Study in Political Communication* (New Brunswick: Aldine Transaction, 2014), 146, 158; Cater, *Fourth Branch of Government,* 131; Donald A. Ritchie, *Reporting from Washington: The History of the Washington Press Corps* (Oxford: Oxford University Press, 2005), xiv.

36. Cater, *Fourth Branch of Government,* 125, 130–134; Montague Kern et al., *The Kennedy Crises: The Press, the Presidency and Foreign Policy* (Chapel Hill: University of North Carolina Press, 1983), 80–81; William Greider, "The Not-Very-Secret Secrecy Game," *WP,* July 9, 1971, A1; David E. Pozen, "The Leaky Leviathan: Why the Government Condemns and Condones Unlawful Disclosures of Information," *Harvard Law Review* 127 (2013): 512–635.

37. Robert W. Merry, *Taking on the World: Joseph and Stewart Alsop—Guardians of the American Century* (New York: Penguin Books, 1996); Oliver Pilat, *Drew Pearson: An Unauthorized Biography* (New York: Harper and Row, 1973); Larry J. Sabato, *Feeding Frenzy: How Attack Journalism Has Transformed American Politics* (New York: Free Press, 1991), 30–41; David Greenberg, "Sex and the Married Politician," *Atlantic Monthly,* October 2011, 52–55.

38. Michael Janeway, *Republic of Denial: Press, Politics and Public Life* (New Haven, CT: Yale University Press, 1999), 80; Oxie Reichler, "Those Homemade Iron Curtains," *NR,* July 1951, 19; Alan Barth, "Needed: Irresponsibility," *NR,* March 1963, 7.

39. "Editorial," *EP,* March 28, 1959, 6; Joseph Alsop and Stewart Alsop, *The Reporter's Trade* (New York: Reynal, 1958), 76; Merry, *Taking on the World,* 300; Warren Zimmerman, "Washington Focus," *EP,* May 14, 1960, 15; "Press Hounded Everyone, Says Herter on U2 Story," *EP,* June 4, 1960, 73; Gordon Eliot White, "The Story's Out," *EP,* May 14, 1960, 15; *Government Information Plans and Policies, Part 1: Hearings before a Subcommittee of the Committee on Government Operations,* 88th Cong. 66 (1963); Clarence R. Wyatt, *Paper Soldiers: The American Press and the Vietnam War* (Chicago: University of Chicago Press, 1995), 20; Schudson, *Discovering the News,* 172.

40. James T. Patterson, *Grand Expectations: The United States, 1945–1974* (New York: Oxford University Press, 1996), 494; *Government Information Plans and Policies: Hearings before a Subcommittee of the Committee on Government Operations,* 88th Cong., 1st Sess. (March 19, 25, 1963), 57; Kern et al., *Kennedy Crises,* 106; W. Joseph Campbell, *Getting It Wrong: Ten of the Greatest Misreported Stories in American Journalism* (Berkeley: University of California Press, 2010),

68–84; Dom Bonafede, "The Press in the Cuban Fiasco," *NR*, July 1961, 5–6; James Reston, "US and Cuba, the Moral Question," *NYT,* April 12, 1961, 40; Neal D. Houghton, "The Cuban Invasion of 1961 and the U.S. Press in Retrospect," *Journalism and Mass Communication Quarterly* 42 (1965): 422–432.

41. Jules Witcover, "Where Washington Reporting Failed," *CJR,* Winter 1970–1971, 9; Wyatt, *Paper Soldiers,* 92, 170; Don Stillman, "Tonkin: What Should Have Been Asked," *CJR,* Winter 1970–1971, 22; Daniel C. Hallin, *The "Uncensored War": The Media and Vietnam* (New York: Oxford University Press, 1986), 60, 91–92, 101; Kathleen J. Turner, *Lyndon Johnson's Dual War: Vietnam and the Press* (Chicago: University of Chicago Press, 1985), chap. 5; William M. Hammond, *Public Affairs: The Military and the Media, 1962–1968* (Washington, DC: Government Printing Office, 1988), 152; *Government Information Plans and Policies, Part 1: Hearings before a Subcommittee of the Committee on Government Operations,* 88th Cong. 75 (1963); "Less than 40% of People Follow Vietnam Events," *WP,* May 27, 1964, A18; Foreign Affairs Division, Legislative Reference Service, *Security Classification as a Problem in the Congressional Role in Foreign Policy* (Washington, DC: Government Printing Office, 1971), 29; "Study of U.S. Role in Laos Demanded," *NYT,* September 19, 1969, 1; "Wide U.S. Role in Laos since 1964 Disclosed," *Boston Globe,* April 20, 1970, 1; Marilyn Young, *Vietnam Wars, 1945–1990* (New York: HarperCollins, 1991), 131.

42. Turner, *Lyndon Johnson's Dual War,* chap. 4; Ben Bagdikian, "Press Agent—But Still President," *CJR,* Summer 1965, 13; Walter Lippmann, "Credibility Gap—How It All Began," *Boston Globe,* March 28, 1967, 13; Wyatt, *Paper Soldiers,* 115–122; Kern et al., *Kennedy Crises,* 187; William M. Hammond, "The Press in Vietnam as Agent of Defeat: A Critical Examination" *Reviews in American History* 17 (1989): 312–323; Hallin, *"Uncensored War";* Witcover, "Where Washington Reporting Failed," 9; A. H. Raskin, "What's Wrong with American Newspapers?" *NYT Magazine,* June 11, 1967, 28.

43. In the Senate, Thomas Henning's Subcommittee on Constitutional Rights also campaigned for government transparency.

44. Robert Okie Blanchard, "The Moss Committee and a Federal Public Records Law, 1955–1965" (Ph.D. diss., Syracuse University, 1966), 54–56, 156; Sam Archibald, "The Early Years of the Freedom of Information Act: 1955 to 1974," *PS: Political Science and Politics* 26 (1993): 728; Robert O. Blanchard, "A Watchdog in Decline," *CJR,* Summer 1966, 19.

45. J. R. Wiggins, "Secrecy, Security and Freedom," *NR,* July 1958, 3; *Report of the Commission on Government Security,* xix; "House Group Says Secrecy Hurts Science," *EP,* April 26, 1958, 86; Galison, "Removing Knowledge," 237–238; William A. Korns, "Secrecy and Security," *Editorial Research Reports,* August 7, 1957, 580; Parks, "Secrecy and the Public Interest," 36–44; Background Outline: Recent Developments in Government Information Control Procedures, n.d., box 142, folder: Freedom of Information 2a, Salinger Papers; *Government Information Plans and Policies, Part 1: Hearings before a Subcommittee of the Committee on Government Operations,* 88th Cong. 35 (1963).

46. Blanchard, "Moss Committee," 64, 89–90, 109, 108; Archibald, "Early Years," 727; Herbert N. Foerstel, *Freedom of Information and the Right to Know:*

The Origins and Applications of the Freedom of Information Act (Westport, CT: Greenwood, 1999), 22–23; "FoI Center Proposed to Lead Battle for the Right to Know," *EP,* March 22, 1958, 9; "Editorial," *EP,* March 22, 1958, 6.

47. Harold L. Cross, *The People's Right to Know: Legal Access to Public Records and Proceedings* (New York: Columbia University Press, 1953), vii, 198; William T. Stone, "Secrecy in Government," *Editorial Research Reports,* December 21, 1955, 899; Pope, "Cult of Secrecy," 9; J. R. Wiggins, "The Role of the Press in Safeguarding the People's Right to Know Government Business," *Marquette Law Review* 40 (1956–1957): 78.

48. Cross, *People's Right to Know,* xiii; Harold L. Cross, "Where Stands the Battle Line on Press Freedom?" *NR,* October 1954, 46.

49. "The Right to Know," *NYT,* January 23, 1945, 18; "Moss Committee Vital to Public Information," *EP,* January 26, 1957, 62.

50. My emphasis. Grosjean v. American Press Co., Inc., 297 U.S. 233, at 243 (1936); James S. Pope, "Freedom Is Indivisible," *NR,* January 1953, 30–31; "Note: Access to Official Information: A Neglected Constitutional Right," *Indiana Law Journal* 27 (1952): 211–212.

51. Wallace Parks, "The Open Government Principle: Applying the Right to Know under the Constitution," *George Washington Law Review* 26 (1957): 10; Pope, "Freedom Is Indivisible," 31.

52. Legal scholar Adam Samaha has rightly pointed out that questions of secrecy and access scramble the distinction between negative and positive liberties. Adam M. Samaha, "Government Secrets, Constitutional Law, and Platforms for Judicial Intervention," *UCLA Law Review* 53 (2005): 952–953.

53. Wiggins, *Freedom or Secrecy,* 132; Wiggins, "Safeguarding the People's Right to Know," 80–81; Harold L. Cross, "Where Stands the Battle Line on Press Freedom?" *NR*, October 1954, 44–45.

54. Cross, *People's Right to Know,* 128–129; *Availability of Information from Federal Departments and Agencies, Part 1: Panel Discussion with Editors, Hearings before a Subcommittee of the Committee on Government Relations,* 84th Cong. 36 (1955). On early American secrecy, see Sagar, *Secrets and Leaks,* 20–21; Rozell, *Executive Privilege,* 24; Gerald L. Grotta, "Philip Freneau's Crusade for Open Sessions of the U.S. Senate," *JQ* 49 (1971): 667–671.

55. Cross, *People's Right to Know,* 246.

56. Ibid., 222; "Is a Congressional Committee Entitled to Demand and Receive Information and Papers from the President and the Heads of Departments Which They Deem Confidential in the Public Interest?" n.d., box 88, file: Executive Privilege 2, RC; Quist, *Security Classification of Information,* vol. 1, 12; Pope, "Cult of Secrecy," 8–9; "Congress Given Bills to Open Public Records," *EP,* January 19, 1957, 12; "Eisenhower Signs Information Bill," *NYT,* August 13, 1958, 15; "Shop Talk at Thirty," *EP,* December 6, 1958, 76; George Penn Kennedy, "Advocates of Openness: The Freedom of Information Movement" (Ph.D. diss., University of Missouri–Columbia, 1978), 92; Blanchard, "Moss Committee," 117–120, 133.

57. House Report 1497, May 9, 1966, 5, Senate Report 813, October 1, 1965, 3, both in box 36, folder PL 89–487, S1160, Reports on Enrolled Legislation, LBJ

Library; Cross, *People's Right to Know,* 223–228; "Procedure Act Sanctions US Secrecy," *EP,* April 26, 1958, 78.

58. Kennedy, "Advocates of Openness," 95–96, 120–122; Harold C. Relyea, "Freedom of Information, Privacy and Official Secrecy: The Evolution of Federal Government Information Policy Concepts," *Social Indicators Research* 7 (1980): 137–156; *Freedom of Information and Secrecy in Government, Part 1: Hearing before the Subcommittee on Constitutional Rights of the Committee on the Judiciary on S.921,* 85th Cong. 4 (1958).

59. "Information Bill Faces Stiff Test," *WP,* August 10, 1965, A12; "White House Opposition Stalls Information Bill," August 9, 1965 clipping, box 44, folder FE 14–1, WHCF; Bill Moyers on the Freedom of Information Act, April 5, 2002, www.pbs.org/now/commentary/moyers4.html; Statement on S.1160, March 16, 1966, p. 2, box 44, folder FE 14–1, WHCF; *Federal Public Records Law, Part 1: Hearings before a Subcommittee of the Committee on Government Operations,* 89th Cong. 5–6 (1965); Lee White to Sam Archibald, August 27, 1965, folder: Executive Privilege, box 22, Office Files of Harry McPherson, LBJ Library; Phillip S. Hughes to White, March 10, 1965, Hughes to White, August 12, 1965, Hughes to White, October 4, 1965, all in box 44, folder FE 14–1, WHCF; "Information Freedom Bill Backed in Senate," *WP,* March 3, 1964, A7; "Shop Talk at 30," *EP,* August 29, 1964, 72.

60. "Hill Drive on to Reduce Secrecy in Government," *WP,* February 18, 1965, A22; "Senate Again Votes a Bill on News Flow," *NYT,* August 1, 1964, 18; "An Information Bill Is Passed by Senate," *NYT,* October 14, 1965, 36; "Editors Told Johnson Tries to Scuttle Freedom of Information Measure," *WP,* February 22, 1966, A15; Paul Wieck, "Chill Threatens Press Bill," *Albuquerque Journal,* July 11, 1965, 5; Moyers to Lee White, December 15, 1965, box 44, folder FE 14–1, WHCF.

61. Lee C. White Memorandum, January 15, 1966, box 25, folder FE 14–1, WHCF; *Freedom of Information, Executive Privilege, Secrecy in Government, Volume 2: Hearings before the Subcommittees on Administrative Practice and Procedure,* 93rd Cong. 122–126 (1973); Blanchard, "Moss Committee," 200–206; "Disclosure Bill Gains Approval of House Unit," *WP,* April 28, 1966, A12; Bryce Nelson, "House Votes Information Access Bill," *WP,* June 21, 1966, A1; House Report 1497, May 9, 1966, 6, Senate Report 813, October 1, 1965, 3–4, 10, William Feldesman to Wilfred H. Rommel, June 22, 1966, Chairman of AEC to Charles Schultz, June 24, 1966; Deputy Secretary of Defense to Charles Schultze, June 28, 1966, John Gardner to Charles Schultze, June 23, 1966, all in box 36, folder PL 89–487, S1160, Reports on Enrolled Legislation, LBJ Library; Milton P. Semer, Memorandum for the President, July 1, 1966, box 25, folder FE 14–1, WHCF.

62. Samuel Archibald to Milton P. Semer, June 20, 1966, box 25, folder FE 14–1, WHCF; Robert Kintner, Memorandum for the President, June 24, 1966, box 15, folder: Handwriting President Johnson, June 1966, Notes Instructions Doodles (4 of 5), Handwriting File, LBJ Library; Robert E. Kintner to Milt Semer, June 23, 1966, box 62, folder: LE/AG—LE/FG 410, Legislation (2 of 2), LBJ Confidential File, LBJ Library.

63. Statement by the President upon Signing the "Freedom of Information Act," July 4, 1966, APP; Statement by the President, n.d., box 44, folder FE 14–1, WHCF;

Statement by the President upon Signing S.1160, July 4, 1966, box 120, folder: Press Release Drafts, July 1966 (3 of 3), White House Press Office Files, LBJ Library.

64. ASNE Annual Report Press Release, April 20, 1967, box 25, folder FE 14–1, WHCF; Memorandum for Executive Departments and Agencies Concerning Section 3 of the Administrative Procedure Act, Preliminary Draft, May 15, 1967, p. vii, box 25, folder FE 14–1, WHCF; Frank M. Wozencraft, "The Freedom of Information Act and the Agencies," *Administrative Law Review* 23 (1971): 129–131; Kenneth Culp Davis, "The Information Act: A Preliminary Analysis," *University of Chicago Law Review* 34 (1967): 761–816.

65. "Moss Committee Vital to Public Information," *EP,* January 26, 1957, 62; Quist, *Security Classification of Information,* vol. 1, 2002, 44.

66. Roscoe Drummond, "Half a Law," *Christian Science Monitor,* July 11, 1966, 16; Arthur Sylvester to Pierre Salinger, n.d., box 143, folder FOIA (3b of 4), Salinger Papers, JFK Library.

67. Wyatt, *Paper Soldiers,* 46, 232.

8. Leaks, Mergers, and Nixon's Assault on the News

1. Tom Wicker, "The Press as Ostrich," *NYT,* October 26, 1972, 43; Rick Perlstein, *Nixonland: The Rise of a President and the Fracturing of America* (New York: Scribner, 2008), 61; David Greenberg, *Nixon's Shadow: The History of an Image* (New York: W. W. Norton, 2003); Stanley I. Kutler, *The Wars of Watergate: The Last Crisis of Richard Nixon* (New York: W. W. Norton, 1990), 70–71.

2. A combined *World-Journal-Tribune* lasted only a year; it was a paper "born to die." A. H. Raskin, "What's Wrong with American Newspapers?" *NYT Magazine,* June 11, 1967; John P. Patkus, "The Newspaper Preservation Act: Why It Fails to Preserve Newspapers," *Akron Law Review* 17 (1984): 446; Donald F. Turner, "Antitrust Division Activity in Newspaper Industry," February 10 1967, box 88, folder: Antitrust Newspapers, RC; David R. Davies, *The Postwar Decline of American Newspapers, 1945–1965* (Westport, CT: Praeger, 2006), 115.

3. Elizabeth MacIver Neiva, "Chain Building: Consolidation of the American Newspaper Industry, 1953–1980," *Business History Review* 70 (1996): 26–32; John H. Carlson, "Newspaper Preservation Act: A Critique," *Indiana Law Journal* 46 (1971): 394; Jon G. Udell, *Economics of the American Newspaper* (New York: Hastings House, 1978), 69–71, 112–115; Robert G. Picard, "U.S. Newspaper Ad Revenue Shows Consistent Growth," *Newspaper Research Journal* 23 (2002): 21–33; Benjamin M. Compaine, *Papers and Profits: A Special Report on the Newspaper Business* (White Plains, NY: Knowledge Industry Productions, 1971), 11–14, 40, 123.

4. The Times-Mirror Company and the *Wall Street Journal* were earlier instances. Anthony Smith, *Goodbye Gutenberg: The Newspaper Revolution of the 1980's* (Oxford: Oxford University Press, 1980), 48; Gilbert Cranberg, Randall Bezanson, and John Soloski, *Taking Stock: Journalism and the Publicly Traded Newspaper Company* (Ames: Iowa State University Press, 2001), 25–33; Sam Kuczun, "Ownership of Newspapers Increasingly Becomes Public," *JQ* 55 (1978): 342–344;

Compaine, *Papers and Profits,* 137; James D. Squires, *Read All About It! The Corporate Takeover of America's Newspapers* (New York: Random House, 1993), 21.

5. A. J. Liebling, *The Press,* 2nd ed. (New York: Pantheon Books, 1975), 3–5; Raskin, "What's Wrong with American Newspapers?"; Neiva, "Chain Building," 26–32; Eli M. Noam, *Media Ownership and Concentration in America* (Oxford: Oxford University Press, 2009), 139.

6. Stuart C. Babington, "Newspaper Monopolies under the Microscope: The Celler Hearings of 1963," *American Journalism* 28 (2011): 113–137; Keith Roberts, "Antitrust Problems in the Newspaper Industry," *Harvard Law Review* 82 (1968): 341; "17 Antitrust Cases Filed against Papers since 1890," *WP,* August 2, 1977, D7; William Orrick, "Memo for the AG Re USA v. Hearst Publishing Co Inc," n.d., "Proposed Civil Complaint Charging Hearst and Chandler," July 18, 1963, both in box 109, folder: LA Newspaper Case, RC; David Halberstam, *The Powers That Be* (New York: Alfred A. Knopf, 1979), 291–292; CBS Reports, "Death in the City Room," Transcript, January 25, 1962, box 116a, folder 4: Monopoly and the Newspaper Crisis, NGNY.

7. Charles J. Romeo and Aran Canes, "A Theory of Quality Competition in Newspaper Joint Operating Agreements," *Antitrust Bulletin* 57 (2012): 373; Warren Christopher, Memo for Larry E. Temple, February 8, 1968, box 24, Executive Folder JL 2–1, WHCF; William H. Orrick Jr., "Joint Publishing Agreements in the Newspaper Industry," Donald F. Turner, "Antitrust Division Activity in Newspaper Industry," February 10, 1967, and Donald F. Turner, "Memo for the AG re San Francisco Newspapers," July 30, 1965, all in box 88, folder: Antitrust Newspapers, RC.

8. Citizen Publishing Co. v. United States, 394 U.S. 131 (1969); "Preserving Press Diversity," *NYT,* January 31, 1970, 30; Glenn Becker, "Failing Newspapers or Failing Journalism: The Public vs. the Publishers," *University of San Francisco Law Review* 4 (1970): 466–467.

9. "Hearing Set in June on Bill to Help Failing Newspapers," *WP,* June 1, 1967, E6; "Senate Unit Sets Newspaper Study," *NYT,* June 18, 1967, 56; "Executive Scores News Trust Bill," *NYT,* August 8, 1967, 17; Newspaper Preservation Act, 15 U.S.C. §1801 (1970).

10. "Would Fight Own Fight, Foe of Press Bill Says," *WP,* July 19, 1967, A2; "Executive Scores News Trust Bill," *NYT,* August 8, 1967, 17; "Trust Exemption for Press Opposed," *NYT,* April 17, 1968, 19; Thomas J. Murphy to Leonard Farbstein, March 18, 1969, box 97, folder 6: Failing Newspaper Act, NGNY; 91 Cong. Rec. S2009 (January 30, 1970); "Aide Says Nixon Opposes Easing of Trust Laws for Weak Papers," *NYT,* June 21, 1969, 30; "Senate Panel Opens Its Hearings on Newspapers," *NYT,* July 13, 1967, 18; Committee on the Judiciary, *Newspaper Preservation Act,* S.Doc. 91–535, at 6–8, 13–14 (1969).

11. Donald F. Turner, "Antitrust Division Activity in Newspaper Industry," February 10, 1967, box 88, folder: Antitrust Newspapers, RC; "Capitol Gets Bills on Paper Mergers," *NYT,* March 13, 1969, 94; "Bill to Aid Failing Newspapers Advances," *WP,* May 26, 1969, A7; Arthur E. Rowse, "The Press Dummies Up," *The Nation,* June 30, 1969, 818; Jim Cesnik to Tom Murphy, July 11, 1969, box 97, folder 6: Failing Newspaper Act, NGNY; Ben H. Bagdikian, *The Media Monopoly,* 5th ed. (Boston: Beacon Press, 1997), 90–101; Becker, "Failing Newspapers or

Failing Journalism," 466; "Senate Approves Newspaper Plan," *NYT,* January 31, 1970, 3; "Newspaper Bill Clears House Unit," *NYT,* July 1, 1970, 29; Randy Brubaker, "The Newspaper Preservation Act: How It Affects Diversity in the Newspaper Industry," *Journal of Communication Inquiry* 7 (1982): 94.

12. Felicity Barringer, "A 1970's Act to Preserve Faltering Newspapers Seems Only to Delay the Inevitable End," *NYT,* August 16, 1999; Janice E. Rubin, "The Newspaper Preservation Act," *Congressional Research Service,* April 5, 1989; Romeo and Canes, "Theory of Quality Competition," 376–377, 407–408; Patkus, "Newspaper Preservation Act," 447–450; Robbie Steele, "Joint Operating Agreements in the Newspaper Industry: A Threat to First Amendment Freedoms," *University of Pennsylvania Law Review* 138 (1989): 283.

13. Patkus, "Newspaper Preservation Act," 437–441; Rubin, "Newspaper Preservation Act," 4–6; Steele, "Joint Operating Agreements," 300–302, 309; "Antitrust and the Press," *WP,* August 22, 1967, A16; Squires, *Read All About It!,* 123.

14. John C. Busterna, "Trends in Daily Newspaper Ownership," *JQ* 65 (1988): 835; Brubaker, "Newspaper Preservation Act," 91; Patkus, "Newspaper Preservation Act," 447; Neiva, "Chain Building," 26–32.

15. David C. Coulson, "Antitrust and the Media: Making the Newspapers Safe for Democracy," *JQ* 57 (1980): 82–84; John C. Busterna, "Anti-Trust in the 1980s: An Analysis of 45 Newspaper Actions," *Newspaper Research Journal* 9 (1988): 37–49.

16. Jerome A. Barron, "Access to the Press—A New First Amendment Right," *Harvard Law Review* 80 (1967): 1641, 1660, 1678; Tornillo v. Miami Herald Publishing Co., 287 So.2d 78 at 87 (1973); Miami Herald Publishing Co. v. Tornillo, 418 U.S. 241 at 256 (1974).

17. Red Lion Broadcasting Co. v. Federal Communications Commission, 395 U.S. 367 (1969); Lee C. Bollinger, *Images of a Free Press* (Chicago: University of Chicago Press, 1991); Margaret A. Blanchard, "The Institutional Press and Its First Amendment Privileges," *Supreme Court Review* (1978): 241; Coulson, "Antitrust and the Media," 82–83; Federal Communications Commission v. National Citizens Committee for Broadcasting, 436 U.S. 775 (1978); Adam Candeub, "Media Ownership Regulation, the First Amendment, and Democracy's Future," *UC Davis Law Review* 41 (2008):1547–1611; Patricia Aufderheide, "Shifting Policy Paradigms and the Public Interest in the U.S. Telecommunications Act of 1996," *Communication Review* 2 (1997): 259–281; Eric Klinenberg, *Fighting for Air: The Battle to Control America's Media* (New York: Metropolitan Books, 2007), 34–35; Les Brown, "Press Freedom for Cable TV Is Urged in Whitehead Report," *NYT,* January 17, 1974, 1.

18. Compaine, *Papers and Profits,* 39; Udell, *Economics of the American Newspaper,* 65–66; John Cowles, "Fewer Papers Means Better Papers," July 1951, in *Reporting the News: Selections from the Nieman Reports,* ed. Louis M. Lyons (Cambridge, MA: Belknap Press of Harvard University Press, 1965), 160.

19. David Rudenstine, *The Day the Presses Stopped: A History of the Pentagon Papers Case* (Berkeley: University of California Press, 1996), 15–65; Daniel Ellsberg, "Randy Kehler: Haverford, August 1969," December 22, 1988, "Janaki: Princeton, April, 1968," n.d., "Daniel Ellsberg: Personal Commitment/Political

Action," *Creation,* November–December 1988, p. 15, all in box 50, folder 2, HZ; Rudenstine, *Day the Presses Stopped,* 33–65; Halberstam, *Powers That Be,* 567–570.

20. Rudenstine, *Day the Presses Stopped,* 66–258.

21. Ibid., 111–117, 139–168, 240, 273; "Brief on Behalf of National Emergency Civil Liberties Committee as Amicus Curiae," June 21, 1971, box 37, folder 23, HZ.

22. Rudenstine, *Day the Presses Stopped,* 268–276; 289, 292.

23. New York Times Co. v. United States, 403 U.S. 713 at 715, 717, 748–750 (1971).

24. New York Times Co. v. United States, 403 U.S. 713 at 726–727, 730.

25. Sanford J. Ungar, *The Papers & the Papers: An Account of the Legal and Political Battle over the Pentagon Papers* (New York: E. P. Dutton, 1972), 250–270; Erwin Knoll, "The H-Bomb and the First Amendment," *William and Mary Bill of Rights Journal* 3 (1994): 705–714.

26. New York Times Co. v. United States, 403 U.S. 713 at 730, 733, 752.

27. William L. Claiborne, "Government Secrets and the Press," *WP,* April 20, 1972, C3.

28. "A Beautiful Day for America," *Boston Globe,* July 1, 1971, 26; Rudenstine, *Day the Presses Stopped,* 75; New York Times Co. v. United States, 403 U.S. 713 at 762.

29. Daniel Ellsberg, "Secrecy and National Security Whistleblowing," *Social Research* 77 (2010): 788; Melville B. Nimmer, "National Security Secrets v. Free Speech: The Issues Left Undecided in the Ellsberg Case," *Stanford Law Review* 26 (1974): 311–333; Indictment in U.S. of America v. Anthony Joseph Russo Jr., Daniel Ellsberg, U.S. District Court for the Central District of California, March 1971, box 37, folder 24, HZ; Kutler, *Wars of Watergate,* 112–116; "Text of Judge Byrne's Ruling Ending Trial of Ellsberg, Russo," *Boston Globe,* May 12, 1973, 9.

30. "The Ellsberg Case's Meaning," *Boston Globe,* May 14, 1973, 10; Sanford J. Ungar, "With Questions Unanswered," *WP,* May 14, 1973, A2; Sanford J. Ungar and Leroy F. Aarons, "Most Ellsberg Jurors in Favor of Acquittal," *WP,* May 13, 1973, A1.

31. Max Holland, *Leak: Why Mark Felt Became Deep Throat* (Lawrence: University of Kansas Press, 2012), 68.

32. Michael Schudson, *Watergate in American Memory: How We Remember, Forget, and Reconstruct the Past* (New York: Basic Books, 1992), 105; Kutler, *Wars of Watergate,* 226; James J. Kilpatrick, "GOP Has Explaining to Do in Watergate Caper," *Los Angeles Times,* August 9, 1972, E9; Tad Szulc, "From the Folks Who Brought You the Bay of Pigs," *NYT,* June 25, 1972, E2; Louis W. Liebovich, *Richard Nixon, Watergate and the Press* (Westport, CT: Praeger, 2003), 65–66; Richard Nixon: "The President's News Conference," June 22, 1972, APP; Greenberg, *Nixon's Shadow,* 161, 164–165; Alicia Shepard, *Woodward and Bernstein: Life in the Shadow of Watergate* (Hoboken, NJ: John Wiley and Sons, 2007), 51–52.

33. Mark Feldstein, "Watergate Revisited," *American Journalism Review,* August–September 2004, cited from www.ajr.org/article_printable.asp?id=3735; Carl Bernstein and Bob Woodward's stories included "Bug Suspect Got Campaign Funds," *WP,* August 1, 1972, A1; "Mitchell Controlled Secret GOP Fund," *WP,* Sep-

tember 29, 1971, A1; "Campaign Fund Is Confirmed," *WP,* October 27, 1972, A6; "Alleged GOP Saboteur Tied to Nixon Official," *WP,* October 31, 1972, A2.

34. Alfred E. Lewis, "5 Held in Plot to Bug Democrat's Office Here," *WP,* June 18, 1972, A1; Shepard, *Woodward and Bernstein,* 32–36; Carl Bernstein and Bob Woodward, *All the President's Men* (New York: Simon and Schuster, 1974), 35; Walter Rugaber, "Calls to GOP Unit Linked to Raid on the Democrats," *NYT,* July 25, 1972, 1.

35. Carl Bernstein and Bob Woodward, "Key Nixon Aide Named as 'Sabotage' Contact," *WP,* October 15, 1972, A1; Bernstein and Woodward, *All the President's Men,* 159, 232–233; "Anti-democratic Spying Tied to High Republicans," *NYT,* October 16, 1972, 1; "More Fumes from the Watergate Affair," *Time,* October 23, 1972, 25; Shepard, *Woodward and Bernstein,* 57; "Bugging Witness Tells Inside Story on Incident at Watergate," *Los Angeles Times,* October 5, 1972, A1; Holland, *Leak,* 114–115; Seymour Hersh, "Trial Continues Tomorrow: Report 4 Defendants Still Paid in Bug Case," *NYT,* January 14, 1973, 34.

36. Walter Rugaber, "Motive Is Big Mystery in Raid on Democrats," *NYT,* June 26, 1972, 1; Holland, *Leak,* 31–33; Shepard, *Woodward and Bernstein,* 54; Richard Perez-Pena, "2 Ex-Timesmen Say They Had a Tip on Watergate First," *NYT,* May 24, 2009, B4.

37. Bernstein and Woodward, *All the President's Men,* 47, 61, 101, 299; Bob Woodward and Carl Bernstein, "Stans Denies GOP Money Funded Watergate Break-In," *WP,* August 9, 1972, A1; Carl Bernstein and Bob Woodward, "Justice Completes Watergate Probe," *WP,* September 9, 1972, A1.

38. By the time his identity was made public in 2005, Felt was an old man and no longer in full control of his faculties, so it is hard to assess his motives. Holland, *Leak;* Bob Woodward, *The Secret Man: The Story of Watergate's Deep Throat* (New York: Simon and Schuster, 2005), 15–26, 48–50, 217; Bernstein and Woodward, *All the President's Men,* 131; Beverley Gage, "Deep Throat, Watergate and the Bureaucratic Politics of the FBI," *Journal of Policy History* 24 (2013): 157–183.

39. Woodward, *Secret Man,* 120–121; Edward Jay Epstein, "Did the Press Uncover Watergate?" *Commentary,* July 1974, www.edwardjayepstein.com/archived/watergate.htm; Holland, *Leak,* 79–81, 180.

40. Carl Bernstein and Bob Woodward, "Bug Memos Sent to Nixon Aides," *WP,* October 6, 1972, A1; Bernstein and Woodward, *All the President's Men,* 178–180, 270; Robert Barkdoll, "White House Denies Story of Secret Fund," *Los Angeles Times,* October 26, 1972, A16; Carl Bernstein and Bob Woodward, "Testimony Ties Top Nixon Aide to Secret Fund," *WP,* October 25, 1972, A1; Holland, *Leak,* 53; Epstein, "Did the Press Uncover Watergate?"

41. Woodward, *Secret Man,* 92; W. Joseph Campbell, *Getting It Wrong: Ten of the Greatest Misreported Stories in American Journalism* (Berkeley: University of California Press, 2010), 123; Bernstein and Woodward, *All the President's Men,* 199, 279–280, 330; Shepard, *Woodward and Bernstein,* 68.

42. Kutler, *Wars of Watergate,* 260–358.

43. Ibid., 369; "Senators Press Nixon on Secrecy," *NYT,* January 17, 1973, 81; "Executive Silence Stirs Democrats," *NYT,* January 19, 1973, 14; "Historian Tells Senators Meeting on Executive Privilege, You Are the Superior Power," *NYT,*

April 13, 1973, 19; "Ervin Notes Role," *NYT,* April 19, 1973, 1; Richard Nixon, "Statement about Executive Privilege," March 12, 1973, APP; "Kleindienst Sees Wider Executive Shield," *NYT,* April 11, 1973, 1; "Text of Letters and Orders on Nixon Refusal to Respond to Subpoenas," *NYT,* July 27, 1973, 9; Richard Nixon, "Address to the Nation about the Watergate Investigations," August 15, 1973, APP.

44. U.S. v. Nixon, 418 U.S. 683 (1974); Mark J. Rozell, *Executive Privilege: Presidential Power, Secrecy and Accountability,* 3rd ed. (Lawrence: University Press of Kansas, 2010), 55–72.

45. Alexander M. Bickel, *The Morality of Consent* (New Haven, CT: Yale University Press, 1975), 80–83.

46. Snepp v. United States, 444 U.S. 507 (1980); Mary-Rose Papandrea, "Lapdogs, Watchdogs and Scapegoats: The Press and National Security Information," *Indiana Law Journal* 83 (2008): 281–282, 296; Philip Weiss, "The Quiet Coup," *Harper's Magazine,* September 1989, 54–65; Stuart Taylor Jr., "U.S. Court Backs Conviction in Spy Satellite Photos Case," *NYT,* April 5, 1988, A1; Linda Greenhouse, "Appeal Rebuffed in Rare Spy Case," *NYT,* October 18, 1988, A27.

47. Landmark Communications, Inc. v. Virginia, 435 U.S. 829 (1978); Jason M. Shepard, *Privileging the Press: Confidential Sources, Journalism Ethics and the First Amendment* (El Paso, TX: LFB Scholarly Pub LLC, 2011), 168–169; Blanchard, "Institutional Press and First Amendment Privileges," 236; Papandrea, "Lapdogs, Watchdogs and Scapegoats," 274–276; Jennifer K. Elsea, "Intelligence Identities Protection Act," *Congressional Research Service Report,* April 10, 2013.

48. Heidi Kitrosser, "Free Speech aboard the Leaky Ship of State: Calibrating First Amendment Protections for Leakers of Classified Information," *Journal of National Security Law and Policy* 6 (2013): 409–446; Ellsberg, "Secrecy and National Security Whistleblowing," 773–804.

49. Shepard, *Privileging the Press,* 2–6; Hugh M Culbertson, "Veiled News Sources—Who and What Are They?" *ANPA News Research Bulletin,* May 1975, 9; Betty Medsger, *The Burglary: The Discovery of J. Edgar Hoover's Secret FBI* (New York: Alfred Knopf, 2014); David E. Pozen, "The Leaky Leviathan: Why the Government Condemns and Condones Unlawful Disclosures of Information," *Harvard Law Review* 127 (2013): 512–635; Richard Halloran, "A Primer on the Fine Art of Leaking Information," *NYT,* January 14, 1983, A16; Elie Abel, *Leaking: Who Does It? Who Benefits? At What Cost?* (New York: Priority Press Publications, 1987).

50. Kutler, *Wars of Watergate,* 109; Howard Zinn, "Testifying at the Ellsberg Trial," *The Zinn Reader: Writings on Disobedience and Democracy* (New York: Seven Stories, 1997), 426; Rudenstine, *Day the Presses Stopped,* 330; Shepard, *Privileging the Press,* 189; Bickel, *Morality of Consent,* 83–85; Branzburg v. Hayes, 408 U.S. 665 (1972); Geoffrey R. Stone, "Why We Need a Federal Reporter's Privilege," *Hofstra Law Review* 34 (2005): 44; Pozen, "Leaky Leviathan," 538–539.

51. In 1998, a limited Intelligence Community Whistleblower Protection Act was passed. Papandrea, "Lapdogs, Watchdogs and Scapegoats," 245–248; Pozen, "Leaky Leviathan"; Stephen I. Vladeck, "The Espionage Act and National Security Whistleblowing after Garcetti," *American University Law Review* 57 (2008): 1531–1546.

52. Committee on Government Operations, *Administration of the Freedom of Information Act,* H.R. Rep. No. 92–1419, at 8, 76; Ralph Nader, "Freedom from Information: The Act and the Agencies," *Harvard Civil Rights and Civil Liberties Review* 5 (1970): 5; EPA v. Mink, 410 U.S. 73 (1972); Gregory L. Waples, "The Freedom of Information Act: A Seven-Year Assessment," *Columbia Law Review* 74 (1974): 931–932; Arthur M. Schlesinger Jr., *The Imperial Presidency* (Boston: Mariner Books, 2004), 364–365.

53. *Administration of the Freedom of Information Act,* 21–22, 73, 76; George Penn Kennedy, "Advocates of Openness: The Freedom of Information Movement" (Ph.D. diss., University of Missouri–Columbia, 1978), 146–149; Waples, "Freedom of Information Act," 958; Louis M. Kohlmeier, "The Journalist's Viewpoint," *Administrative Law Review* 23 (1971): 143–145; Samuel J. Archibald, "The Freedom of Information Act Revisited," *Public Administration Review* 39 (1979): 315.

54. *Freedom of Information Act Amendments,* H.R. Rep. No. 93–1380 (1974) (Conf. Rep.).

55. Ibid., 2, 12; Kennedy, "Advocates of Openness," 182–185; Gerald R. Ford, "Veto of Freedom of Information Act Amendments," October 17, 1974, APP; Herbert N. Foerstel, *Freedom of Information and the Right to Know: The Origins and Applications of the Freedom of Information Act* (Westport, CT: Greenwood, 1999), 47–48; James M. Naughton, "House Overrides Two Ford Vetoes by Huge Margins," *NYT,* November 21, 1974, 1.

56. Steven Aftergood, "National Security Secrecy: How the Limits Change," *Social Research* 77 (Fall 2010): 843; Foerstel, *Freedom of Information,* 49, 72–77.

57. Steve Weinberg, "Freedom of Information: You Still Need a Can Opener," *The Nation,* April 19, 1975, 463; Peter Irons to Howard Zinn, February 14, 1977, box 51, folder 16, HZ; "Coalition of Journalists for Open Government, Frequent Filers: Businesses Make FOIA Their Business," July 3, 2006, www.gfaf.org/resources/who_uses_foi.pdf; Michael Doyle, "Missed Information: The Reporting Tool that Reporters Don't Use," www.johnemossfoundation.org/foi/doyle.htm; Foerstel, *Freedom of Information,* 52–56, 71–78, 109–110; Jason Ross Arnold, *Secrecy in the Sunshine Era: The Promise and Failure of US Open Government Laws* (Lawrence: University Press of Kansas, 2014), 72–77, 152; Office of Information and Privacy Law, U.S. Department of Justice, "Agencies Rely on Wide Range of Exemption 3 Statutes," September 3, 2003, www.justice.gov/oip/blog/foia-post-2003-agencies-rely-wide-range-exemption-3-statutes.

58. Adam M. Samaha, "Government Secrets, Constitutional Law, and Platforms for Judicial Intervention," *UCLA Law Review* 53 (2005): 938–940, 972; Philip J. Cooper, "The Supreme Court, the First Amendment, and Freedom of Information," *Public Administration Review* 46 (November–December 1986): 625; David E. Pozen, "The Mosaic Theory, National Security and the Freedom of Information Act," *Yale Law Journal* 115 (2005): 638–639; Robert P. Deyling, "Judicial Deference and De Novo Review in Litigation over National Security Information under the Freedom of Information Act," *Villanova Law Review* 37 (1992): 67–112.

59. Potter Stewart, "Or of the Press," *Hastings Law Journal* 26 (1975): 631–637; Pittsburgh Press Co. v. Pittsburgh Commission on Human Relations, 413 U.S. 376 (1973); Saxbe v. Washington Post Co., 417 U.S. 843 (1974); Pell v. Procunier,

417 U.S. 817 (1974); Houchins v. KQED Inc., 438 U.S. 1 (1978); Blanchard, "Institutional Press and First Amendment Privileges," 239; Anthony Lewis, "A Public Right to Know about Public Institutions: The First Amendment as Sword," *Supreme Court Review* (1980): 1–25; Lee C. Bollinger, *Uninhibited, Robust, and Wide-Open* (New York: Oxford University Press, 2010), 24–29.

60. New York Times v. Sullivan, 376 U.S. 254 (1964); Anthony Lewis, *Make No Law: The Sullivan Case and the First Amendment* (New York: Random House, 1991), 154.

61. Brandenburg v. Ohio, 395 U.S. 444 (1969); Joseph Burstyn, Inc. v. Wilson, 343 U.S. 495 (1952); Cohen v. California, 403 U.S. 15 (1971); Miller v. California, 413 U.S. 15 (1973); Roth v. United States, 354 U.S. 476 (1957).

62. Virginia State Board of Pharmacy et al. v. Virginia Citizens Consumer Council, Incorporated et al., 425 U.S. 748 (1976); Buckley v. Valeo, 424 U.S. 1 (1976); First National Bank of Boston v. Bellotti, 435 U.S. 765 (1978); Mark Graber, *Transforming Free Speech: The Ambiguous Legacy of Civil Libertarianism* (Berkeley: University of California Press, 1991), 185–215.

63. Thomas I. Emerson, *Toward a General Theory of the First Amendment* (New York: Vintage, 1966), 3–4; Alexander Meiklejohn, *Free Speech and Its Relation to Self-Government* (New York: Harper and Brothers, 1948), 25; Robert H. Bork, "Neutral Principles and Some First Amendment Problems," *Indiana Law Journal* 47 (1971): 1–35. Emerson was open to an affirmative right to know, but only where it complemented, and did not interfere with, the individual right to expression. Thomas I. Emerson, "Legal Foundations of the Right to Know," *Washington University Law Quarterly,* 1976, 1–23.

64. Marc Weingarten, *The Gang That Wouldn't Write Straight: Wolfe, Thompson, Didion and the New Journalism Revolution* (New York: Crown, 2006), 84–87, 124–132; Shepard, *Woodward and Bernstein,* 93.

65. Jack Newfield, "Journalism: Old, New and Corporate," in *The Reporter as Artist: A Look at the New Journalism Controversy,* ed. Ronald Weber (New York: Hastings House, 1974), 55–56; Nat Hentoff, "Behold the New Journalism—It's Coming after You!," in Weber, *Reporter as Artist,* 51.

66. There were, of course, earlier examples of journalism borrowing from literary techniques: Lillian Ross, James Agee, James Hersey, and others. But Mailer's was the earliest piece that was later included in the canon of 1960s New Journalism.

67. Norman Mailer, "Superman Comes to the Supermarket," in *Smiling through the Apocalypse: Esquires History of the Sixties,* ed. Harold Hayes (New York: McCall, 1970), 3; Weingarten, *Gang That Wouldn't Write Straight,* 55; Dan Wakefield, "The Personal Voice and the Impersonal Eye," in Weber, *Reporter as Artist,* 41.

68. Leonard Wallace Robinson, "The New Journalism," in Weber, *Reporter as Artist,* 68–69; Hentoff, "Behold the New Journalism," 50; Weingarten, *Gang That Wouldn't Write Straight,* 234.

69. James Boylan, "Declarations of Independence," in *Media Voices: An Historical Perspective,* ed. Jean Folkerts (New York: MacMillan, 1992), 446–447; Edwin Diamond, "Reporter Power Takes Root," *CJR,* Summer 1970, 12–18.

70. John Brady, "Gay Talese: An Interview," in Weber, *Reporter as Artist,* 110; Wakefield, "Personal Voice and Impersonal Eye," 42.

71. Ronald Weber, "Some Sort of Artistic Excitement," in Weber, *Reporter as Artist,* 21; Newfield, "Journalism," 61; Timothy Crouse, *The Boys on the Bus* (New York: Ballantine, 1972); Hunter S. Thompson, *Fear and Loathing on the Campaign Trail* (New York: Grand Central Publishing, 1973).

72. Jack Newfield said that Wolfe "has no politics." Newfield, "Journalism," 63; Leonard Wallace Robinson, "The New Journalism," in Weber, *Reporter as Artist,* 69; Gay Talese, *Fame and Obscurity* (New York: Dell, 1981); Tom Wolfe, *The Kandy Kolored Tangerine-Flake Streamline Baby* (New York: Picador, 2009); Dwight MacDonald, "ParaJournalism, or, Tom Wolfe and his Magic Writing Machine," in *Masscult and Midcult: Essays against the American Grain* (New York: New York Review of Books, 2011), 236–268; Morris Dickstein, *Gates of Eden: American Culture in the Sixties* (New York: Basic Books, 1977), 140–141.

73. David McHam, "The Authentic New Journalists," in Weber, *Reporter as Artist,* 119; Robinson, "New Journalism," 71–72; Brady, "Gay Talese," 84, 94.

74. Brady, "Gay Talese," 106; Scott Sherman, "The Long Goodbye," *Vanity Fair,* November 30, 2012, www.vanityfair.com/culture/2012/11/1963-newspaper-strike-bertram-powers.

75. Weingarten, *Gang That Wouldn't Write Straight,* 270–294.

76. Aggressive questions remained in the minority, however. Steven E. Clayman, Marc N. Elliott, John Heritage, and Laurie L. McDonald, "Historical Trends in Questioning Presidents," *Presidential Studies Quarterly* 36 (2006): 561–583; Steven E Clayman, Marc N. Elliott, John Heritage, and Megan K. Beckett, "A Watershed in White House Journalism: Explaining the Post-1968 Rise of Aggressive Presidential News," *Political Communication* 27 (2010): 229–247.

77. Thomas E. Patterson, "Bad News, Bad Governance," *Annals of the American Academy of Political and Social Science* 546 (1996): 97–108; Thomas E. Patterson, "Doing Well and Doing Good," *Joan Shorenstein Center on the Press, Politics and Public Policy Report,* 2000, http://shorensteincenter.org/research-publications/reports/; James L. Aucoin, "The Reemergence of American Investigative Journalism, 1960–1975," *Journalism History* 21 (1995): 3–15; Carey McWilliams, "Is Muckraking Coming Back?" *CJR*, Fall 1970, 8–15; Katherine Fink and Michael Schudson, "The Rise of Contextual Journalism, 1950s–2000s," *Journalism* 15 (2014): 3–20; Michael J. Socolow, "A Profitable Public Sphere: The Creation of the New York Times Op-Ed Page," *Journalism and Mass Communications Quarterly* 87 (2010): 281–296; "Op-ed page," *NYT,* September 21, 1970, 42.

78. Fink and Schudson, "Contextual Journalism"; Carl Sessions Stepp, "Then and Now," *American Journalism Review,* September 1999, 60–75; Kevin G. Barnhurst and Diana Mutz, "American Journalism and the Decline in Event-Centered Reporting," *Journal of Communication* 47 (1997): 27–53.

79. Doug Underwood, *When MBAs Rule the Newsroom: How the Marketers and Managers Are Reshaping Today's Media* (New York: Columbia University Press, 1993), 20; David H. Weaver, Randal A. Beam, et al., *The American Journalist in the 21st Century: U.S. News People at the Dawn of a New Millennium* (Mahwah, NJ: Lawrence Erlbaum Associates, 2007), 2; Squires, *Read All About It!,* 91; Gilbert

Cranberg, Randall Bezanson, and John Soloski, *Taking Stock: Journalism and the Publicly Traded Newspaper Company* (Ames: Iowa State University Press, 2001), 24–33, 90–92.

80. C. Edwin Baker, "Ownership of Newspapers: The View from Positivist Social Science, Research Paper R-12," *Joan Shorenstein Center,* September 1994; Weaver et al., *American Journalist,* 2, 28; Robert W. McChesney and John Nichols, *The Death and Life of American Journalism: The Media Revolution That Will Begin the World Again* (New York: Nation Books, 2010), 32–40; Andrew Kohut, "Self-censorship: Counting the Ways," *CJR,* May–June 2000, 42–43; G. Pascal Zachary, "All the News? Many Journalists See a Growing Reluctance to Criticize Advertisers," *Wall Street Journal,* February 6, 1992, A1; Steve Singer, "Auto Dealers Muscle the Newsroom," *Washington Journalism Review,* September 1991, 24–28; Mary Ellen Schoonmaker, "The Real Estate Story: Hard News or Soft Sell?," *CJR,* January–February 1987, 25–30; Joanne Angela Ambrosio, "It's in the Journal. But This Is Reporting?" *CJR,* March–April 1980, 34–36.

81. Jane Delano Brown et al., "Invisible Power: Newspaper News Sources and the Limits of Diversity," *JQ* 64 (1987): 51–52; Daniel C. Hallin et al., "Sourcing Patterns of National Security Reporters," *JQ* 70 (1993): 755–758; Rozell, *Executive Privilege,* 97; W. Lance Bennett, "Toward a Theory of Press-State Relations in the United States," *Journal of Communication* 40 (1990): 103–127; Jonathan Mermin, *Debating War and Peace: Media Coverage of U.S. Intervention in the Post-Vietnam Era* (Princeton, NJ: Princeton University Press, 1999); Eleanor Randolph, "How Newshounds Blew the Iran-Contra Story," *WP,* November 15, 1987, C1; Mark Hertsgaard, *On Bended Knee: The Press and the Reagan Presidency* (New York: Farrar, Straus and Giroux, 1988), quote at 101; Edward S. Herman and Noam Chomsky, *Manufacturing Consent: The Political Economy of the Mass Media* (New York: Pantheon, 1988).

82. Patterson, "Doing Well and Doing Good."

83. Greenberg, *Nixon's Shadow,* 172–177; Larry J. Sabato, *Feeding Frenzy: How Attack Journalism Has Transformed American* Politics (New York: Free Press, 1991); Matt Bai, *All the Truth Is Out: The Week Politics Went Tabloid* (New York: Alfred A. Knopf, 2014).

84. Campbell, *Getting It Wrong,* 127–129; Greenberg, *Nixon's Shadow,* 176.

9. Sprawling Secrecy and Dying Newsrooms

1. Paul Starr, "An Unexpected Crisis: The News Media in Post-industrial Democracies," *International Journal of Press/Politics* 17 (2012): 234–242. Starr distinguishes freedom of information from press freedom and thinks it is improving; I include freedom of information as part of a positive vision of press freedom, and am less optimistic.

2. R.A.V. v. City of St. Paul, 505 U.S. 377 (1992); Snyder v. Phelps, 562 U.S. 443 (2011); United States v. Stevens, 550 U.S. 460 (2010); Dahlia Lithwick and Christian Turner, "It's Not My Gun. It's 'Free Speech,' " *Slate,* November 12, 2013, www.slate.com/articles/news_and_politics/jurisprudence/2013/11/open_carry

_demonstrations_is_carrying_a_gun_to_a_protest_protected_by_the.html; Christopher Finan, *From the Palmer Raids to Patriot Act: A History of the Fight for Free Speech in America* (Boston: Beacon, 2007), 168–305; Geoffrey R. Stone, *Perilous Times: Free Speech in Wartime: From the Sedition Act of 1798 to the War on Terrorism* (New York: W. W. Norton, 2004), 550–557.

3. Citizens United v. FEC, 558 U.S. 310 (2010); Kathleen M. Sullivan, "Two Concepts of Freedom of Speech," *Harvard Law Review* 124 (2010): 143–177.

4. Sorrell v. IMS Health Inc., 131 S.Ct. 2653 (2011); Jack M. Balkin, "Digital Speech and Democratic Culture: A Theory of Freedom of Expression for the Information Society," *New York University Law Review* 79 (2004): 27; Jebediah Purdy, "The Roberts Court v. America," *Democracy: A Journal of Ideas* 23 (Winter 2012), www.democracyjournal.org/23/the-roberts-court-v-america.php?page=all; Adam Liptak, "First Amendment, 'Patron Saint' of Protesters, Is Embraced by Corporations," *NYT,* March 23, 2015; Robert Post and Amanda Shanor, "Adam Smith's First Amendment," *Harvard Law Review Forum* 128 (2015): 165–182; Tim Wu, "The Right to Evade Regulation," *New Republic,* June 3, 2013.

5. Reno v. American Civil Liberties Union, 521 U.S. 844 (1997); Douglas W. Vick, "The Internet and the First Amendment," *Modern Law Review* 61 (1998): 414–421.

6. Pew Research Journalism Project, *State of News Media 2014,* www.journalism.org/packages/state-of-the-news-media-2014/; Yochai Benkler, *The Wealth of Networks: How Social Production Transforms Markets and Freedom* (New Haven, CT: Yale University Press, 2006); Matthew Hindman, *The Myth of Digital Democracy* (Princeton, NJ: Princeton University Press, 2008); cf. Aaron Shaw and Yochai Benkler, "A Tale of Two Blogospheres: Discursive Practices on the Left and Right," *American Behavioral Scientist* 56 (2012): 459–487.

7. Pew Research Journalism Project, *How News Happens: A Study of the News Ecosystem of One American City,* January 11, 2010, www.journalism.org/2010/01/11/how-news-happens/; Steven Waldman and the Working Group on Information Needs of Communities, *Information Needs of Communities: The Changing Media Landscape in a Broadband Age,* Federal Communications Commission Report, July 2011, 6.

8. *How News Happens; Information Needs of Communities,* 10–11, 40, 262.

9. Leonard Downie Jr. and Michael Schudson, "The Reconstruction of American Journalism," *CJR,* October 19, 2009; Paul Starr, "Goodbye to the Age of Newspapers (Hello to a New Era of Corruption," *New Republic,* March 4, 2009, www.newrepublic.com/article/goodbye-the-age-newspapers-hello-new-era-corruption.

10. These processes were already in play, obviously, with the rise of cable, the transformation of the magazine industry from general interest to specialty publications, and the broader specialization of niche consumption in the postwar American economy. But the Internet radically accelerated them.

11. Pew Research Journalism Project, *The State of the News Media 2013,* www.stateofthemedia.org/2013/newspapers-stabilizing-but-still-threatened/newspapers-by-the-numbers/.

12. Warren Buffett to Shareholders of Berkshire Hathaway Inc., February 25, 1985, www.berkshirehathaway.com/letters/1984.html. By 2013, newspaper prices

had fallen so low that he reconsidered. Jack Shafer, "So Warren Buffett Likes Newspaper Again?" *Reuters Blog,* May 18, 2012, http://blogs.reuters.com/jackshafer/2012/05/18/so-warren-buffett-likes-newspapers-again/.

13. Robert W. McChesney and John Nichols, *The Death and Life of American Journalism: The Media Revolution that Will Begin the World Again* (New York: Nation Books, 2010), 37, 285; James D. Squires, *Read All About It! The Corporate Takeover of America's Newspapers* (New York: Random House, 1993), 100.

14. Aisha Gani, "Blendle: Will the 'iTunes of Journalism' Strike a Chord Worldwide?" *Guardian,* October 29, 2014; Joseph Lichterman, "A Money-Back Guarantee," *Nieman Lab,* April 21, 2014, www.niemanlab.org/2014/04/a-money-back-guarantee-how-blendle-hopes-to-convince-dutch-news-readers-to-pay-by-the-article/; Rick Edmonds, Emily Guskin, et al., "Newspapers: Stabilizing but Still Threatened," *The State of the News Media* 2013, Pew Research Center Project for Excellence in Journalism, www.stateofthemedia.org/2013/newspapers-stabilizing-but-still-threatened/#fnref-12990–9; "New York Times Now Gets More Revenue from Subscribers than Advertisers," *Business Insider,* February 8, 2013, www.businessinsider.com/the-new-york-times-now-gets-more-revenue-from-subscribers-than-advertisers-2013–2; Ravi Somaiya, "New York Times Co. Profit Falls Despite Strides in Digital Ads," *NYT,* February 3, 2015; Rick Edmonds, "Gannett Earnings Report Hints at Coming Problems with Paywalls," *Poynter Institute,* February 4, 2014, www.poynter.org/news/mediawire/237601/gannett-earnings-report-hints-at-a-coming-problem-with-paywalls/; Michael Nevradakis, "Behind the Paywall: Lessons from US Newspapers," *Guardian,* March 27, 2013, www.theguardian.com/media-network/2013/mar/27/behind-paywall-us-newspaper-websites.

15. *Information Needs of Communities,* 16; *State of News Media 2014.*

16. www.propublica.org/about/.

17. Barack Obama, "Transparency and Open Government," Memorandum for the Heads of Executive Departments and Agencies, www.whitehouse.gov/the_press_office/TransparencyandOpenGovernment/; *Information Needs of Communities,* 202.

18. Yochai Benkler, "A Free Irresponsible Press: WikiLeaks and the Battle over the Soul of the Networked Fourth Estate," *Harvard Civil Rights—Civil Liberties Law Review* 46 (2011): 311–397; Peter Maass, "How Laura Poitras Helped Snowden Spill His Secrets," *NYT Magazine,* August 13, 2013.

19. Obama, "Transparency and Open Government."

20. Most put the previous count at three, missing the little-known case of John Nickerson. "Spy Case Dropped, Nickerson Admits Leak on Missiles," *NYT,* June 26, 1957, 1; Mike German and Jay Stanley, *Drastic Measures Required: Congress Needs to Overhaul U.S. Secrecy Laws and Increase Oversight of the Secret Security Establishment,* ACLU Report, July 2011, 10–11; Leonard Downie Jr. and Sara Rafsky, *The Obama Administration and the Press: Leak Investigations and Surveillance in Post-9/11 America,* Special Report for the Committee to Protect Journalists, October 10, 2013; Jane Mayer, "The Secret Sharer," *New Yorker,* May 23, 2011; Charlie Savage, "Nine Leak-Related Cases," June 20, 2012; Cora Currier, "Charting Obama's Crackdown on National Security Leaks," ProPublica, July 30, 2013,

www.propublica.org/special/sealing-loose-lips-charting-obamas-crackdown-on-national-security-leaks; Charlie Savage and Emmarie Huetteman, "Manning Sentenced to 35 Years for a Pivotal Leak of U.S. Files," *NYT*, August 21, 2013.

21. Scott Shane and Charlie Savage, "Administration Took Accidental Path to Setting Record for Leak Cases," *NYT*, June 19, 2012.

22. Barack Obama, "Executive Order 13587," October 7, 2011, www.whitehouse.gov/the-press-office/2011/10/07/executive-order-13587-structural-reforms-improve-security-classified-net; "Federal Agencies Embrace New Technology and Strategies to Find the Enemy Within," *WP*, March 7, 2014; Downie and Rafsky, "Obama Administration and the Press"; Marisa Taylor and Jonathan S. Landay, "Obama's Crackdown Views Leaks as Aiding Enemies of U.S.," McClatchy DC, June 20, 2013, www.mcclatchydc.com/2013/06/20/194513/obamas-crackdown-views-leaks-as.html.

23. Steven Aftergood, "National Security Secrecy: How the Limits Change," *Social Research* 77 (2010): 842; Benkler, "Free Irresponsible Press"; Mary-Rose Papandrea, "Lapdogs, Watchdogs and Scapegoats: The Press and National Security Information," *Indiana Law Journal* 83 (2008): 261.

24. David Brooks, "The Solitary Leaker," *NYT*, June 10, 2013; Ginger Thompson, "Early Struggles of Soldier Charged in Leak Case," *NYT*, August 8, 2010; Jeffrey Toobin, "Edward Snowden Is No Hero," *New Yorker*, June 10, 2013, www.newyorker.com/news/daily-comment/edward-snowden-is-no-hero; Derek E. Bambauer, "Consider the Censor," *Wake Forest Journal of Law and Policy* 1 (2011): 34–39.

25. Later, larger portions of the documents were released directly online, apparently because of a sequence of negligent practices and accidents. Benkler, "Free Irresponsible Press"; Yochai Benkler, "A Public Accountability Defense for National Security Leakers and Whistleblowers," *Harvard Law and Policy Review* 8 (2014): 118, Christian Stocker, "Leak at WikiLeaks: A Dispatch Disaster in Six Acts," *Der Spiegel Online*, September 1, 2011, www.spiegel.de/international/world/leak-at-wikileaks-a-dispatch-disaster-in-six-acts-a-783778.html.

26. Maass, "How Laura Poitras Helped Snowden."

27. Reporters Committee on Freedom of the Press, *Homefront Confidential: How the War on Terrorism Affects Access to Information and the Public's Right to Know*, RCFP White Paper, 6th ed., September 2005, 51–57; Jason M. Shepard, *Privileging the Press: Confidential Sources, Journalism Ethics and the First Amendment* (El Paso, TX: LFB Scholarly Pub LLC, 2011), 73–104; Ravi Somaiya, "Head of AP Criticizes Seizure of Phone Records," *NYT*, May 19, 2013; Jonathan Mahler, "Reporter's Case Poses Dilemma for Justice Department," *NYT*, June 27, 2014; Joanna Walters, "James Risen Calls Obama 'Greatest Enemy of Press Freedom in a Generation,'" *Guardian*, August 17, 2014; Sari Horwitz, "Holder Tightens Investigators' Guidelines in Cases Involving News Media," *WP*, January 14, 2015; Matt Zapotosky, "Prosecutors Will Not Call Reporter in Leaks Case," *WP*, January 12, 2015.

28. Matt Zapotosky, "Former CIA officer Jeffrey Sterling Convicted in Leak Case," *WP*, January 26, 2015.

29. Geoffrey R. Stone, *Top Secret: When Our Government Keeps Us in the Dark* (Lanham, MD: Rowman and Littlefield, 2007), 1; Walter Pincus, "Senator May Seek

Tougher Law on Leaks," *WP,* February 17, 2006; Jeffrey Kuhner, "Assassinate Assange?" *Washington Times,* December 2, 2010; Diane Feinstein, "Prosecute Assange under the Espionage Act," *Wall Street Journal,* December 7, 2010; "Assange Appeal Rejected by Sweden's Supreme Court," *Guardian,* May 11, 2015.

30. Spencer Ackerman, "Senior US Congressman Mike Rogers: Glenn Greenwald Is a 'Thief,'" *Guardian,* February 4, 2014; Greenwald comments in questions at speech at Sixth and I Synagogue, Washington, DC, May 14, 2014; Ed Pilkington, "Bradley Manning's Treatment Was Cruel and Inhuman, UN Torture Chief Rules," *Guardian,* March 12, 2012; Ed Pilkington, "Guardian and Washington Post Win Pulitzer Prize for NSA Revelations," *Guardian,* April 14, 2014; Downie and Rafsky, "Obama Administration and the Press."

31. David E. Pozen, "The Mosaic Theory, National Security and the Freedom of Information Act," *Yale Law Journal* 115 (2005): 646–648; Papandrea, "Lapdogs, Watchdogs and Scapegoats," 242; Reporters Committee on Freedom of the Press, *Homefront Confidential,* 58–59; Jason Ross Arnold, *Secrecy in the Sunshine Era: The Promise and Failure of US Open Government Laws* (Lawrence: University Press of Kansas, 2014), 67–69, 81–85; Scott Shane, "Official Secrecy Reaches Historic High in the US," *NYT,* July 4, 2005; German and Stanley, *Drastic Measures Required,* 8–9.

32. Barack Obama, "Freedom of Information Act," www.whitehouse.gov/the-press-office/freedom-information-act; German and Stanley, *Drastic Measures Required,* 8–10, 14–15; Information Security Oversight Office, Report to President, 2013, 20–21, www.archives.gov/isoo/reports/2013-annual-report.pdf; Arnold, *Secrecy in the Sunshine Era,* 25; Geoffrey Stone, "Our Untransparent President," *NYT,* June 26, 2011; Downie and Rafsky, "Obama Administration and the Press."

33. Elisabeth Bumiller, "Bush Aides Set Strategy to Sell Policy on Iraq," *NYT,* September 7, 2002; Walter Pincus, "Records Could Shed Light on Iraq Group," *WP,* June 9, 2008; Michael Isikoff and David Corn, *Hubris: The Inside Story of Spin, Scandal and the Selling of the Iraq War* (New York: Crown, 2006), 34–36; Dana Priest, "A Clash on Classified Documents," *WP,* March 31, 2004, A12; Daniel Okrent, "The Public Editor: Weapons of Mass Destruction? Or Mass Distraction," *NYT,* May 30, 2004; "The Times and Iraq," *NYT,* May 26, 2004; Charles Lewis and Mark Reading-Smith, "False Pretenses," Center for Public Integrity, January 23, 2008, cited from www.publicintegrity.org/2008/01/23/5641/false-pretenses.

34. Dean Starkman, "The Hamster Wheel," *CJR,* September 14, 2010; McChesney and Nichols, *Death and Life,* xiii–xviii; *How News Happens; State of News Media 2014;* Michael Sebastian, "Wall Street Journal Adopts Native Ads," *Advertising Age,* March 20, 2014, http://adage.com/article/media/wall-street-journal-introducing-native-ads-site/292044/.

35. James Curran, Shanto Iyengar, et al., "Media System, Public Knowledge and Democracy: A Comparative Study," *European Journal of Communication* 24 (2009): 5–26; Steven Kull, Clay Ramsay, and Evan Lewis, "Misperceptions, the Media and the Iraq War," *Political Science Quarterly* 118 (2003–2004): 572, 575; Tom Zeller, "How Americans Link Iraq and Sept 11," *NYT,* March 2, 2003; Michael X. Delli Carpini and Scott Keeter, *What Americans Know about Politics and Why It Mat-*

ters (New Haven, CT: Yale University Press, 1996), 62–134; "Public Knowledge of Current Affairs Little Changed by News and Information Revolutions: What Americans Know: 1989–2007," Pew Research Center, April 15, 2007, www.people-press.org/2007/04/15/public-knowledge-of-current-affairs-little-changed-by-news-and-information-revolutions/.

36. *Information Needs of Communities,* 21; Thomas E. Patterson, "Young People and the News," *A Report from the Joan Shorenstein Center on the Press, Politics and Public Policy,* July 2007; Markus Prior, "News v. Entertainment: How Increasing Media Choice Widens Gaps in Political Knowledge and Turnout," *American Journal of Political Science* 49 (2005): 577–592.

37. Pew Research Center, "One Reason Some Americans Give up on News Media: Less Information," May 14, 2013, www.pewresearch.org/daily-number/one-reason-some-americans-give-up-on-news-media-less-information/; Lada Adamic and Natalie Glance, "The Political Blogosphere and the 2004 U.S. Election: Divided They Blog," Proceedings of 3rd International Workshop on Link Discovery, Eleventh ACM SIGKDD International Conference on Knowledge Discovery and Data Mining (New York: ACM Press, 2005), 36–43; Michael Cooper, "Campaigns Play Loose with Truth in a Fact Check Age," *NYT,* August 31, 2012; James Bennett, "We're Not Going to Let Our Campaign Be Dictated by Fact-Checkers," *Atlantic,* August 28, 2012, www.theatlantic.com/politics/archive/2012/08/were-not-going-to-let-our-campaign-be-dictated-by-fact-checkers/261674/; Jodi Dean, "Communicative Capitalism: Circulation and the Foreclosure of Politics," in *Digital Media and Democracy: Tactics in Hard Times,* ed. Megan Boler (Cambridge, MA: MIT Press, 2008), 101–121.

38. For a similar, though not identical, formulation, see Lee C. Bollinger, *Uninhibited, Robust, and Wide-Open: A Free Press for a New Century* (New York: Oxford University Press, 2010), 61–62.

39. For examples of the rhetoric of "creative destruction," see McChesney and Nichols, *Death and Life,* 75–79; Michael Kinsley, "Life after Newspapers," *WP,* April 6, 2009; Edward Lopez, "Is the Decline of Newspapers a Market Failure," Foundation for Economic Education, September 22, 2010, http://fee.org/freeman/detail/is-the-decline-of-newspapers-a-market-failure; Jeff Jarvis, "How Not to Save the News," *New York Post,* June 3, 2010, http://nypost.com/2010/06/03/how-not-to-save-news/.

40. Owen Fiss, "Why the State?" *Harvard Law Review* 100 (1987): 781–794; Cass R. Sunstein, *Democracy and the Problem of Free Speech* (New York: Free Press, 1995); Ben Scott, "A Broad, Positive View of the First Amendment," in *The Case Against Media Consolidation: Evidence on Concentration, Localism and Diversity,* ed. Mark N. Cooper (Stanford, CA: Creative Commons, 2007); McChesney and Nichols, *Death and Life;* Victor Pickard, *America's Battle for Media Democracy: The Triumph of Corporate Libertarianism and the Future of Media Reform* (New York: Cambridge University Press, 2015).

41. Rodney Benson, "Public Funding and Journalistic Independence: What Does Research Tell Us?" in *Will the Last Reporter Please Turn Out the Lights: The Collapse of Journalism and How to Fix It,* ed. Robert W. McChesney and Victor Pickard (New York: New Press, 2011), 314–319.

42. They proposed this scheme, with differing details, in *Death and Life of American Journalism,* and John Nichols and Robert W. McChesney, "Death and Life of Great American Newspapers," *The Nation,* March 18, 2009; Bruce Ackerman, "One Click Away: The Case for the Internet News Voucher," in McChesney and Pickard, *Will the Last Reporter Please Turn Out the Lights,* 299–305.

43. Yochai Benkler, "Give the Networked Public Sphere Time to Develop," in McChesney and Pickard, *Will the Last Reporter Please Turn Out the Lights,* 225–237.

44. Even proponents of the scheme, while committed civil libertarians, have seen a need to impose some limits. When McChesney and Nichols first proposed the voucher, qualifications included a cap on advertising and minimum publication schedules; in the subsequent book, it was limited to nonprofit newspapers that crossed a certain threshold of vouchers. Ackerman proposes looser and more speech-protective limits, and would allow vouchers to be sent on commercial papers—but vouchers could not be used for pornographic sites, and papers would need to carry libel insurance.

45. Frederick Schauer, "The Exceptional First Amendment," in *American Exceptionalism and Human Rights,* ed. Michael Ignatieff (Princeton, NJ: Princeton University Press, 2005), 29–56.

46. Jon G. Udell, *Economics of the American Newspaper* (New York: Hastings House, 1978), 122–124.

47. Walter Lippmann, *Public Opinion* (Miami, FL: BN Publishing, 2007), 101.

48. *St. Louis Post-Dispatch, St. Louis Post-Dispatch Symposium on Freedom of the Press: Expressions by 120 Representative Americans,* reprinted from December 13 to December 25, 1938 issues (no publication details, 1938), 45.

49. Sari Horwitz, "Media Shield Act Moves on to the Full Senate," *WP,* September 12, 2013; Jason Leopold, "Lawmakers Unveil Major Changes to FOIA," Al Jazeera America, June 24, 2014, http://america.aljazeera.com/articles/2014/6/24/reform-freedom-informationact.html; Sophia Cope, "Congress Must Pass FOIA Reform Legislation," *Electronic Frontier Foundation,* March 19, 2015, www.eff.org/deeplinks/2015/03/congress-must-pass-foia-reform-legislation; Benkler, "Public Accountability Defense," 281–326.

50. Arnold, *Secrecy in the Sunshine Era,* 5, 21–22; David H. Morrissey, "Disclosure and Secrecy: Security Classification Executive Orders," *Journalism and Mass Communication Monographs* (February 1997): 33; Press Release, Senator Jeanne Shaheen, "Shaheen Calls on White House to Increase Transparency, Reduce Wasteful Spending by Reforming Classification System" (May 30, 2013); Robert P. Deyling, "Judicial Deference and De Novo Review in Litigation over National Security Information under the Freedom of Information Act," *Villanova Law Review* 37 (1992): 81; Morton H. Halperin and Daniel N. Hoffman, *Top Secret: National Security and the Right to Know* (Washington, DC: New Republic Books, 1977), 51–54.

51. Executive Order 12065, Executive Order 12356, APP.

52. German and Stanley, *Drastic Measures Required,* 47; Deyling, "Judicial Deference and De Novo Review under the FOIA," 88–89; Halperin and Hoffman, *Top Secret,* 55–85; Foreign Affairs Division, Legislative Reference Service, *Security Clas-*

sification as a Problem in the Congressional Role in Foreign Policy (Washington, DC: Government Printing Office, 1971), 39; Christina E. Wells, "National Security Information and FOIA," *Administrative Law Review* 56 (4): 1217–1220.

53. Executive Order 13526, December 29, 2009, APP.

54. Herbert Lin, "A Proposal to Reduce Government Overclassification of Information Related to National Security," *Journal of National Security Law & Policy* 7 (2014): 443–464; Elizabeth Gotein and David M. Shapiro, *Reducing Overclassification through Accountability* Brennan Center for Justice, October 4, 2011, 19–20, www.brennancenter.org/publication/reducing-overclassification-through-accountability; Richard F. Johnson and Kay Marmorek, "Access to Government Information and the Classification Process—Is There a Right to Know?" *New York Law Forum* 17 (1971): 840; *Security Classification as a Problem in the Congressional Role,* 34; Steven Aftergood, "An Inquiry into the Dynamics of Government Secrecy," *Harvard Civil Rights and Civil Liberties Law Review* 48 (2013): 525–527; James S. Pope to Joseph Short, copied to Benton, n.d., folder: Executive Order Re Classified Information, 285-M, miscel., box 928, Truman OF. On capture problems, see Rahul Sagar, *Secrets and Leaks: The Dilemma of State Secrecy* (Princeton, NJ: Princeton University Press, 2013).

55. Benkler, "Public Accountability Defense."

56. Walter Lippmann, *Liberty and the News* (Princeton, NJ: Princeton University Press, 2008), 59.

ACKNOWLEDGMENTS

The start of an academic career, particularly in the current economy, is an uncertain and turbulent thing. Writing a book, on the other hand, requires security, stability, and support. I am glad to have the opportunity to thank the institutions, teachers, colleagues, friends, and family who have helped provide the shelter and guidance that allowed me to finish this work.

This book began in the History Department at the University of Chicago, where I was lucky enough to receive several years of funding that allowed me to relocate from Sydney and begin my studies. A generous fellowship from the Truman Library Institute allowed me to devote my final year in graduate school to writing. A postdoctoral fellowship at the Center for Cultural Analysis (CCA) at Rutgers University allowed me to participate in Meredith McGill and Henry Turner's wonderful "public knowledge" seminar and gave me the space to reconceptualize the scope of this book. The CCA also helped me organize some crucial adjuncting work that kept me afloat at the end of the fellowship. On two occasions, I had the pleasure of spending a semester at the Tamiment Library at New York University. A fellowship at the Center for the US and the Cold War helped me begin the project in 2008; a fellowship at the Frederic Ewen Academic Freedom Center in 2013 helped me bring it to completion. I also want to thank the American Society for Legal History, which awarded me the Paul Murphy Prize in the History of Civil Liberties in 2013. The award was an invaluable psychological and financial boost at a time when I needed both. The archival research for the book would not have been possible without generous support from the Franklin and Eleanor Roosevelt Institute, the LBJ Foundation, the Truman Library Institute, the Marshall/Baruch Foundation, and the University of Chicago History Department. Last, but certainly not least, I want to thank my new institutional home in the Department of History and Art History at George Mason University—I can't believe how lucky I am to have landed in such a collegial and supportive place, and to be working with so many great people.

I have learned from wonderful teachers over the course of my studies. At the University of Sydney, Stephen Robertson inspired a rather underwhelmed law student and politics major with his history courses, supported my first stabs at historical research, and encouraged me to apply to the States for grad school. Without his guidance, support, and example, I doubt I would be here today. Amy Dru Stanley and James Sparrow, my mentors at Chicago, have in their own ways shaped my approach to history and to this project immeasurably. My thanks to both of them for the inspiring example of their scholarship, and for their willingness to push me to be a better historian. Adam Green and Mark Bradley read early drafts of these chapters closely, and their questions and comments opened up many new avenues. I also learned a great deal from my other teachers at the University of Chicago, especially George Chauncey, Michael Geyer, Neil Harris, Mae Ngai, and Moishe Postone. Geoffrey Stone let me audit his First Amendment class, which changed the trajectory of this book.

I've had the pleasure of discussing this project with many colleagues, all of whom have helped shape my work. Since we met at a conference in Sydney in 2008, Paul Kramer has been an amazing source of advice and inspiration on all matters professional and intellectual. David Greenberg shared his knowledge of media and political history, and generously extended me opportunities to present my work. I've learned a great deal from the fantastic scholarship of Laura Weinrib and Jeremy Kessler, and from their generous readings of my work. Too many people have provided feedback at workshops, at conferences, or over coffee or drinks for me to list here. But my thanks to Hadji Bakara, Chris Dietrich, Kate Epstein, Dan Ernst, Dina Fainberg, David Farber, Ellen Goodman, Daniel Immerwahr, Deepa Kumar, Dan Leab, Shaul Mitelpunkt, Molly Nolan, Amy Offner, David Rabban, Ellen Schrecker, Michael Schudson, John Witt, and Marilyn Young, as well as all the participants of the University of Chicago Social History Workshop, the CCA Seminar on Public Knowledge, the Rutgers Center for Historical Analysis Seminar on Networks of Exchange, the Tamiment Cold War Seminar, the Legal History Forum at Yale Law School, and the Lees Seminar at Rutgers-Camden. And deep thanks to all my students at Chicago, Rutgers, and Mason who helped me work so much of this out in the classroom.

Working with Harvard University Press has been a real privilege and a real pleasure. I want to thank Joyce Seltzer for seeing potential in this book and for doing so much to help me realize it. From our first talks about my proposal to our last-minute conversations about the title, I've benefited greatly from Joyce's expert advice and editing. The manuscript was much improved by the careful reading it was given by two anonymous reviewers, and by the careful copyediting of Ellen Lohman and Ashley Moore. And many thanks to Brian Distelberg for all of his help in guiding the manuscript (and its author) through the production process so smoothly.

Many friends have helped inspire, support, and encourage me over the years—over beers, I'll thank you personally. But some names need to be named: Mikey Slezak and Amy Corderoy; Richard and Alex Del Rio; Jake Smith, Gwyn Troyer (and Zara); Peter Simons and Celeste Moore; Darryl Heller, Saskia Rombouts, and Itxaso. You have all been incredibly close friends and shared your homes with me more times than I can count while I was writing this book. Special thanks go to

Justin Evans. Justin has been a constant and inspiring interlocutor, a not-too-shabby matchmaker, and, with Judy Choi, a great friend and host. At a late stage in the writing process, he selflessly read a much longer version of this manuscript, and his incredible editorial eye made the arguments and prose much sharper than they would otherwise have been. It is a source of both excitement and sadness that all these great people are now scattered across so many different cities. One day, I hope in vain, we can all live in the same place.

Luckily, my best friend has been able to travel with me. Emily Jane Weaver has put up with deadlines, multiple moves, and seemingly endless discussions of press freedom with more calm and enthusiasm than I will ever be able to understand. Nothing I write here could begin to thank her for all the ways she has supported and encouraged me over the years. But I simply couldn't have written this book without her, and she's made the past few years far more fun than I had any right to expect. Thanks, Em, for everything.

Thanks as well to the rest of the Weaver clan for welcoming me warmly—thanks to Dee and John, Maeghan and Eric, Ursula and Joe, and Johnny for so many great times in Maine, and to Maeghan, John, and Ursula for expert moving help (more than once).

As for my family in Sydney, I don't know where to begin. Grad school and academia are opaque processes at the best of times; when the Pacific is in the way, I think they make little sense at all. While my sister's own journey through a PhD program has given her some idea of what I'm up to, I regret that Anna and I have spent so little of our adult lives on the same continent. For my parents and grandparents, well, I still don't have a good answer when they ask me why I chose to leave Sydney for the frigid Midwest—although the looming presence of Hearst in these pages suggests that Mum may not be totally off-base when she blames that childhood trip to the West Coast. As I've come to better appreciate the impact and ramifications of my decision to leave home, I'm beginning to better appreciate just how deep my parents' faith in me has always been, and how unconditionally they have supported me. This book is a product of that faith and support. As a poor token of appreciation, it is dedicated to them.

INDEX